DAILY LIFE IN

CIVIL WAR AMERICA

Recent Titles in
The Greenwood Press Daily Life Through History Series

The Hellenistic Age: From Alexander to Cleopatra
James Allan Evans

Imperial Russia
Greta Bucher

The Greenwood Encyclopedia of Daily Life in America, Four Volumes
Randall M. Miller, general editor

Civilians in Wartime Twentieth-Century Europe
Nicholas Atkin, editor

Ancient Egyptians, Second Edition
Bob Brier and Hoyt Hobbs

Civilians in Wartime Latin America: From the Wars of Independence to the Central American Civil Wars
Pedro Santoni, editor

Science and Technology in Modern European Life
Guillaume de Syon

Cooking in Europe, 1650–1850
Ivan P. Day

Victorian England, Second Edition
Sally Mitchell

The Ancient Greeks, Second Edition
Robert Garland

Chaucer's England, Second Edition
Jeffrey L. Forgeng and Will McLean

The Holocaust, Second Edition
Eve Nussbaum Soumerai and Carol D. Schulz

DAILY LIFE IN

CIVIL WAR AMERICA

Second Edition

DOROTHY DENNEEN VOLO

AND JAMES M. VOLO

The Greenwood Press Daily Life Through History Series

GREENWOOD PRESS
An Imprint of ABC-CLIO, LLC

A B C ☰ C L I O

Santa Barbara, California • Denver, Colorado • Oxford, England

Library of Congress Cataloging-in-Publication Data
Volo, Dorothy Denneen, 1949–
   Daily life in Civil War America / Dorothy Denneen Volo and James M. Volo. — 2nd ed.
       p. cm. — (The Greenwood Press Daily life through history series)
   Includes bibliographical references and index.
   ISBN 978-0-313-36603-1 (hard copy : alk. paper) — ISBN 978-0-313-36604-8 (ebook) 1. United States—History—Civil War, 1861-1865—Social aspects.
2. United States—Social life and customs—1783–1865. I. Volo, James M., 1947–
II. Title.
   E468.9.V6   2009
   973.7'11—dc22   2009025495

13 12 11 10 9   1 2 3 4 5

This book is also available on the World Wide Web as an eBook.
Visit www.abc-clio.com for details.

ABC-CLIO, LLC
130 Cremona Drive, P.O. Box 1911
Santa Barbara, California 93116–1911

This book is printed on acid-free paper ∞

Manufactured in the United States of America

CONTENTS

INTRODUCTION TO THE REVISED EDITION

The federal capital at Washington was highly valued as a symbol by 19th-century Americans. Carefully laid out in a district allocated from within the boundaries of Maryland in order to salve the pride of the South, the nation's capital city had been under construction since the turn of the century. Americans pointed proudly to the imposing structure of the Capitol building, as well as the General Post Office, the Bureau of the Treasury, the Smithsonian Institution, and the Executive Mansion, as representative of a vigorous young nation preparing to take its place among the leading countries of the world.

Unfortunately, Washington was also symbolic of other things. The plans for the city, like the basic founding concepts of the nation itself, were as pretentious as they were visionary, and in 1860 both lay unfulfilled and disordered. Sprawling along the banks of the Potomac with the "Old City" of Alexandria, Virginia, across the water, the great buildings of the new capital remained incomplete even after the expenditure of vast sums of money and six decades of effort. The Capitol building lay unfinished with its original dome removed—a scaffolding and a towering crane representative of restructuring and rethinking. The wings of the building were "stretched bare and unfinished, devoid even of steps." The imposing obelisk of the Washington Monument lay as a mere foundation. Blocks of marble, lumber, cast iron plates, and the tools of workmen strewn about the district gave quiet testimony to the fact that the plan for the nation's first city, like the social and political plan for the American nation itself, was incomplete and open to revision.[1]

At the head of the James River, one hundred miles south of Washington and in sharp contrast to it, was Richmond, Virginia. As the third largest city in the South, Richmond had proven an elegant state capital with fine buildings and traditional architecture. Although the city was cultivated and cosmopolitan, it was also the center of Virginia's economy, with mills, railways, and trading establishments. In 1861 Richmond was the finest city in the South and one of the better places in which to live in the entire country. Within a few months of secession, though, Richmond had been made the capital of the new Confederate nation, and its tenor changed dramatically. The city teemed with soldiers, wagons, and government officials. Defenses in the form of artillery emplacements, trenches, and earthworks rimmed its suburbs. The South's only major foundry, the Tredegar Iron Works, turned out cannon, rails, and plates for armored gunboats. But in a mere four years the once stately city would be a ruin comparable to the broken hulk of Berlin at the end of World War II. Its people would be described as looking "hungry, gaunt, ghastly, and yellow." Even the young were so pale and thin that it was "pitiful to see."[2]

In response to secession, it had been expected that the main Federal army would march on the main Confederate army before summer 1861, win the ensuing battle, take Richmond, and end the rebellion. Only gradually did the dire reality of the situation take hold. The lists of dead and wounded from the battle of Bull Run (July 1861)—the largest number of casualties in American history to that time—shocked the public and stunned the general staff. The federal Army of the Potomac—the largest American force ever to take the field in wartime—had lost the battle, and the US military went silent for several months thereafter while its generals absorbed the lessons they had learned. During this time, with the exception of the Battle of Ball's Bluff, which the Confederates also won, there was little more than skirmishing and raiding. Civilian morale concerning the war remained unexpectedly high, and the soldiers in their naiveté exhibited more confidence and energy than their officers. As the war unfolded, however, giant armies trudged across the hinterland in efforts to defend the Confederacy or dismantle the Old South with its characteristic lifestyle. Ultimately one in four men engaged in battle were dead, wounded, or missing. Parts of the South were said to actually stink with the odor of death. While bullets, artillery, and bayonets destroyed the opposing forces, the effects of war wrecked havoc on the lives of civilians also.

The War of Southern Secession, a civil war, had come to America. It would be one of the most tragic events in the nation's history, resulting from a dispute among its citizens over just what the new country should look like. For four years the country passed through a traumatic military and social upheaval that touched the lives of its people in many ways. More than 600,000 soldiers died from wounds and disease, and an incalculable number of civilian lives were permanently disrupted by war. Such matters have sent historians delving in the depths of old newspaper columns, official records, letters, and memoirs to unearth the details of constitutional pressures, agricultural and industrial production, social development, and political evolution, thereby producing over the intervening decades an enormous and ever-growing body of printed work. More than 100,000 volumes have been written about the American Civil War.

Although no event in American history has had so much written about it, much of the research has dealt with battles, operations, commanders, and military personalities. When a nation is at war—especially when it is at war with itself—it is not just the soldiers whose lives are changed. The lives of the civilians who remain behind, whether they are joined to the battle by the ties of love or not, are altered just as irrevocably. This book is designed to dovetail with other texts that focus on the widespread activities of armies and states in conflict while it attends to the events of daily life. It is hoped that the work will integrate into the body of military knowledge the details of the lifestyles of the people who populated the great northern cities or lived amid the ruins of the South through almost 1,500 days of conflict.

Of great weight, and equal importance, are the details of soldier life in the camps and on campaign. Nonetheless, the devotees of warfare will find this work almost devoid of descriptions of specific battles except insofar as they provide a basis for comparisons or a chronology for events. It is not the desire of the authors, however, to write a book about the Civil War without a sniff of gunpowder in the air. It is the vagaries and hazards of military life as the soldiers would have experienced them in their own microcosm rather than in a giant overview composed of the endless movement of regiments and armies that are emphasized. The chapter on the ordeals of combat, for instance, is drawn almost solely from firsthand accounts of the actual experiences of the soldiers who fought.

The research for the sections of this book dealing with politics, clothing, mourning, amusements, religion, and the household has led to untold diaries, letters, journals, maps, tracts, and old newspapers as well as to museums, historic places, antique shops, and old bookstores. Additional primary documents and internet sources have been consulted in producing the revised edition, which includes two completely new chapters dealing with a renewed emphasis on the effects of the war on children and families and on the activities of civilians on the home front. There is also an expanded discussion of the significance of pacifist groups, Copperheads, and anti-Confederate border residents.

Many of these personal reminiscences, diaries, and photographs were formerly hidden on dusty library shelves, in the vaults of antiquarian societies, or in the personal collections of those who are devotees of the 19th-century Victoriana. Many of these sources have been made available through the Internet in a way undreamed of a single decade ago when the first edition of this work was written. Many of these sources, and the text itself, lend themselves to further directed study by students and persons interested in expanding their knowledge of the period. Among the items suggested for further directed study are the analysis of original documents such as diary and journal entries, poems, newspaper articles and illustrations; mathematical exercises based on period data; graphical interpretation and the analysis of charts and tables; and the expression of alternative interpretations of political, economic, and/or military events based on packets of information. The authors—devoted historians and teachers for more than four decades—hope that they have extricated the germ of truth from these and other sources without distorting a genuine picture of daily life in Civil War America.

NOTES

1. Margaret Leech, *Reveille in Washington* (New York: Harper & Brothers, 1941), 5–6.

2. James H. Croushore, ed., *A Volunteer's Adventure, by Captain John W. De Forest* (New Haven: Yale University Press, 1949), 35.

CHRONOLOGY

March 1820	The Missouri Compromise admits Maine and Missouri as free and slave states, respectively, and prohibits slavery in the territories north of 36°30' north latitude.
May 1822	Denmark Vesey is executed for plotting a slave uprising.
December 1828	First nullification crisis. South Carolina nullifies the Tariff of 1828.
January 1831	William Lloyd Garrison begins publishing The Liberator.
August 1831	Nat Turner, a radical slave preacher, is killed as he leads a bloody slave revolt in Virginia.
November 1832	South Carolina nullifies the Tariff of 1832. President Jackson utilizes the Force Bill against South Carolina, but Henry Clay provides a compromise.
December 1833	The American Anti-Slavery Society is organized.
August 1839	The Cuban slave ship Amistad is brought into New Haven, Connecticut, by a U.S. naval vessel.

March 1841	The Africans from the Amistad are freed by the Supreme Court to return to Africa.
July 1845	The Republic of Texas formally agrees to annexation to the United States.
May 1846–February 1848	The Mexican-American War. General Winfield Scott marches victoriously into Mexico City. The Treaty of Guadalupe Hidalgo ends the war by giving a half million square miles of the West to the United States.
September 1850	The Compromise of 1850 extends the bounds of legal slavery and strengthens the Fugitive Slave Act.
June 1851–March 1852	Harriet Beecher Stowe's *Uncle Tom's Cabin* appears first as a serial and finally as a complete novel.
January 1854	The Kansas-Nebraska Act, which would repeal the Compromise of 1850 and substitute the concept of popular sovereignty, is endorsed by Northern Democrats.
February 1854	Anti-slavery proponents form the Republican Party in reaction to the Kansas-Nebraska Act.
May 1854	The Kansas-Nebraska Act is passed by Congress and signed by President Pierce.
December 1855	A virtual civil war over slavery exists along the border between Kansas and Missouri.
May 1856	Senator Charles Sumner is beaten with a cane by Rep. Preston Brooks of South Carolina in the Senate Chamber of the Capitol. Fiery abolitionist John Brown kills five pro-slavery men at Pottawotamie Creek in Kansas.
March 1857	The Supreme Court hands down its decision against Dred Scott and declares the Missouri Compromise of 1820 unconstitutional.
June 1858	In Illinois, the Republican Party chooses Abraham Lincoln to run for the Senate against Stephen Douglas. Lincoln gives his famous "House Divided" speech.

October 1859	John Brown is seized by federal troops led by Col. Robert E. Lee at Harper's Ferry. By December he is tried, convicted of treason, and hanged.
May 1860	The Republican Party nominates Lincoln for president.
November 1860	Lincoln wins election in a four-way race.
December 1860	South Carolina votes to secede from the Union, beginning a rush by some Southern states to form the Confederacy.
April 1861	With the bombardment of Fort Sumter, Lincoln calls for 75,000 volunteers to defend the Union. Virginia joins the Confederate States, followed by Arkansas, North Carolina, and Tennessee. The American Civil War has begun.
April-June 1861	West Virginia supports the Union. Although federal soldiers are killed in Baltimore, Maryland repudiates secession. Col. Thomas J. Jackson seizes the federal arsenal at Harper's Ferry. Missouri and much of Kentucky come under federal control.
July 1861	Battle of First Manassas, or First Bull Run, in Virginia. After the surprising defeat of the federal forces only minor skirmishing takes place for several months between the opponents on either side of the Potomac, in Missouri, and in Kentucky.
October 1861	Gen. Winfield Scott passes command of the federal forces to Gen. George B. McClellan.
November-December 1861	The Trent Affair. Possible war looms between the federal government and Great Britain over the seizure of Confederate diplomats from a British vessel. The crisis is averted when the men are released at year's end.
February 1862	Forts Henry and Donelson fall to Gen. Ulysses S. Grant. Grant demands "unconditional and immediate surrender."

March 1862	Gen. Thomas "Stonewall" Jackson begins a three-month campaign in the Shenandoah Valley against three federal armies that will become a model of tactics and strategy for students of military science. The CSS Virginia and USS Monitor battle in Hampton Roads, Virginia.
April 1862	The Battle of Shiloh in Tennessee is the bloodiest of the war to this point, but New Orleans falls to federal naval forces and troops with little opposition.
June and July 1862	The Seven Days Battles begin McClellan's failed Peninsular campaign.
September 1862	Battle of Second Manassas or Second Bull Run. Battle of Antietam. Lincoln drafts the Emancipation Proclamation.
December 1862	Battle of Murfreesboro, Tennessee, or Stones River. First Battle of Fredericksburg.
January 1863	Emancipation Proclamation takes effect.
April 1863	Richmond Bread Riot.
May 1863	Battle of Chancellorsville. Second Fredericksburg.
July 1863	Battle of Gettysburg. Fall of Vicksburg. The so-called High-Water Mark of the Confederacy.
September 1863	Battle of Chickamauga.
November 1863	Battle of Chattanooga.
March 1864	Gen. U. S. Grant becomes commander of federal forces.
May 1864	Battle of the Wilderness. Battle of Spotsylvania Courthouse. May is the bloodiest month of the war.
June 1864	More than 7,000 men fall in twenty minutes at the Battle of Cold Harbor.
June-July 1864	The so-called Atlanta Campaign begins. The siege of Petersburg begins.

November 1864	Lincoln defeats McClellan in the presidential election.
January 1865	Lincoln begins his second term with Andrew Johnson of Tennessee as vice-president.
April 1865	Lee surrenders at Appomattox Courthouse. John Wilkes Booth assassinates Lincoln.
June 1865	The last of the Confederate forces under Gen. Stand Wati and Gen. Joe Shelby formally surrender.

PART I

HISTORY, POLITICS, AND SLAVERY

1

THE HISTORIAN'S WAR

"An irrepressible conflict between opposing and enduring forces."

—William H. Seward

19TH-CENTURY AMERICA

At the outbreak of the war, all but the most astute observers thought that the question of national unity would be settled in a single afternoon of combat. But in the first great battle of the war, the intrinsic drama of Americans locked in mortal combat diverted everyone's attention from the fact that indecisiveness had crept into warfare over the centuries. From 1861 to 1865, Yankees were "bushwhacked" in western Virginia and Rebels were "sniped at" near Washington. Federal "Red Legs" and Confederate "Partisans" mauled one another across the plains of Kansas and Missouri and were held in contempt by the politicians on both sides.

Simultaneously, giant armies trudged across Northern Virginia, Louisiana, and middle Tennessee in efforts to either defend or dismantle the Old South and its characteristic lifestyle. The war policies of both governments so extended into the lives of the local populations that people came to look seriously upon the result as "the hard hand of war." Meanwhile, the terrible cost of war, measured in thousands of lives, afflicted the North with such a palpable weariness that Abraham Lincoln despaired of winning reelection in 1864. He began to lay plans for turning the federal government over to a successor who would end the war by simply declaring it finished.[1]

The Battle of Gettysburg, the bloodiest ever fought on the North American continent, has long been a focal point of Civil War historians. Taken with the simultaneous fall of Vicksburg, the Confederate stronghold on the Mississippi, the federal victory at Gettysburg should have been one of the most decisive military actions in history. Yet the internecine struggle continued, seemingly powered by the undiminished will of the Southern people to prevail. "We shall not give up the contest," said one Confederate officer after the fall of the Southern stronghold at Port Hudson, "and I think we shall tire you out at last." From the rousing partisan raids of cavalier clad horsemen in Tennessee to the dreary siege warfare of the Petersburg trenches, the obstinate refusal of the ragged troops to be forced from a thousand battlefields left the issue of what constituted the American nation undecided for four long years. Yet only about a dozen engagements of the war are considered worthy of general interest in today's classrooms and lecture halls.[2]

The Civil War attracted historians like no other time in American history. Nineteenth-century Americans of every sort—and of many social classes—documented their lives in great detail in diaries, letters, and journals. The public record of the war was available in almost countless newspapers and illustrated magazines. Photographs, engravings, and woodcuts abound, and the state and national governments kept generally precise records that can be found in the volumes of military correspondence and paperwork and among the data collected by the public census.

A central theme of all recorded history has been the use or abuse of power–how it lurks in the shadows behind the professed idealism of politicians and the compelling reasons they expound when they bring their nations to war. Such words often cloak those who wield political power and redistribute it among themselves as a consequence of success or failure on the battlefield. The ancient Greek historian of the Peloponnesian Wars (fourth century B.C.), Thucydides, urged historians to embrace skepticism in their analysis of great events and to look to personal or national self-interest rather than publicized grievances and high-sounding intentions when writing of warfare. Whenever a conflict breaks out in American history, its own generation of historians often rushes forward to record it with preconceived theories that often require for their support facts that are not in evidence while ignoring some of the so-called "realities on the ground" that might confound their pet hypothesis.

Immediately after the Civil War, the public was swamped with war stories, journals, memoirs, and battle descriptions. Former army commanders renewed wartime arguments about tactics and strategies in print—the pen and the printing press their only weapons. Battlefield opponents, and sometimes former comrades, aired the dirty laundry of their respective commands before an awaiting public. The politicians, who brought on the Civil War through their intransigency or through an inability to find solutions to the crises of slavery, secession, cultural upheaval, and other national problems, were often the main characters in their own histories of the struggle, and they must be read in our own generation with proper Thucydidian cynicism.[3] Personal letters, diaries, and journals written by so-called average people are less prone to these problems, but they too must be viewed critically because they often exhibit personal bias and ethnic, regional, or racial prejudices. Nonetheless, the words of the 19th century can not be dismissed out-of-hand simply because the modern generation of historians dislikes what they represent or feels uncomfortable in providing a fair and balanced historical view of certain hot-button topics.

Southern apologists, particularly, tried to rationalize their lost cause by finding unexploited opportunities, scapegoats, excuses, and martyrs. For quite some time—in fact for almost as long as the veterans of the war lived—this was the stuff of Civil War history. In 1881, Francis M. Palfrey—a federal veteran and war historian embittered by the increasingly sympathetic light in which the Confederate Army was being portrayed—wrote, "A few more years, a few more books, and it will appear that Lee and Longstreet, and a one-armed orderly, and a casualty with a shotgun, fought all the battles of the rebellion and killed all the Union soldiers except those who ran away."[4]

In the 1940s and 1950s, historians became mesmerized by the idea of identifying the reasons for the conflict, setting off a new wave of printing. Yet the causes proved so lost in a maze of interrelated factors and so obscured by the hidden agendas of those who wrote, or rewrote, history that there was no possibility of identifying all of them. Historians found that more than two years before the outbreak of hostilities, Americans had already identified, to their satisfaction at least, a very powerful cause for the bloody struggle that loomed between the increasingly antagonistic sections of their country. "It is an irrepressible conflict between opposing and enduring forces," declared William H. Seward. Some modern historians still agree with this outspoken anti-slavery Republican, but others disagree, believing the war could have been avoided by compromise. Nonetheless, it seems certain, from the distance of generations, that some form of civil upheaval was inevitable.[5]

In recent years, a more meaningful debate has centered on the people who found themselves caught in undercurrents of history so strong and compelling that they were unable to avoid conflict. This discussion has sparked several interesting lines of research into the nature of American society before and during the conflict, and historians have studied constitutional theory, politics, economics, geography, and society in an attempt to understand the wartime generation. Research in these areas has been particularly helpful in producing a mass of documentary evidence concerning the lives of the people of the Civil War era.

This research has made it clear that secession, and not slavery, was the precipitating controversy of the war. Although anti-slavery was a promi-

The Hard Hand of War: Sketch artist Henry Lovie's view of the condition of refugee families driven from their homes in the border states, as printed in *Leslie's Illustrated Magazine*.

nent reform movement of the period, other causes, such as temperance, women's rights, religious revival, public education, concerns for the poor, and prison reform, were as zealously pursued by activists. Of these, only slavery and disunion became politically charged issues in the antebellum period, and as the middle ground of compromise on such issues was eroded, only the extreme positions became viable, until disunion brought on armed conflict. Universal abolition, never an overall war aim of the Northern war effort, was not even recognized by the proclamation of emancipation of 1863. As expressed by one abolitionist, the prominence of secession as a cause of the war becomes obvious: "Who cares now about slavery. Secession, and the Oligarchy built upon it, have crowded it out."[6] A Federal officer serving in the field noted, "The nearer [the men] approach death the stronger is their hatred of Secession & the dearer is the sight of the true flag."[7]

The case for secession had flourished for more than seven decades, and it would seem, from an unbiased reading of the record, that the secessionists had at least an arguable case on their side. By comparison, the case for a perpetual union was a recent product of the sectional conflicts of the 1850s. Moreover, its fundamental legal principles were far from perfect, and the logic behind its arguments was fraught with ambiguity. Unfortunately, the specific legal status of secession was never adjudicated by a court due to the haste with which both North and South resorted to armed conflict.

SOWING THE SEEDS OF CONFLICT

How did the nation come to such an impasse? Historians have long held that part of the answer may lie in the questions about the nature of the American nation that had been left undecided by the Founding Fathers. Of these questions, the continuation of slavery and the political relationship between the state and national governments had resisted resolution. The crux of the slavery issue revolved around the question of whether the United States had been founded as a free republic that allowed slavery or as a slaveholding republic with pockets of freedom. The question of "states' rights" held at issue whether the state or the national government was ultimately sovereign. Since both situations had existed simultaneously for decades, which was the aberration?

The Founders produced a loose-knit union of sovereign states under the Articles of Confederation which had resulted from their dedication to the historic concepts of personal, political, and property rights. The limitations of the Articles became almost immediately apparent, however, and the Constitutional Convention of 1787 was called to amend them. The delegates chose, instead, to write a totally new underpinning document.

To provide for free and open discussion, no minutes of the deliberations were taken. If not for the personal notes taken by the delegates, nothing of the constitutional debates would be known today. The lack of explicit and indisputable records from the convention created a problem during the antebellum political wrangling. Advocates of one position or another tended to use self-serving and selective excerpts from the writings of the Founding Fathers. Those who supported abolition, for instance, invoked Jefferson's phrase, "All men are created equal," while those who opposed it were quick to point out that Jefferson had also written that "blacks ... are inferior to the whites in the endowments both of body and mind."[8]

Free from the intensity of the debate that was prevalent in the 1850s, it is clear today that the primary desire of the framers of the Constitution was to design a government that would possess only those powers necessary to carry out the common needs of the thirteen states and relieve the obvious weaknesses in the Articles. There was considerable disagreement about the exact limits of the relationship among the new federal government, the older states, and the individual citizen. In this regard, the delegates invoked the concept of state sovereignty, but republicanism, social pluralism, and constitutionalism were deemed the primary characteristics for a new government by the majority. Slavery and the possibility of future disunion were considered secondary issues. Few observers at the time thought that the questions raised about the fundamentals of American society and government would come to be "settled only at the cannon's mouth."[9]

The idea of limited federal power was much older than the slavery debates of the 19th century and was recognized as an unresolved issue at the time. Would the united states, melted down into one nation, be practicable or consistent with freedom? Thomas Jefferson warned that if the federal government was allowed to define the limits of its own powers, the result would be "not short of despotism." The anxiety over the exact extent of federal authority was serious enough to require the addition of a separate Bill of Rights defining the limits of governmental power alluded to in the principal document. Without a Bill of Rights, it was deemed impossible to achieve the adoption of the Constitution by the delegates or to ensure its ratification by the states. Nonetheless, even a radical politician like Patrick Henry refused to sanction the new Constitution, saying, "I smell a rat!"[10]

It is important in this discussion to emphasize the contrast between "rights" and "powers." Ironically, many strong reservations about "powers" came from the Northern states during the ratification debates. The Massachusetts legislature expressed a fear that the Constitution might be interpreted so as to extend the powers of Congress, and Rhode Island proposed a remarkable statement of states' rights similar in sentiment to that used by Southern secessionists two generations later. Even New England politicians resorted to their rights and threatened secession if their demands were not met. Among the Southern states, the people of Virginia required that the powers granted the national government under the Constitution "be resumed by the states, whensoever the same shall be perverted to their injury or oppression."[11] Both Thomas Jefferson and James Madison believed that the states were "not united on the principle of unlimited submission to their general government" but reserved "each State to itself, the . . . right to their own self-government."[12]

The concept of states' rights was clearly a separate issue from that of slavery in the minds of the Founders of the Constitution. Although Southerners frequently invoked states' rights as a symbol in their turmoil over slavery, the concept was first elaborated in the tariff nullification crises of the 1820s and 1830s. Nonetheless, states' rights advocates seem to have been able to keep the two questions of sovereignty and slavery distinct. In much of the North, however, the questions of states' rights and the continuation of slavery became a single issue on which it was impossible to have divergent views.

The Constitution clearly recognized and protected the right of a citizen to own slaves. Only by the most tortured of legal arguments could slavery have been considered illegal under the original founding document. Moreover, the Tenth Amendment explicitly forbade the federal government to intervene in state affairs. For this reason alone, the South proclaimed that the federal government had no justification in law to interfere with slavery. The Supreme Court, often top-heavy with Southern justices, had generally sided with the South on these questions, and Southerners had prevented any changes in law by maintaining control of the Senate.

Historians feel that when the South perceived a possible loss of this legislative and judicial advantage, it resorted to secession as a remedy.

A DIVIDED ECONOMY

A favorite area of study by the historians of the 1970s was economics. On the surface, at least, the Southern section of the country was doing well in 1850. The South shared with the rest of the country a common language, an identification with many basic legal principles, and a growing body of literature, music, and history. Indeed, both cultures can be seen as basically moral, righteous, and eminently Protestant. Each side viewed itself as truly patriotic and dedicated to the Constitution. But the economies of the industrialized North and the agrarian South were becoming increasingly difficult to reconcile. Southern nationalists, in particular, deplored the increasing dependence of their economy on Northern manufacturing and shipping. By the 1850s, canal and railroad construction had strengthened the economic position of the Northeastern cities to the detriment of Southern ports. Farmers in the Northwest were now able to bypass traditional Southern trading outlets and ship directly to the East Coast. Consequently, the political allegiance of the Northwest had also shifted and upset the traditional political balance of the government in favor of the North.

The South's importance as a comprehensive producer of agricultural products was also waning in this period, being replaced by the farms of Michigan, Iowa, Kansas, and Missouri. Tobacco remained an important crop in North Carolina and Kentucky, but the tobacco plantations of Virginia and Maryland were feeling the effects of depressed prices and depleted soils. The largest Southern crop was corn, which was consumed locally by man and beast. Rice was a valuable export item, and the rice plantations of South Carolina and Georgia were still prosperous in the 1850s.

Southern cotton production had originated along the coast and moved into the backcountry of South Carolina and Georgia by the end of the 18th century, but it quickly spread into all the states that were to become members of the Confederacy. The significance of cotton in the money-conscious 19th century resulted primarily from the fact that it was a cash crop. By mid-century more than five million bales were being produced annually, causing cotton to be termed the "king" of agricultural exports. The Southern cities, particularly New Orleans, Mobile, Savannah, and Charleston, continued to flourish because of their dedication to the export of cotton. In 1853, New Orleans was described in a child's geography text as "remarkable for the number of ships and steamboats that crowd its levee, or [land] along the river."[13] Yet on the eve of the war, New York was exporting more cotton to Europe than Charleston, much of it transshipped from other Southern ports including New Orleans. Seventy-five percent of all cotton came from plantations, as did almost all of the rice, sugar, and tobacco. The success of the plantation economy, and the cotton plantations in particular, therefore, was vital to the continuation of the genteel Southern lifestyle.

MODERNIZATION

Cultural and social changes were sweeping the North in the 1840s and 1850s. Industry and urbanization had moved the North toward a more modern society with an unprecedented set of novel social values, while the South had essentially lagged behind, clinging to the traditions of the 18th century.

Historians have noted that the differences between the folk culture of the South and the modern culture of the North certainly fueled the broad-based reform movements of mid-century and may have ignited the turmoil over state sovereignty and slavery. The debate surrounding these questions, driven by an intensely partisan press, "not only aroused feelings of jealousy, honor, and regional pride, but raised fundamental questions about the future direction of the American society."[14]

The most obvious modern element in the North was the rapid growth of its urban centers as more and more people flocked to the cities to find work in the factories. Although the class structure was still dominated by the old social elite, a new middle class was striving to become socially acceptable, and it was becoming increasingly difficult for the community to distinguish between the two. Unfortunately, the distinctions between these and the urban lower classes continued to be characterized by sharp contrasts in wealth, ethnic origin, and religion.

The lower classes of the North were exceedingly poor and were composed largely of immigrants. Many of the poorest immigrants were Irish Catholics. The Irish were the first truly urban group in America, living in crowded slums rife with crime and disease, and experiencing severe religious prejudice at the hands of the Protestant majority. "Help wanted" advertisements often stated, "Irish need not apply." One of the ironic characteristics of the new modernism in Northern society was the simultaneous existence of anti-slavery sentiment and severe ethnic prejudice among upper-class Protestants. This is especially surprising in view of the prominence of social reform movements in the North.

The South was a structured society tied to tradition and continuity rather than to progress and change. Southerners strove to maintain a romanticized version of the old aristocratic order as it was before the American Revolution. They were remarkably intolerant of social reform and disdainful of activism, yet they thought of themselves as well mannered, chivalrous to women and children, religious, and protective of all that was still fundamentally good in America. They lionized the stratified, but benevolent, social order portrayed in the 19th-century romance novel. To paraphrase the immensely popular Sir Walter Scott, the lower classes retained enough "insolence" to tell the aristocrats that any breach of proper formality between them was dishonorable to both. At all levels of Southern society individual liberty, manliness, and respect for authority and position were held in such high esteem that one put his life and personal honor on the line to protect them.[15]

The vast majority of Southern citizens were small farmers who planned their lives around rural activities and seasonal chores such as barn raising, quilting bees, planting, haying, and harvesting. Their concept of time was based on sunrise, noon, spring, or summer, and they set their appointments or ended the workday by this standard. Free white laborers and artisans were paid at the completion of a task, and rarely by the clock or calendar. The system provided continuity in the work relationship between employer and employee, and it was not unusual for one family to be employed by another in the same capacity for several generations. Family members usually cooperated in completing chores. This togetherness was thought to foster feelings of kinship and traditional family values. Fathers and mothers worked beside their children and grandchildren in an idyllic, if not a mechanically efficient, simplicity.

While many Northerners were still farmers, a growing segment of the population was becoming tied to the cities and factories. Middle-class men who had grown up in the first half of the century could remember a childhood spent living in a family working environment, either on the farm, in a cottage at the mill, or in a room behind the family shop. But as the century progressed men's work increasingly took place in the special atmosphere of business premises such as the factory or office. Fathers commonly left the home to work for 10 to 14 hours, and their children rarely saw them during daylight hours. A father's work and workplace became foreign to his children. This tendency to "go to work," rather than to work at home, led to the virtual removal of men from the home environment, leaving it the sole province of the female. The modern 19th-century home increasingly came to focus almost solely on the wife and children. The evolution to a female-dominated household may help to explain the growing formalism and rigid authoritarianism that Victorian fathers demanded when they were present.[16]

With the general availability of the pocket watch, these men increasingly lived their lives by the clock. They valued these timepieces as heirlooms. The last significant act of many Civil War soldiers was to ensure that their pocket watches were passed on to their sons. Factory workers were expected to work in shifts dictated by the public clocks that came to be prominently displayed on towers, in the streets, and on the factory walls. In 1847, John A. Thayer of Stoughton, Massachusetts, published one of the first books of tables for the calculation of wages "at various prices, either by the day, week, or month, for different lengths of time."

The idea of being "on time" represented a significant change in the life-style of most city dwellers, and since the North was the most urbanized section of the country, being on time became characteristic of Northern life.[17]

Conversely, Southerners, who had no need to work by the clock, were often viewed as shiftless and lazy. Southern laborers feared the develop-ment of the unprecedented "work for wage" economy of the cities, and they saw Northern wage earners as degraded and enslaved persons. A Northern woman living on a Southern plantation wrote to her mother in Massachusetts,

All the alarm and anxiety I feel now is for you & and for all the people of the North who depend upon their daily wages for a living. What is to become of them? I never sit down to the table, but I think of the many, to whom a small portion, even of our abundance, would be so acceptable. The Abolitionists talk about the poor negro—I dare say not one white person in ten throughout the whole North had such a dinner for Christmas as did [my slaves] yesterday.[18]

The city worker sold himself into economic bondage for a wage, and the expansion of a similar work for wage system was dreaded by Southerners almost as much as abolitionists dreaded the expansion of slavery. South-ern whites were clearly anxious to maintain their status as freemen, even if this required that they be very poor freemen. Many in the laboring class believed that the North was determined to enslave them to the factory system or counting house. The modern egalitarian society of the North was viewed with disdain and seen as degenerate and immoral. Rising crime rates in the cities, flagrant and open prostitution, and the squalid conditions of the urban lower classes were proffered as proof of Northern inferiority.

The unmodernized South was led by a privileged planter class whose elite lifestyle was maintained at the expense of the rest of society. This planter aristocracy relied on its kinship network and social status as means to personal success. Southern culture and institutions were seen by outsiders as backward, inefficient, and harmful to the American nation as a whole. Nonetheless, the Southern elite voluntarily assumed the role of benefactor and knight errant to all other levels of their society. Like cava-liers on a quest, Southern men felt obliged to counsel and defend not only their own families, but also all females and minor children placed under their protection. This obligation was extended to their slaves in an ambig-uous, but serious, way. Many Southerners were genuinely concerned for the physical and moral welfare of their slaves, but only in terms of contin-ued racial separation and subjugation.

Failing to acknowledge the good in Southern society because it was tied to slavery, Northern reformers made no attempt to hide their universal disapproval of all things Southern. They became increasingly acrimonious, alienating, and violent in their rhetoric as the war approached. These social reformers were widely viewed as interventionists, fanatics, anarchists, or worse by the Southern population.

POLITICS AS USUAL

The most modern element in American life in the first half of the century was a vigorous interest in politics. Politics became a great national pastime, almost a hobby, shared by both the North and the South. This interest crossed many of the old social and economic lines to engage devotees from many classes, with sharp debates resulting on an almost daily basis. Unfortunately, restraint was conspicuously absent from the political process of the 1850s.

Historians have observed that this widespread participation almost certainly added to the furor for war. Antagonists on all sides assailed their opponents with arguments taken from the law, the Bible, literature, pamphlets, election speeches, and the press. When unprepared to rebut these arguments on an equal footing, the opponents often resorted to ridiculous remarks and unsupported allegations. A Southern observer wrote of the period: "The hot headed politician and preacher seemed to be molding public opinion without any regard to the country as a whole. Both North and South proved, from their point of view, the righteousness of their positions by resorting to both the Bible and the Constitution."[19]

Politics became increasingly characterized by intemperate and abusive language, or even fisticuffs, especially when the subject turned to inflammatory issues such as slavery. When Senator Charles Sumner, a man of "wicked tongue" and "intemperate language" with regard to slavery, was beaten with a cane by Congressman Preston Brooks in the Senate, the blows were struck not only in the halls of Congress, but in the barbershops, parlors, and taverns of every small town and city.[20]

The great flaw in the work of historians of the antebellum period was that they could not explain how the geographic sections of the nation could share so many important cultural and political characteristics and still be mutually antagonistic to the point of shedding blood. The actual causes of the war are complex and multidimensional, and any discussion along these lines inevitably remains totally academic. It is clear that the nation did not go to war simply because of slavery any more than it did over disputes involving temperance, urbanization, poverty, politics, or economics. Possibly, historians should look to the cumulative effect of all the various disputes as a cause of the war. Nonetheless, the work done by these researchers has proved helpful in documenting the characteristics of daily life in this period.

NOTES

1. See Virgil Carrington Jones, *Gray Ghosts and Rebel Raiders* (New York: Galahad, 1956), 45–46, 166; Russell F. Weigley, *The Age of Battles: The Quest for Decisive Warfare from Breitenfeld to Waterloo* (Bloomington: Indiana University Press, 1991), xii-xiii; Mark Grimsley, *The Hard Hand of War: Union Military Policy Toward Southern Civilians, 1861–1865* (Cambridge: Cambridge University Press, 1995), 5; and Thomas A. Lewis, *The Guns of Cedar Creek* (New York: Bantam, 1991), 25.

2. Croushore, 146; Joseph B. Mitchell, *Decisive Battles of the Civil War* (New York: Fawcett, 1955). A short list of these might include First Manassas/Bull Run (July 1861), Shiloh (April 1862), the Seven Days Battles (June and July 1862), Second Manassas/Second Bull Run (September 1862), Antietam (September 1862), Murfreesboro/Stones River (December 1862), Fredericksburg (December 1862), Chancellorsville (May 1863), Chickamauga (September 1863), Chattanooga (November 1863), the Wilderness (May 1864), Spotsylvania (May 1864), Atlanta (July 1864), and Petersburg (July 1864).

3. See Victor David Hanson, *A War Like No Other: How the Athenians and Spartans Fought the Peloponnesian War* (New York: Random House, 2005), 5–7.

4. Steven H. Newton, *Lost for the Cause, The Confederate Army in 1864.* (Mason City, IA: Savas Publishing Company, 2000), 3.

5. William H. Seward, from a speech given in Rochester, New York, on October 25, 1858, as quoted in David Donald, *The Civil War and Reconstruction* (Boston: Heath, 1961), 124. This speech provides the basis for the irrepressible conflict theory of Civil War causation.

6. Lewis, 163, quoting federal Col. Charles Russell Lowell in March 1861.

7. Stephen W. Sears, ed., *For Country, Cause, and Leader: The Civil War Journal of Charles B. Hayden* (New York: Ticknor & Fields, 1993), 25.

8. Emory M. Thomas, *The Confederacy as a Revolutionary Experience* (Columbia: University of South Carolina Press, 1991), 11.

9. Calvin Colton, ed., *The Private Correspondence of Henry Clay* (Cincinnati: N.p., 1856), 313. From a letter written by former president John Quincy Adams to Clay.

10. James R. Kennedy and Walter D. Kennedy, *The South Was Right* (Gretna, LA: Pelican, 1995), 164.

11. Ibid., 162.

12. Ibid., 164–165.

13. S. Augustus Mitchell, *An Easy Introduction to the Study of Geography* (Philadelphia: Thomas, Cowperthwait & Co., 1853), 49.

14. Richard H. Sewell, *A House Divided: Sectionalism and the Civil War, 1848–1865* (Baltimore: Johns Hopkins University Press, 1988), xi.

15. Sir Walter Scott, *The Fair Maid of Perth* (New York: Harper, 1831), 9. The actual quote reads: "Yes—respect; and who pays any respect to me?" said the haughty young lord. "A miserable artisan and his daughter, too much honored by my slightest notice, have the insolence to tell me that my notice dishonors them."

16. John Tosh, "New Men? The Bourgeois Cult of Home," *History Today* 46 (December 1996): 9–15.

17. John A. Thayer, *The Practical Expedite or Time-Book Companion* (Stoughton, MA: Privately published, 1847).

18. Wilma King, ed., *A Northern Woman in the Plantation South, The Letters of Tryphena Blanche Holder Fox, 1856–1876* (Columbia: University of South Carolina Press, 1993), 131.

19. William A. Fletcher, *Rebel Private: Front and Rear* (1908; reprint, New York: Meridian, 1997), 2.

20. John S. Bowman, ed., *The Civil War Almanac* (New York: Bison Books, 1983), 383–384.

2

POLITICS: THE NATIONAL HOBBY

"Both North and South seemed to be swayed by the demagogue."

—Confederate Private William Fletcher

THE POLITICS OF DIVISION

In the 1940s a group of historians suggested that the Civil War was caused by the blundering of a generation of politicians and social agitators. Certainly some of what they said was true. Compromise had proven successful in keeping the various sections of the country together for eight decades, and a modicum of moderation on both sides might have prevented bloodshed. These "blundering generation" theorists were very helpful in explaining how the war came to be.

During the 1840s, the Whigs and Democrats, the two oldest political parties in the United States, had reached agreement on several issues that had plagued the early republic. The tariff, the National Bank, and the regulation of internal commerce rank high among these divisive issues. Americans celebrated their limited form of federal government and considered any of its remaining weaknesses essential to the safeguarding of personal and political freedom.

The next decade was one of rapid economic and social change in America, and politics was gaining a more general audience than at any time since the Revolution. The Whigs and Democrats were searching for new issues that would mobilize the voters behind the old party structure.

This attempt to underscore the meaning of the old parties was to have far-reaching consequences as political and social agendas began driving forward proposals that required strong federal action. One unforeseen consequence of trying to bolster the parties was that, ironically, it eventually led to the virtual dissolution of both.

In August 1846, David Wilmot, a Democrat from Pennsylvania, introduced an amendment to an appropriation bill requested by President James K. Polk that stipulated that slavery and involuntary servitude would be barred from all lands acquired from Mexico as a result of the war. Wilmot framed his measure in terms of its appeal to the white working-class rather than as any humanitarian benefit to blacks. Its central commitment was to congressional prohibition of slavery from all federal territories, a position that Lincoln and the Republican Party would adopt in the 1850s. The Wilmot Proviso split both Whigs and Democrats along sectional lines and polarized Northerners and Southerners against each other. It failed to pass in 1846. Reintroduced in later years, it often passed the House, where Northerner supporters outnumbered the Southerners who opposed it, only to be buried in the Senate, where the two sections had an equal number of seats. By the start of 1850, 14 of 15 northern state legislatures had instructed their states' congressmen to impose the Proviso on any territories organized in the Mexican Cession while increasing numbers of Southerners vowed to secede should Congress ever pass it into law. The proviso tended to equate opposition to slavery and its extension with opposition to the war. This brought hundreds of anti-slavery activists into the antiwar movement, among them a vast number of women from the religious denominations of the North and Northeast who provided the movement with a "great silent army of volunteers and fund-raisers."[1]

In the 1850s, the Democratic Party became divided over the issue of the extension of slavery. The Northern branch of the party favored "popular sovereignty," wherein the voters decided for or against the extension of slavery to new states or territories. The Southern branch preferred an unequivocal assertion that the Constitution absolutely protected the practice of slavery. Stephen A. Douglas became the leader of the Northern group, while Jefferson Davis led the Southern position. When Congress voted to ease the tensions over slavery with the passage of the Compromise of 1850, Davis voted against every provision of the bill except that which strengthened the Fugitive Slave Law. When Davis introduced legislation that would have condemned Northern interference in Southern "domestic institutions," the Douglas faction refused to support their own party.

An example of this political realignment can be seen in the reaction to the passage of the Kansas-Nebraska Act in 1854. A product of the optimism of the Northern Democrats and Stephen Douglas, the Kansas-Nebraska Act seemingly sabotaged the political compromises that had characterized the previous decades of American politics. The Fugitive Slave Law established "dubious democratic procedures for capturing runaways" in the free states, and now the Kansas-Nebraska Act established "dubiously democratic proslavery barricades" in the territories.[2] The measure was popular among Northern Democrats, and the Southern Democrats gave it support, but its passage ultimately caused a split in the party. Moderates in the North felt betrayed. Outraged by the act, Northern voters began to speak of the existence of a "slave power conspiracy." In response, moderates in the South began to harden their position and seriously consider disunion. With the next election cycle in 1856, it became obvious that the "Slave Power" forces had reached their peak.

While the Northern Democrats were hurt by the response to the act, the Whigs were devastated by it. The Southern wing of the Whig Party, sympathetic to compromise on the slavery issue, bolted, thereafter aligning themselves with the Southern Democrats; and the Whig Party, already weak after years of deterioration, was left in disarray and all but destroyed. A serious misreading of the temper of the voters had taken place, and they were left simmering in anger at the old parties. Significantly, this political upheaval came at a time when the old party system was already suffering from weakening voter support and poor party discipline. Yet in the wake of the disaster that followed the Kansas-Nebraska Act, interest in politics and political discussions increased, and several new parties moved in to fill the void.

Among these, two major new parties stood out: the Nativists and the Republicans. The Nativist, or American, Party rose very rapidly in popularity but failed in carrying its agenda to the national scene. The Republicans, after a false start in 1856, managed to win the White House in 1860, a victory that would bring the country to civil war.

Nativist propaganda was widely promulgated throughout the nation, and even those who disagreed with Nativist positions were well aware of them. Nativists were solidly Protestant and radically anti-Catholic in their rhetoric. For support, they tapped into the growing fear and resentment that paralleled the rapid changes taking place in American society. Nativist rhetoric portrayed Catholics, and especially the Catholic immigrants, as crime-ridden and intemperate, a drag on the economy, and a danger to the fabric of society. They viewed the acceptance of Catholics by the Northern wing of the Democratic Party as proof that the old political system would fail to support traditional American values. By tapping into a growing sense of resentment of politics as usual, out of touch with the pulse of the people and dedicated only to entrenched interests, the Nativists found an agenda designed to ensure the defeat of the old parties.

The Nativists were deeply immersed in the evangelical movement, and they were strongly supported by some of the finest established families of the North. Politically, they made some gains at the state level, especially in Massachusetts, only to have the party collapse after a few years because it failed to generate enough voter support nationally. Nativists were particularly embarrassed by their inability to bring about the passage of more stringent immigration laws. They did poorly with Southerners, who were more accepting of immigrants and more tolerant of Catholicism than many in the North. More generally, the Nativists failed because of their lack of political experience, their association with several prominent old party Whigs, and their violent anti-Catholic rhetoric, which bothered many politically active Protestants.

The Republican Party benefited from the collapse of the Nativists. Developing more slowly, it avoided a similar meteoric rise and fall. While Nativists generally identified with social and cultural ideals, the motivations of the Republicans were purely those of political ambition. Even early Republicans were astute politicians. The party agenda called for a restructuring and expansion of government on all levels. The positions taken on abolition, urbanization, extension of the vote, and free labor were all carefully crafted to foster a positive public impression of the party and to increase its power and prestige.

Free labor seems to have been the most fundamental element of the Republican belief system and identity. It embodied the ideals of a classless, socially mobile society within the framework of a harmonic and expansive economic system, all deeply rooted in personal prosperity and capitalism. While Northern Democrats espoused many of these same principles, Republicans were more optimistic about the future of a highly industrialized America and were certain that the new society and culture of the North would ultimately supplant that of the South to the betterment of the nation as a whole.

The Republican Party benefited greatly from the rising tide of sectional resentment. The Kansas-Nebraska Act was a godsend for the Republican Party. In 1856, they almost won the presidency with an anti-Slave Power agenda. They used the passage of the act and the subsequent decision of the courts in the Dred Scott case as symbols verifying the existence of a slave power conspiracy. Not only was such a conspiracy dangerous in itself, but it was clear evidence that the old powers wished to spread slavery to every corner of the land. In this regard, Republicans were in the unique position of being able to stand as the defenders of an idealized Northern culture, untainted, as were the Democrats, by former associations with the South.

An important part of the Republican arsenal of ideals was its characterization of the Southern planter class as the "slave aristocracy," viciously suppressing the mass of the Southern white population and all blacks, and denying them the benefits of true political democracy. The Republicans were able to transform the fears of papistry, slave power, and the unrestrained expansion of slavery into issues that could be blamed on the Democrats, North and South. The Republicans promised that *they* would never willingly allow the slaveowners to pass any national proslavery laws.

The Northern Democrats also used the symbols of progress, opportunity, and mobility to considerable effect. However, they had to defend their party's historic position on slavery. Southern planters were portrayed by the Democrats as favoring progress and opportunity, but only for whites, and some movement was made in the Southern states toward the expansion of the vote for white males. But the Democratic Party was often viewed as part of the problem, deeply involved in the political corruption of the day and supporting a widespread system of patronage. Voters were generally disenchanted with the party's "politics as usual" agenda, and many viewed the Democratic toleration of Catholics as self-serving and insincere. The Northern Democrats, although considerably weakened, were able to remain a political force until the outbreak of the war. The Southern branch maintained itself by championing the resistance to outside intervention in Southern lifestyle and culture, which were inexorably linked to slavery.

The 1856 election proved to be the death knell of the old two-party system. In the presidential race, the Republicans championed the slogan "Free Speech, Free Press, Free Soil, Free Men, Fremont and Victory." John C. Fremont may have been made a national hero for his role in mapping and exploring the West, but he was an unacceptable presidential candidate in the South. Governor Henry A. Wise warned that if Fremont won the 1856 election, Virginia would secede. Consequently, the Democrats, fearing to incur the wrath of the Northern voter by nominating Stephen A. Douglas, the author of the Kansas-Nebraska Act, decided to run James Buchanan of Pennsylvania. Buchanan won the election against Fremont due to the entry into the race of a weak candidate from the American Party, a coalition of Nativists and Know-Nothings. This third party candidate was former president Millard Fillmore. Buchanan received only a minority of the popular votes for president, yet he handily won the Electoral College.

As a new party, the Republicans had not had time to organize an electoral victory behind Fremont. Nonetheless, by the end of the decade the Republican Party had become the foremost instrument of anti-slavery sentiment in the country. Its condemnation of the slave power forces, coupled with the Kansas-Nebraska Act and the Dred Scott decision, brought it adherents. The events, both real and fabricated, taking place in "Bleeding Kansas" and the schemes of fanatical abolitionists like John Brown to forcibly liberate slaves and promote slave insurrections tended to radicalize even the most moderate politicians.

Northern office seekers, with their sights set on 1860, began calling for an assault on the traditions and honor of the South with all the enthusiasm that their rhetoric could convey. Such attacks fueled Southern indignation, created a desire for vindictive satisfaction, and led Southern moderates to retrench their positions. Southern radicals began to call for disunion as the best means of protecting sectional interests. "Both North and South seemed to be swayed by the demagogue," observed William Fletcher, who would go on to fight as a Rebel private.[3] Under the perceived weight of "accumulated wrongs and indignities," the South was swept up in a reckless euphoria for secession and the establishment of the Confederacy.[4]

THE ELECTION OF 1860

James Buchanan's legacy as the 15th president of the United States was to follow, rather than to lead, the country to the brink of civil war. Buchanan entered office knowing that he was unpopular with most of America. He was seemingly unwilling or powerless to control the radicals of either the North or the South. He had an honest desire for peace, but he was a pro-Southern unionist and as such was willing to make concessions to the South to maintain at least the semblance of national unity. Nevertheless, pro-Southern forces thought his concessions too harsh, while Northerners found him weak and pusillanimous. Buchanan was saddled with a cabinet divided by controversy over the same issues that split the country, and his vacillating policies did little but engender both social and political turmoil.

The rising star of national politics in the 1850s was a young former Whig politician from Illinois. Abraham Lincoln had not rushed to join the first groups that formed the Republican Party, but in 1854, in a speech in Peoria, Illinois, he began to speak out against the Kansas-Nebraska Act. The deep crusading tenor of this speech was closely linked to Lincoln's ambition for office. Instead of casting his fortunes with the Republicans, who were expounding on the issue of expanding slavery into the territories, he mistakenly continued to identify himself with the nearly defunct Whig Party. Viewed as an old party candidate, he lost the 1854 Senate election in a close race.

Immediately thereafter, he transferred his allegiance to the Republicans and helped to organize the party in Illinois. It was no surprise when Lincoln was chosen by the Republicans to face Stephen A. Douglas in the 1858 race for the Senate. Lincoln began his campaign with his famous "House Divided Against Itself" speech. In this address, Lincoln gave the most radical speech of his entire life, calling for the country to become all free or all slave. Never again did he express such radical views. His words were widely interpreted as a declaration of war on Southern institutions. In a highly publicized series of debates, Douglas carefully pointed out that the country had been split for quite some time on the issue of slavery and could continue to be so indefinitely if the hotheads on both sides would leave well enough alone. By espousing moderation, Douglas narrowly won the race, but Lincoln's stance had catapulted the young lawyer into a position of leadership in the Republican Party. By aligning himself with the influential radical wing of the party, he went on to engineer the Republican national convention in 1860 and received the party's presidential nomination instead of William H. Seward, an abolitionist who had recently moderated his position in an attempt to garner the nomination.

The radicals who joined the Republican Party did so largely because of the slavery issue. Seward's shifting positions—he would too optimistically underestimate the number of southern unionists after the firing on Ft. Sumter—cost him the support of the Republican radicals. The radicals generally came from the agricultural areas of the Midwest or the cosmopolitan urban centers of the Northeast. The latter seemed especially absorbed by the concept of the immediate abolition of slavery and the granting of full civil rights to blacks—objectives that they sought during the period known as Radical Reconstruction (1865–1877). They saw no room for compromise in these matters and were willing to destroy the party if necessary to attain their goals. If the Union did not stand for liberty, it too was expendable.

While Lincoln had used the radicals to gain the nomination, he immediately began to modify his radical image to make himself more acceptable to other factions of the party. The moderates made up the majority of the Republican Party, but there was a wider variety in their beliefs than among the radicals. The moderates tried to control the party by holding a balance of power. They emphasized that slavery was a territorial issue and were willing to leave slavery alone in areas of the South where it had long been established. Many believed in gradual emancipation and foreign colonization efforts by black freemen. By failing to center himself within the party spectrum, Lincoln essentially drove moderate Republicans toward the radical position. Certainly this is the light in which the South viewed the Republicans and Lincoln during the election. Southerners began to preach of "Black Republicanism" as a counterpoint to the charges of a "slave power conspiracy."

Lincoln probably would not have won the presidency in 1860 had the election not become a four-way race. The Democratic Party split between two candidates: pro-slavery John C. Breckinridge, a former vice-president of the United States; and Stephen A. Douglas, a moderate, who attempted to reprise his defeat of Lincoln in 1858. The fourth candidate, on the ticket of the new Constitutional Union Party, composed of former Whigs and Nativists, was John Bell of Tennessee. Tariffs, homesteads, railroads, immigrants, and political corruption all figured in the campaign, but slavery and the fear of disunion remained the pivotal questions. When it became obvious to the candidates, based on the results of gubernatorial elections in Pennsylvania and Indiana, that Lincoln was going to win, Bell accepted the inevitable secession of his home state of Tennessee, and Breckinridge proclaimed dedication to immediate disunion; but Douglas, to his credit, disavowed any ideas of secession, saying, "If Lincoln is elected, he must be inaugurated."[5]

Lincoln won the election with just under 40 percent of the popular vote and 59 percent of the electoral votes. He carried eighteen states; yet, with the exception of coastal California, not one of them was below the Mason-Dixon line. This result reinforced his position as a sectional leader rather than a national one. Significantly, Douglas, who beat both Breckinridge and Bell with 30 percent of the popular vote, represented the views of at least some of the electorate in all parts of the country although he received a mere four percent of the electoral votes. Besides Mississippi, the only other state won by Douglas was New Jersey. This seemingly strange pairing effectively ended the influence of Douglas and the Northern Democrats. Breckinridge, with 18 percent of the popular vote, carried every state that would come to be in the Confederacy except Mississippi and Virginia. The former vice-president also carried Maryland and Delaware. Bell captured the states of Kentucky, Tennessee, and Virginia and received 13 percent of the popular vote. Notwithstanding this result, 70 percent of the voters had shown support for at least a moderate stand against slavery, but they almost all resided in the North.

President-elect Lincoln first came to Willard's Hotel in Washington, and he stayed there rather than at a rented house for 10 days prior to his own inauguration in 1861. The First Family occupied Parlor No. 6, a pricey corner suite of rooms on the second floor. The bill for the stay was more than $770. Diarist George B. Loring spotted Lincoln at Willard's when the president-elect made his first public appearance in the nation's capital. "I was standing in the upper hall of Willard's hotel, conversing with a friend and listening to the confused talk of the crowded drawing-room adjoining. As we stood there, a tall and awkward form appeared above the stairs, especially conspicuous, as it came into view, for a new and stylish hat. It was evidently President Lincoln, whom neither of us had seen before. As soon as his presence was known, the hall was thronged from the drawing rooms. He seemed somewhat startled by the crowd, did not remove his hat, wended his way somewhat rapidly and with mere passing recognition, and took shelter in his room."[6]

In his inaugural address, Lincoln tried to reassure the South that the federal government would "never interfere with the domestic institutions of the states." He saw no constitutional means by which the federal government might outlaw slavery in the southern states. "I have no purpose, directly or indirectly to interfere with the institution of slavery in the States where it exists. I believe I have no lawful right to do so, and I have no inclination to do so." Lincoln hoped instead to "nudge" slavery out of existence.[7] The border states had been selling increasing numbers of slaves south for decades, and the isolation of slavery to the so-called Cotton States of the Deep South was not too far in the future. Southerners would have to decide the issue within their own states. Slavery might last for a century, thereafter collapsing under its own weight. Free blacks would be dispatched to Africa.[8]

A group of moderate Virginia residents declared that "the election of a sectional president even with odious and dangerous sentiment" would not of itself be sufficient cause for secession. All three defeated presidential candidates from the 1860 election—Douglas, Bell, and Breckinridge—called on Lincoln at the Willard's in the first days of his presidency. Only Douglas, himself a Northern Democrat, stood squarely behind the president, and he was one of the first public figures to suggest that those who did not embrace the war effort were traitors. "There are but two parties, the party of patriots and the party of traitors."[9] Shortly thereafter, the president met with delegates from 21 of the 34 states in one of Willard's drawing rooms in an unsuccessful attempt to avoid civil war through negotiation. Lincoln begged the Southerners for a fair trial, and he guaranteed that under his administration only they would decide the fate of slavery inside their states. Yet many Southerners saw the election result as "an alarming indication" of the ripening schemes of abolitionists to "plunder" and "outrage" the Southern way of life with their growing fanaticism. The abolitionists exacerbated the seriousness of the situation by taunting Virginia as a "Plunderer of Cradles—she who has grown fat by selling her own children in the slave shambles: Virginia! Butcher—Pirate—Kidnapper—Slavocrat—the murderer of John Brown and his gallant band—at last, will meet her just doom." Secessionists warned that Virginia could soon expect an invasion of armed abolitionists and would become, as it subsequently did, the primary theater of the military campaign to eradicate slavery.[10]

SECESSION

In light of subsequent events, it seems certain that the election of Lincoln in 1860 was the precipitating event that led to secession and ultimately to the Civil War. Lincoln, following the generally unpopular Buchanan, was the second minority president elected in succession, which suggests a growing lack of faith in the national government. But the question of secession had appeared much earlier than 1860, and from many unexpected quarters. It had first been suggested by the New England colonies in their dispute with James Madison over the War of 1812. The most serious confrontation between the federal government and the states, however, had come in the nullification crisis of the 1830s. South Carolina had actually raised troops to withstand the implementation of the Tariff of 1832. The question of secession had been a political issue in the national elections in both 1852 and 1856. Virginia had threatened secession in 1856, and South Carolina had threatened to secede in both these years.

While the concept of state nullification was a moderate position compared to secession, its logical conclusion would have rendered the federal government impotent. John C. Calhoun, a brilliant legal mind, realized that, even in a democracy, 49 percent of the people could be tyrannized by the other 51 percent if the majority were well organized behind a single issue. Therefore, if the majority was to rule, the minority must be

willing to assert its rights. In this case, the right was that of state nullification. The administration of Andrew Jackson had reacted to nullification
with the passage of a Force Bill (1833) authorizing the president to send
troops to South Carolina if the state persisted in its refusal to allow the
collection of the tariff and in its marshalling of an armed force in the form
of a state militia. The crisis was averted by the passage of a compromise
federal tariff acceptable to South Carolina, and the nullification of the
Force Bill by the state. While disunion was averted by this face-saving
device, the entire scenario would be played out again in 1860 with very
different results.

In the nullification crisis, the South found a new weapon with which
to enforce its will on the national government. The threat of secession
thereafter dominated the rhetoric of Southern politicians. The radical
politicians of the South raised the concept of states' rights to the level of
political gospel during the decade of the 1850s. Many Southern leaders
espoused secession only sporadically, and usually only during an election
campaign. Those who did otherwise did not achieve lasting prominence.
However, with the help of the Southern radicals called "fire-eaters," what
had started as an intriguing political device soon got out of hand.

FIRE-EATERS

Although there were numerous radicals actively pursuing disunion in
all the Southern states, some fire-eaters are worthy of separate consideration, as they were conspicuously in the forefront of the clamor for secession and served as consistent and effective proponents of disunion.

Edmund Ruffin was an aged Virginian who had taken up the torch of
secession in mid-life and allowed his quest to become an obsession. Ruffin
devoted twenty years to the espousal of secessionist doctrine. He became
a professional fire-eater, traveling widely, speaking to public gatherings,
and writing prolifically on this sole theme. Ruffin was in his mid-sixties
by the time secession became a reality, but he was still active in the cause
and had the honor of firing the first shot on Fort Sumter.

As early as 1828, Robert B. Rhett of South Carolina was urging resistance
to the supposed despotic rule of the federal government. Rhett was one of
the earliest and most outspoken of the fire-eaters railing against Andrew
Jackson's Force Bill and urging armed resistance. He introduced amendments to the U.S. Constitution to protect Southern rights, and in 1844 he
led an abortive tariff nullification movement. Rhett used his Charleston-
based newspaper, the *Charleston Mercury,* to plead with the Southern states
to secede en masse in defense of states' rights and Southern culture. When
these supplications fell on deaf ears, he urged South Carolina to set an
example and secede alone, believing that the rest of the South would follow. His long dedication to the cause earned him the appellation "Father
of Secession."

William L. Yancey of Alabama was one of the best spoken of the disunion apologists. Yancey had lived as a youth in the North and never tired of using his personal experiences to reinforce the perception of its moral and cultural degradation. In the 1830s he became convinced that the South could no longer protect itself from the degrading Northern influences that seemed to be gaining control of Congress. When the Democrats refused to include a pro-slavery plank in their 1848 election platform, he became an ardent and unapologetic secessionist, urging immediate disunion. He hammered relentlessly on the themes of Southern unity of action and immediate disunion. The Southern states, he said, "all united may yet produce spirit enough to lead us forward, to call forth a Lexington, to fight a Bunker's Hill, to drive the foe from the city of our rights." It was Yancey, in the spring of 1860, who engineered the split in the Democratic convention that all but ensured the election of an anti-slavery Republican.[11]

Of the prominent fire-eaters, few went on to serve in battle, choosing rather to remain in politics. William Barkesdale of Mississippi, however, was a notable exception. Barkesdale, a true fire-eater, had been a vociferous and effective proponent of secession. The Southern war office made him a brigadier general, and he proved one of the most effective political commanders in the war. The tenacity with which his Mississippi regiments opposed the river crossing of federal troops during the Battle of Fredericksburg won him great renown. Barkesdale was killed during the Battle of Gettysburg as he fought in the peach orchard.

THE SOUTHERN RADICAL PRESS

In calling for secession, the fire-eaters were aided by a highly partisan and radical press. Public orations, debates, and harangues were a popular instrument of the fire-eaters and were well attended. Yet these forums addressed only those who could be present, producing a somewhat transient enthusiasm for the particular topic of discussion. Therefore, the 19th-century citizen favored the newspaper as a more individualized form of communication. Newspapers gained influence steadily during the first half of the century. An amazingly large number of local publications appeared. Speeches were printed in their entirety within a few days of being given. Printed political arguments, essays, letters to the editor, and discussions among dedicated readers—both genuine and planted for effect—flowed in the wake of every issue.

People read alone or in small groups, with the leisure to reread and analyze what was printed. The power of the press to influence a wider audience than could be assembled at any one place and time was not to be underestimated. Some papers tried to remain neutral, but others sought out political alliances either because of the agenda of the editors, or, more commonly, in order to attract a lucrative trade in political advertising and public printing. Neutrality on any topic of public interest often doomed a newspaper to failure. "We have perfect unanimity in the press," wrote one Southern observer. Local newspapers commonly filled their pages with reprinted articles and speeches reported in other journals from around the country, often with biting editorial preambles.[12]

Besides Rhett's *Charleston Mercury,* several newspapers were actively stressing Southern independence. *DeBow's Review,* a monthly commercial publication located in New Orleans, urged the South to diversify its economy and to build railroads, factories, and canals, thereby freeing itself from dependence on the North. By mid-century *DeBow's* was increasingly seen as a vehicle for secessionist propaganda. *The Richmond South,* edited by Roger A. Pryor, and its sister paper, the *Enquirer,* edited by Henry A. Wise, both stressed secessionist themes. *The Richmond Examiner* was described as firing "shot and shell" at those moderate on secession. The *Whig* went "into the secession movement with all its might." *The Dispatch,* once neutral and conservative, threw "all its powers, with its large circulation, into the cause" by 1860.[13] Southern nationalism was hawked by the respected *Southern Literary Messenger,* once edited by Edgar Allan Poe, and even the *Southern Quarterly Review* was pleading the cause of disunion.

Secessionist sentiment pervaded the churches, the shops, and even the schools. Pro-secession radicals smashed unfriendly presses, banned books, and fought duels with Unionists. The fire-eaters turned every news article, pamphlet, sermon, and play into a propaganda piece for secession. Even minor confrontations with the Unionists, or with the abolitionists, were declared a crisis upon whose immediate resolution rested the very survival of the South. Warfare in Kansas, the publication of *Uncle Tom's Cabin,* and the anti-slavery raid of John Brown at Harper's Ferry gave credence to the tales of the fire-eaters. When there was no crisis, the radicals were fully capable of fabricating one. Southern leaders in Congress proposed the reopening of the transatlantic slave trade in 1859 without hope of the question being resolved in their favor so that the radicals might use the issue to good effect as propaganda.

THE ACT OF DISUNION

Secessionists had proclaimed South Carolina the leader of disunion since the 1830s, and it remained the natural home of secession throughout the period. The nullification crisis had all but eliminated any pro-Union feeling in the state. Radicals claimed that if South Carolina were to act for itself, the secession of the entire South would be "three-fourths finished." The Palmetto State had renewed its threat to secede in 1859 by inviting its sister slaveholding states to consider a course of concerted action. Many in the Deep South thought that the border states—Virginia, Maryland, Kentucky, and Tennessee among them—would ultimately join a new confederacy in their own time. Nonetheless, a positive decision was deferred pending the outcome of the 1860 election. This view was held by both the North and the South and was one of the few things that evoked widespread unanimity. It is not clear what result a Lincoln defeat or a Breckinridge, Douglas, or Bell victory would have meant to the secession movement. However, in its declaration the Secession Convention listed as one of the reasons for its secession "the election of a man to the high office of President of the United States whose opinions and purposes are hostile to slavery." Certainly, a Republican victory had been a signal for action.[14]

The eight states with Southern sympathies initially stood against the Confederacy and were willing to give Lincoln a chance. These included the Border states of Maryland, Delaware, Tennessee, and Kentucky, and the Middle South of Virginia, Arkansas, North Carolina, and Missouri. In the four Middle South states, only Arkansas and Virginia called a state convention to consider secession before the Fort Sumter crisis. Arkansas rejected secession by a narrow margin, but in Virginia the vote was 2 to 1 against disunion. Elsewhere Missouri, Tennessee, and Kentucky "shouted no," North Carolina voters "whispered no," and Maryland and Delaware did not formally consider the question. "Thus as Abraham Lincoln began his presidency two-thirds of southern whites remained rooted in the Union."[15]

Some secessionists, including William Yancey, began the movement toward disunion on the eve of the presidential election by calling for part,

The Secession Congress: On December 20, 1860, South Carolina voted to dissolve the Union. The state had threatened to secede many times in the past without acting on the threat, but the election of Lincoln made secession a reality.

if not all, of the South to make an immediate break with the North. These men were willing to leave Virginia and the other border states, thought to be soft on the question of secession, in the Union in order to save the rest of the South from further Northern degradation. A border composed of states in the Union, yet amicable to slavery, might prove more effective to a new confederacy than confederated states that were lukewarm to disunion. The new nation would thereby have a border free of hostile abolitionists, and it was thought that neutral border states might be unwilling to allow the predicted Northern invasion to be marshaled in their territory. Other Southerners cautioned that some precipitate action might limit the time needed to build consensus for the Confederacy and to establish firm control of former Federal instillations in the South like forts, ports, armories, and depots.

On the afternoon of December 20, 1860, the South Carolina Convention passed an Ordinance of Secession. Five additional Southern states quickly followed its example: Mississippi, Florida, Alabama, Georgia, and Louisiana. In February, Texas came on board. At first, it appeared that only these seven states would secede, and early Confederate flags sported only seven stars. Lincoln's decision to contest the surrender of Fort Sumter in Charleston and Fort Pickens in Pensacola provoked many of the formerly undecided states to secede, yet it was Jefferson Davis who decided to fire the first shot of the war. In April, after the bombardment of Fort Sumter and Lincoln's call for 75,000 volunteers to defend the Union, Virginia joined its sisters voting 6 to 1 for disunion. A Confederate officer's teenage wife wrote in her journal, "Dear Old Virginia, long did she strive to keep her place in the Union, but trampled rights, a broken Constitution, and a dishonorable Government compelled her to join her sister states in a new Confederacy." This news was followed in May and June by the secession of Arkansas (13 to 1), Tennessee (2 to1), and North Carolina, whose legislature agreed unanimously.[16] When Lincoln had become president, the Confederacy had contained seven states with approximately 33 percent of all the white residents of the South. In less than six months his policies had helped the Confederacy to grow to eleven states and 63 percent of southern whites.[17]

The presence of federal troops in nearby Washington virtually tied Maryland and Delaware to the Union. Western Virginia and most of Eastern Tennessee were solidly against secession from the Union, but only West Virginia was willing to make a break with the rest of Virginia, becoming a distinct state in June 1863. Secessionist sentiment in Missouri and Kentucky was somewhat split. As large areas of these states were quickly brought under federal control, actual secession was impractical. Eleven states had actually seceded; nonetheless, when the new Confederate battle flag was designed, it sported thirteen stars, the last two representing the fiction that Missouri and Kentucky were willing but unable to join their sisters. Certainly, the western reaches of Missouri and the southwest corner of Kentucky were populated by secessionists, but neither was able to form a viable government. The use of thirteen stars was thought to reinforce the symbolic connections between the infant Confederacy and the American Revolution.

Although the radicals and fire-eaters had set secession in motion, they soon lost control of the new Southern nation. Few fire-eaters served successfully for any time in the new government. More moderate heads prevailed. Jefferson Davis, the first president of the Confederacy, had been a strong advocate of states' rights, but he was far from being considered a radical. Alexander Stephens, a recent convert to disunion, was chosen to serve as the Confederate vice-president. Other moderates like Judah P. Benjamin and Robert E. Lee would lead the prosecution of the war.

Nonetheless, disunion was very popular in the South, not only among the social and political elite, but also with the average white Southerner. "The unanimity of the people was simply marvelous. So long as the question of secession was under discussion opinions were both various and violent. The moment secession was finally determined upon, a revolution was wrought. There was no longer anything to discuss, and so discussion ceased. Men got ready for war, and delicate women with equal spirit sent them off with smiling faces."[18]

In 1861, after Lincoln's call for a Northern mobilization of 75,000 men, a clerk from the Confederate War Department noted, "From the ardor of the [Southern] volunteers . . . they might sweep the whole Abolition concern beyond the Susquehanna, and afterwards keep them there."[19] All seemed to understand the consequences if the cause of secession did not succeed. Southerners could not, without a complete sacrifice of their honor, do anything else but fight on to victory or utter defeat. "This is the irrevocable blow! Every reflecting mind here should know that the only alternatives now are successful revolution or abject subjugation."[20]

The function of honor, as an important component in the Southern rationale that led to secession and war should not be minimized. While no one can exactly define the reason for which each Confederate soldier fought, their diaries and letters suggest that the defense of Southern honor, which had been disparaged by Northern fanatics, was high on the list. Rebel private Carlton McCarthy noted, "When one section of the country oppresses and insults another, the result is . . . war!"[21] With respect to the secession of Virginia, General Robert E. Lee wrote, "We could have pursued no other course without dishonor. And sad as the results have been, if it had to be done over again, we should be compelled to act in precisely the same manner."[22]

Northerners responded to the act of disunion in a variety of ways. A young woman wrote, "The storm has broken over us . . . How strange and awful it seems." In the North the stock markets fell and banks began to

An artist's conception of the parade of the Federal Volunteers through the streets of New York—a scene repeated in many cities and small towns in the North.

call in their loans. Many businessmen, forgetful of their recent enthusiasm for abolition, panicked at the specter of near bankruptcy. Yet initially the majority of the people celebrated the coming of the storm with fervor and enthusiasm: "We have flags on our papers and envelopes, and have all our stationery bordered with red, white and blue. We wear little flag pins for badges and tie our hair with red, white and blue ribbons and have pins and earrings made of the buttons the soldiers gave us." Women gathered to sew uniforms and made up "scrap lint and roll up bandages" in the churches and the local courthouses.[23]

Troops paraded through the streets of large cities and small towns. "It seemed," wrote Theodore Winthrop, "as if all the able-bodied men in the country were moving, on the first of May, with all their property on their backs, to agreeable, but dusty lodgings on the Potomac." Soldiers in gray and blue, and in the garish uniforms of Zouaves, Chasseurs, and Dragoons, carried their regimental flags past the White House. Six regiments from three different states arrived in Washington in such close succession that their separate parades formed "a continuous procession." The War Department could not provide for all the volunteers arriving in the capital, and placed them in warehouses and markets to sleep until proper camps could be arranged on the ring of hills around the city. Like irresponsible children, some soldiers joined the gaily dressed and carefree crowds that roamed the city, even to the grounds of the Executive Mansion, waving flags to the strains of patriotic songs such as "Yankee Doodle," "The Girl

I Left Behind Me," and "Columbia, the Gem of the Ocean." Lincoln's call for volunteers had been answered with a vengeance.[24]

A young Michigan volunteer remembered the holiday atmosphere that he encountered as he headed South with his unit in early June 1861:

We shook hands with everybody and bid them goodbye, and the desire on the part of others was equally great. . . Our journey through Ohio was a glorious one. Every hat and handkerchief and apron and bonnet along the road was thrown into the air. All manner of shouts and cheers of encouragement. Hurrah for Michigan, hurrah for the union, God bless you, farewell, give 'em h—l, etc. greeted us at every step . . I observed one thing in particular, to wit, that there are an immense number of pretty women in Ohio . . Our whole reception was such as only the soldiers of liberty and civilization receive. The whole country where we pass is in a blaze of patriotism.[25]

When the Michigan unit reached Baltimore, Maryland—a so-called border state—the streets were as densely crowded. "The children and ladies cheer in great numbers for the union and several wave flags. The men are much more careful what they do." Marylanders had attacked Federal troops (the 6th Massachusetts) marching through the city with blood shed on both sides, and the young Michigan soldier was ordered to load his gun with a live round, "the first ball that I ever intended for a human mark." The troops marched down the streets of Baltimore in silent wariness. "Cheers for Jeff Davis [Confederate President] are heard occasionally from groups of 3 or 4 . . We pass over the way pursued by the Mass. 6th and saw the place where those who were killed fell." A group of the Michigan volunteers caught a "secessionist," searched his home, and would have killed him had they found a so-called "secession flag," but their officer stopped them and placed a guard on the man's home to protect it.[26]

NOTES

1. Daniel Walker Howe, *What God Hath Wrought: The Transformation of America, 1815–1848* (New York: Oxford University Press, 2007), 650, 767.

2. William E. Freehling, *The South vs. The South: How Anti-Confederate Southerners Shaped the Course of the Civil War* (New York: Oxford University Press, 2001), 35.

3. William A. Fletcher, *Rebel Private: Front and Rear* (1908; reprint, New York: Meridian, 1997), 2.

4. Carlton McCarthy, *Detailed Minutiae of Soldier Life in the Army of Northern Virginia, 1861–1865* (1882; reprint, Lincoln: University of Nebraska Press, 1993), 3. Originally printed in 1882, this is one of the most readable Confederate accounts of the daily life of the soldier. For a more detailed discussion of the disunion debate in the South, see Sewell, 68–78.

5. Richard H. Sewell, *A House Divided: Sectionalism and the Civil War, 1848–1865* (Baltimore: Johns Hopkins University Press, 1988), 76.

6. "Abraham Lincoln at the Willard Hotel," Abraham Lincoln Online, http://showcase.netins.net/web/creative/lincoln/sites/willards.htm (accessed January 2008).

7. William E. Freehling, *The South vs. The South: How Anti-Confederate Southerners Shaped the Course of the Civil War* (New York: Oxford University Press, 2001), 36.

8. See the statements of Georgia's Henry L. Benning in Ibid., 36.

9. Jennifer L. Weber, *Copperheads: The Rise and Fall of Lincoln's Opponents in the North* (New York: Oxford University Press, 2006), 14.

10. Ervin L. Jordan, Jr., *Black Confederates and Afro-Yankees in Civil War Virginia* (Charlottesville: University Press of Virginia, 1995), 16. Attributed to the Charlottesville Review, March 15, 1861, as reported in the Winchester Republican, March 22, 1861.

11. Emory M. Thomas, *The Confederacy as a Revolutionary Experience* (Columbia: University of South Carolina Press, 1991), 28.

12. Earl Schenck Miers, ed., *A Rebel War Clerk's Diary, by John B. Jones, 1861–1865* (New York: Sagamore Press, 1958), 14.

13. Ibid.

14. Thomas, 30.

15. Freehling, 40–41.

16. Civil War Times Illustrated, March-April 1991, 12.

17. Freehling, 43.

18. George, C. Eggleston, *A Rebel's Recollections* (1874; reprint, Bloomington: Indiana University Press, 1959).

19. Miers, 8.

20. Ibid., 1.

21. McCarthy, 2.

22. Kennedy and Kennedy, 155.

23. Caroline C. Richards, *Village Life in America, 1852–1872* (Gansevoort, NY: Corner Book, 1997), 130–131.

24. Margaret Leech, *Reveille in Washington* (New York: Harper & Brothers, 1941), 66–77.

25. Stephen W. Sears, ed., *For Country, Cause, and Leader: The Civil War Journal of Charles B. Hayden* (New York: Ticknor & Fields, 1993), 18–20.

26. Ibid., 22.

3

THE AMERICAN ZION

"Boston rules Massachusetts, Massachusetts rules New England, and New England rules the nation."
— William Lloyd Garrison

THE PERFECT NATION

From the opening of the 19th century, Northerners persisted in an effort to portray the American Republic in idealistic terms that reflected openness, unpretentiousness, and ease of ascent. Even though the reality was far from the ideal, America continued to be viewed as a Zion for the world, and the non-utopian inconsistencies, most evident in Northern urban life, were excused as temporary problems with which the nation would come to terms in time. Socially conscious Northerners declared that America was the archetype of the perfect nation, with its expansive borders, rich and prolific soil, abundant raw materials, citizens blessed with industry and enterprise, and institutions and forms of government more free and equal than any in Europe.

This view was periodically bolstered throughout the prewar period by advances on many fronts. The nation had doubled in size with the Louisiana Purchase of 1803. Texas had been annexed, California had been added, and the northern boundary of Oregon had been settled. In 1853, the Gadsden Purchase from Mexico filled out the familiar continental boundaries of the United States. The nation had accomplished its Manifest Destiny by stretching from sea to sea in less than three-quarters of a century. American industry was becoming the ideal of the world, and American clipper ships were masters of the seas. The major cities of the North were connected by rail, canal, or steamship, and the modern marvel of telegraphy crisscrossed the eastern half of the country by 1850.

Even in the face of severe social, political, and economic problems, Northerners sang the praises of their unique American way of life and soft-pedaled the traditional life of the South with its rural ways and race-based slavery. However, social inequities were not confined to the South. In the cities of the Northeast the disparities between the immigrant and the native born, the wealthy and the impoverished, and the educated and the ignorant were growing. Urbanization brought crowding and disease. Technological advancement led not only to labor-saving devices and to better systems of transportation and communications, but also to derailments, steamboat explosions, and factory disasters. Increasing industrialization exploited white labor on a level that seemingly rivaled the evils of slavery.

For remedies, concerned Americans looked to a national government unfamiliar with dealing with social problems. The Founding Fathers had predicted that the republic could not meet all the imponderable requirements of an expanding society without modification. For this reason, they had provided for amendments to the federal Constitution. Yet basic changes in the role of government were found to be unacceptable to many citizens; therefore, a quiet attempt began to perfect the American system incrementally rather than radically. As many problems were predominantly local in nature, 19th-century Americans began by tinkering with their state governments. Each state had its own constitution reflecting a regional consciousness generally more accepting of amendment than the founding federal document, which required a greater unity of the national mind.

During the first half of the century, the political deficiencies that threatened the national utopia had become highlighted. Many voters came to a personal reappraisal of the traditional system of American self-government. Rapidly changing social circumstances fueled this dissatisfaction. Growing political partisanship was the natural outgrowth of these efforts to correct the situation with a minimum of turbulence. A growing lack of consideration among politicians for the public good underscored the need for leaders independent of partisan politics to decide on the new direction of the nation. The decision to change the basic character of the state to conform with visionary social principles quickly became a moral imperative to be pursued regardless of the consequences.

In a reactionary effort permanently to shield the new American utopia from the reach of later partisan politicians, legislatures in a few Northern states amended their constitutions in ways better left to well-thought-out and specific legislation. Politicians were pressed by reformers to present amendments affecting the most minute details of daily life. Requirements for officeholding, taxation, and enfranchisement were changed, and limits on police power, legislative prerogatives, and judicial authority were enacted. By mid-century most state and local offices had been made elective instead of appointive. This feature of local government allowed the electorate to replace those officials with whom they became displeased and had the effect of further democratizing the process. By mid-century adult white males could vote in every state in the Union, and election turnouts often rose above 70 percent of the eligible voters.

In the Northern states the rise of urbanization, immigration, and manufacturing led to changes in property qualifications for officeholding and voting. Often masked as an attempt to protect the rising middle classes, such efforts were often designed to limit the influence of large employers to control the votes of their workers. Officeholding became a good deal more widespread than previously was the case, and "rotation in office" came to be viewed as a leading principle of a republican form of government. It was seen as a way of enlarging the ranks of public servants to include those outside the sphere of the landed gentry or the social elite.[1]

By contrast, the South had moved to ensure and perpetuate the influence of the planter class. Reformers generally discounted the views of the planter class as being particularly detrimental to the national good because of their support of slavery. Nonetheless, the old aristocratic Southern families had a firm hold on the structure of local and state government, and resisted any attempts at change. The mass of Southern voters generally applauded this restraint, choosing to support their leaders in a defense of the traditional American way of life. Although small farmers and shopkeepers found their way into government, the big planters continued to control a disproportionate share of the public offices.[2]

GROWING GOVERNMENT

In 1821, Thomas Jefferson had expressed concern over the increasing presence of government at all levels of American life, and many of his worst fears came to be realized. As a consequence of political and social tinkering, the number of public offices on the local and state levels of government began multiplying at an alarming rate. Government expansion into areas of life heretofore untouched by bureaucracy was disheartening to many. Local government, particularly, came to control a wide range of economic activity in a given region. Local regulations governed innkeeping, markets, bakeries, port fees, and hauling rates, and the growth of trade and manufacturing opened additional areas to control. The state acted in the licensing of trades and professions, the setting of standards, and the inspection of products. In the absence of strong federal policies, regulating banking and credit and providing for a system of uniform taxation and revenue collection became major concerns of the state authorities. Strangely, the composition and implementation of such sweeping regulatory changes were left largely in the hands of people from outside the upper classes of society. This generally enhanced the influence of bankers, corporation presidents, and money brokers.

Personal aggrandizement and financial enhancement threatened to dictate much of the new governmental regulation. As most Northern voters were not influential or prosperous men, state legislatures began bestowing privileges on small groups of well-heeled political supporters. These privileges often took the form of charters for banks and corporations, rights of way for turnpikes and railways, lucrative monopolies for the construction and operation of canals, and favorable regulatory legislation. By means of bounties, exemptions, and subsidies, government officials were becoming increasingly involved in business. "The state governments regulated business, promoted business, and engaged in business," wrote one observer.[3]

By mid-century there were signs that the people were finding the unceasing intervention by government in their daily affairs tiresome. Political opponents were refused charters or licenses and were hounded by the minions of the controlling party until their taxes were paid, while the delinquencies of political allies were often overlooked. At the same time that state funds were stretched to the limit and local credit was less readily available, many state-supported enterprises were poorly run or did not live up to expectations. Governments began spending beyond the level of revenue, and the public debt increased everywhere.

The control of state politics gradually shifted and, in many cases, came to reside in unexpected hands. The petty politician was suddenly faced with unexpected opportunities in municipal government. Day-to-day politics became the domain of the man who had a hand on the pulse of local opinion. Political neophytes were attracted to positions as selectmen, sheriffs, justices, collectors, inspectors, and deputies of all kinds. Positions in the state capital or county seat often attracted lawyers who were there to enact other business. Sometimes the caliber of these officeholders was questionable. Genius, dedication to the commonwealth, and talent often lay neglected as offices were increasingly filled by the ambitious, the reprobate, the dishonest, or those who could barely read and write.[4]

The most influential officeholders operated from an ever-growing urban base. Established families in the North clutched at the reins of power, but the new class of municipal officeholders successfully manipulated the ever-changing social structure in the cities by rallying the population to one cause or another. A European observer of the American political system noted, "To gain votes, one must descend to maneuvers that disgust men of distinction. One must haunt the taverns, drink and argue with the mob; that is what is called Electioneering in America."[5]

In an effort to garner wider public support for their agendas, politicians consciously moved the decision-making process from the gatherings of a few influential individuals to the open conventions of political parties. Although the smoke-filled back room still played its role, the politicians recognized a need to develop a following in the electorate and a political platform from which to launch their schemes. Inevitably, these tactics led to the benefits of an extended franchise and the removal of property qualifications for officeholding. As the process expanded to include persons never before allowed to participate in politics, many were attracted to socially acceptable outlets for their newfound zeal. As the traditional emphasis on sin and salvation in many New England churches came to be replaced by the more secularized obligations of social justice and humanitarianism, the great cities of the North, and Boston in particular, became hotbeds of political activism.

The American people appear to have had an unlimited faith in their ability to perfect the human condition and provide a model social setting for all. This optimism, somewhat misplaced in light of future events, placed a heavy burden on the social elite to ease the sharpening contrasts between the ideal American society and the realities of social misery that were becoming more visible in the city streets.

The influence of these social and moral pressures on the attitudes of the middle and upper classes should not be underestimated. Discontent and frustration with the inertia of the political process induced many Americans to join and support a number of reform movements. The perpetuation of social ills was ascribed to a lack of public will in implementing the appropriate cures. Reformers were absolute in their belief in the efficacy of these cures and demanded their immediate implementation. "A new type of despotism" emerged from the imperative to reform. Although it was based on intellectual and emotional forces rather than on physical compulsion, the reform movement, in many of its guises, was willing to suppress personal liberty, tradition, and even constitutional principles to correct the social ills in America.[6]

While there remained a strong belief in American individualism, personal strength of character, and the ability of a man to overcome the handicaps of his environment, such concepts were identified more and more with conservative resistance to social reform. Some Northerners and many in the South, unconvinced that poverty and disease among the lowest level of the social order posed a menace to their communities, were also distressed by the radical way social activists approached their task. Opposition forces found many of the reform proposals unrealistic, grandiose, sanctimonious, and antagonistic to traditional American concepts of personal rights and freedoms.

URBANIZATION

In 1800, the entire United States was essentially a rural country. Less than 6 percent of its population of 5 million lived in towns with populations larger than 2,500. Only Philadelphia and New York had populations greater than 25,000. The settlement of the Mississippi Valley and the Northwest during the first half of the 19th century had contributed to a vast internal migration. By 1850, the country had 23 million inhabitants, and more than 30 percent of the population lived in towns with more than 2,500 persons. Although two-thirds of the population was still involved in agriculture, the expansion of commerce and industry had drawn a large number of people into towns that were both old and new. The urban population became the fastest growing segment of the population.

Cities as distinct as Providence and Chicago were experiencing similar rates of growth due to their importance in trade. A number of small coastal towns became booming cities by mid-century in response to America's rise to maritime greatness in the clipper ship era. Boston, Salem, Portland, and New Haven, for example, were all active coastal trading cities in 1850. Boston alone was the terminus for no fewer than seven railroads. Westward expansion and the successful navigation of the western rivers by steamboats made a number of inland ports equally important. These included Pittsburgh, Cincinnati, Louisville, Memphis, Natchez, and St. Louis. The number of towns having more than 10,000 people increased from 6 to more than 60 in less than half a century.

The cities that had been the largest at the turn of the century remained so and experienced the greatest rates of population growth. By 1850, New York City boasted a population of more than half a million. Philadelphia, Boston, Newport, Baltimore, New Orleans, and Charleston had grown to hold hundreds of thousands of persons. Nonetheless, Southern cities had attracted less than 10 percent of the population of the region. The physical size of the American city also increased, from a radius of less than a mile to four or five miles. Northern cities were characterized by a well-defined and established business district, socially and ethnically segregated residential areas, and the beginnings of the suburb.

The Southern cities grew along the perimeter of the region's heartland and tended to materialize after the surrounding area was well settled. These cities grew as planters and farmers came in from their outlying and relatively isolated holdings to take advantage of the social and cultural benefits cities offered. Coastal and river cities in the South also had a large itinerant population of traders, bargemen, and clerks, but Southern cities tended to avoid the development of slums and ghettos. Outside of the almost self-sufficient plantations, small towns in the rural South offered a few amenities such as a doctor, a tradesman, or a small store or two, but nothing more. Consequently, Southern towns often appeared shabby and run-down to visitors unfamiliar with rural life.

Immigration from abroad outstripped the physical expansion of the cities and stressed their infrastructure to the limit. This remarkable influx of foreigners had an incalculable effect on the nature of Northern culture. Poverty, disease, crime, and ignorance became concentrated in the slum districts of Northern cities as immigrants drew together in the security of their own communities. Antebellum immigration reached its peak between 1845 and 1855. More than three million immigrants, 10 times as many as had come to America since the founding of the republic, entered the country. Most congregated in the cities of the North. One had only to walk through an ethnic ghetto to discover the overwhelming atmosphere of social decay and moral degeneration—a condition Southerners quickly pointed to as evidence of the failure of Northern culture. Even the reformers believed that the standard of living among these immigrants had to be improved if the squalor of the cities was not to become a permanent feature of Northern society. Their predictions were borne out by the subsequent decades of urban poverty.

Many Americans could not escape the view that the decay and degeneracy were due to the immigrants themselves. Immigrant populations seemed to tolerate—if not frequent—taverns, beer halls, saloons, dance halls, gambling establishments, and houses of ill repute with amazing disregard for traditional American standards of conduct. A tone of condescension and disdain even entered the rhetoric of the reform movements. Many reformers attributed widespread social nonconformity among immigrants to social degradation rather than differences in ethnic character. They therefore misguidedly directed their reform campaigns against the foreign-born instead of toward the correction of social injustice in the American system. By mid-century a strong ultra-Americanism had coalesced in the form of "American Only" organizations such as the Nativist Party.

There were three major countries of origin for the immigrants that entered America at this time. These were, in descending order of their proportion in the immigrant population, Ireland, Germany, and Great Britain. Together, they provided about 85 percent of all immigrants to the United States up to the beginning of the Civil War. The influx of Italians, Jews, and eastern Europeans would not become significant until late in the century. With the exception of the Germans, the majority of immigrants spoke English. There was therefore little in the way of a language barrier to frustrate economic success or attract prejudice. Immigrants from Great Britain assimilated fairly well into surroundings dominated by an American upper class that had strong English origins.

The Irish, who also spoke English, had an unfortunate history of poor relations with their cousins in Great Britain that followed them to the New World. The Irish were the first truly urban immigrants in American history, banding together in inner-city neighborhoods that quickly took on all of the outward appearances of slums. Many established Americans saw this development only in prejudicial terms and blamed the slum-like conditions on the Irish themselves, ignoring the anti-Irish bigotry of employers and landlords. In addition to being the victims of social prejudice, the Irish were also accused of voting illegally, of selling their votes to unscrupulous politicians, and of engendering crime and immorality. Cyrus Byington, a Presbyterian minister, noted that compared to the Irish in Boston "the negroes. . . are princes."[7] Ironically, many of the worst and most unruly elements among the urban street gangs chose to enter the army in 1861 thereby relieving for a short period some of the crime that had plagued city residents.

RELIGION

A matter of primary concern influencing this bias was the difference in religious background among immigrants. The United States had been predominantly Protestant and Christian from its inception. Although the population was mainly Episcopal (Anglican or Church of England) in colonial times, the American Revolution had shed many of the country's links with the established Church in England. The Founding Fathers had almost all been Protestants, but this Protestantism had been essentially related to Puritanism as represented by the Congregational churches. In the colonial period, Scotch-Irish immigrants had added an element of Presbyterianism, and later the Baptist Church became popular. Both of these were largely within the same religious tradition. Protestantism remained the dominant mode of religious affiliation into the 19th century, with the Episcopal Church remaining strong in the South. The predominantly Lutheran Germans and Scandinavians were the first to introduce a new element to the religious mix. Nonetheless, their churches were essentially Protestant, and they assimilated with little fuss into the American social fabric.

At the time the nation was founded, Jews made up such a small proportion of the population that their presence was mathematically insignificant. However, in 1845 a European economic depression caused many Jews to immigrate to North America. German Jews made up the largest portion of this wave of immigration, with the majority clustering in the urban centers of America. For example, the Lower East Side of Manhattan—famous for its tenement houses, neighborhood groceries, and clothing stores—became an enclave of Judaism. Between 1850 and 1860, the number of American Jews tripled, to 150,000—a significant number, but still less than one-half of one percent of a population of 32 million Americans.

The German Jews brought with them to America the idea of Reform Judaism. In their synagogues, they introduced innovations in the ritual, used both German and English, and allowed men and women to be seated together. Nonetheless, most still observed the traditional dietary laws in their homes. Apparently, Jews experienced little overt anti-Semitism. This may have been due to their isolation and their small number. . A significant number of Jewish individuals played important roles as government officials and army officers in the war.[8]

However, it was the Christian religious revival at the beginning of the century that most affected American society. Evangelism, with its strong emotional appeal, was particularly influential among 19th-century Americans. By the 1830s, Methodist and Baptist churches had become the two largest denominations in the country. Methodism, in particular, offered a new view of theology. The tenets of Methodism were more comforting and humanitarian than the stern predestination and selective salvation of the Puritans. The older denominations, which stressed the total depravity of man, seemed to be at odds with the democratic spirit of America. By mid-century most American Protestants had come to believe in their free will to choose a path to salvation by placing themselves in a position to receive God's grace if they were worthy of it. This belief was to have a profound effect on the way soldiers faced death in battle as they strove to be worthy of God's protection by exhibiting courage and steadiness under fire.

The newer religions stressed repentance, individual awakening, and conversion, and reflected the same trends in secular society. Unitarians and Disciples of Christ broke away from established churches, while Mormons and Adventists sprang from the soil of America itself. Mormons were so feared and hated in America that they were driven to isolation in the West in the prewar years.

Only the Quaker sect, one of the oldest in America, seems to have had a unanimous position on the questions of the war—renouncing violence and supporting abolition. Both the Baptists and the Methodists split along sectional lines in the 1840s over doctrinal and organizational controversies exacerbated by the issue of slavery. The other church sects were equally unable to maintain a strong spirit of fellowship. There was an increased tension in religious circles between social activism and private religious expression. Some of the community's leaders opted for positions in secular organizations rather than religious ones in an attempt to effect social change. Ordinary people, however, remained more interested in matters of spirituality.[9]

Added to this confusion were the new immigrants, particularly the Irish, who were predominantly Catholic. In the 1830s the Roman Catholic Church was possibly the only religion in America not divided over doctrine. The Church was intolerant of criticism, unapologetically authoritarian, resolute, and unalterable in its structure. It was the oldest religion in the Western world, and it demanded the unquestioned obedience of its members to the will of the Pope. It was the Catholic Church that grew fastest because of the mass immigration of the 1840s and 1850s.

Catholic believers were prospering. They established an educational system that still exists as well as colleges and seminaries that provided some of the best higher education available in the country at the time. A European touring the United States in 1831 said of the Catholic colleges in Maryland: "These colleges are full of Protestants. There is perhaps no young man in Maryland who has received a good education who has not been brought up by Catholics."[10]

A "Protestant crusade" to stem the growing influence of the Catholics in America began in the 1820s and grew in proportion to the increase in Catholic immigration. This movement, truly reactionary and discriminatory, was rooted in a traditional abhorrence of the Roman church and was aimed at the recent Catholic American immigrant. Americans feared the power of the Catholic Church. Even in the South, where concern over immigration and papal absolutism was marginal, due in large part to a significant minority population of French and Spanish ancestry, the authoritarian structure of the Catholic Church was viewed as incompatible with American principles and capable of marshaling Catholic immigrants against traditional American institutions.[11]

REFORM MOVEMENTS

The majority of reform movements initiated prior to the Civil War were essentially benevolent. Philanthropic reforms focused almost solely on the visibly degraded elements of society whose condition proved an embarrassment to the nation. These included paupers, drunkards, orphans, illiterates, Indians, slaves, prostitutes, and prisoners. Reform activities were popular primarily with the middle and upper classes, and were characterized by a laudable "urge to remedy visible social ills, alleviate suffering and discourage behavior that was considered immoral."[12] Although reform movements were common to urban areas generally, the home of reform was Boston. Many social reformers agreed that "Boston rules Massachusetts, Massachusetts rules New England, and New England rules the nation."[13]

Many different types of people were drawn into these reform movements. Some community leaders opted for positions in these highly visible secular organizations solely to improve their social standing. Some obviously enjoyed the work because it satisfied their own aspirations and salved their feelings of frustration. Others crossed the lines between reform movements, working on one social ill and then another. William Lloyd Garrison, for example, began as a temperance advocate in 1828, founded the American Anti-Slavery Society in 1833, and took up the causes of feminism and radical pacifism in the 1840s. Ultimately, Garrison claimed that he was willing to destroy the Constitution in the name of abolition, and he disrupted church services and political meetings to make his point.[14]

Much of the resistance to reform was based in a natural social inertia, but some of it was caused by the inability of the activists to articulate the scope and righteousness of their agenda to the public. The activists proved most controversial in their insistence on immediate and total reform and in their unwillingness to compromise. This was particularly true of the radical abolitionists. Moreover, reformers demanded that the government supplement intellectual persuasion with legal coercion in many areas. Nonetheless, the majority of social reformers were motivated by a genuine sense of moral obligation and national pride.

THE TEMPERANCE MOVEMENT

The growing popularity of the temperance movement can serve as an example in this regard. From colonial times, a moderate use of strong drink was considered acceptable by all but the most radical portions of the population. The colonial population, magistrates, and clergy, in the absence of potable water, had consumed alcohol in prodigious quantities. In 1644, Connecticut ordered all but the smallest towns to establish a tavern or inn for travelers constrained for want of entertainment, and in 1656 the General Court of Massachusetts made towns liable to a fine for not sustaining a licensed public house. The importance of the tavern to its neighbors was far greater than it was to any itinerant travelers that happened upon it. It was there for the comfort of the community, for the interchange of news and opinions, and for the incidental sociability it provided among the townspeople. The tavern was often the unofficial center of community life.

In the 18th century, the consumption of alcohol had not yet taken on any negative associations; colonial New England imported four million gallons of molasses each year. Half of this was distilled into a very satisfying rum in the 60 distilleries in Massachusetts, and 95 percent of the rum produced was consumed locally. Besides domestically produced rum and beer, there were imported wines, brandies, and liqueurs of many types. Whiskeys, gins, and other distilled beverages were not particularly popular in America except as home brews intended to deny import duties to the government.

A copy of the *Temperance Recorder* of August 1834. From the authors' collection.

Nonetheless, alcohol quickly became a target of 19th-century social reformers. When Secretary of War Jefferson Davis criticized the use of a statue of the Goddess of Liberty to adorn the top of the United States Capitol in 1850, one of the proffered recommendations for a substitute was a statue of the Goddess of Temperance. While the proposal was dismissed by the officials in Washington, the temperance crusaders, undaunted by the rebuff, put their movement into high gear. The failed campaign nonetheless produced a good deal of positive propaganda. Newspapers ran stories of drunken street brawls and bitter domestic scenes brought on by alcoholic consumption. Illustrations portrayed the general doom of the drunkard in its many guises in the shadow of the unfinished Capitol.

Immigrant families, following European custom, often used alcohol as a cultural prerogative, giving beer, light wines, and rum to children to "strengthen the blood" and prevent disease. Nonetheless, the dangers of immoderate drinking were real, and alcoholism could end in disaster. Many men actually drank away their wages, leaving their wives and children destitute. For the alcoholic, suicide became a cliché. Strong drink was often cited as the cause for eternal damnation and earthly licentiousness, as well as spouse abuse and rape.

In fact, the temperance movement was very closely allied with women's issues and may have mirrored a rising tide of women's discontent with their place in the social order. Women took up the temperance struggle by forming prayer groups and railing against saloons with their bottles, mirrors, and portraits of reclining nudes. A melodramatic scene printed on the cover of *Harper's Weekly* in 1858 showed a young wife and children, the alcoholic head of the family missing, turned out of their tenement into the cold. Whether the mother was widowed or abandoned—there was no suggestion of waywardness or immoral propensities in her appearance—the picture emphasized, once again, the message of a close connection between women's issues and social activism on many fronts.[15]

Alcohol was viewed as both the cause and the balm of the economic despair found among the poor in the urban slums. As the root cause of their problems, regular appearances in the local tavern with "jolly companions" were considered the "ultimate attainment of the confirmed drunkard." Conversely, temperance was equated with love, purity, truth, fidelity, marital stability, economic prosperity, social position, and religious salvation.[16]

The temperance movement was set back for a time by the defection of activists to the abolitionist cause and the exigencies of living in a war-torn nation. Yet the temperance reformers increased the stakes of their game and insisted on total abstinence from alcohol in any quantity or strength and supplemented their demands with calls for its legal prohibition. Temperance forces succeeded in passing prohibition legislation in a half dozen Northern states, but many of these laws were subsequently found to be unconstitutional. Not until the 20th century did temperance legislation find solid ground in an amendment to the federal constitution. This shift from moderate and sometimes symbolic goals to conclusive ones, carved into the legal fabric of the nation, was typical of many of the reform movements of the 19th century.

THE PREVENTION OF PAUPERISM

One of the earliest reform organizations was the Society for the Prevention of Pauperism. In a country supposedly blessed with economic abundance, it was difficult to understand the causes and conditions that led to poverty among a large segment of the population. In the 19th century it was clear that people recognized a difference between the "poor," who had small incomes, and those known as "paupers," who were so destitute as to be on the public dole. Americans in colonial times had adopted a calm and complacent cure for such poverty. Disinclined to design large programs to relieve poverty, and reluctant to lay blame upon the poor for their condition, the colonials quickly and without tedious investigation simply provided support for the destitute. This support often took the form of financial aid, food, firewood, or clothing brought to the homes of the needy. If the recipients were disabled or suffering from extreme age, the support was funneled through the households of relatives or friends.

A period illustration of poor boys shoveling snow for the rich in hope of receiving a tip.

Traditional American culture, still in vogue in the South, exhibited a broader acceptance of the poor than was found in industrialized and urbanized areas in the North. Eighteenth-century Americans, in sharp contrast to 19th-century reformers, viewed a well-ordered society as hierarchical, with each social level enjoying its own special privileges and obligations. Unfortunately, this conception made the poor a permanent fixture of the social order. If the poor were "always with us," asserted the Founding Fathers using a biblical reference to justify the continued presence of the unfortunate in a supposedly enlightened social order, then "let God be praised" for the opportunity to help them.

Southern attitudes in the 19th century continued to reflect much the same perspective. The black slave was visibly marked by God to show his natural place in the social order. The place of the laborer or the artisan in Southern society was part of the natural order, not a demeaning or disparaging imposition from which one sought to escape. Moreover, the leadership of society was equally well established in the leading families of the South as a natural consequence of God's will. Of course, the needy were much less conspicuous and more sparsely concentrated in the largely rural areas of the South in the 19th century, much as they had been in colonial America, and the task of providing for their support under trying circumstances was thereby made less onerous.

Beginning in the 1820s, poverty came to be seen as unnatural in a bountiful America. Moreover, an implicit faith in the perfection of America left many among the socially conscious with the notion that poverty was capable of eradication if the systematic roadblocks and reluctance to change in the old order were removed.

Nonetheless, if colonials had made little effort to eliminate poverty, at least they did not punish and seek to isolate the poor. Colonial complacency quickly gave way in the 19th century to a heightened suspicion of the poor themselves. "Surely the poor were partly to blame for their own misery, having succumbed to the vice of idleness or intemperance. Yet. . . they were not inherently depraved but rather were the victims of the numerous temptations set before them by society." As religious thought became increasingly secular, God's will and the ravages of original sin no longer seemed satisfactory explanations for the condition of the poor.[17]

Reform advocates railed against towns that licensed grog shops and saloons. They defamed politicians who allowed gambling halls and dens of iniquity to flourish. Moreover, they castigated the poor themselves. New York's Society for the Prevention of Pauperism found that most of the poor of the city required support because they were so "depraved and vicious." The poor were increasingly viewed as human raw material "to be acted upon, to be improved, manipulated, elevated and reformed."[18]

Of course, none of the reformers thought to ask the poor what they felt were the primary causes of their condition. The poor may have listed unfair labor practices, ethnic or religious bias, and unscrupulous landlords as causes of their plight, but they were generally quiet on the subject. The reform movement of the 19th century was characterized as one of activism of the "haves" for the "have nots" rather than a demand for reform from those who were oppressed. This form of personal protest would not become popular until late in the century.

Activists formed a sort of reform elite that not only had the conceit to decide what areas of society needed reformation but also attempted to differentiate between the worthy poor, whose lot was due to misfortune, and the corrupted and unworthy idlers. Widows with small children were almost universally viewed as worthy of public assistance. An investigatory committee in 1827 unhesitatingly reported that the vice found in large eastern cities was attributable in large part to the actions of the poor themselves. The reformers concluded that eliminating the stain of poverty from the fabric of American society would require the isolation of the poor from their sources of temptation and the instruction, by force if necessary, of the destitute in the habits of industry and labor. This grandiose plan resulted in the institution of a series of almshouses. The poor, regardless of the particular circumstances of their plight, would receive aid only while confined within the almshouse. Once inside, they would be taught order, discipline, and responsibility.

A group of New England philanthropists was assured in 1843 that the almshouse was "a place where the tempted are removed from the means of their sin, and where the indolent, while he is usefully and industriously employed. . . is prepared for a better career."[19] Notwithstanding these assurances, the almshouses failed to relieve the problem of prolonged poverty or its symptoms. The truly depraved and corrupted among the poor avoided such institutions. Almshouses became filled to overcrowding with the helpless, the decrepit, the abandoned, and the very young. The emphasis on rehabilitation and personal reformation, initially a primary goal of the antipoverty reformers, quickly became irrelevant as the most heart-rending members of the poor community were hidden behind brick walls. A committee in New York reported in 1857 that the general conditions found in such institutions had degenerated into a cruel and punitive system of custodial care.

Social conservatives, North and South, particularly deplored the development of free public schools that admitted children from many class, ethnic, and family backgrounds, and inculcated in them a set of novel values that stressed social equality. The development of the public schools was paralleled by the institution of a Catholic school system in the immigrant-filled cities of the North. Such notions were seen as a threat to traditional fundamental values and represented a clear danger to the status quo, to be avoided at all costs.[20]

The dimensions of the schemes put forth by the reformers of the 19th century were exceeded only by the depth of their failure. The poor remained in their crime-ridden environment, alcohol flowed freely until the

20th century, and the freed slaves remained on the bottom rung of social and economic life. Yet, despite the incongruity between the utopian ideals of the reformers and the consequences of reality, mindless social tinkering and disgraceful forms of public altruism persisted and proliferated until well after the Civil War. Only the uncompromising conviction of the reform activists of the correctness of their self-proclaimed solutions to America's social ills, and their unrelenting hounding of public officials, could have kept such failed social experiments in existence.

THE VALUE OF A DOLLAR

In order to set a standard for the study of the Northern economy in the later half of the 19th century, it is important to evaluate the worth of a U.S. dollar. Oddly, the value of a dollar was exactly the same in 1860 as it was in 1900. There had been inflation during the Civil War, and it took $1.96 dollars to equal an 1860 dollar in purchasing power in 1865. However, the monetary history of the U.S. dollar during the rest of the century was one of deflation from this high. It is safe to assume that an 1860 U.S. dollar (USD) was equivalent to approximately $18 (USD) in 2008 currency. Oddly, the intrinsic worth of the present U.S. dollar is less stable than it was during much of the 19th century because it is presently unsupported by precious metals (gold or silver) as was the 1860 dollar.

The average family income in the United States in 1860 in modern dollars (2008) was a remarkably low $7000, or just under $400 dollars in 1860 money. People generally worked for less than might be thought, and the overwhelming majority of families had little income in the form of hard cash. Nonetheless, they were also largely farm families that extracted much of their sustenance from the land. On the other hand, a family with an average income of $2500 in 1860 dollars could afford to hire a cook, a housemaid, and a nurse for the children. Doctors, lawyers, and civil servants—considered the "middle of the middle class"—made between $1500 and $2500 annually depending on whether they practiced in rural or urban areas of the country respectively.[21]

Family income was the measure by which sociologists and social reformers in both Britain and the United States differentiated between the "poor" and the "very poor" or destitute. Acting out of concern for an understanding of the working-class unrest that gripped Europe in 1848, statisticians and sociologists began about 1850 to take data and to conduct studies of family income and expenditures in order to shed light on any differences. One of the major figures in this field was Ernst Engle (not Friedrich Engle, the colleague of Karl Marx). Ernst Engle formulated the idea of poverty studies in which family income was compared to family expenditure as a measure of a *standard of living.* Two English sociologists, Charles Booth and B. Seebohm Rowntree, were the first to show that poverty was not simply a matter of low income. Booth and Rowntree, separately, devised the concepts of *primary poverty* and *secondary poverty*—those with barely enough means for independent living, and those whose income was insufficient to meet their daily needs, respectively.

In the 19th century, every man worked for his living, but not all men worked in the same way. Almost everyone below the uppermost classes of society needed to make a living through the application of their own physical labor. Workers at this time could be divided into several categories, among them laborers, farmers, clerks, craftsmen, machine operators, shopkeepers, metalworkers, and mariners. There were also those who dealt in the extraction trades like mining, timbering, or fishing. Before the Civil War, clerks and machine operators represented a numerous, but decided minority of city workers. In some urban areas, unskilled laborers made up to 40 percent of all workers. Craftsmen and shopkeepers have often been considered a privileged class somewhat akin to small businessmen, but many of the persons involved in crafts or shopkeeping were actually women, not the middle-class employers of apprentices and journeymen, but petty proprietors with just enough income and business acumen to rest on the lower rung of middle-class status.

The constant influx of immigrants, who were willing to take on the most onerous and lowest paid jobs, effectively drove the native working classes to middle class status; and as an incoming tide raises all boats, the Northern middle class found itself raised to a social level undreamed of in the previous century. Nonetheless, entry into the upper classes in America required both money and the acceptance of those already considered the social elite. Many families were barred, therefore, from further upward mobility, and the middle class consequently expanded.

Employment opportunities were not equally available to all classes and levels of society. Young men of the upper class preparing for life in a profession—physician, engineer, or lawyer—expected to be able to maintain a standard of living and social status commensurate with their services to the community. Churchmen and teachers, always resentful of the parsimony of the community, expected a salary that reflected their educational qualifications and a respectful place in the scheme of social hierarchy. Those born to wealth might lead an indulgent life or work as managers of the family business or plantation without regard to the willingness of their neighbors to provide them an income. They formed the highest rungs of the economic ladder because of their birth or family connection. Industrialization brought a new category of worker into the mix. This was the factory manager, or overseer, who directed the labor of others in the mills and manufactories.[22]

THE NORTH FINANCES THE WAR

Under the influence of the gold coming from California in 1849 and 1850, the American economy regained much of the prosperity that had been lost in the prolonged depression of 1837. The economy again experienced minor downturns in 1854 and 1858, but silver and gold discovered in the Washoe area of the Sierra Nevada's in 1859 (known as the Comstock Lode or Nevada Bonanza) relieved the distress somewhat, the economy was still reeling from its latest bout with the so-called Panic of 1858 when war broke out. Development and exploitation of existing mines was particularly important during the war years as both North and South tried to fill their war chests by mining precious metals.

Owing to the initial expectation of a short war, the Federal government raised its war chest chiefly by taking loans and issuing paper money and bonds. The government generally failed to raise enough funds through these methods running in deficit throughout the conflict. Expenses ran eight times the revenue from taxes. After encountering serious difficulties in marketing government bonds, Secretary Simon P. Chase authorized the firm of Jay Cooke and Company to be the sole subscription agent for the sale of Federal bonds. Through his network of sub-agents, his many newspaper advertisements, and his vivid speeches appealing to workingmen to put their savings into the war effort, Cooke quickly marketed the bonds both in the United States and in Europe. He was thereafter known as "the financier of the Civil War."

Nonetheless, the money raised by selling bonds was inadequate. In August 1861, the Federal government required each state in the Union to fill a revenue quota for the war based on population. How each state raised the money was left to its own devices. It was hoped that $20 million would be raised through this means, but only $17 million was forthcoming.

Another source of war funding was found in the adoption of a personal income tax, the first tax of its kind ever levied by the United States government. As first envisioned, it fixed a three percent tax on family incomes over $800, but by June 1864 the exemption fell to $600 and the minimum rate rose to five percent on incomes up to $5,000, quickly setting a pattern for federal income taxes to come. The rates increased progressively to 7.5 percent on incomes between $5,000 and $10,000, and 10 percent on those over $10,000. During the three war years—1863, 1864, and 1865—the income tax yielded only $55 million.

In order to raise addition funds, the Federal government established an excise tax. This was an internal revenue tax that was added to the price of a broad range of items, and it served as the main source of Federal financing for the war. Ostensibly, the seller paid a tax on the sale price of the item, and the purchaser paid a personal property tax on its ownership. Of course, as with most taxes of this type, the purchaser ultimately paid the entire tax in the form of high sales prices. These taxes were applied to a list of commodities that included a three percent tax on malt liquor, spirits, tobacco, and stamps as well as on manufactured items made of cotton, wool, flax, hemp, iron, steel, wood, and stone. Meats were taxed at 30 cents per butchered steer, 10 cents per hog, and 5 cents per sheep. Carriages, billiard

Indices of Prices and Real Wages During the Civil War (1860 = 100 USD/CSD)

Year	Union (USD)		Confederate (CSD)	
	Prices	*Real Wages*	*Prices*	*Real Wages*
1860	100	100	100	100
1861	101	100	121	86
1862	113	93	388	35
1863	139	84	1,452	19
1864	176	77	3,992	11
1865	175	82		

Source: Roger Ransom, "Economics of the Civil War," *EH.Net Encyclopedia*, ed. Robert Whaples. http://eh.net/encyclopedia/article/ransom.civil.war.us (accessed April 2009).

tables, gold and silver plate, yachts, and other top-tier items were charged an additional luxury tax. Moreover, many professions and trades were forced to pay fees for licenses, and many forms of entertainment were required to collect taxes as part of their ticket price. Railroads, banks, insurance companies, and telegraph companies were required to pay at rates and in ways best fitted to their individual business operations. The law was so extensive and so minute in its detail that it required 240 pages and more than 20,000 words to express its provisions. In 1864 and 1865, these excise taxes yielded close to $210 million.[23]

Although buoyed by the influx of precious metals from mines in California and the Mountain West, in 1862 the Lincoln administration began to issue paper currency as a wartime economic measure. Called "greenbacks," more than $450 million in engraved paper bills were issued. Ever since the days of the Federalists, paper currency had been issued by the government, but it had always been backed at a specific rate by specie ($20 per troy ounce of gold) held in government vaults. Lincoln's greenbacks were based only on the good credit of the United States government. Inevitably, in the midst of a war of disunion, a difference between gold value and paper currency value appeared on most commodities, and trading in currency became complex and volatile.

Gold being the universal liquidator of commerce, the first premium on gold coins and bullion was seen when importers of foreign goods were required by their suppliers overseas to pay in gold rather than paper. Domestic commodities and internal business exchanges were less affected than foreign ones. The premium set in motion a speculative trade in greenbacks and gold futures that caused the value of both to fluctuate. In January 1862, gold opened at a mere 1.5 cent premium, but the premium quickly increased as Federal armies failed to quell the rebellion. Exactly two years later, it was at 52 cents per dollar, and in June 1864, the gold premium stood at more than 95 cents. In other words, almost two paper dollars were needed to make the equivalent of one dollar in gold. In July 1864, the premium reached its greatest excess at $2.85 of paper currency for $1 in gold money.

Finding their shops swamped with business customers trading in dollars and gold, Wall Street money brokers in New York, who commonly dealt in foreign currency exchanges, moved into a suitable building that was dubbed the Gold Exchange. There were numerous reasons for the fluctuations in gold premium. Indeed the whole gold market was as sensitized to the political and economic pulse of the country as was the stock market. Changing currents in fiscal policy, debates in Congress, international crises, battle results, changes in army or government personnel, rumors, and many other factors affected the price of gold and had the inverse affect on greenbacks. When the Confederate forces under Gen. Jubal A. Early were loose in Maryland and threatening the Federal Capitol on July 11, 1864, the paper price of gold reached $2.85 per $1.00 in gold money. Early was met by a hastily improvised force under Federal Gen. Lew Wallace (best known as the author of the novel *Ben Hur*), and when Early turned away from Washington, the premium price of gold fell, some say in proportion to his distance from the capitol. Although the Gold Exchange was a wartime phenomenon, it remained in operation for seventeen years. After a long fight in Congress and the courts over the conversion of greenbacks to gold, specie payments were resumed in 1879, and the price of gold was again fixed by the government at $20 per ounce with an ounce of silver at $1.

It should be noted that when comparing international monetary values during the 19th century, the normal exchange rate of $5 (USD) per British pound sterling (£1) was commonly used. Except during the war years, the difference between the dollar and the pound was largely a function of their value in gold rather than of the unsupported strength of the currency as it is today. Specie-backed dollars were simply smaller units of value than specie-backed pounds.

NOTES

1. This is similar to the effort to set term limits in the 1990s.
2. Richard H. Sewell, *A House Divided: Sectionalism and the Civil War, 1848–1865* (Baltimore: Johns Hopkins University Press, 1988), 3.
3. Don E. Fehrenbacher, *The Era of Expansion, 1800–1848* (New York: John Wiley & Sons, 1969), 76.
4. Oscar Handlin and Lilian Handlin, *Liberty and Expansion, 1760–1850* (New York: Harper & Row, 1989), 123.
5. J. P. Mayer, ed., *Journey to America, by Alexis de Tocqueville*, Trans. George Lawrence (New Haven: Yale University Press, 1960), 254.
6. Fehrenbacher, 98.

7. Clyde A. Milner II and Floyd A. O'Neil, eds., *Churchmen and the Western Indians, 1829–1920* (Norman: University of Oklahoma Press, 1985), 30.

8. Frank L. Byrne and Jean Powers Soman, eds., *A Jewish Colonel in the Civil War: Marcus M. Spiegel of the Ohio Volunteers* (Lincoln: University of Nebraska Press, 1994), 2–3.

9. Anne C. Rose, *Victorian America and the Civil War* (Cambridge: Cambridge University Press, 1994), 54–60.

10. Mayer, 78.

11. It was not until the election of John F. Kennedy in November 1960 that the Catholic taboo was broken, but questions were raised regarding the Mormon religion of presidential candidate Mitt Romney in 2008.

12. Fehrenbacher, 111.

13. George M. Frederickson, ed., *Great Lives Observed: William Lloyd Garrison.* (Englewood Cliffs, NJ: Prentice-Hall, 1968), 148.

14. Rose, 54–60.

15. David J. Rothman, "Our Brother's Keepers," *American Heritage,* December 1972, 39.

16. Ibid., 39–40.

17. See Ibid., 38–42, 100–105.

18. Ibid., 41.

19. Attributed to Dr. Walter Channing. As quoted in Ibid., 42.

20. These views were widely compared to the views of the 17th-century radicals of the English Civil Wars known as Levelers.

21. Schollander Wendell and Wes Schollander. Forgotten Elegance, *The Art, Artifacts, and Peculiar History of Victorian and Edwardian Entertaining in America* (Westport, CT: Greenwood Press, 2002), 217.

22. Volo and Volo, 2007: 73–74.

23. Randall J. G. and David Donald, *The Civil War and Reconstruction* (Boston: D.C. Heath and Company, 1961), 344–345.

4

ON BEHALF OF SOUTHERN INDEPENDENCE

"We have changed our constituent parts, but not the system of our government."

—Confederate President Jefferson Davis

SOUTHERN NATIONALISM

Patriotism and nationalism were powerful motivations in Civil War America. A growing Southern nationalism accompanied the development of the Confederate States of America. Nationalism was on the rise throughout Europe in the 19th century, and Confederates were quick to draw parallels between their struggle to found a Southern nation with those of the Dutch Republic and the Portuguese against Spain; the Italian revolutions in Sicily and Naples led by Garibaldi; the Polish rebellion against the power of Russian imperialism; and the ongoing Piedmontese struggle against Austria. Confederate diplomats held forth these examples to the world in the hope of gaining international support and recognition for their fledgling country.

The North had similar nationalistic views, but they were more capitalistic and utopian than those of its Southern counterpart. The Northern nation was dedicated to physical liberty, freeing the slave from his bonds, separating the poor from their circumstances, and relieving the alcoholic from his dependence on liquor. By contrast, the Southern nation was more dedicated to an abstract liberty defined by traditional political ideology and personal freedom of action unrestricted by governmental intervention.

As the two cultures diverged during the first half of the 19th century, their separate concepts of which social, political, and cultural characteristics should be indicative of America's ideal national identity diverged also.

Several of the competing characteristics came to be mutually exclusive and served as focal points for controversy. These included questions of slavery or abolition; economies dedicated to the growth of agriculture or industry; social elitism or social mobility; limited suffrage or democratization; personal religion or societal morality; patriarchy or matriarchy; personal responsibility or governmental action; and conservative or progressive politics. Forces representing different opinions on these questions were in almost continual conflict by mid-century.

Although the questions of slavery or abolition stood out at the time, Southern nationalism was fueled not only by the endorsement of continued slavery, but also by a growing contrast between a conservative Southern culture and a progressive Northern industrial society increasingly in favor of popular suffrage, a changing role for women, widening democracy, and social reform.

The creation of Southern nationalism and the establishment of a national identity separate from that of the North came to be viewed as necessary for the survival of the Southern culture, with or without the challenge of war. Many historians have continued to view the nationalist trappings of the Confederacy as a kind of mask for the Southern defense of slavery. Nonetheless, Southerners were strikingly self-conscious about the need to explain themselves and publicly define their position on this question. Slavery was an embarrassment to some Southern apologists; yet, at the time, slavery and national identity may have been truly inseparable in the minds of most Southerners.

Historically, the South had been neither democratic nor purely aristocratic. Instead, Southern politics had reached a balance much closer to the classical Roman concept of the republic, a public order in which the power rested with an elite group of people who ruled for the good of all. When the war began, the South was a distinct political entity with a fully operational government, at least at the state and local levels. Confederate nationalism, although novel as a collective entity, had deep roots in a distinctive antebellum Southern ideology. The "plantation aristocracy" had successfully dominated Southern society for many years by applying their wealth and political influence to the wheels of government. Their numbers were so small that no more than 50,000 persons—men, women, and children—in a population of several million qualified as part of this class. Economic security, once the hallmark of plantations, which stood like agricultural city-states, was no longer a certainty. The historic political power of the planter class had largely been conveyed during the decades after the Revolution to a new moneyed aristocracy vested in industry, commerce, banking, and railroads.

Small farmers had so worn out their land that they looked to cast their lot with the expansionists who were moving into the territories. Many middle-class Southerners migrated with their manners and culture to states such as Kentucky, Southern Ohio, Mississippi, Southern Indiana, and Texas. Planters with modest holdings were able to maintain their gracious style of living by establishing subsidiaries to their planting operations. Sawmills, gristmills, distilleries, and even country stores were run on plantations. The sons of these planters turned to new professions such as law and medicine. Some went into the city to deal in tobacco-related industries, and some turned to the military as an honorable profession in keeping with the traditions of the aristocrat. This may help to explain the large number of Southern gentlemen who received their education at military academies such as West Point or Virginia Military Institute.

Southerners willingly tried all expedients to support their culture, even though the system had long ago become economically archaic. The large landowners hoped, at the very least, to maintain their social status under such conditions. As the traditional prerogatives faded from the landed families, they were replaced by a defense of a lifestyle that was increasingly becoming a social anachronism.

This distinctiveness provided a rather warped view of the South, but many Americans accepted it as a valid interpretation of Southern culture and acted accordingly upon it. No one would have cared how archaic the plantation system was becoming, but slavery was the one anachronism that many concerned Americans could not accept. Although the aristocratic Southern way of life was practiced by a small minority of the population, the lifestyle of the planter class came under attack by the forces of democratization, industrialization, and abolition. The very intensity of the attack, endured for several decades by the planter aristocracy, helped to define a narrow set of characteristic social customs as particularly "Southern."[1]

With the increasing likelihood of secession, the large planters moved quickly to ensure that Southern nationalism reflected their particular interests, and they strove to protect their cherished way of life under the new government. However, the planters clearly understood that they could not act alone effectively. Practical considerations made them more dependent than ever before on the white masses. Conservative and elitist tendencies were altered by this need to create a popular consensus. Politicians, journalists, and clergymen undertook, therefore, to enlist the support of the small slaveholders and the non-slaveowning white majority in the establishment of a new nation. They used an astonishing mix of political and religious language in an attempt to excite an ardent and enduring enthusiasm across the entire population for the Confederate government and its institutions. However, they carefully avoided presenting secession ordinances and state constitutions to the masses for ratification lest their plans fail the test of public support.[2]

Ordinary citizens quickly recognized that their support was needed for secession and that their physical assistance would be required on the battlefield. They sought to trade their support for reforms in taxation, governmental structure, and social and political access under the new government which had been denied to them in former years. However, it was the political, social, and religious elite who most effectively interjected their concerns into the new Southern nation, and they were successful in exporting their ideals beyond the battlefield soldier to the mass of the Southern people.

"If the Confederate experience did nothing else, it gave Southerners, many for the first time, a sense of corporate identity," noted an observer of the process.[3] Even the citizens of Tennessee, who had previously disavowed the idea of secession, overwhelmingly voted in favor of separation from the Union once Lincoln called for troops to suppress the rebellion. Hundreds of suggestions poured in from all levels and classes of Southern society when a committee of the Confederate Congress asked for designs for a new national flag. Nine out of ten of these were from women. A Southern woman's diary noted in April 1861: "Upon returning to my boarding-house. . . I found the ladies making secession flags. Indeed, the ladies everywhere seem imbued with the spirit of patriotism, and never fail to exert their influence in behalf of Southern independence."[4] Women wore secession flags as part of their daily costume in the streets. Southern ladies formed gunboat societies that sponsored dances, bake sales, rummage sales, and auctions to raise money for the building of ironclads for the infant Confederate navy to use in defending the harbors and waterways. Southern women were intensely aware of the need to maintain a Southern tradition and culture that "had roots several decades deep," and their diaries and letters are replete with nationalistic themes.[5]

The strongest feature of Southern nationalism was to be found on the battlefield. The South was ripe for war. The *Baltimore American and Commercial Advertiser* reported on April 22, 1861, that hundreds of impetuous young Marylanders had left the city in wagons, carriages, and buggies or on horseback to cross over into the Confederacy and wage war against the invaders from the North. Although volunteers dedicated themselves to the defense of their individual states, the Southern army quickly showed a new unity and esprit de corps. For the first time in their lives many young men traveled away from their homes and interacted with people who were not also neighbors or relations. They accepted strangers as brethren, bonded to them by a larger identity. An analysis of the surviving letters and diaries of Confederate soldiers suggests that many expressed a patriotic allegiance to the Confederacy as a "country." Soldiers typically referred to sacrificing themselves on the "altar" of their country. Nonetheless, Rev. Wm. H. McIntosh warned that Jesus had foretold "the destruction of Jerusalem," and had admonished his flock to continue to look toward the salvation of their souls. "I might speak of the duty which you owe to others. . .[but] in these days some entertain the wicked delusion that he who dies for his country will be saved by virtue of his patriotism."[6]

Southern men were equally expressive in their desire to defend their state, their home and hearth, and their families. The conflict between the love of those things familiar, personal, or close and dedication to the more abstract and intangible new nation troubled many Confederates, but the paradox brought forth by this dichotomy of motivation was not insoluble. The urge to defend one's state and family, which brought many volunteers to the battlefield in 1861, took on greater scope when the Federals launched a massive invasion of the South in 1862. Those from Tennessee and Louisiana who had fought initially to liberate their homes from the "varlet's threat" quickly extended their commitment to the Southern nation as a whole, particularly when their principal cities fell to federal forces. Many Confederates came to realize that the defense of their home and hearth was best prosecuted by winning the war, even if that meant fighting on fields foreign to their domestic concerns. A Southern soldier wrote of both his nationalism and his identity as a Southerner: "My country shall be freed from the fiendish vandals who thirst for the extermination of a people who are actuated by motives . . . far above those that influence and characterize the enemy."[7] Individuals may have continued to do things as Texans or Floridians, but on the whole they identified themselves as Confederates united in the defense of an independent Southern nation.

REESTABLISHING THE AMERICAN REVOLUTION

The nationalist movement with which the South most closely identified was the American Revolution, and references were consistently made to it throughout the prewar period and through the Civil War years. Southerners viewed their struggle as a continuation of that of 1776. They felt that the original Revolutionary dream had not been completely fulfilled and that the original Constitution had been corrupted by Yankee degeneracy and immorality. It is important to note that many of the expressions of Revolutionary ideals credited to Southern apologists in the 19th century were also found with surprising regularity in diaries, journals, and letters from the front to loved ones at home. As these contemporary documents were not written for publication or for use as propaganda, it is hopeless to hold the position that their regular appearance in private letters is anything but a heartfelt outpouring of genuine sentiment.

It was commonly held that the fires of revolution, first kindled in Massachusetts, would have gone out had it not been for the sympathy, aid, and manpower provided by Virginia and South Carolina. There was a factual legitimacy to this claim. The views of Henry "Light Horse Harry" Lee, a Revolutionary War hero, devoted friend of Washington, and the father of Robert E. Lee, were typical of those of many Southerners. He wrote that the American victories in New Jersey, New York, and Pennsylvania were inconsequential in the ultimate attainment of independence. Indeed, although he participated actively in these campaigns, Lee felt that much of the martial effort in the North resulted in a string of abject failures, wherein even the victories proved indecisive in securing independence. The signal victories of the war over the British forces, and the ultimate victory at Yorktown, were perceived to have been Southern victories, and the outcome of the Revolution had been decided south of the Mason-Dixon Line. Many Southerners were of the opinion that they were, thereby, the natural guardians of Revolutionary ideals.

Southern political and military leaders of the American Revolution were held in awe. Thomas Jefferson, Patrick Henry, and Richard Henry Lee were viewed as the political giants who had fathered independence. The figure of George Washington was consistently recalled in this regard both in public documents and in private papers. Besides Washington, a litany of Southern battlefield heroes was commonly called forth to support the myth. The military legacy of a successful militia uprising against the overwhelming force of the regular British army, whether martial mythology or historical reality, was to have far-reaching effects in the organization of the infant Confederate army.

Southerners argued that it was illogical for the North to enshrine radical revolutionaries such as Sam Adams and Patrick Henry as Founding Fathers, but consider Edmund Ruffin a demented old man and William Yancey a traitor when they championed the same political ideals that led to revolution in 1775. The political concepts that fired a just revolution in the 18th century were no less valid in the 19th century.

The new Confederate Constitution was closer to the U.S. Constitution than it was to a revolutionary document. With the exception of a few omissions and changes in phraseology, the two documents are almost identical. As the purpose of disunion was to establish a government that would preserve Southern culture and society as it was, this is not surprising. The act of secession was a conservative political uprising, and the Confederate Constitution has been described as "a theoretical time capsule that embodies the distinctive principles of republican government."[8] These principles tended to focus on the Anti-Federalist view of the government which had been obscured by the development and implementation of Federalist political theory since 1789. Jefferson Davis wrote, "We have changed our constituent parts, but not the system of our government."[9] This statement exemplifies the true nature of the Confederacy as the Southerners saw it. The new government was to be a continuation of those ideals fostered in the first American Revolution which had been altered by a fanatical and immoral North.

However, as champions of a new revolution and defenders of the Southern nation, the Confederates gave up much of what they held dear. The South embraced a centralized government fully as determined to control the reins of government as that in Washington. The concept of states' rights was sacrificed—not without the determined resistance of some state governments—for the defense of the country as a whole. Southern cities swelled in size, urbanization increased, factories and manufacturing took on a new importance, and men and women went to work much like the wage earners of the North. Ultimately, even slavery changed as the Confederate Congress provided for the enlistment of black soldiers and dallied with bartering black emancipation for foreign recognition in the name of independence.

The planter aristocracy was sorely tested, and in many cases their social and financial prominence did not meet the challenge. Although wealth and social position maintained their hold on the structure of Southern society, the military created new avenues to prominence. Many aristocratic families lost scions to the fates of battle, while many of the masters of plantations proved unfortunate choices as military leaders.

The infant national government brought prominence and power to many of those who had been outside the upper classes of society before the war. Alexander Stephens, who was from a poor Georgia family, nonetheless became the vice-president of the new country. Judah Benjamin, outside the pale of acceptability in the North because of his Jewish ancestry, rose to be one of the most capable members of the Confederate cabinet and a respected and loyal friend of President Jefferson Davis. The greatest hero in the South during the war was an orphan and an impoverished

A *Leslie's* illustration by William Waud of the undiminished nationalism of the people of New Orleans even in the face of the loss of the city to Federal occupying forces. Note the prominence of the Confederate national flag and its similarity to that of the United States.

college professor who raised himself to the rank of lieutenant general—
Thomas J. "Stonewall" Jackson.

Before secession, the majority of manufactured goods needed in the
South came from the Northern states. Those not made in the North were
imported from Europe and entered the country through Northern ports
to be shipped south by means of railroads, river steamers, and coasting
vessels. The prospect of war with the North ended any hope of continuing this trade. At the same time imports from Europe, which had been
negligible before the war, were now becoming vital to the life of the new
Southern nation. Since the Confederacy had no large-scale shipbuilding
industry, lacking both facilities and shipwrights, and since the small facilities that did exist were totally dedicated to the building of gunboats and
ironclads, the effort to develop a substantial trade with Europe focused
on foreign vessels as carriers and made the new nation as dependent on
foreign powers as it had been on the North.

Below the mouth of the Chesapeake Bay, the Southern coast was largely
a ridge of sand occasionally broken by the mouths of rivers which discharged sediment into the bays and inlets that could afford ships a safe
haven. This silt was incorporated into a natural series of banks, shoals,
and sandbars inimical to deepwater shipping. As a consequence there
were few harbors in the South that were not subject to continually shifting
navigational obstructions, and few large ports capable of receiving oceangoing vessels had developed.

Two of the best ports available to the South—Norfolk, Virginia, and New
Orleans, Louisiana—were quickly taken by federal forces. Norfolk gave
access to Richmond by way of the James River, and New Orleans ranked
first as a Southern port in terms of wealth, volume of trade, and the number of alternate entrances to its harbor for oceangoing vessels. The federal
government further hampered the Southern effort to import necessities by
blockading the few good remaining ports along the coast. Of these, Wilmington, North Carolina; Charleston, South Carolina; Savannah, Georgia;
Mobile, Alabama; and Galveston, Texas, were the most important. Each of
these, with the exception of Galveston, was connected by rail to the rest of
the South. After June 1863, Wilmington proved the most important element
in the Confederate supply system both because of its rail connections and
because of its geographical location near the focus of the war in the east.

FINANCING DISUNION

The dedication to states' rights by its several member governments
made a wide-ranging system of centralized revenue measures difficult
for the Confederacy. The governments of several Confederate states railed
at any policy that came out of Richmond smelling of federalism. For instance, none of the paper notes issued in the Southern states was classified
as "legal tender," a status that would have made it mandatory for citizens

to accept the paper currencies as payment for all debts and for use in all monetary transactions for goods and services. Instead, these currencies were structured to be promissory notes or interest-bearing notes that relied solely on the good faith and confidence of the people in their state (and the state of the war), not on the dictate of a central government.

The three principal methods used to finance the Southern war effort were direct taxation, bonds and loans, and treasury notes. The Confederate government in Richmond was reluctant to rely on the first of these because it might too greatly stress the loyalty of the Southern people who were paying the cost of its defense with their economic life-blood or the actual lives of their sons and fathers. This was especially true in large areas of the Confederate states like Tennessee, Missouri, and Louisiana that were being overrun by Northern armies early in the war. The Federal armies, and particularly its blockading navy, kept import and export duties from bringing in much revenue. A direct tax on real estate, slaves, and other luxury property was enacted, but offsetting exemptions were allowed for funds paid to the individual states in both Confederate currency and specie. Less than $18 million in the equivalent of Confederate state dollars (CSD) was realized from direct taxation.

The Confederacy imposed an excise and license tax similar to that of the North in 1863, but it included taxes on additional items important to the Southern economy like naval stores, turpentine, sugar, molasses, and salt. Southern salt works were a priority target for the invading Federals. Only five months into the war, the Southern papers began to fret over a shortage of salt, which was worth its weight in gold.

The same legislation created an income tax of 1 percent on the first $1500 over a base exemption of $1000 to 15 percent on all incomes over $10,000. No tax was levied on land or slaves, but after reserving certain stores for their own use, all farmers and planter were required to pay to the central government one-tenth of their wheat, corn, oats, rye, buckwheat, rice, sweet and Irish potatoes, cured hay and fodder, sugar, molasses, cotton, wool, tobacco, beans, peas, and bacon. The legislation was expanded in 1864. This tax-in-kind means of financing and supplying the troops was very unpopular in some states and was tolerated in others. Everywhere it proved burdensome and inefficient to deal in bulk commodities rather than in cash. North Carolina and Georgia complained bitterly that their produce and materials should be used only for their own state troops. A final tax of 25 percent was levied on all coins, bullion, and foreign moneys exchanged in the Confederate states in February 1865. This came much too late to reenergize lagging Southern revenues. Since so much of the levy was paid in kind, it is difficult to attach a dollar amount to the revenue generated by these taxes. Nonetheless, it has been estimated that the Confederacy raised about one percent of its income from these sources.[10]

The south was more successful in borrowing money secured by its paper pledges known as *Cotton Bonds*. The Confederacy imported a remarkable amount of military supplies from Europe through the Federal naval blockade. More than 400,000 rifles, 3 million pounds of lead, and 2 million pounds of saltpeter for gunpowder production, as well as food, clothing, shoes, accouterments, medicines, and paper, were brought through the blockade. To pay for these supplies more than 500,000 bales of cotton were shipped out of the South during the war, and cotton bonds for additional bales worth millions of Confederate dollars (CSD) were issued to creditors mostly located in England and France.

Alexander H. Stephens, confederate vice-president, proposed the sale of cotton as a way of financing the war. His initial plan entailed taking two million bales of cotton from the 1861 crop, paying $100 million (CSD) for them in eight percent bonds issued to the growers, adding to them two million more bales purchased at the prewar market price, and shipping the whole four million bales to Europe. Here the cotton would be stored until shortages at the textile mills in England and France caused by the expected Federal blockage increased the market price to a staggering $1 billion. This would net the Confederacy a neat $800 million in a single operation. The plan was creative but hopelessly optimistic. Yet it might have been feasible if the four million bales and the ships to move them had been available and left unmolested by the Federal navy.

The South was much more successful in carrying out its cotton financing schemes on paper. Its first loan, based on cotton bonds, was for $15 million in 1861, and it was taken up domestically by the South's own loyal citizens. The residents of New Orleans picked up two-fifths of the issue. A $100 million loan was taken later the same year; this was taken up by the planters themselves and was paid in paper currency and produce, especially raw cotton. The most famous of these loans was arranged in 1863 by a French Financier named Erlanger, who sold Confederate bonds backed by cotton futures in the European financial markets for a sizeable profit. The bonds had a purchase price of $90 U.S. dollars (USD) or their equivalent in specie, and Erlanger undertook them at a $13 discount. They rose to $91.75 (USD) in May 1863 and never saw such a level again. The value of the bonds fluctuated widely following the good or ill fortunes of Confederate armies in the field. In December of 1863 after the effects of Gettysburg and the fall of Vicksburg had set in, they bottomed at $35.50 (USD), rebounded somewhat in 1864 when Confederate forces under Jubal Early threatened Washington, D. C., and settled thereafter at near half their issue price until Spring 1865. They then quickly plummeted to single digits, and at the final surrender of confederate forces in May 1865 were worth only $8 (USD).

BLOCKADE RUNNERS

A unifying feature of the Southern nation in its struggle with the North was the continued existence of the blockade runners. Often called the "lifeline of the Confederacy," the blockade runners were largely foreign-owned vessels that attempted to evade the federal blockade and bring military and other goods into Southern ports. The inability of the federal navy to stop these vessels served as a rallying point for Southern nationalism. The Confederacy imported a remarkable amount of military supplies through the blockade. To pay for these supplies more than 500,000 bales of cotton were shipped out of the South during the war and bonds worth millions of Confederate dollars were issued to creditors.

The price of consumer goods was most directly affected by the blockade. From 1860 to 1863 the monthly cost of feeding a small family was reported to have gone from $6.55 to $68.25.[11] The following prices were recorded in the months indicated by a concerned observer: In May 1862: meat—50 cents per pound; butter—75 cents per pound; coffee—$1.50; tea—$10; boots—$30; men's shoes—$18; ladies' shoes—$15; shirts—$6; room and board for one—$30 to $40 per month; and house rent per year—$1,000.[12] In September 1862: firewood—$16 per cord; coal—$9 per load; blankets—$25; sheets—$15; and bleached cotton shirting—$1 per yard.[13] In March 1863: cornmeal—$8 per bushel; chickens—$5 each; turkeys—$20 each; turnip greens—$8 per bushel; bacon—$1.50 per pound; bread—20 cents per loaf; and flour—$39 per hundredweight barrel.[14]

With a scarce supply of gold and the value of the Confederate dollar down to $18.50 per federal greenback by November 1863, the Southern government began impressing items of all kinds—"horses, wagons, hogs, cattle, grain, potatoes—leaving the farmers only enough for their own subsistence."[15] In March 1863 the Confederate War Department issued a schedule of standardized prices for impressed goods that reflected only half of their market value. Some counties were so alarmed by this development that they threatened to take steps to prohibit the export of foodstuffs from within their boundaries to the rest of the country.

The eventual success or failure of the Confederacy was largely dependent on the will of the people to support the war by enduring privation and tolerating wartime prices. Unfortunately, profits and patriotism were often in conflict when it came to blockade running. Of course, without profits there would have been no blockade runners at all. Yet the huge profits brought by private rather than military goods continued to hamper the ability of the Confederacy to use the blockade runners to their best advantage. Nonmilitary goods vied for scarce cargo space on the runners and sold for incredibly high prices in the marketplace, thereby fueling inflation. For a short time the Richmond government tried to enforce regulations reserving a large fraction of the cargo space in each blockade runner for military goods. This plan was aided by the dedication of Wilmington as a port of entry for military imports, while Charleston was left in the hands of private shippers.

The average lifetime of a blockade runner was two round trips. Besides a small number of sailing vessels, just under 300 individual steam-powered vessels tested the blockade, and two-thirds of these were either captured or destroyed. Nonetheless, of 1,300 attempted runs, over 1,000 were successful, and the supply line was maintained until the very last months of the war. Regardless of the inefficiencies of the blockade running system, no battle or campaign of the war was lost by the Confederacy for lack of arms or ammunition, due almost solely to the success of the runners.[16]

THE BREAD RIOTS

A severe food shortage seems to have developed in urban areas of the South in the latter part of March 1863. Initially a group of women in Salisbury, North Carolina, demanded that store owners charge them no more than the fixed price the government would ordinarily pay for foodstuffs and goods. Some of the merchants obliged the ladies by lowering their prices. There were several such episodes in the South at the same time. The most significant took place in the capital city of Richmond, where Mary Jackson promoted a concerted action by the women of that city to influence the price of goods and foodstuffs.

Beginning at the Belvidere Hill Baptist Church, the women, armed with persuaders such as pistols, knives, and hatchets, and led by Mary Jackson, marched on Capital Square in protest. Here the governor of Virginia, John Letcher, spoke to the crowd and expressed his sympathy, but he offered no concrete solution to their problem. As the crowd disgorged from the square, the gathering of women clearly became a mob and began to loot the stores and take the goods of the merchants. Seemingly no attempt was made to buy articles at any price, including prices fixed by the government. A number of merchants simply tried to close their doors, and at least one, a Mr. Knott, tried to appease the women by handing out packages of sewing needles—considered a luxury item at the time.

This episode was widely reported in the antigovernment papers and the Northern press as a "bread riot." Although there is no indication that any bread was taken or asked for, some foodstuffs, including bread, meat, and rice were distributed to the needy by the Young Men's Christian Association. "Boots are not bread, brooms are not bread, men's hats are not bread, and I have never heard of anybody's eating them," retorted a government clerk to the reports.

The riot was not a particularly large affair, and from its beginning at the Belvidere Church to its end in the downtown merchant quarter, it lasted little more than two hours. Nonetheless, President Davis had gone so far as to threaten to have the mob fired upon by the Public Guard which had mobilized in the streets. The Richmond Examiner suggested that future rioters be shot on the spot. The City Council initiated a formal investigation of the affair and found the riot to be totally unjustified. Several of the instigators of the protest were arrested. Of these, twelve women were

THE SOUTHERN QUEST FOR RECOGNITION

In March 1861, several Confederate diplomats were dispatched to Europe, carrying letters from the Confederate government promising advantageous treatment with regard to Southern cotton. The price was recognition of the Confederate States of America. These men were received cordially but coolly in Britain and France. In May, Queen Victoria extended "belligerent rights" to Confederate vessels and neutral shipping carrying military supplies and raw materials to the South, infuriating the Federal government.

In November, James M. Mason and John Slidell sailed from Cuba on the British ship *Trent.* The next day, in international waters, a United States warship overtook the *Trent,* and Mason and Slidell were brought under arrest to Boston. The British threatened war, but by the time the two Southern diplomats reached London and Paris, the furor had died. Neither man was greatly effective in their diplomatic mission.

Several Confederate agents were successful in other ways. James D. Bullock built and armed a number of Confederate vessels in Britain. Edwin De Leon, former U.S. Consul to Egypt, sailed to Europe to oversee Southern propaganda efforts in Britain and France. He was critical of his colleagues' efforts, however, and became convinced that recognition by Britain was impossible as long as the South supported slavery.

There was also a Confederate effort made to annex the Mexican states of Nuevo Leon, Baja California, Sonora, and Chihuahua. This was not a new idea; Southerners had howled with rage when the United States failed to demand these states at the end of the Mexican War. In 1861, many southerners thought their inclusion in the Confederacy would strengthen the South, but they failed to realize the added necessity of defending the new territory and the additional coastline, a proposition that could hardly have been fulfilled by an infant government already strained by its war effort in the East.

convicted of misdemeanors, and four men and one woman, Mary Jackson, were convicted of felonies.[17]

Southern nationalism, and the traditional "Old South," died as surely in the city streets and farmyards as it did on the battlefields. The Southern landscape was littered with debris—skeletons of horses and mules left unburied, human remains washed from their shallow graves, broken muskets, and wagon wheels decorated the sides of rutted ditches that once were pleasant lanes through the countryside. Homes had been shelled or dismantled to build fortifications, roads, and bridges. Parts of the South were said actually to stink with the odor of death.

The immediate cause of defeat was a lack of sufficient manpower for the Confederate armies, but the inability of the civilian population to withstand any more war after four years of mourning their loved ones ensured that the war would not long endure. For four brief years Southerners, charged with a spirit of revolution and nationalism, took charge of their own destiny. In the aftermath of the war, the unique Confederate identity would never be the same again. Yet the new South, rising from the ashes of the old, would reassert many of its traditional ideologies from the postwar years to the present.[18]

NOTES

1. Drew Gilpin Faust, *The Creation of Confederate Nationalism: Ideology and Identity in the Civil War South* (Baton Rouge: Louisiana State University Press, 1988), 3–4.

2. Ibid., 15, 36.

3. Emory M. Thomas, *The Confederacy as a Revolutionary Experience* (Columbia: University of South Carolina Press, 1991), 114.

4. Faust, Nationalism, 8; Earl Schenck Miers, ed., *A Rebel War Clerk's Diary, by John B. Jones, 1861–1865* (New York: Sagamore Press, 1958), 3.

5. James M. McPherson, *For Cause and Comrades: Why Men Fought in the Civil War* (New York: Oxford University Press, 1997), 95. See Croushore, 30.

6. W. H. McIntosh, "James C. Sumner, the Young Soldier Ready for Death," Rare Book Collection, University of North Carolina at Chapel Hill. http://docsouth.unc.edu/imls/mcintosh/mcintosh.html (Accessed April 2008).

7. James West Smith, "A Confederate Soldier's Diary: Vicksburg in 1863," *Southwest Review* 28 (1943): 304, 312.

8. Marshall L. DeRosa, *The Confederate Constitution of 1861* (Columbia: University of Missouri Press, 1991), 17.

9. Thomas, 40.

10. Randall J. G. and David Donald, *The Civil War and Reconstruction* (Boston: D.C. Heath and Company, 1961), 258.

11. Douglas O. Tice, "Bread or Blood: The Richmond Bread Riot," *Civil War Times Illustrated*, February 1974, 12.

12. Miers, 79.

13. Ibid., 99.

14. Ibid., 178.

15. Ibid., 310–312.

16. For a detailed discussion of blockade running and its effect on the South, see Stephen R. Wise, *Lifeline of the Confederacy: Blockade Running During the Civil War* (Columbia: University of South Carolina Press, 1988).

17. Tice, 14–16.

18. Thomas, 127.

5

THE PECULIAR
INSTITUTION: SLAVERY

"I feel that it is degrading the human race to have white men
for servants."
                                    —A Congressman from Maryland, 1831

THE SLAVE TRADE

History inexplicably continues to blame the English for creating a system
of "American" plantation slavery when the system is documented to have
existed before the New World was discovered and more than a century
before the English set foot in any colony of their own. The African slave
trade was begun by Arab and Muslim traders in the 15th century, and the
Portuguese adapted slavery to their immensely profitable sugar plantations in the islands of the eastern Atlantic before the discovery of the New
World. Three-quarters of all the Africans brought to the New World were
imported by either Spain or Portugal.

Unfortunately, the early history of slavery in North America is poorly
documented and inconclusive. It seems certain that none of the founders of
the first English colonies anticipated a dependence on black slaves. While
the first Negroes brought to the English colonies were formerly thought to
have been exclusively slaves, recent research suggests that many of them
were actually indentured servants or free craftsmen. It is equally clear,
however, that there were distinctions made between black and white laborers and servants in even the earliest English colonies; however, in a

The slave patrol at work. All blacks, free or slave, were required to have a pass when off the plantation and not accompanied by a white. Failure to obey the slave patrol could end in detention or even death. Sketch by F. B. Schell.

society where whites were often degraded and treated as brutally as slaves, social distinctions often proved more important than racial ones.[1]

The distinction between free blacks, black indentured servants, and black slaves quickly blurred. Free blacks seem to have preferred to live in an urban setting and were twice as likely to live in cities as slaves, who were primarily agricultural workers. In cosmopolitan areas, free blacks and slave craftsmen found opportunities for employment, exposure to black culture and religion, and the company of other freemen. However, the majority of free blacks lived on the margins of poverty and were subject to detention and questioning by the authorities without cause. They were continually encouraged to sell themselves back into slavery.[2]

By the beginning of the 18th century, race-based slavery firmly established itself in English North America in place of indentured service. Historians have been hard pressed to explain the sudden shift from white indentured labor to black slavery, as indentured servants were less expensive to maintain and generally more tractable workers. One theory suggests that whites became unwilling to undergo the physical hardships required of work on another man's plantation, opting instead to hack out a living for themselves on the frontier. The absurd theory that the black race was better suited to the hot climate of the South than the white was put to rest by John Quincy Adams: "Europeans cultivate the land in Greece and in Sicily; why should they not do so in Virginia or the Carolinas? It is not hotter there."[3]

The Fraction of Incomes Derived from Slavery in the Confederate States

State	Percent of the Population That Were Slaves	Per Capita Earnings of Free Whites (USD)	Slave Earnings per Free White (USD)	Fraction of Earnings Due to Slavery
Alabama	45	120	50	41.7
South Carolina	57	159	57	35.8
Florida	44	143	48	33.6
Georgia	44	136	40	29.4
Mississippi	55	253	74	29.2
Louisiana	47	229	54	23.6
Texas	30	134	26	19.4
Cotton States (Avg.)	46	163	50	30.6
North Carolina	33	108	21	19.4
Tennessee	25	93	17	18.3
Arkansas	26	121	21	17.4
Virginia	32	121	21	17.4
Other States (Avg.)	29	111	20	18.1
All CSA States (Avg.)	38	135	35	25.9

Source: Roger Ransom, "Economics of the Civil War," *EH.Net Encyclopedia*, ed. Robert Whaples. http://eh.net/encyclopedia/article/ransom.civil.war.us (accessed April 2009).

During the 18th century, slave labor proved profitable only on large-scale plantations that produced a cash crop. At the time, only tobacco and sugar seemed to satisfy this requirement. Growing tobacco had saved the Virginia and Carolina colonies from extinction once the quest for gold and precious metals had been quelled by failure. Tobacco was used as cash, in lieu of cash payments, and as collateral for loans. Tobacco bonds, which encumbered the profits of future crops, were even accepted in lieu of taxes. But intensive tobacco farming was hard on the soil, stripping it of valuable nutrients that could not easily be replaced in an era before synthetic fertilizers. The production of sugar was particularly lucrative, but sugar cultivation was hard on the slaves, who suffered ghastly levels of mortality in the pest-infested humidity of the cane fields. If a large planter of tobacco or sugar were fortunate enough to have three good agricultural years in a row, he could become fabulously wealthy.[4]

Fortunes made in growing sugar and tobacco altered the entire state of colonial society. Whites living in the Southern colonies developed a class structure based on "all the ideals, all the passions, all the prejudices of an aristocracy." Many built manor houses that rivaled the great homes of Europe. So common were these residences that a substantial immigrant population made up of Italian stonemasons, bricklayers, and plasterers came to reside in the South, and was supported almost solely by this form of construction.

Rich Southerners maintained their "planter aristocracy" through the Revolution and into the 19th century. Certainly, there were upper and working classes among the whites, but nowhere was the equality between white men so complete as in their ability to force Negroes to work without working themselves. The laws of the new republic lent authority to the white man by divesting the black of two-fifths of his very humanity.[5]

Of the 10,000 plantations that came to rely on slave labor in the antebellum period, fewer than 10 percent had more than one hundred slaves. The institution of slavery had been in decline for some time before the war, particularly among the small tobacco planters who had worn out their soil. A South Carolina planter in 1831 reported: "It is an extraordinary thing how far public opinion is becoming enlightened about slavery. The idea that it is a great evil and that one could do without it is gaining ground more and more . . . We have seen it abolished in the State of New York, then in Pennsylvania; it holds on to a precarious existence in Maryland; there is talk against it in the Legislature of Virginia."[6]

The importation of slaves into the United States was outlawed in 1808, but the ownership and selling of slaves within the confines of the country continued. Not until 1848 was slavery abolished in most of New England. This was accomplished by gradual emancipation and not without considerable turmoil over the incorporation of free blacks into New England society. It is an amazing facet of the war that the New England states should so strongly oppose slavery in 1860 when they had tolerated or supported it a mere 12 years earlier.

Cotton saved the plantation system and breathed new life into slavery. By mid-century cotton accounted for two-thirds of the exports of the country and created an unprecedented demand for agricultural laborers. The widespread adoption of the cotton gin, which economically removed the seeds from desirable long staple varieties of cotton, resurrected the plantations of the Deep South in the antebellum period. A slave, who could process 100 pounds of cotton per day without the cotton gin, could produce 1,000 pounds of fiber in the same time with it. Estimates show that by 1860 there were more than 3.6 million black slaves in those states that were to form the Confederacy. Profits from cotton in the Carolinas and from sugar in Louisiana provided a financial bulwark for slavery in the Deep South.

The archaic plantation system would have faded into obscurity were it not for the ability of slavery to provide the labor needed to produce these crops.

Virginia, noted for its production of tobacco rather than as a cotton producer, became a major supplier of slaves to other areas of the South. In 1860 the estimated value of all the slave property in the Old Dominion alone was more than $300 million dollars.[7] Virginians found that they could make more profit selling slaves than using them as laborers. In the three decades before the war, more than a quarter million slaves were "sold south" from Virginia alone. In 1860 young black men aged 19 to 24 could bring between $1,300 and $1,700 in the slave market; and young women between 16 and 20, from $1,200 to $1,500. Slaves with skills brought higher prices. Blacksmiths, wheelwrights, and furniture makers sold at a premium, as did particularly comely young women. Children, the aged, and the unskilled brought less. A healthy child four months old was considered worth $100 in North Carolina. The average price for a slave, taking all ages and sexes into account, has been estimated to have been $1,500. The largest number of slaves purchased was young men. Few women, children, or older slaves saw regular trading. This difference helps to explain the high average of $1,500. To place these values in perspective, it should be noted that a white overseer on a moderate-sized plantation could expect to receive a salary of only $200 to $500 for an entire year's work.[8]

Outside the Deep South economic and moral attitudes toward the "peculiar institution" had begun to change before the turn of the century. In the border states the importance of slavery as an institution continued to erode. Topography was a leading indicator of whether or not slavery was widely practiced. The border states of Kentucky and Tennessee had few slaves, as they were too mountainous to grow cotton economically. But parts of solid slave states like Alabama, Georgia, and Virginia were populated by virtually no one who was not white. One county in western Virginia was so removed from slavery that there was not a single black person, slave or free, within its bounds in 1860. Whites in these areas were often more interested in keeping out immigrants from Europe than in maintaining slavery.[9]

Nonetheless, as an institution, race-based slavery had a long lifeline. So-called "black belts" could be found in 1/4 part of Kentucky, 1/5 of Maryland, and 1/10 of Missouri. Delaware had a slave population only 1/62 part of its total residents. White belts consumed far more of the border states, especially in their northern halves. In Maryland and Delaware slaves were found mostly in the cities, serving as tradesmen, artisans, and household help. More than 90 percent of Delaware's blacks and 49 percent of those in Maryland lived as freedmen in 1860. Nonetheless, many borderites evidenced a characteristic contradiction of being soft on slavery but hard on abolitionists. They also believed that blacks had their place in the social scheme of things and should maintain it. "I feel that it is degrading the human race to have white men for servants," said a border state congressman. "When one comes to change my plate, I am always tempted to offer him my place at table."[10]

PLANTATION SLAVERY

Historians are greatly divided on the extent of the various physical mistreatments to which slaves were exposed, and the psychological effects of being held in bondage can only be surmised. A Northern visitor to the South testified, "It is almost impossible to believe that human nature can endure such hardships and sufferings as the slaves have to go through."[11] Though slavery was certainly a great evil and was oppressive everywhere, the burden imposed on the individual slave varied greatly depending on the master and the region of the country in which the slave resided. Profession and practice with regard to slavery were so complex that they were frequently radically different things, and generalizations in this area must be carefully drawn. Unquestionably, the practices that served to underpin the institution of slavery in the South were becoming more harsh as the century progressed. This was especially true with respect to questions of black education, manumission, provision of physical care, and the status of blacks, both free and slave.

There seems to have been a striking difference between the treatment of slaves in the small towns and cities of the South and that of blacks held on large plantations. Both the material mistreatment of the "whip-driven" slave on the plantation and the freedom enjoyed by urban slaves, as well as black freemen, were exaggerated by anti-slavery advocates at the time and subsequently by some serious historical scholars. Notwithstanding such exaggeration, there was almost certainly a relative disadvantage to being a plantation slave.

The systemic abuse of black freemen was generally limited to the rural areas of the South and was much less common before the war than after.[12] Southern blacks lived hard lives, yet many displayed fortitude, courage, and a sense of dignity throughout. Nonetheless, on the eve of the Civil War there were blacks in the South, themselves free, who owned slaves, used slave labor in their businesses, and condoned slavery. Black slave masters, especially shippers, tradesmen, and artisans, owned many of their fellow Negro workers, an arrangement often entered into in lieu of an apprenticeship agreement. Incredibly, many of the free Negro tradesmen and artisans invested heavily in these slaves. This was especially true of free Negroes who owned shipping concerns where slaves served as shipwrights, sailmakers, and stevedores. It has been documented that in 1830 more than 2,000 black slaves were owned by free Negro masters in New Orleans alone.[13]

The campaign to emancipate these slaves raised interesting questions about the sympathies of free Negroes who owned slaves. Black masters, who sometimes also owned the members of their families, had their rights recognized in law in most states. They could therefore stabilize their workforce and provide a modicum of legal protection for their loved ones. These men were highly educated, cultured, and sophisticated in their outlook, and they were decidedly against any form of gradual emancipation without indemnification. At the beginning of the war many of them were openly Confederate in their outlook.[14]

The available evidence about the conditions surrounding slavery comes to us from a variety of sources, some of which hardly inspire confidence as to their reliability. Slave biographies and narratives based on oral interviews are one major source of information. Many of these were taken down in the 1920s and 1930s by historians desperate to document the details of slave life before its participants faded away. These narratives were given by people who were, on the average, over eighty years old and had been children when the Civil War began. Additional sources are found in the letters, diaries, and contemporary writings of the slaveholders, and in the collections of plantation records, Freedmen's Bureau documents, and other written material dealing with the slave trade and plantation management that survived the war. Each of these must be subjected to the same type of evaluation by which all sources of historical information are judged.[15]

Slave autobiographies, in particular, have been extensively used by historians, and perhaps too uncritically, because they are few in number. Under close scrutiny they often turn out to be carefully crafted propaganda pieces, rooted in truth but designed by the abolitionists to appeal to all the dissimilar reform groups of the North. In the 1860s there was an explosion of handwritten testimony from slaves recently freed by federal troops. New Orleans fell to federal troops early in the war, and there was an active attempt to document the system of slavery in the area around that city. While historians know more about slaves in New Orleans during the war than in any other Southern city, it was hardly an archetype of Southern slavery. New Orleans boasted the largest black community of any city in the country at the time, composed of numerous free black businessmen and artisans, urbanized former slaves, and recent refugees from the plantations.

Nonetheless, the data that were compiled are useful, particularly since the slaves could not be expected to leave much in the way of other written documentation. Much of the material collected took the form of anecdotal statements by former slaves assembled by well meaning, but not unbiased, investigators.[16] It is not enough to say that all sources are biased. Some sources suffer from other limiting characteristics beyond their obvious intent, such as the author's selective memory or his desire to make himself seem heroic. It is almost impossible to correct the data that we have for the prejudice of "untrained, negligent, or incompetent" 19th-century researchers. Such data have been used by scholars, authors, playwrights, and screenwriters to distort the picture of slavery beyond our ability to know the truth.[17]

The accounts of slave society written by slaveowners are used sparingly and with great caution by historians even though they are plentiful and vastly superior sources of detailed information. These sources of information about slavery reside largely in the daily reports of plantation activities and the internal records of slave trading establishments. Considering them along with published tracts on the "Management of Negroes," private letters and papers of slaveholders, and advertisements for fugitives, we can at least surmise an accurate picture of what slaves looked like and did, even if we cannot get a reliable view of how they felt or what they thought. These sources provide firsthand accounts, rather than hearsay evidence, of slavery. They are contemporary with the events and are considered by most open-minded historians to have been written "with the substantial integrity needed for accuracy in business accounts."[18]

If we properly discount the reliability of the self-serving firsthand documents produced by slaveowners and their apologists, must we not take into account the subjective influences brought to bear on the autobiographies and narratives of slaves published and recorded by abolitionists? One outstanding slave autobiography, favorable to slavery, is almost totally ignored by historians as "obviously unreliable," yet there is no clear evidence that the feelings expressed therein are bogus or recorded under duress. The pamphlet, Slavery and Abolitionism, as Viewed by a Georgia Slave, by Harrison Berry, a shoemaker and slave, warned against the promises of the abolitionists and pointed to the potential poverty that blacks would experience if let free in an anti-black society. In urging his fellow blacks to be submissive to their owners, Berry was perhaps the only person to address the nation directly on the subject of bondage while still a slave, and he seemingly never disavowed these sentiments.[19]

The "Narrative" of Frederick Douglass is a commonly referenced work in this regard. Douglass was a slave in Baltimore for more than 20 years, and his book, published by the American Anti-slavery Society, was replete with descriptions of the physical abuses of slavery, including whippings, rape, unwarranted punishments, and cold-blooded murder. The work appealed to a wider audience of reformers than just those who favored emancipation. Proponents of women's rights, temperance, public education, and immigration reform all found something to stir them in Douglass' work.

Southern readers pointed with incredulity to many of Douglass' childhood memories of the whipping and murder of his fellow slaves. As he carefully omitted corroborating details from the incidents, many whites were convinced that the stories were patently false. His accounts of two slaves being murdered in unrelated incidents by individual masters on adjoining plantations within hours of one another rang false to all but the most dedicated of abolitionist ears. Nevertheless, between 1845 and

1850 the book sold more than 30,000 copies and was regarded by many in the North as a true picture of slavery in Maryland. A *New York Tribune* reviewer, himself an abolitionist, praised the book upon its publication for its simplicity, truth, coherence, and warmth.

SLAVE CLOTHING

It would be an error to generalize about the standards of slave attire before the war based on Civil War documents. The physical appearance of slaves in the war-torn South was widely documented by the illustrated newspapers of the day and, to a lesser extent, by the science of photography; however, little of their condition prior to the war had been so documented. Drawings are valuable, but often reflect the bias of the artists, who tended to portray blacks as the North expected to see them. The photographers of the period, notorious for staging their shots, took very few pictures of common slaves. An exception to this is the series of photos taken immediately after the war that documents the scarred condition of an elderly man's back.

Slaves were a valuable form of property, and, as such, their owners had a financial incentive to keep them in good health. Plantation slaves were often clothed in coarse but durable trousers, shirts, and skirts made from "Negro-cloth," usually a form of coarse linen. Shoes were purchased for the plantation workers by the barrel, and most former slaves complained of rarely having had shoes that fit well. In 1839 a visitor from the North testified as follows: "The allowance of clothing on [one] plantation, to each slave, was given out at Christmas for the year, and consisted of one pair of coarse shoes, and enough coarse cloth to make a jacket and trousers ... The slaves on this plantation, being near Wilmington, procured themselves extra clothing by working Sundays and moonlighting nights." The women received the same allowance of cloth as the men. It is certain that slaves were provided with better clothing before the war than after the federal blockade took effect.[20]

SLAVE WORK WEEK

Slavery called for long hours of work and trying conditions by modern standards. Most slaves worked from sunup to sundown in the fields, or until the work was finished when working indoors. During harvest or corn husking, slaves could be found working into the early hours of the morning. Slaughtering, in late fall, was a bloody and offensive task that allowed no interruption for rest. Nonetheless, the testimony of former slaves suggests that there was time to do extra work "on the side." The work week ran from Monday to Saturday noon and respected the Sabbath. Attendance at church services in clean clothes was required. Most blacks were restricted to the plantation and lived in the village of shanty

A *Leslie's* illustration by Edwin Forbes of so-called "contrabands"—slaves who have fled to the federal lines. Federal officials were hard pressed to decide the status of these unfortunates, and General Benjamin Butler decided he could hold them as contraband of war.

huts provided for them. Any slave found off the plantation without a pass ran the danger of being "whipped on the spot" by the slave patrol, and if he resisted capture he could be shot. Slave housing was poor; heat in winter and ventilation in summer were generally haphazard, if not altogether absent. The plantations were therefore a strange combination of labor camp, racial community, and Christian mission.[21]

SLAVE FOOD

The food provided for slaves was of poor quality by modern standards, and the diet was periodically unbalanced. Yet even the slave narratives suggest that foodstuffs were often abundant. Much of the food given to slaves was thought to be offensive or unwholesome. Whites normally did not eat chicken necks, gizzards, or pig's feet; and the small intestines of hogs, made up into chitlins, and kush, a mixture of bacon fat and corn-meal, were considered less than appealing to the delicate palates of white slaveowners. Wheat flour, white bread, and beef were almost unknown to slaves. Nonetheless, ham and gravy, fried chicken, ashcake, and hoe-cake—all standards in modest white households—were also found in slave kitchens. To supplement their diet, slaves were allowed to grow their own vegetables and to catch fish, squirrels, raccoons, opossums, and rabbits.[22]

Slaves were periodically issued molasses, salt pork, okra, peas, collard greens, turnips, and black-eyed peas. These foods supplemented a steady diet of cornmeal, fresh or parched corn, and potatoes or yams. Salted codfish was a staple of the slave diet in many localities. Purchased from the New England fisheries, it was identical to a familiar staple item in many European communities, especially those along the Atlantic and Mediterranean coasts of Spain and Italy. Surprisingly, slaves seem to have received sufficient calories and nutrients from this diet to allow for the heavy labor to which they were put.

SLAVE ENTERTAINMENT

Slaves had no form of entertainment outside of that which they provided for themselves. As their work was tiring to the point of exhaustion, the very idea of leisure activities was displaced by a need for rest, if not sleep. Nonetheless, slaves found personal tasks to perform in their non-laboring hours. Mending clothing, tending gardens, fishing and hunting, and caring for children and relatives took up much of their time. There were opportunities for enjoying music, dancing, storytelling, and simple sports such as footraces. Amusements included pitching horseshoes, gambling, cockfighting, and playing at marbles, checkers, or games of African origin. A good deal of time was spent in community activities such as church services, visits to the sick and elderly, and other comparable family activities.

LEGAL RIGHTS FOR SLAVES AND DISCIPLINE

Unlike white employees, slaves were not free to change their condition should it become too burdensome. They could be physically chastised by their masters for many forms of disobedience, for insolence involving a white person, and for petty crimes. Incredibly, masters did not have unlimited legal power over their slaves. A slave accused of a felony could not be purposely mutilated, maimed, or killed as a punishment without the intervention of a court. The jurisdiction of these courts varied from place to place, but, generally, their procedures were set down in the Black Codes.

Of course, a slave defendant was not entitled to a jury trial. However, a hearing officer was required to determine the merits of the case and to act as a finder of fact. The county would then mete out punishment to slaves found to be guilty of serious crimes. As the hearing officers came from the community of free white slaveholders, questions of guilt or innocence were often moot. Nonetheless, the slave was allowed to make a defense. In such a case, the defendant needed to rely upon his own testimony or the testimony of other slaves. Slaves could not subpoena whites to testify. Both the Black Codes and custom gave great leeway to the officers of the court in determining the nature of any punishment.

As slaves were valuable property, masters looked down on any form of physical punishment that permanently devalued their slaves. Some masters intervened on behalf of their slaves even when their guilt had been firmly established. Hamstringing, various forms of dismemberment, and death, while not complete figments of the abolitionists' imaginations, were uncommon punishments for mere disobedience or petty crime. If only for economic reasons, the master wanted to maintain a chastised but physically capable slave in his employ, not a handicapped cripple. Punishments most often took the form of an informal laying on of the ever-present lash, while a hitching up to the whipping post for a formal flogging was reserved for major offenses. Masters also had the option of selling the unrepentant slave to the far South, into the interior, or to the disease-infested sugar plantations in lieu of punishment. The slaves themselves attest to such goings-on, and in very few narratives are such events absent.

Slaveowners rarely punished their bondsmen personally. This was left to the overseer. Much of the physical abuse distributed to slaves came from these often coarse and uncultivated men. Overseers came and went on individual plantations, and "some were too severe on the Negroes . . . brutified by their employment, [and] little better than the Negroes they managed."[23] These white men were aided by slave drivers, who, although black slaves themselves, could apply the lash with pitiless regularity and were used to chase down fugitives. Some blacks, like the slave drivers, were often characterized as "white folks' servants," devoted to the master and his family and alienated from the general slave community. They were viewed by other slaves with disgust, as it was feared that they might curry favor with the master at the expense of other slaves by betraying them.

Ostensibly, flogging was the most widespread form of cruelty practiced by these persons, yet Americans believed even the most outrageous tales of immense abuse. Corporal punishment in many forms was highly evident throughout white society even in the North. Schoolmasters caned their disobedient or lazy students; fathers accompanied their progeny on repeated trips to the woodshed with razor strop or belt in hand; prisoners were ruthlessly beaten with sticks and whips by their jailers; and soldiers and sailors were frequently punished by flogging, sometimes to the point of death. Notwithstanding these facts, slaves were certainly exposed to excessive and unwarranted cruelty through no fault of their own.

While on an intellectual level Southerners claimed racial superiority for the white race, they nonetheless depended on the Negro to tend their animals, repair their vehicles, cook their food, and care for their children. White slaveowners were intimately involved with blacks almost all of their lives. In the isolation of the great plantations, it was possible that most of a white person's dealings, in human terms, were either with family members or with blacks. Some slaves were able to accompany their owners on trips to the town or city, and, once there, they were sent off on their own, with a pass, to do their master's business. It is strange to consider that white slaveowners, who so underestimated the value of human beings as to enslave them, were also able to entrust their bondsmen with the well-being and protection of their property and families. This fact seems to say much more about the humanity and responsibility exhibited by the slaves themselves than about their masters.

Race-based slavery promoted a type of equality among all white Southerners regardless of their social status. The lowliest white man could find comfort in the knowledge that he was the legal superior of even the wealthiest black freeman. Yet many slaveowners found it undesirable to have lower-class whites living on the fringes of plantations, where the slaves could be "impaired by contact with white labor."[24] Although it is uncertain with how much respect these whites viewed the Negro freeman, it would be common for them to have to deal with free blacks as laborers, tradesmen, and artisans. The working white population in much of the South exhibited far less abhorrence of blacks than did many in the upper and middle classes in the North.[25]

DRAFT RIOTS

European immigrants showed a particularly strong prejudice against the Negro. This was most obviously manifest during the 1863 New York City draft riots. Beyond a few recruiters and government officials who happened to be in the wrong place at the time, the targets of the mostly Irish rioters were generally Negroes.[26] Harper's reported that "no class of our foreign population is more jealous of its own liberties than the Irish, and there is also none which more strongly resents every liberty accorded to the Negro race." One black was "seized by the mob, and, after his life had been nearly beaten out, his body was suspended from a tree, a fire kindled under him, and, in the midst of excruciating torments, he expired." There may have been upwards of seventy black victims among the servants and workers of the hotels and restaurants in New York. An observer noted, "These things were done deliberately, and not in the heat of passion. . . and were moved by a political prejudice."[27]

By comparison, Southerners were generally ambivalent in their attitude toward Negroes, requiring considerable formality from them, but treating them with disdain or paying them no mind at all. In some circumstances slaves were able to earn a small amount of cash by doing extra work, turning their talents to a particularly artful or craftsman-like project, or receiving the equivalent of tips. One slave, "a money making and saving boy," was said to have accumulated more than $500 in this manner, only to have it stolen by a foraging party of black federal soldiers. Very elderly slaves,

unable to work in their old age, were often "pensioned off," being provided with a small sum of cash or being given a shack and a regular issue
of food on the plantation. Some states had laws requiring slaveowners to
make such provisions so that elderly slaves, and those freed under manumission provisions, did not become a burden on society.[28]

BLACK CHURCHES

Even in the absence of physical abuse or brutality, the institution of slavery did great harm to the bondsman. Southern blacks countered by drawing great strength from a number of traditional and cultural sources. In
the years before the abolition of the slave trade, new arrivals from Africa
exhibited a heavy dependence on their own tribal religions. In Louisiana
and the West Indies many African religious practices came to be fused into
a widespread religion known as Voodoo, "which penetrated into every
level of Black society." Slaves bought charms and amulets in order to control their masters, obtain money, ensure love or good health, or bring harm
and even death to enemies and nonbelievers. The New Orleans Delta reported in 1854 that the participants "strip themselves naked and then
commence a strange, wild sort of Indian dance." Wild orgies, the drinking
of blood, necromancy, and human sacrifice were all attributed to Voodoo
by white observers.[29]

White society deemed such activities pagan, innately evil, and incon-
sistent with its own dedication to Christianity. Many African religious
practices were rooted in a communication with the natural world and the
joyful expression of an overt sexuality that shocked the more prudish Protestants. By extension, whites came to be intolerant of all forms of African
culture that they did not understand. Slaveowners, even benevolent ones,
effectively stripped the black of his tribal religious culture. Slaves were
expected to exhibit moral behavior reflecting the mores of the God-fearing
Christians whom they served. The responsibility for Christianizing the
slaves, baptizing their infants, and nurturing in them a fear of the Lord
was seriously regarded by whites. Many slaves were therefore forced to
attend conventional religious instruction for the good of their souls.

White Southerners used their religion to validate the concept of race-
based slavery, but their religion made the masters neither more humane
to their slaves nor more likely to emancipate them.[30] Some of the most
brutal masters were avid churchgoers. A Southern woman wrote in her
journal with regard to slaveowning, "The purest and holiest men have
owned them, and I see nothing in the scriptures which forbids it."[31] White
ministers often preached to the blacks in a manner calculated to make the
slave satisfied with his lot as an expression of the will of God. It was not
unusual for the white clergy to own one or two slaves as servants. Sometimes slaves were provided by the congregation as part of the living given
to the minister. Some churches, especially the Methodists and Baptists of

the South, thought the social issues surrounding slavery scarcely worth consideration when contrasted to the saving of the heathen soul. Since many of the white man's churches upheld slavery, many blacks became suspicious of organized religions with white origins.[32]

There were churches established exclusively for slaves by their owners, but the presiding white ministers, who were in the forefront of defending slavery from the pulpit as the natural and correct place for the black race, were generally disliked. Most free Negroes in New Orleans attended the Catholic Church, where they enjoyed an almost equal standing with the white congregation. Separate black congregations grew in number among many sects because the white congregations of their denomination did not welcome black freemen. A growing army of black ministers was thereby able to found parishes among the freemen and slaves of the South. The African Methodist Episcopal (A.M.E.) Churches had the most prominent black ministers of the period. In New Orleans there was a congregation supported by more than 600 slaves of the Methodist Church, and the black Baptist Church had 500 members. White authorities feared any large meeting of blacks and broke up these religious services on a regular basis for the most trivial of reasons.

There were two very different types of religious services common to black churches. In the upper-class churches, populated by large numbers of freemen, there was a great dedication to religious form and ceremony. The services were less passionate and affected a greater intellectual appeal and attention to social problems than in the lower-class churches. The communicants of the lower-class churches were primarily composed of slaves and poor Negroes who held a strong belief in the power of God in their everyday lives. They emphasized revelations, visions, dreams, and outward expressions of redemption. Worship was often accompanied by shouts, cries, dancing, and other forms of joyful noise. Nonetheless, in each form, some of the African music, folk heritage, and dance survived. With time, blacks were able to blend many of their African beliefs with the biblical teachings of Christianity. Both types of worship, although generally dividing the black community along class lines, served to uphold the structure of black life in a nation that cared little for Negroes except as chattels and laborers. The church proved to be one of the more durable black institutions.

THE SLAVE FAMILY

Another important social institution among blacks was the family. That the slave family was an incredibly unstable institution was only partially due to the influence of whites. A former slave noted, "There were on this plantation about seventy slaves, male and female: some were married, and others lived together as man and wife, without even a mock ceremony . . . The slaves, however, think much of being married by a clergyman." Since marriage was considered a legal medium by which property was handed down, and the slave had no property, the law saw no reason to recognize the union of slaves as binding. Some morally scrupulous planters encouraged slave marriage as opposed to the immorality of open promiscuity.[33]

Investigators in New Orleans during the federal occupation recorded more than 500 marriages that had taken place while the couples involved had been slaves. Of these, fewer than 100 had remained unbroken. While some unions lasted from 20 to 40 years, the average length of a slave marriage was a mere 5.6 years. Records indicate that 70 percent of these marriages ended due to death or personal choice, and only 30 percent of the slave unions were broken up by the planters. Many planters professed an aversion to breaking up slave families because the practice increased unrest among the blacks; however, the extravagant lifestyle of the planters, coupled with the regularity of foreclosures on mortgages and demands for the repayment of loans, caused most slaves to see the auction block at least once in their lives. Slaves could be bought or sold, rented out, gambled away, or left in a will as an inheritance to almost anyone. The law did not provide for the continuity of the slave family as a unit.

Slave children did not belong to their parents but generally were considered the property of the mother's master. The father and the father's master, should he be a different person, were denied any standing in regard to the offspring of slave unions. "Women were generally shown some indulgence for three or four weeks previous to childbirth . . . [and] they are generally allowed four weeks after the birth of a child, before they are compelled to go into the field, they then take the child with them."[34] The offspring of a free man with a slave woman was thereby a slave, yet the offspring of a slave with a free woman was considered to be freeborn even if the woman were black. Even the children of a white master by a slave mother were born slaves. In the case of a dispute in this regard, with very few exceptions, whenever a slave's human rights came into conflict with a master's property rights, the courts invariably decided in favor of the master. The first activity of many refugee slaves during the war was to begin a search for their missing mates or children.

MISCEGENATION

One of the unique features of slavery in this period was the pervasiveness of miscegenation,[35] or interracial sexual activity. The desire of white men to have sexual contact with black females was seemingly so common in the South that no social stigma was attached to it; whereas, illicit liaisons between whites, extending even to white couples who were engaged to be married, were roundly condemned. White men involved in sexual relationships with black women, slave or free, seem to have received a special dispensation from Southern society. Indeed, a man who openly kept a white mistress would be turned out of society; yet, if he chose a "colored" one, and produced a whole family of mixed-race children from the relationship, he was seemingly absolved from any shame and highly regarded by his fellows.

Mixed-race sexual relations were not unknown in the North, and black-white marriages were legally void in several Northern states. Nonetheless, Northerners viewed miscegenation as a form of moral degeneracy, singularly "Southern," and rooted in the immorality of slavery. A European traveler to America found that blacks treated those of mixed race with disdain and hate. "They think them much closer to the Whites than to the Blacks."[36] An antebellum abolitionist author confidently reported that half the slave population of the South was mixed with white blood, and his assertion was accepted as gospel by willing readers. Statistical analysis suggests, however, that fewer than 10 percent of the slaves in the South were of mixed ancestry, and a portion of these had Native American blood. Only a small percentage of the children born to slaves in a given year were fathered by white men. A high incidence of illegitimacy among poor populations, as well as a lack of careful records, makes the question of establishing absolute paternity difficult to answer.

Over time there developed an absurd theory that a single drop of black blood polluted the human being. Yet some Southerners suggested the equally preposterous notion that miscegenation improved the black population by breeding "whiteness" into it and would gradually eliminate the black race from America by dilution. Abolitionists spread the probably specious story of a slaveowner who offered a white man "twenty dollars for every one of his female slaves, whom he would get in the family way."[37] The extent of miscegenation is somewhat obscured by the methods used by 19th-century investigators to quantify the mixed-race population of the South as mulattos, quadroons, and octoroons by the criteria of the outward appearance of the skin and the absence or presence of certain defining racial features. A large population of mixed-race persons "passing for white" may also have obscured any meaningful estimates at the time.

Some white men, abjuring any justification for the satisfaction of their lustful desires, simply considered every slave cabin a bordello. In 1851 a Louisiana court recognized the virtual helplessness of the female slave in this situation, finding that she was "particularly exposed to the seductions of an unprincipled master."[38] A free black of New Orleans ascribed a loss of all feelings of morality and chastity among female slaves to this helplessness: "The practice of indiscriminate sexual intercourse . . . was so universal that a chaste colored girl at the age of seventeen was almost unknown."[39]

The anti-slavery audiences of the North were horrified by descriptions of a planter who proposed intercourse with his female slave. If she would not comply, he could send for the overseer and have her flogged. "Seeing that her case was hopeless, her back smarting with the scourging she had received, and dreading a repetition, [she] gave herself up to be the victim of his brutal lusts."[40]

Notwithstanding such anecdotal evidence to the contrary, slave women rarely needed to be beaten into submission in such a manner. Consent was never more than a minor factor in any relationship between master and slave, and rape would seem a more straightforward and timely answer to the bestial needs of this particularly unethical master. No court would have heard a case of rape brought by a black slave against a white man.

Evidence suggests that female slaves were more often bribed, cajoled, or simply seduced by their masters or their master's sons. When the harsh realities of servitude were the only available alternative, any romantic notions involving the practices of miscegenation should best be avoided as sentiment rather than as an unbiased assessment of the situation in which these young women were placed.[41] Notwithstanding this reservation, there is documentary evidence, as well as anecdotal accounts, that some white Southerners demonstrated a long commitment to their black mistresses, recognized their mixed-race offspring, and attempted to provide for their upkeep and well-being. Often this took the form of a public admission after death, and many interracial alliances were recognized in a planter's will. The white children of such masters often went to great lengths to undo those parts of their father's will favorable to their biracial siblings.

The openness of many of these liaisons scandalized the social and religious elite everywhere. Nonetheless, some men of wealth seemingly relied on the common practice of supplying themselves with a quadroon mistress for short-term affairs. "They [the mistresses] are furnished with a Chamber and a sitting room and servants, and the comforts and elegancies of life. It generally costs from $1500 to $2000 a year to keep a quadroon."[42] The slave market records show that mixed-race, "light-skinned girls" brought far higher prices at auction than did prime field hands. In a documented case, $8,000 was paid for a "particularly beautiful Negro woman." Moreover, to those who lacked the price of a slave or the wherewithal to maintain a mistress, the services of black prostitutes were sold at a premium, and comely slave girls brought exaggerated prices on the block from whoremongers who then hired them out as concubines.[43]

Southern ladies universally frowned upon any husband who was too open in his lustfulness, and while it seems that they could do little to enforce their displeasure on the male population at large, they could become quite angry and vengeful when the husband was theirs. More than one planter, taken with the beauty of a comely black slave, was forced to sell her or otherwise remove her from the reach of his wife. Evidence suggests that many of the petty lashings and beatings visited on the slaves were brought on by the vengeance of a jealous plantation wife taken out on the concubines and mixed-race children of her husband.

The question of how common sexual affairs between slaves and masters actually were, as opposed to how often they appear as titillating tidbits of gossip in journals and letters, is undecided. It is certain that the abolitionists exaggerated the universality of the documented cases. Southern sla-veowners went to great lengths to structure laws and cultural norms that would prohibit such interaction. Many slaveholding states passed anti-miscegenation measures providing severe social penalties for white men who openly bedded black women and massive physical retaliation upon any black men who had sexual relations with white women. Although these measures ostensibly prohibited all interracial unions, for the white male they only made the offspring of his intercourse illegitimate.

The concept of white women sleeping with black men, a possible consequence of the moral hypocrisy surrounding such practices, was a proposition too explosive for the delicate egos of white males. White women were expected to respond to blacks as they would to any ani-mate property, such as pets. The diaries and letters of young women and girls are full of references to the indelicacy of naked blacks, even adult males. Young women were expected to steel themselves into viewing the naked slave as a dehumanized object, no more indelicate than livestock in the barnyard.[44] Documented cases of the daughters of wealthy planta-tion owners bearing mixed-race children are rare, and, when found, are accompanied by tales of social rebuff and revulsion. Only after the war did liaisons involving white women and black men become more com-mon and open to public knowledge; nonetheless, such women were uni-versally labeled "sluts."[45]

NOTES

1. David Brion Davis, *Slavery in the Colonial Chesapeake* (Williamsburg: Colonial Williamsburg Foundation, 1994), 5.

2. A freeman could sell himself as an indentured servant for life, contract his conditions of employment, choose his master, and retain the cash under the laws of Virginia and other colonies.

3. J. P. Mayer, ed., *Journey to America, by Alexis de Tocqueville,* trans. George Lawrence (New Haven: Yale University Press, 1960), 61.

4. Davis, 4, 6, 22.

5. Mayer, 61.

6. Ibid., 116. Comments are attributed to an American diplomat, Joel R. Poin-sett (1779–1851).

7. Ervin L. Jordan, Jr., *Black Confederates and Afro-Yankees in Civil War Virginia* (Charlottesville: University Press of Virginia, 1995), 5–11, 21.

8. The view that slaves were bred for sale is not universally accepted by histo-rians. In a 1980 work, Kenneth M. Stampp of the University of California, Berkeley, wrote, "No conventional historian of the past generation claimed that slaves were bred in the Old South in the manner here described." Stampp, *The Imperiled Union* (New York: Oxford University Press, 1980), 92. The authors have deferred in this regard to the more recent work of Ervin L. Jordan.

9. William E. Freehling, *The South vs. the South: How Anti-Confederate South-erners Shaped the Course of the Civil War* (New York: Oxford University Press, 2001), 23.

10. Mayer, 61.

11. Horatio T. Strother, *The Underground Railroad in Connecticut* (Middletown: Wesleyan University Press, 1962), 201. From the narrative of Nehemiah Caulkins, a Northern visitor to North Carolina, published by Theodore Weld in 1839.

12. Richard H. Sewell, *A House Divided: Sectionalism and the Civil War, 1848–1865* (Baltimore: Johns Hopkins University Press, 1988), 15; Jordan, 9, 22.

13. John W. Blassingame, *Black New Orleans* (Chicago: Chicago University Press, 1973), 33.

14. Ibid.

15. The Smithsonian Institution has audiovisual tapes and films of former slaves whose ages were close to 100 years when they were recorded.

16. Alice Dana Adams, *The Neglected Period of Anti-slavery in America* (Boston: Corner House, 1973), 75, 77; Jordan, 14.

17. Stampp, *Imperiled Union*, 81.

18. Ibid., 43–45.

19. Harrison Berry, *Slavery and Abolitionism, as Viewed by a Georgia Slave* (Atlanta: M. Lynch, 1861).

20. Strother, 197.

21. Ibid., 203.

22. Recent archeological studies of slave quarters in Virginia have found evidence that some slaves may have been allowed the use of firearms.

23. Walter Sullivan, *The War the Women Lived: Female Voices from the Confederate South* (Nashville: J. S. Sanders, 1995), 5.

24. Kenneth M. Stampp, *The Peculiar Institution* (New York: Vintage, 1956), 150–151.

25. Jordan, 22.

26. Blassingame, *Black New Orleans*, 20–21. Arguably, this is a phenomenon still present in American society, with new immigrant groups vying for the last practical social level that will sustain survival.

27. Alfred H. Guernsey and Henry M. Alden, ed., *Harper's History of the Great Rebellion* (New York: Gramercy Books, 1866), 652.

28. Dolly Sumner Lunt, *A Woman's Wartime Journal* (Atlanta: Cherokee, 1994), 26.

29. Blassingame, *Black New Orleans*, 5–6.

30. Frederick Douglass, *Narrative of the Life of an American Slave, Written by Himself* (1845; New York: Penguin, 1968), 67.

31. Lunt, 38.

32. In a research study of New England towns done in 1987 under a grant from the Connecticut Council for the Humanities, it was found that many ministers and preachers had households which were comprised of both slaves and free blacks under the same roof.

33. See Theodore Weld, *American Slavery as It Is* (New York: N.p., 1839).

34. Strother, 195.

35. Although mixed-race sexual relations have an ancient history, Webster's dictionary claims that the word "miscegenation" did not appear in print until 1864.

36. Mayer, 116.

37. Strother, 207.

38. Quoted in Blassingame, *Black New Orleans*, 83.

39. Quoted in Ibid.

40. Strother, 206.

41. There is considerable disagreement over the level of true affection found between such couples. Noted Civil War historian Eugene D. Genovese claims that many slaves fell in love with their masters and vice versa. In *The Plantation Mistress: Woman's World in the Old South* (New York: Pantheon Books, 1982), Catherine Clinton finds such a conclusion lacking in sensitivity with regard to the dynamics of sexual exploitation. The authors have decided to defer to Clinton's view.

42. Herbert A. Kellar, ed., "The Diary of James D. Davidson," *Journal of Southern History* 1 (1935): 348. Davidson was a visitor to Louisiana in 1836.

43. *New Orleans as It Is* (New Orleans: N.p., 1850), 35–45. See Blassingame, *Black New Orleans*, chap. 1.

44. Clinton, 111, 208–209, 221.

45. See Ibid. 199–222.

6

ABOLITION

"I want to see those hot-headed abolitionists put in the front rank and shot first."

—A federal soldier in 1861

THE ANTI-SLAVERY MOVEMENT

Attacks on slavery in the early years of the republic had been based on the ideals set forth in the Declaration of Independence and the incompatibility of slavery with the concept that "all men are created equal." Many Americans freed their slaves during and immediately after the Revolution—a circumstance not confined to the North. Following the Revolution a large number of Southerners spoke about the abolition of slavery in abstract terms, and others were sufficiently dedicated to its ultimate eradication to provide for private manumission of their slave property. Widespread allegiance to slavery as an institution was rarely expressed at this stage of American history. That was to come later in the turmoil over states' rights.

Yet early opposition to emancipation, including that of Thomas Jefferson, was based largely on the racist concept that the inherent inequality in the races would prevent their living in peace and prosperity together. Nonetheless, while President Jefferson had made the international trade and transportation of slaves from Africa illegal in 1808 by signing the U.S. Slave Trade Act, the act was a response to the total emancipation of slaves in Britain and its colonies, not a homegrown upwelling of anti-slavery sentiment. The British had accomplished this through the indemnification of its slaveowners for their "property" by the crown—a solution to the problem of continued slavery that was neither economically feasible in America nor acceptable to the radical forces of abolition, who demanded immediate and uncompensated emancipation of all slaves. Jefferson was simply signing on to the slave trade ban in the hope of protecting American shipping and commerce for unwarranted detention at sea by the Royal navy.

SUPPRESSION OF THE SLAVE TRADE

From the start, the Slave Trade Act proved unenforceable largely because of Jefferson's opposition to an advanced program of naval shipbuilding. The lack of ships denied the U.S. government any power to halt the slave trade where it was at its weakest: in the Middle Passage at sea, away from any coastal safe-havens into which a slave-ship might scurry to avoid capture. At the same time, rising cotton prices and rising demand for cotton fiber in Europe was expanding the use of slave labor in the American South beyond the so-called natural increase of the slave population. Consequently, slave ships continued to take blacks from West Africa and the Caribbean and secretly bring them into American ports for black-market sale and trade.

The British Royal Navy actively patrolled the West coast of Africa in order to suppress the slave trade. This often meant overhauling and boarding slavers flying the U.S. flag. The efforts of the U.S. Navy to suppress the international slave trade through cooperation with the Royal Navy were initially hindered due to the antagonism left over from the Revolution, and all efforts were suspended during the War of 1812. Under several treaties between 1817 and 1830, the Spanish and Portuguese also made the slave trade illegal. The plantation South despised these agreements, but the U.S. Navy was, nonetheless, required to help enforce them.

In 1820 Congress passed a new bill that allowed severe punishment for violation of the Slave Trade Act. Slaving at sea was thereafter considered an act of piracy and any American caught could be punished with death. The navy was empowered to seize slave ships wherever they were found. President James Monroe allocated $100,000 to enforce the act, immediately sending a small flotilla of warships to the African coast. This was the first occasion on which the United States acted against slavery as an international partner with Britain. It was common for abolitionist forces in America to complain that the navy was not taking the law seriously. They pointed out that while the Royal Navy went out of its way to actively patrol African and Caribbean waters for slavers, the Americans only seemed to enforce the restrictions when it was convenient. They pointed to the fact that the American navy had captured "only" 10 slavers in its first season of patrolling. At least 6 of these were registered in Baltimore, Charleston, or New York.

Nonetheless, Sir George Collier, commander of the British anti-slavery squadron, reported that the American navy on all occasions acted with the greatest zeal and the most perfect unanimity with His Majesty's forces with respect to stopping the slavers. In 1821, Collier reportedly that the British ships employed on the coast of West Africa were too slow to compete with the speedy American-built vessels of the slavers. He also reported seeing slaves throwing themselves overboard during the capture of a slave ship. He later wrote that the enslaved Africans were "linked in shackles by the leg in pairs, some of them bound with cords; and several had their arms so lacerated by the tightness that the flesh was completely eaten through."[1]

Among those Americans sent to patrol the waters off West Africa was Lt. Matthew C. Perry, whose family had been associated with the establishment of the American Colonization Society in 1816. It was he that escorted the first group of former black slaves as settlers to African Liberia. In 1821 the 10-gun schooner *Shark* was launched from the Washington Navy Yard with the specific objective of eliminating piracy and slave trading in the reef-filled waters of the Caribbean, and Perry was chosen as the speedy schooner's commander. Perry had entered the navy as a midshipman in 1809 and was promoted Lieutenant in 1813. Perry acquired the courtesy title of Commodore in 1841. Although his older brother, Oliver Hazard Perry, was a famed American commodore and the "Hero of the Battle of Lake Erie" (1813), Matthew Perry had to wait 34 years to receive his own genuine Captaincy (1847) during the war with Mexico.

In the 1830s a commercial liaison was formed between slavers in Cuba and the builders of quick sailing Baltimore Clippers in the United States. Nicholas Trist, the American Consul in Havana from Virginia, was found to be deeply involved in fraudulently authenticating these sales in an effort to hide the paperwork trail from builder to slaver. Trist was removed from his post in 1841. The trade flourished in the interim, however, because it was almost impossible to prove that the Americans were in a conspiracy to trade slaves. Until 1835, the anti-slavery squadrons of both the U.S. and British navies were allowed to seize only slave-ships that had slaves actually on board, even if it was obvious from their equipment that they intended to trade in slaves.[2] This often resulted in slaves being thrown overboard weighted by their chains to drown at the ocean's bottom as soon as a chase of the slave-ship commenced. The inhumanity of the slavers in disposing of the evidence in this manner was remarkable. In 1843 a permanent African Squadron under Matthew C. Perry was sent to patrol all known slave harbors on the west coast of the continent in order to catch the slavers with their cargoes intact, but the squadron was called away to serve in the Gulf during the Mexican War of 1846.

When his health began to fail due to chronic alcoholism, Matthew Perry was advanced to rear admiral on the so-called retired list. He died in 1858, but he left his mark on the navy of the Civil War Era, nonetheless. From 1838 to 1840 as commander of the steam frigate *Fulton,* Perry made a number of important experiments with steam-powered naval operations. In 1853 he was sent with a squadron to show the American flag in the Pacific where he helped to open Japanese ports to American shipping for the first time. In 1855 Congress voted him a reward of $20,000 in appreciation of his work in Japan. Perry used part of this money to publish a report on the expedition titled *Narrative of the Expedition of an American Squadron to the China Seas and Japan.* The reports of his services in Japan helped to foster an interest in the Far East among many Americans at a time when most of the nation was looking inward.

GRADUALISM AND COLONIZATION

Proponents of emancipation looked to gradualism and colonization, rather than immediate emancipation and inclusion, to relieve the supposed incongruities of the races living peacefully together. Gradual emancipation provided that children born as slaves could be freed on attaining maturity, having been given a skill or education in the interim so that they might provide for themselves. Similarly formed legislation had quietly obliterated slavery throughout the New England states by mid-century—the last being Connecticut in 1848. Private parties among anti-slavery proponents (as opposed to the more formal organizations) largely favored the removal of free blacks to colonies established far from the Americas. The African city of Monrovia was founded as a "freemen's colony" in 1821 in this manner. Less dramatic suggestions were also made to remove freed blacks to the Indian Territories, Florida, the Caribbean Islands, and Central America.

While many Northerners were against slavery, they were also remarkably prejudiced against blacks. They were averse to having them live in their communities and inclined to leave the issue of universal emancipation alone. Radical abolitionists—always a minority among anti-slavery advocates—were loath to accept the slow pace of gradual emancipation and were becoming increasingly militant in their frustration as the war approached. This militancy was not universally shared even among anti-slavery proponents. An anti-slavery speaker, Elijah P. Lovejoy, was murdered by a mob in the free state of Illinois in 1837, and Abolitionist speakers were threatened with tar and feathers in New England towns as late as 1850.[3]

The treatment of blacks in Northern states was often brutish, and they were despised and treated with contempt. It was widely held that free blacks would come North to compete for scarce jobs in the cities, and an economic downturn in 1857 did not help to relieve this fear. In the decades after independence, towns and cities had been flooded by thousands of freed blacks, some of whom had fought in the Revolutionary army, and any plan for a general abolition of slavery had to deal with the touchy problem of free blacks living in a white-dominated, racist society. This led many sympathetic whites to fear for the ultimate welfare and safety of a black population suddenly foisted on an unfriendly America should the radicals attain their goal of universal emancipation.[4]

Immediately after the firing on Ft. Sumter, there were reports of armed anti-abolition organizations forming in New England, the home of abolition. One anti-abolitionist from New Haven, Connecticut promised that he would raise and equip two companies of 100 men each to fight for the South. Former Connecticut governor Thomas Seymour wrote, "Free the blacks and enslave the whites; that seems to be the policy of the Lincoln dynasty. If freemen are pleased with this, they may get enough of it." Feelings against abolition ran deep. Wendell Phillips, staunch abolitionist, was pelted with eggs in 1862 while trying to deliver an antislavery speech. James Gordon Bennett of the *New York Herald* wrote, "If this is a war of ideas then let the abolitionists fight for their ideas, and let all others stand back." While the bigotry was unforgivable and the rhetoric inflammatory and unhelpful, the sentiments were not surprising.[5]

The fact that antiwar sentiment existed also caused a flurry of accusations regarding disloyalty elsewhere. Two men in Union County, Illinois claimed that their region was the most pro-slavery in the state. Many Democrats readily admitted forming units for the personal safety of the residents in their area. Former president Franklin Pierce was accused of being a member of a group whose secret objective was to overthrow the federal government. Secretary of State William H. Seward wrote to Pierce requiring an acceptable explanation of the rumor. Reports of disaffection were made to state governors scrambling to fill the office rolls of their volunteer units. Governors, especially in the border regions and the states of the Midwest, were earnestly urged to send troops to disband newly formed Copperhead militias that may or may not have existed, and for which task the governors had no available troops in any case.

Even among those who volunteered to fight for the preservation of the Union, there was little sympathy for the abolitionists. Wrote one federal soldier at the beginning of the war, "I don't blame the South an atom. They have been driven to desperation by such lunatics as Garrison and Phillips, and these men ought to be hung for it." Another federal recruit said, "I want to see those hot-headed abolitionists put in the front rank and shot first."[6]

There had been a growing recognition throughout the 19th century, however, that slavery was a great moral and social evil that must be ended. But it was also true that slavery had become uneconomical for the smaller planters leaving it largely the realm of politically influential and wealthy planters. As early as 1816, several Southern states, Virginia, Geor-

gia, Maryland, and Tennessee included, had asked that a site for colonization by freed blacks be procured, and they had jointly petitioned the
federal government for financial aid to offset the monetary loss involved
in emancipating their slaves. The British government had successfully indemnified its slaveowners for their loss when the slave trade was ended in
1808, but a similar arrangement was not possible in antebellum America,
either financially or politically.

In 1817 the American Colonization Society was formed to encourage
free blacks to return to Africa. The organizational meeting was held in no
less a prestigious place than the chambers of the House of Representatives. Among its founders were Henry Clay, Andrew Jackson, and Francis
Scott Key. The society drew its initial support from all sections of the country and from both slavery and anti-slavery advocates. Colonization societies outnumbered abolition societies in America right up to the opening
of the war. Within two decades of its founding, more than 140 branches
of the American Colonization Society were formed in the Southern states,
with the majority of chapters in Virginia, Kentucky, and Tennessee. In the
North approximately 100 societies were formed—radical abolition seemingly stealing some of the colonialists' thunder, the majority established
in the states of Ohio, New York, and Pennsylvania. Only in Massachusetts
did immediate abolition have a greater following than colonization. Of
all the states, only Rhode Island and South Carolina had no colonization
societies—both had been major import markets in the days of the Atlantic
slave trade. Unquestionably, the intervention of Northern moralists into
the evolution of anti-slavery at this point provided a "fateful check" to any
hope of abolition without considerable turmoil.[7]

A minority of free blacks espoused great interest in their African homeland, yet a larger number were interested not in Africa, but in other areas
outside the United States. Canada, Central America, and Haiti were all
mentioned as possible sites for black emigration. Several prominent free
blacks, such as poet James M. Whitfield, the Rev. Henry H. Garnet, and Dr.
Martin R. Delancy, called for an emphasis on black nationalism and militant black unity. It was feared that in the United States blacks could always
expect to be crawling in the dust at the feet of their former oppressors.[8]

Colonization was very popular politically. At the time, it was estimated
by the proponents of colonization that slavery could be abolished by 1890.
During the debates with Stephen Douglas in 1858, Lincoln had expressed
both support for colonization and a belief in an inherent inequality among
the races. He disclaimed any hopes for "social and political equality of the
White and Black races," and disavowed any plan to make "voters or jurors
of Negroes, nor of qualifying them to hold office, nor to intermarry with
white people." Most important, he pledged his support for colonization
of freed slaves, saying, "There is a physical difference between the White
and Black races which I believe will forever forbid the two races living together on terms of social and political equality." True to his word, in 1862,

one year before the Emancipation Proclamation, the president signed a congressional appropriation of $100,000 for the purpose of encouraging black colonization.[9]

Some slaveowners claimed that slavery could not continue to exist if it did not expand, but others, like Georgia's Henry L. Benning, prophesized in 1861 that within a decade it would wither away in the border states and be isolated in the "Cotton States" within 25 years. "The day is not distant when the Cotton States . . . will be the only Slave states." Thereafter, Benning warned, the states of the North, Midwest, and border areas would combine to secure three-fourths of the seats in congress, and, with a "free labor" majority, would come the knockout punch of an antislavery constitutional amendment. He had "a presentiment that [slavery was] a doomed institution." The only way slaveowners had to protect their investment in "slave property" was to get rid of it and sell it South "until it gets to the bottom."[10]

But the abolitionists demanded immediate, unreimbursed emancipation and integration of freed blacks into white society, not gradualism and separation. No price, including war and disunion, was too great to pay in the cause of ending slavery and racial prejudice. The rhetoric of Wendell Phillips, a leading abolitionist in Massachusetts, provided an example to the South, and all of America, of just how far the radicals were willing to go when he suggested "trampling the laws and Constitution of the country" to gain their ends. Such rhetoric was seen as a call for civil disorder, even violence, on a massive level.[11]

The radical abolitionists berated the gradualists and colonialists as being less than completely dedicated to the cause of emancipation. In *Thoughts on African Colonization* (1832), William Lloyd Garrison went so far as to suggest that the gradualists and colonialists were actually covert supporters of slavery, allowing Northern slaveowners to "sell their slaves south," thereby recouping their considerable investment in slave property. Garrison argued that colonization would make Americans "abominably hypocritical" by allowing free blacks to remain among them only "as inferior beings, deprived of all the valuable privileges of freemen, separated by the brand of indelible ignominy, and debased to a level with the beasts."[12]

Garrison was never restrained in his criticism of any topic he considered iniquitous or unjust, but he was thoroughly nonviolent. In 1831, in the very first issue of his anti-slavery newspaper, the *Liberator,* Garrison stated, "I do not wish to think, or speak, or write, with moderation. . . I am in earnest—I will not equivocate—I will not excuse—I will not retreat a single inch—and I will be heard."[13]

Garrison may have been the most vehement of the radical abolitionists. Although he did not, in any real sense, lead the American anti-slavery movement, he was possibly the most conspicuous of the radicals. In 1845 he wrote, in the highly idealized style typical of the movement, "Be faithful, be vigilant, be untiring in your efforts to break every yoke, and let the oppressed go free. Come what may—cost what it may—inscribe on the banner which you unfurl to the breeze, as your religious and political motto—'No Compromise with Slavery! No Union with Slaveholders!'"[14]

Frustrated in its attempt to convert Southern moderates to abolition and unable to sustain itself any Southern state other than Kentucky, the abolitionist movement of the 1840s was closely focused on a Northern audience. The abolition leadership, however, disagreed among themselves over how best to proceed, and a serious rift developed over the question of tactics. Those who followed Garrison also generally supported pacifism, nonresistance, social utopianism, anarchism, and full women's rights—causes thought by some to be impractical. When an international antislavery convention in London in 1840 refused to recognize women delegates, Garrison dramatically took a seat among the women in the gallery in protest.

The Garrisonians also tended to embrace religious views outside the evangelical mainstream. They tended to be Unitarians, Transcendentalists, or Quakers, who had seceded from their original denominations. They were thought by some to be more closely aligned with the members of certain regional utopian communities such as Hopedale or Northampton in Massachusetts than with the goals of the wider evangelical reform community. Consequently, about half the membership of Garrison's American Anti-Slavery Society split from the organization and formed the American and Foreign Anti-Slavery Society under the leadership of Louis Tappan. The Tappanites had no objection to political activity supporting the Liberty Party and anti-slavery candidates from the major parties. Garrisonians tended to focus on moral and religious agitation, shunning the political arena and the preeminence of constitutional law over moral principles.[15]

Although calls to violence were not characteristic of the abolition movement, the rhetoric of the outspoken radicals was couched in inflammatory and unambiguous terms aimed at ending slavery—"Law or No law, constitution or no constitution."[16] Abolitionists vowed to work with "invincible determination" regardless of the consequences. The radicals publicly disavowed the unsettling concept of slaves shedding the blood of their oppressors, but they recognized that there was "no neutral ground in this matter, and the time is near when they will be compelled to take sides."[17]

In the call for a slave rebellion, the goal of which was "to attack the slave power in its most vulnerable point," the South perceived a very real physical threat. There had been three important black insurrections in the South: the Gabriel revolt in 1800, the Denmark Vesey revolt in 1822, and the Nat Turner revolt in 1831. Only the Turner revolt had led to any deaths among whites, but these had numbered mostly women and children among the sixty or so killed. Coupled with the knowledge of major slave revolts and mass murders in the West Indies, such doings were taken seriously by slaveowners. Abolitionists endorsed John Brown's attempt to foment an armed slave rebellion in Virginia by attacking Harper's Ferry in 1858. Against this background the writings and speeches of the radicals proved truly heavy rhetoric. Brown was arrested by troops under the command of Robert E. Lee. He was tried for treason and hung in 1859. The last official act of Governor Henry A. Wise of Virginia was to sign the death warrant. Wise went on to be a Confederate brigadier general.[18]

Young Kate Stone's diary reflected her fears in an encounter with slaves recently freed by federal forces in April 1863: "Looking out the window, we saw three fiendish looking, black Negroes standing around George Richards, two with their guns leveled and almost touching his breast. He was deathly pale but did not move. We thought he would be killed instantly. But after a few words from George . . . they lowered their guns and rushed into the house . . . to rob and terrorize us."[19]

ABOLITIONISTS

Those who identified themselves as abolitionists generally eschewed allegiance to a particular religious group, but a good number were intimately involved in their religions, particularly the newly formed sect of Unitarianism. However, those belonging to the Congregational, Presbyterian, and Quaker denominations predominated in the movement. The Methodists and Baptists were quite split over the issue, and very few Catholics rose to prominence in the largely Protestant anti-slavery circles. The Quaker sect was probably the most unified in its position against slavery. Yet the crusade for the immediate social and political equality of blacks was championed with a religious fervor by many men and women.

Lewis Tappan, a New York merchant, abandoned his Calvinist roots to become the treasurer of the American Unitarian Association. He was a supporter of the American Board of Commissioners for Foreign Missions and the American Bible Society. In 1833 he established the American Anti-Slavery Society in New York, but split with the Massachusetts-based abolitionists over ancillary issues raised by Garrison. Thereafter, he worked increasingly for the Negro through the American Missionary Association and through support of the Underground Railroad.

Theodore Tilton joined the New York Observer, a Presbyterian weekly, in 1853. However, he found the paper's editorial attitude toward abolition lukewarm and moved on to become the editor of the Independent, a Congregational journal with more radical views on emancipation. Tilton turned the Independent into a first-class journal. He attracted writers such as E. B. Browning, Whittier, Lowell, Garrison, and Seward, and he regularly printed the sermons of Henry Ward Beecher, the prominent pastor of the Plymouth Church in Brooklyn, New York. Tilton and Beecher joined forces in 1861 and used the paper to fight aggressively for emancipation and a more vigorous prosecution of the war. Tilton's promising career was ruined in a failed lawsuit against the preacher in which an affair between his wife and Beecher was made public.

Sidney H. Gay was the editor of the New York Tribune from 1857 to 1865. As a young man, Gay had become convinced that slavery in any form was absolutely and morally wrong. He became a member of Garrison's group of abolitionists and edited the American Anti-Slavery Standard in New York from 1843 to 1857. Stirred by the death of the abolitionist Elijah P. Lovejoy at the hands of a mob in Illinois in 1837, Edmund Quincy shocked his family, who were quite moderate on the issue, by becoming a Garrisonian abolitionist and vice-president of the American Anti-Slavery Society. He was a prominent member of the Nonresistance Society, which agitated for the secession of New England from the Union over the issue of slavery. Quincy was well known in literary circles, and his writings on the subject furnish an interesting history of the abolition movement in America.

Like many of the female radicals of the period, Abby K. Foster was an abolitionist as well as a women's rights activist. Originally from a Quaker background, she began to lecture for abolition in 1837. She conducted her campaign with Angelina Grimké, reportedly becoming the first woman in the United States to address a mixed audience in public. For this she was denounced by the clergy, who considered her a menace to public morals, and her speeches were periodically broken up by mob violence. Her presence as a delegate to the World Anti-Slavery Conference in London in 1840 caused serious disturbances, as women delegates were refused recognition. As a pioneer feminist and a leader of the radical abolitionists, she was a well-known figure in the North and a target for hatred in the South.

Angelina and Sarah Grimké were sisters born to a slaveowning family in South Carolina. Upon their father's death, the young sisters were able to persuade their mother to apportion the family slaves to them as a share of their family estate, upon which they freed them at once. Originally members of the Episcopal Church, they were attracted to the Quaker sect by friends who lived in Philadelphia, but found that they lacked the self-restraint to curb their unequivocal hatred of slaveowners. In 1836 Angelina wrote an Appeal to the Christian Women of the South, which urged Southern women to speak and act out against slavery. In South Carolina the 66-page pamphlet was confiscated and burned by postmasters, and the author was threatened with imprisonment if she returned to the state. Angelina followed this work in 1837 with an Appeal to the Women of the Nominally Free States, in which she strongly insisted that the women residing in free states were equally guilty for the national shame of continued slavery.

Sarah and Angelina began their careers by addressing small groups of women on both feminist and anti-slavery topics, and ultimately entered the lecture circuit. So great was the opposition to women speaking in public that the sisters found that they were spending as much time defending their feminism as preaching their anti-slavery ideals. John Greenleaf Whittier came to their defense, referring to them as "Carolina's high souled daughters" in his writings; however, at the same time, he privately suggested that they limit their efforts to the cause of emancipation.

The efforts of the sisters were important in the development of both the feminist and abolitionist causes, and it is difficult to determine to which cause they were most dedicated. Angelina confirmed her position in the anti-slavery community when she married abolition activist and author Theodore D. Weld in 1838. As a youth, Sarah Grimké found that it was impossible for her to study law because she was a woman. From this situation flowed her natural devotion to the cause of women's rights. In 1838, Sarah wrote Letters on the Equality of the Sexes and the Condition of Women. Her correspondence with her brother-in-law is a source of information about the cause of abolition in this period. As Southern advocates of radical abolition and feminism, the Grimké sisters were particularly detested by traditionally minded Southern women, who took pains to target them in their journals and letters.

Activists were not the only targets of Southern ire. An outspoken Southern woman listed a number of pro-abolitionists among the day's popular writers and politicians in the following diatribe: "On one side Mrs. Stowe, Greeley, Thoreau, Emerson, Sumner, in nice New England Homes—clean, clear, sweet-smelling—shut up in libraries, writing books which ease their hearts of their bitterness to us, or editing newspapers—all of which pays better than anything else in the world." The same woman called anti-slavery "the cheapest philanthropy trade in the world" and castigated the abolitionists for "setting John Brown to come down here and cut our throats in Christ's name."[20]

Contrary to the common Southern perceptions of abolitionists—preaching and teaching "hate as a gospel and the sacred duty of murder and insurrection"—the use of violence to attain emancipation never had a great appeal to the mass of people in the North, and the more provocative tactics and strategies of the radicals rarely had any effect outside of New England. Anti-slavery, as a movement, was far too decentralized and subject to too many local variations to march in lockstep behind the radicals.[21]

Garrison, in particular, was prone to involving himself in factional disputes within the movement. His refusal to endorse a political solution to slavery based on compromise, his attacks on the religious institutions of the nation as supporters of slavery in the 1840s, and his continued characterization of the South as an aggressive enemy of all American institutions left him outside the mainstream of anti-slavery sentiment. He attacked the Constitution as a "guilty and bloodstained instrument," called for the secession of the New England states from the Union, disrupted religious services at "pro-slavery" churches, and castigated the clergy and the anti-slavery moderates as conspiring with Southern slave power. These positions caused a split in the movement in 1840. Nonetheless, Garrison remains a central figure in the controversy that led to the Civil War simply because the South took him seriously and believed that he had a much greater following than reality justified.[22]

BLACK ANTI-SLAVERY ACTIVISTS

One of the many themes of the abolitionists was that the slave was "capable of high attainments as an intellectual and moral being—needing nothing but a comparatively small amount of cultivation to make him an ornament of society and a blessing to his race." Emancipation advocates declared that only the great weight of slavery had deteriorated the natural goodness and intelligence the Negro had brought from Africa. "It has a natural, an inevitable tendency to brutalize every noble faculty of man." Frederick Douglass served as a favorite symbol of the ideally regenerated freeman, and was portrayed as a victim of slavery with a "godlike nature" and a "richly endowed" intellect. Douglass was showcased as a naturally eloquent "prodigy—in soul manifestly created but a little lower than the angels."[23]

From 1841 to 1860, Douglass was the most prominent black abolitionist, "filled by his escape to freedom with noble thoughts and thrilling reflections."[24] Yet, among black activists there were several equally eminent success stories. These included Charles Lenox Remond, one of the first black anti-slavery activists; Williams Wells Brown, the first black playwright; Frances E. W. Harper, a prominent poet; Henry Bibb, a former slave and editor of a Canadian newspaper; John Mercer Langston, a free lawyer from Ohio; Martin R. Delancy, a Harvard-trained physician; and Rev. Henry Highland Garnet, the first black man to speak in the U.S. House of Representatives.

Several black newspapers were printed during the antebellum period that vied for prominence in anti-slavery circles with Garrison's *Liberator*. *The Impartial Citizen* was printed in Syracuse, New York, beginning in 1848; *Colored Man's Journal* was popular in the 1850s in New York City; San Francisco had *Mirror of the Times* in the 1850s; and *The Alienated American* was published briefly in Cleveland, Ohio. One of the earliest papers was *Freedom's Journal*, established in 1827 by John B. Russwurm, the first Negro to receive a degree from an American college.

One of the most popular black papers of the 1850s was *Frederick Douglass' Paper,* later called *Douglass' Monthly Magazine*. Unlike the other black papers, which were locally popular and short-lived, Douglass' work was circulated through 18 states and two foreign countries. It had more than 4,000 subscribers and survived for more than 13 years. Not only did these papers showcase the ability of blacks to write and edit, but they also hinted at the large number of blacks among their subscribers who could read.

SLAVEOWNERS

While Southern slaveholders may have been willing to forego slavery as an institution if their financial investment in slaves was indemnified, the mass of Southern society was totally unwilling to be chastised by self-

This drawing illustrates the status of Negro slaves as they are inspected before an auction in antebellum New Orleans. From the authors' collection.

righteous Northern idealists or to tolerate the integration of blacks into white society as equals. It has been estimated that the large slaveowners comprised as little as three percent of Southern whites, and fewer than six percent owned any slaves at all. The majority of these small slaveholders had fewer than five slaves and labored in the fields beside them. Nonetheless, in 1850 slaveholders represented a majority of the delegates in the legislatures of all but two Southern states. Only in South Carolina were they dominant. In Louisiana and Texas nearly two-thirds of the legislators owned no slaves at all. It is estimated that only 40 percent of all county offices in the Deep South were held by nonslaveholders, giving slaveowners control far out of proportion to their numbers.[25]

The impracticality of blacks being integrated into the fabric of American society in the antebellum period can best be measured by the resistance to racial integration seen in the South after a costly and painful war had forced emancipation upon it. With no solution to the perceived problems of free black participation in white society, and faced with economic ruin if forced to forfeit their considerable investment in black labor,

Southerners were forced to turn any moderate attitudes they may have possessed toward gradual emancipation into a total defense of Southern society against any disruption from without. Impelled by a growing body of public opinion in the North that slavery must be abolished at all costs, the South launched an equally militant defense of the institution, portraying it as a positive good—a civilizing and caring medium for blacks who would otherwise revert to the brutality of their African origins. A Southern woman wrote of her slaveowning relations, "They strive to ameliorate the condition of these Africans in every particular . . . [and] live their own lives in peace [as] if they were African missionaries."[26]

SLAVERY AND THE COURTS

A number of important legal cases involving slaves and the efforts of abolitionists preceded the outbreak of war. Three of the more interesting are the *Amistad* case, the Lemmon case, and the Dred Scott case. That not all of these cases were decided in the same direction suggests some ambiguity within the courts, but it should be noted that some of these decisions were handed down by state courts, while others were decided by federal judges. The depth of the discrepancies found in these decisions was symptomatic of the preoccupation with these matters as an outgrowth of the ongoing disputes tearing at the country.

MUTINY ON THE *AMISTAD*

The *Amistad* was a slave ship belonging to Spanish owners that sailed from Havana in June 1839 for another Cuban port. The master of the ship had on board over fifty blacks, including four children. All of them were so recently imported from Africa that most spoke neither English nor any other European language. On the journey the blacks, under the leadership of a warrior named Cinque, overcame the crew and took control of the ship. In the process, they killed the captain and the ship's cook. With the coerced help of the surviving crew, they proceeded to sail north along the Atlantic coast of the United States.

Some months later, the vessel was found at anchor off the shore of Long Island, New York. A boarding party from the USS Washington commanded by Lt. Cmdr. T.R. Gedney, USN, took the *Amistad* into the port of New London, Connecticut, along with the blacks. Gedney brought a case in the U.S. district court in New Haven for the salvage rights to the ship, which included the fair market value of the "slaves" on board.

John H. Hyde, an abolition sympathizer and the editor of the *New London Gazette,* wrote a story about the incident, making the blacks instant celebrities. The Anti-Slavery Society in Connecticut contacted Roger S. Baldwin, a New York attorney, to defend the rights of the Africans found aboard the *Amistad*. With financing arranged by Louis Tappan, the Committee of Friends of the *Amistad* Africans was formed. The abolitionists brought suit in the Connecticut state courts before Judge Andrew T. Judson, claiming the freedom of the Africans under existing U.S. law, as the United States had joined with Britain to prohibit slave trading in 1808. Under several treaties between 1817 and 1830, the Spanish had also made the slave trade illegal.

The abolitionists' lawyers argued that the blacks had the status of free men on the grounds that they were free-born Africans, not subjects of Spain or any other country. They were in fact of the Mendi tribe and had been kidnapped as free men from their homeland in Sierra Leone, and illegally transported to a Spanish possession, and were therefore free under Spanish law as well. Since the treaties between the United States and Spain did not require that the Africans be returned to Spanish territory, the court ruled that they were at liberty to return to Africa if they wished.

Abolitionist forces were initially elated but quickly became alarmed when it was learned that the Van Buren administration in Washington was determined to overturn this decision so as not to offend the sensibilities of the South in the election of 1840. The case was appealed to the Supreme Court, and Justice Joseph Story delivered its opinion in 1841. The Court awarded Lt. Cmdr. Gedney the salvage rights to the ship and its cargo, but freed the Africans on the grounds that they had always been free men and had never become slaves under Spanish law. This was deft footwork if there ever was any. By declaring that the Africans were free by the law of Spain, the Court was able to sidestep any accusations of freeing slaves or setting precedents for the emancipation of American-born blacks under U.S. law.[27]

It had taken almost three years for the Africans on board the *Amistad* to regain their freedom. In the interim, they were housed in Westville, Connecticut, about two miles outside New Haven. Under the care of the abolitionists, many of the Africans learned to speak and write English, studied the Bible, and became "civilized Christian Men." One was later to serve as an English interpreter in an African mission in Sierra Leone, and one of the female children became a teacher. On November 27, 1841, with money raised for the purpose among interested British abolitionists, 35 of the surviving Africans returned to their homeland along with 5 white missionaries and teachers. A Christian mission to Africa was established there and remained prosperous for many decades. It is interesting to note that little money was raised among American abolitionists for the return trip to Africa even though it seemed supportive of the growing colonization movement.[28]

THE LEMMON CASE

In 1852 Jonathan and Juliet Lemmon decided to move from Virginia to Texas and take the eight slaves that belonged to Mrs. Lemmon with them.

Although the details of the trip are confused and unimportant, it was decided to take a side trip by steamer to New York City and then book a luxury passage from there to New Orleans. The slaves were thereby brought into New York Harbor while New York was a free state. Jonathan Lemmon, conscious of a possible problem, made plans to transfer the slaves to a southbound steamer without actually landing them in New York for fear that the abolitionists would make an effort to rescue them. But his plans failed, and the owners and the slaves were arrested as soon as they touched land and were brought before the New York State courts.

The state argued that Lemmon was a slave trader and that these blacks were confined and held against their will. The attorneys for the Lemmons argued that they had the right under federal law to transport their "property" anywhere in the country. Moreover, it was argued that the slaves had never touched free soil except for the purpose of passage and transit. Justice Elijah Paine granted the state's writ, citing the anti-slavery statutes of New York as his authority. He ordered the eight slaves freed. Paine's decision was greeted with approbation by the New York press, free blacks, and abolitionists everywhere. Nevertheless, a group of New York businessmen raised funds to compensate the Lemmons for their loss. The Lemmons received $5,200 in indemnification and returned to Virginia, while the former slaves were secretly whisked off to Canada to ensure their future safety. In March 1860 the New York State court of appeals chose to rehear the Lemmon case, and ruled again in favor of the slaves. Southern slaveowners were horrified by the decision and threatened to take it to the Supreme Court. However, the outbreak of the war prevented the case from ever being heard again.[29]

THE DRED SCOTT DECISION

In 1857, in a much more celebrated case, the Supreme Court decided that the Missouri Compromise was unconstitutional, and that a black slave, Dred Scott, taken from slave territory in Missouri to free soil in Illinois, "had never ceased to be a slave" and so could not claim his freedom in a federal court because he lacked standing as a citizen with the right to sue.

Upon the death of his original master, Scott had passed from his owner to the man's widow and her new husband, an abolitionists congressman who persuaded him to sue for his freedom in the Missouri courts on the grounds that he had lived in the so-called free states of Illinois and Minnesota four a total of four years. The Missouri court initially granted him his freedom, but the case was appealed and reversed in the Missouri Supreme Court. It then moved on to the U.S. Supreme Court for final disposition in 1857.

The 7–2 decision effectively denied the right of Congress to prohibit slaveowning "anywhere within the United States." The opinion written by Chief Justice Roger B. Taney was probably most significant as it suggested that blacks could not be citizens even if they were born free. The Constitution, according to Taney, had been made "by and for white men" and it was "useless and mischievous for the opponents of slavery to quote the Declaration of Independence, for its great words were never meant to include Negroes." Not only was Scott not free, but no black, free or slave, could legally bring suit in a federal court.[30]

In fact, Scott could have been freed at any time by his master, and was given his freedom soon after the Supreme Court decision. But there was little joy in the achievement for Scott or the abolitionists that had manipulated the case in the hope of having slavery outlawed through the courts. An outburst of protest greeted the Dred Scott decision in the North, and the Republicans made it a cornerstone of their 1860 presidential election campaign. Scott worked as a janitor in Barnum's Hotel in St. Louis for a time, but he died of tuberculosis within a year of gaining his freedom.

FUGITIVE SLAVES

Current conventional wisdom among historians credits the black counterculture of the slave quarters rooted in tribal traditions for the success of African-Americans in resisting slavery. This masterful reconstruction of plantation life has been found wanting by historians. "Those pivotal consequences of the runaway's resistance have eluded superb historians only because their histories of slavery end in 1860, before Civil War fugitives' agency in emancipation became unmistakable and shattering."[31] The most remarkable resistance to exploitation was the fugitive or runaway slave. Fugitives helped to weaken the system under which whites controlled the black population of the slave states by shattering the aura of security that surrounded whites in the South. On a half dozen occasions—certainly not more—fugitives had slit the throats of their masters requiring that they be hunted down and punished as a lesson to other blacks. This required the maintenance of slave patrols and slave hunters, the posting of rewards, and the establishment of meaningful public punishments as deterrents.

More importantly, when a single slave escaped without informing the others, no person or group could betray them, and since the runaway resisted non-violently, no cause was created to go about slaughtering innocents in the slave quarters. "Better still, some northern whites aided unarmed runaways." Over 5,000 slaves made the run each year and the majority came from the border states, forcing the South to look beyond its reach to capture fugitives. Failure to establish a deterrence outside the South would create a "void in the plantation gates." Stephen Douglas noted, "Slavery cannot exist a day or an hour anywhere unless it is supported by local police regulations." Slaveowners, realizing this reality in 1850, demanded that the federal government close the open borders through the Fugitive Slave Law that would make antislavery agitation and aid to a runaway illegal everywhere in the nation. While slavery was

Federal authorities initially put escaped slaves to work digging entrenchments and fixing railroads. Some Northern artists had an unfortunate habit of showing blacks in a stereotypical manner that mirrored the expectations of the Northern public. Sketch by W. T. Crane of *Leslie's*.

ended only by a long and costly war, fugitive slaves provoked this debate that ultimately helped to bring about the war. The Fugitive Slave Law brought Southern-inspired limits to white democracy in the North turning virtually all Northerners into informants and slave-catchers, and increasing their discomfort with the peculiar institution by "dragooning them into personally enslaving a fellow human being."[32]

Estimates show that by 1860 there were more than 3.6 million black slaves in the states that were to form the Confederacy. Profits from cotton in the Carolinas and from sugar in Louisiana provided a financial bulwark for slavery in the Deep South. The archaic plantation system would have faded into obscurity were it not for the ability of slavery to provide the labor needed to produce these crops. In early 1861, Federal forces coming upon the first trickle of escaped slaves returned them to Confederate lines in obedience to the Fugitive Slave Act of 1850, but Gen. Benjamin F. Butler, a swashbuckling pro-war democrat from Massachusetts, side-stepped the law by declaring the blacks "contraband of war" and open to seizure. Lincoln reluctantly approved the ruling, and blacks thereafter abandoned the plantations in the hundreds or thousands whenever Federal forces were nearby. At first it seemed that the slaves had traded one master for another, but Congress passed a series of laws that further refined their status. The term "freedman" was adopted in official correspondence after the publication of the Emancipation Proclamation in January 1863, but, to the soldiers in the field, escaped slaves remained known as "contrabands." After 1863, black men were also free to enter the armed service of the United States. The First South Carolina Volunteers was the first Northern regiment composed entirely of escaped slaves and black refugees.

FROM SLAVERY TO CONTRABAND

Reforming the system of slavery into one that recognized freedmen as equals was no simple task. No one knew what to do with the flood of escaped or newly freed blacks that came streaming into the Federal lines at the beginning of the war. Such a volume of displaced persons, especially women and children, had not been anticipated. In the spring of 1861, the first of this wave of escaped slaves to appear were those that came to Fortress Monroe, an old Federal installation near Norfolk, on the southeastern tip of Virginia. They had been working on nearby Confederate fortifications, and took advantage of the proximity of Union lines to flee. By July 1861, at least 900 slaves had gained their freedom at Fortress Monroe, but while they had been given food and shelter, they had also been put to work on the Federal entrenchments.

Over the next four years, tens of thousands of African Americans changed their status from slaves to contrabands by fleeing to Union army posts and occupied territory. Many of these were house servants and skilled craftsmen from local plantations who thought they had the most to gain through freedom and the best chance to integrate into the black community in the North. Most escaped to northern and southeastern Virginia, the Sea Islands off South Carolina, parts of Tennessee, and other places taken over by Union forces early in the war. Thousands fled south. At least 50,000 crowded into enclaves along the Mississippi River, from Cairo, Illinois all the way south to New Orleans, Louisiana, one of the first cities to have fallen to Federal forces (April 1862). There was an active attempt to document the system of slavery in the area around that city. While historians know more about slaves in New Orleans during the war than in any other Southern city, it was hardly an archetype of Southern slavery. New Orleans boasted the largest black community of any city in the country at the time, composed of numerous free black businessmen and artisans, urbanized former slaves, and recent refugees from the plantations.

In the enclaves, some of the temporary camps grew into functioning villages with schools, churches, and shops. Freedman's Village, built along the Potomac River on the site of Robert E. Lee's property in Arlington, Virginia (and now occupied by Arlington National Cemetery), was created to relieve the severe crowding among 10,000 or so black refugees living in the District of Columbia. The government built whitewashed duplexes for the refugees in the village, employed them in workshops and on government farms, and provided a school, chapel, and hospital.

Another model contraband camp grew near Corinth, Mississippi where slaves from northern Mississippi and Alabama and southern Tennessee began arriving after the Federal victory at nearby Shiloh (April 1862). The contrabands built themselves log cabins along the streets laid out and numbered by the army engineers. The little town was even divided into wards. Like Freedman's Village, the camp at Corinth soon had a school, hospital, stores, an administrative office, and a church. Within a few months, some of the African American men had been organized into a kind of militia, relieving white troops of the necessity of guarding the camp. A number of American Missionary Association workers came to Corinth to teach and to preach, and by the summer of 1863 there were nearly 400 pupils attending school. The Union Christian Church of Corinth, as the missionaries called their little chapel, regularly attracted hundreds of worshipers to services that sometimes featured the preaching of four black ministers recently escaped from slavery. More than 300 children attended Sunday School classes. Families were also encouraged to grow their own food in individual gardens. A little cotton field and a large field of vegetables for the hospital were also maintained. The Corinth camp, by the summer of 1863, had become a fully functioning little town.

However, most contrabands did not experience such well-organized and improving conditions. In some places, freed slaves had to live in old packing crates, tobacco barns, sod huts, and, if they were lucky, abandoned houses. Single rooms sometimes housed six families. The supplies that were supposed to be distributed to the contrabands were sometimes sold on the black market by army officers or other officials, and the medical care in the camps (usually provided by army surgeons) was unreliable. Many camps offered material deprivations to the escaped slaves rivaling if not exceeding those of the plantations from which they had escaped.

A northern woman working at a hospital for freedmen in the middle of a muddy field near Washington began her description by writing, "If I were to describe this hospital it would not be believed." In this place "are gathered all the colored people who have been made free by the progress of our Army." The overburdened hospital cared for "all cripples, diseased, aged, wounded, inform, from whatsoever cause." Their patients included black army teamsters beaten nearly to death by white soldiers and desperate mothers carrying dying children into camp. Up to 50 sick, injured, or simply exhausted men, women, and children arrived each day. At least one baby was born daily, but nurses had "no baby clothes except as we wrap them up in an old piece of muslin. . . This hospital consists of all the lame, halt, and blind escaped from slavery."[33]

Conditions in some makeshift camps were even worse. An agent for the Cincinnati Contraband Relief Commission revealed the horror of some contrabands' lives when he described a temporary shelter near Davis Bend, Mississippi. In an open cattle shed lived 35 "poor wretched helpless Negroes." The band consisted of a nearly blind man, 5 women, and 29 children all under the age of 12 years.

Not surprisingly, the death rates in the teeming camps soared, especially among the children. Out of the 4,000 black refugees living in Helena, Arkansas, in 1863–1864, about 1,100 died. In Memphis, 1,200 out of 4,000 contrabands died in only three months, while the camp at Natchez suffered a nearly 50 percent mortality rate in 1863. To make matters worse, Confederate guerrillas frequently attacked defenseless contraband settlements, sometimes kidnapping and selling men, women, and children— each of whom brought as much as $100 on the slave market.

The blacks living in government camps—men, women, and children— rarely received food and shelter free of charge. Contraband of all ages had to work in return for the security, rations, and housing the army provided. By the age of 10 or 12, as they had as slaves, freed-children took their places in the fields alongside older African Americans. Yet many of these newly freed children—not to mention adult contrabands—also had access to schools. After living their entire lives in a society that actually made it illegal for them to learn to read or write, the contraband eagerly crowded into schools of all sizes and in all conditions almost as soon as they reached Federal lines. An escaped slave opened one of the first schools for black students in Norfolk in the fall of 1861. Two years later, there were 21 teachers in 11 schools with 3,000 day and night students of all ages. Scores of individuals, missionary associations, and even the army, sponsored or staffed schools throughout the occupied South; over 1,400 men and women were teaching in 975 schools for blacks in the year after the war ended. These schools ranged in size from a few girls being taught by a lone teacher (sometimes the young daughters of Union army officers) to the 1,422 in public schools run by the military in New Orleans and more than 14,000 in schools operated in rural parishes in southern Louisiana.

A number of the teachers in contraband schools were African American—some escaped slaves themselves. In fact, the American Missionary Association's first school in Norfolk opened under the leadership of Mary Smith Peake, the free daughter of a white man and a mulatto woman. The school would later become Hampton Institute, the alma mater of Booker T. Washington. Some teachers were former slaves, such as "Uncle" Cyrus White, who taught school in Beaufort for several months in 1863; William D. Harris, a plasterer; and his assistant, Amos Wilson, who taught at Grosport, North Carolina. Most black teachers came from the North in the employ of the AMA. Edmonia Highgate of Syracuse, New York had been a teacher and a principal in Norfolk before the war. Her colleague and a former slave, Sara G. Stanley, came from Cleveland via Oberlin College to teach at the AMA school at Camp Baker in Washington. Northern publications produced flash cards and textbooks for contraband schools; The

American Tract Society even published a monthly magazine, *The Freedman*, to be distributed to black soldiers and to be used in contraband schools.

NOTES

1. See "Heroes of the Squadron: Sir George Collier," http://www.royalnaval-museum.org/visit_see_victory_cfexhibition_collier.htm (Accessed March 2008).

2. Dumas Malone, ed. *Dictionary of American Biography* (New York: Scribner's Sons, 1943). The information on prominent abolitionists that follows is taken largely from this source.

3. James Truslow Adams, ed. *Album of American History* (New York: Charles Scribner's Sons, 1946), 66–81. The infant U.S. government promised to free black slaves that fought the British at the end of the Revolutionary War. They kept their word and provided pensions for the veterans. The British made similar promises, but chose to send black volunteers as slaves to the West Indies at the close of the conflict. See David O. White, *Connecticut's Black Soldiers of the Revolution* (Chester: Pequot Press, 1973).

4. Jennifer L. Weber, Copperheads, *The Rise and Fall of Lincoln's Opponents in the North* (New York: Oxford University Press, 2006), 23.

5. John D. Billings, *Hardtack and Coffee* (Boston: G.M. Smith, 1887), 20.

6. Adams, 105, 107. Data taken from the table on p. 106.

7. John W. Blassingame, *The Clarion Voice* (Washington: National Parks Service, 1976), 18.

8. See Ibid., 18–20.

9. William E. Freehling, *The South vs. The South: How Anti-Confederate Southerners Shaped the Course of the Civil War* (New York: Oxford University Press, 2001), 37–38.

10. Frederick Douglass, *Narrative of the Life of an American Slave, Written by Himself* (1845; New York: Penguin, 1968), xvii.

11. William Lloyd Garrison, *Thoughts on African Colonization* (Boston: N.p., 1832), 134.

12. William Lloyd Garrison, "The First Editorial by William Lloyd Garrison," *The Liberator* January 1, 1831, http://www.wfu.edu/~zulick/340/garrisonlibera-tor1.html.

13. Douglass, xiv.

14. Daniel Walker Howe, *What God Hath Wrought: The Transformation of America, 1815–1848* (New York: Oxford University Press, 2007).

15. Garrison, *The Liberator* (Boston), December 15, 1837.

16. Ibid.

17. Ibid., May 31, 1844.

18. Walter Sullivan, *The War the Women Lived: Female Voices from the Confederate South* (Nashville: J. S. Sanders, 1995), 91–92.

19. C. Vann Woodward, *Mary Chesnut's Civil War* (New Haven: Yale University Press, 1981), 245.

20. Clifford Dowdey, *The Great Plantation* (Charles City, VA: Berkeley Plantation Press, 1957), 300.

21. Garrison, *The Liberator,* March 31, 1832.

22. Douglass, vi, 24.

23. Ibid., vi.

24. Ibid., vii.

25. Dowdey, 300; C. Van Woodward, 245.

26. Fred J. Cook, "The Slave Ship Rebellion," *American Heritage,* February 1957, 60–64, 104–115.

27. Howard Jones, *Mutiny on the Amistad* (New York: Oxford University Press, 1987), 3–21.

28. Ervin L. Jordan, Jr., *Black Confederates and Afro-Yankees in Civil War Virginia* (Charlottesville: University Press of Virginia, 1995), 13–14.

29. John S. Bowman, ed. *The Civil War Almanac* (New York: Bison Books, 1983), 38.

30. See Freehling, *The South vs. the South,* 25–26.

31. Ibid., 30–31.

32. David S. Heidler, and Jeanne T. Heidler, eds. *Daily Life of Civilians in Wartime Early America, From the Colonial Era to the Civil War* (Westport, CT: Greenwood Press, 2007), 173–175.

33. Ibid., 174.

PART II

SOLDIERS' LIVES

7

BILLY YANK AND JOHNNY REB

"Dearest and most intimate friends and companions."
—Thomas A. Ashby

COMMON SOLDIERS

The men who opposed one another on the battlefields of the Civil War were more alike than different. Generally, the soldiers on both sides came from similar backgrounds, spoke the same language (although sometimes with widely divergent regional accents), had the same political history, cherished the same Constitution, and suffered the same hardships and dangers offered by soldiering. But the differences between Billy Yank and Johnny Reb were nonetheless meaningful enough to sustain four years of bloody conflict and may help to explain the relationship between these enemies.[1]

The great difference between Billy Yank and Johnny Reb seems to have been in their style of fighting—a characteristic noted by many observers, such as federal captain John W. De Forest: "Three points I noted with regard to our opponents," observed federal captain John W. De Forest. "They aimed better than our men; they covered themselves (in case of need) more carefully and effectively; they could move in a swarm, without much care for alignment and touching elbows. In short, they fought more like [Indians], or like hunters, than we. The result was that they lost fewer men, though they were far inferior in numbers."[2]

Applying statistical analysis to the Civil War is difficult at best and foolhardy at worst. Authorities differ, and statistics bristle in the many controversies. Yet the war generated a noble body of data that begs to be interpreted. Still, hard and fast conclusions based solely on these data should be avoided. Facts and figures on the men who faced one another in 1861–62 are largely unreliable when grouped together with those of 1863–64. The volunteers of the earlier period tended to differ significantly from the troops of the later war, which included draftees, substitutes, and bounty claimers. Moreover, it is difficult to ascertain reliable statistics for Southern troops, as they are simply not available for all theaters or periods

Civil war reenactment enthusiasts go to great lengths to portray the era correctly with reproduction (not replica) weapons, clothing, and accoutrements. (Left) Mark Gilbert: Capt. Hatcher's Co. A, Fauquier Mountain Rangers, Turner Ashby's 7th Virginia Cavalry, Wm. E. "Grumble" Jones' Brigade, Army of Northern Virginia. (Right) Keith Curtis and Jim Volo, Co. A, Col. Wm. S. Fish's 1st Connecticut Volunteer Cavalry, Gen. George A. Custer's Brigade, Gen. Phil Sheridan's Division, Army of the Potomac. Dorothy Volo photos.

of the conflict. Similar inherent inaccuracies in the data notwithstanding, some simple facts stand out about the men who fought in the Civil War.[3]

Of all the soldiers that served in the war, it has been estimated that between 30 percent and 40 percent were Confederates, yet a reliable figure for their absolute number can not be obtained because records for the western armies are lacking. Between 1 and 1.5 million men may have served in the Rebel army. In contrast, the records of the United States Government, which are much more complete and reliable, show that federal forces numbered precisely 2.2 million men. Approximately three-quarters of each opposing force were composed of infantry, with cavalry making up 15 percent and artillery about 7 percent. The remaining portion was composed of engineers, medical personnel, teamsters, and other ancillary personnel. About 10 percent of each army served as officers. Only 3 percent of all federal personnel served in the navy, and less than 1 percent served in the minuscule Confederate navy.

The average age of the men at enlistment in the federal army was just under 26. Yet a 27 year-old Michigan man, who was among the first to rush to volunteer in the heady days of 1862, found that he was a half dozen years older than most of his fellows.[4] One study of a million Federal enlistments turned up only 16,000 as old as 44, and only 46,000 of 25 or more, but this includes less than half of the recruits to the Federal cause. According to other authorities, the Union armies were made up as follows: 30 percent of men under 21; 30 percent from 21 to 24; 30 percent from 25 to 30; 10 percent over 30. The Confederates averaged just over 26 years, a remarkable agreement with the average federal figure when the traditional view of the Rebels is of an army composed of old men and young boys. The height and weight of federal recruits is well documented; they averaged 5 feet, 8 inches and 145 pounds. As 19th-century men were about this size on average, it can be presumed that Confederates were of a similar height and weight. Of the federal soldiers, 29 percent were married when they enlisted, while more than 36 percent of their Southern counterparts seem to have been married men. This may reflect a greater mobilization of the available population in the manpower-hungry South.

While many men wrote regularly to their families and expressed pitiable longing and loneliness for them, a federal officer testified about receiving a letter from a destitute wife, anxious for news of her husband's health. The wife had received no word of him in months and only nine dollars since he had enlisted. She and her children had therefore been evicted from their home. "Here are four pages of pathos that make me want . . . to kick him for not deserving them," wrote the officer. "Apparently a fairly educated and quite worthy girl has married a good-looking youth of inferior nature and breeding who has not the energy to toil effectively for her, nor the affection to endure privations for her sake."[5]

While only 5 percent of all federal soldiers were killed or mortally wounded in combat, almost 12 percent of the Confederates suffered a similar fate. The death rate from all causes, including accidents and sickness, was much higher. Six hundred thirty thousand Americans died in the conflict. As many as 25 percent of all Southern soldiers may have died. The North actually suffered more war deaths: almost three men for every two lost by the South. The Battle at Gettysburg had the highest number of casualties in the war, but it was one of the largest battles in terms of the number of men engaged. In terms of the number of wounded and killed as a portion of the forces engaged, the bloodiest battle of the war was Shiloh; the bloodiest single day took place at Antietam; and the greatest losses suffered in the shortest time were at Cold Harbor, where up to 7,000 men fell in just 20 minutes. The single worst one-month period for casualties was May 1864. Almost 100,000 Americans lost their lives or were wounded in battle during this period, and Grant was called a butcher for continuing his campaign. The willingness of Civil War soldiers to face death in a conflict that offered no chance of personal gain remains one of the most remarkable characteristics of the war.

Billy Yank was generally better educated than Johnny Reb, owing, in part, to the greater number of prestigious colleges and universities located in the North and the greater emphasis placed on basic public education at the lower academic levels. While the South had a number of impressive universities, their number was small in proportion to the total in the country, and Southerners were wary of public education. The rate of illiteracy among Civil War soldiers should not be overemphasized, however. Most of the troops could write their names and read from the Bible. However, the spelling and grammar found in letters, diaries, and journals frequently fell well below schoolroom standards. A typical white regiment on either side of the contest probably had few illiterates, and many units had none at all. The highest rate of illiteracy was found among black units. This is to be expected, as many of these soldiers had been denied an education. Nonetheless, there were many well-educated black freemen in the ranks. Even the totally unlettered soldier could easily impose himself on a literate comrade to read a newspaper out loud or to write a letter home for him.

The vast majority of the men who served were neither professional soldiers nor draftees. The largest percentage were farmers before the war. The Southern soldier was more likely to be an agricultural worker of some type than the immigrant recruit from the more highly industrialized North. The available data make no distinction between the plantation owner, the small farm owner or his children, and the paid agricultural worker. The data also ignore all those who were too young to have an occupation when they enlisted, such as teenagers and students. Many of these were listed as unskilled workers.

Skilled laborers made up the second largest group of men to serve in either army. These skilled laborers included carpenters and furniture makers, masons, machinists, wheelwrights and cartwrights, barrel makers and coopers, shoemakers and leather workers, smiths of many kinds, and other skilled tradesmen. The particular trade by which an artisan made his living rarely prepared him for military service. Exceptions to this may have been made for artisans like butchers, blacksmiths, and farriers, who were organized within the service to practice their trades for the army.

Both armies required that men be right-handed, or at least to perform all drills, the manual of arms, and battalion evolutions based on the right hand. Muskets were designed to be fired with the butt placed firmly against the right shoulder, the aim taken with the right eye, and the trigger actuated by the right hand. The cartridge box was worn on the right-rear hip to be accessed with that hand. Handedness was no small consideration because the tactics of the day required men to stand shoulder-to-shoulder in the battle line while loading and firing. Fire by platoon and by rank and file was part of training. Initially, individual firing was thought to cause a breakdown in fire discipline, and any deviation from the drill could cause considerable disruption during combat. Of course, right-handedness was very common in the general population and rarely presented a problem for most left-handed men if they were properly trained.

Oddly, shifting the aim from the front to the right oblique was diffi-cult for soldiers in a right-handed stance because it required them to turn most of their bodies in that direction. The relative ease with which the aim might be altered from the front to the left oblique made the attack from the right wing of the army and the defense from left wing slightly more effec-tive than on the other flank of either battle line. This effect of handedness on the battlefield had been noted since ancient times when warriors at-tacked with spears in their right hands and wore shields on the left arms. The advantage to the right wing caused the entire line to rotate somewhat in a counterclockwise manner when an attack was successfully pressed. It was common for the right and left wings of opposing forces to face one another in battle offsetting the advantages somewhat, but flanking move-ments upon the right of isolated units could be advantageous to the at-tackers and devastating to the defense. The Confederates under Thomas "Stonewall" Jackson successfully pressed their attack on the right flank of the Federal army at Chancellorsville causing its collapse. Commanders often "refused the flank" by setting a company at right angles to the battle line to deter such an attack.[6]

Professional and white-collar occupations made up the largest portion of those who served as officers. Professional men included lawyers, physi-cians, clergymen, engineers, professors, and army and navy officers. The "white-collar" category is somewhat obscured, as it is distinguished from the professional class more by degree than by any other characteristic, and many men often crossed the line between the two. These included bankers, merchants, manufacturers, journalists, clerks, bookkeepers, and schoolteachers.

An 1864 *Leslie's* illustration of the New York City Hall Park Recruiting Office. Although bounties were offered to new recruits, it should be remembered that all those who served in the first two years of the war were volunteers. Courtesy of Library of Congress.

Notwithstanding their civilian occupations, each man came with a set of values that mirrored the home and community he had left behind. The majority of the recruits in the first year of the war were volunteers, and they pledged themselves to serve for three months, expecting that the first major battle would decide the issue of secession. Nonetheless, their commitment to serve, their personal and economic sacrifice, and the distress experienced by their families and loved ones should not be minimized because of this limited initial commitment. The motivation of most volunteers seems to have been rooted in the compelling and deeply personal forces of duty and honor. In 1861 both of these were closely linked with concepts of masculinity, morality, conscience, and romance.[7]

It is strange that federal volunteers most often associated their service with duty, while honor seems to have motivated Confederate volunteers. Although the two are not mutually exclusive, there is some truth in viewing the South as a society with a profound sense of honor, whereas the North was driven by a communal conscience analogous to a compact made with God. Americans of the early 19th century were strongly influenced by such sentiments. The consciousness of duty resonated particularly well with the parallel development of social reform in the North. To shirk duty was to violate the collective conscience and to offend morality by omission. Duty was viewed as a personal responsibility rather than a collective obligation. It served as part of the identity of manhood and established the place of the individual in society. "We all of us have a duty to perform in this life," wrote one volunteer. It was not enough to support the war from a distance when duty required that a man place his life on the line. Many Confederates also cited obligations to duty, but they were much more likely to speak of honor.[8]

Honor was primarily a masculine concept that dealt with one's public image and reputation. There is ample evidence of a link among the romantic themes of adventure, glory, and honor that appeared in the popular literature of the period and the letters and diaries of the Southern volunteers. Nonetheless, Southerners also viewed honor in a contemporary light, and the continued popularity of dueling attests to the vitality of the sentiment in the Southern psyche. Confederate soldiers often wrote of being dishonored in the eyes of their "revolutionary ancestors" should they fail to defend the cause. Nonetheless, the appeals to duty and honor were most often found among the letters and journals of the more literate upper classes.[9]

Among less popular motivations such as adventure, excitement, patriotism, and ideology, Civil War soldiers were also affected by a need to prove their masculinity. Southerners tended to be more boastful in this regard than the Yankees. "They were amiable, gentle, and unselfish in disposition, yet were fearless and daring in spirit, and devoted . . . to those bodily exercises that make the strong and vigorous man," noted one observer.[10] Northerners tended to be more circumspect, worrying whether they would pass the test of manhood posed by battle. The psychological importance of passing this test should not be minimized. Particularly among the young volunteers, the experience of battle, "seeing the elephant" in 19th century terms, was seen as a rite of passage.

Many men looked forward to their first furlough home. One volunteer noted, "The men seem perfectly crazy to go home and show their uniforms. Blue cloth and brass buttons enlist more soldiers than patriotism."[11] A young woman wrote, "It seems very patriotic and grand . . . for one's country to die. . .A lot of us girls went down to the train and took flowers to the soldiers as they were passing through and they cut buttons from their coats and gave [them] to us as souvenirs." Young men quickly repudiated the romance, adventure, and glory surrounding the war once they had "seen the elephant" in battle, but a young man's performance on the battlefield quite literally separated the men from the boys.[12]

Perhaps the many references to sentiment were a reaction to the pressures brought upon the men by the communities and social groups to which they belonged. As volunteers generally served in companies and regiments raised from the eligible men in a local neighborhood, it may have been socially impossible for them to do otherwise. A contemporary commentator noted, "The associations of. . .boyhood and early manhood were with these people . . . [their] dearest and most intimate friends and companions . . . These men found gratification in a military organization composed of those of their own class." A man's behavior in war often established his place in the community in the postwar period.[13]

If the recruits' own motivations for volunteering, as set down in their personal letters and diaries, are not accepted at face value, it is difficult to rationalize how so many individuals could have been willing to die for a cause or how such massive volunteer armies could have been raised. Nonetheless, it remains an extraordinary fact that during the first year of the war all those who enlisted and fought on one side or the other chose to do so.

While the vast majority of soldiers, both North and South, were native-born Americans, a large number of foreigners were to be found in both armies. It has been estimated that between 20 percent and 25 percent of the Union army was foreign born. Millions of Europeans had migrated to North America in the decades before the war, and the majority had settled in the North. Most of these had established themselves in the great urban areas. Close to four million aliens were living in the North when the war began. They tended to identify with that section of the country, and joined the federal forces. As little as four or five percent of the Confederate army was composed of foreigners. There were fewer than one million foreign-born residents in the Confederacy, and therefore they made up a smaller proportion of the Southern forces. The crews of the minuscule Confederate navy were almost entirely recruited from abroad. As a proportion of the available population, however, foreigners seemed to have supported both the North and South equally.

Almost eight percent of the federal generals and two percent of the Confederate generals were foreign born. The government at Washington gave serious consideration to offering the command of its armies to the Italian patriot Giuseppe Garibaldi, who had lived in Staten Island, New York, briefly in the 1850s, but the freedom fighter demurred. Federal general Philip H. Sheridan, who in later years alternately claimed Albany, Boston, and Somerset, Ohio, as his birthplace, was certainly of Irish extraction, and probably was born in Ireland—a difference unimportant until postwar supporters wished him to run for the presidency. The four Solomon brothers from Prussia had fought on the losing side of a revolt in their homeland in 1848. All fought for the federal cause in 1861. One of them was the wartime governor of Wisconsin, while two others served as colonels and the last as a brigadier.[14]

The largest group of foreigners to serve in federal ranks, about 200,000, were of German origin. The Irish were next, numbering about 150,000, followed by the Canadians and the English, each totaling about 50,000 men. Scandinavians, Frenchmen, Italians, and other nationalities also served in small numbers. Although the largest foreign group to serve the Confederacy seems to have been the Irish, other nationalities were also present in the Rebel ranks, including Englishmen, Canadians, Frenchmen, Italians, and Mexicans.

The motivation for foreign-born soldiers to participate in an internecine conflict in the absence of obvious personal advantages is difficult to pin down. Some, like British officer Sir Percy Wyndham, who had once served with Garibaldi in Italy, were simply soldiers of fortune. Men from the socially unacceptable and impoverished immigrant populations may have served in an attempt to win a place for themselves and their families in postwar American society. In this they were at least partially successful—as with the Irish, who came to dominate early 20th-century urban politics. Whatever their motivation, the foreign-born soldiers generally gave a good account of themselves. The Irish troops, in particular, provided some of the most momentous and courageous combat of the war. The fighting reputations of the federal Irish Brigades and the Louisiana Tigers, both composed of working-class Irish immigrants, stand up well beside the reputations of any native-born American unit on either side of the contest. Many units, like these, were solidly foreign or ethnically related in their composition, but others, like the 5th Confederate Regiment, a "foreign legion" serving under General John B. Hood in Tennessee, were composed of men from many nationalities.

Blacks, Jews, and Native Americans were also represented in the service. Throughout the war, blacks were generally made to serve in noncombatant roles at the front in order to free white soldiers for the battle line. A federal officer in occupied New Orleans, where some of the first black regiments, with black and white officers, were raised, expressed the following thought: "The colored troops will probably be kept near here and used to garrison unhealthy positions; they will be called on for fatigue duty such as making roads, building bridges and draining marshes; they will seldom be put into battle." Allotted to white regiments, blacks dug ditches, built fortifications, and served as laborers, wagoners, carpenters, farriers, orderlies, stevedores, track layers, and porters.[15]

Ultimately, the Union had almost 180,000 black soldiers under arms. The acceptance of the "Sable Arm" of the federal army was not immediate, however. Although free blacks were enlisted, they were placed in segregated units largely under the command of white officers who felt that such an assignment would "afford small chance for distinction." Based upon prejudicial notions that they could not equal white soldiers in a fight, these units were often given noncombatant duties far from the front. However, it should be noted that the Union army expected menial services from all its troops regardless of race—a policy that raised some objections among the insecure Irish, who were asked to labor beside the blacks. Ultimately, under severe pressure from Northern abolitionists, black troops were placed in combat roles, where their performance proved laudable, and at times heroic. The best-known black unit was the 54th Massachusetts Colored Infantry, but other black units were raised throughout the occupied South as well as in almost every Northern state. Although the use of black combat troops was not necessary "to win the war," blacks came to represent nine percent of all Union forces—a higher proportion of free blacks in service than were represented by their percentage in Northern society.

Initially, white federal troops were opposed to this policy. Black men wearing the same uniforms as whites had disturbing implications of equality for men whose own status in a recently restructured Northern society was suspect. Many white soldiers, willing to die in order to free a black man from slavery, were unwilling to fight beside him. Federal soldiers from the border states strongly expressed a reluctance to serve in the same army with men who had been considered menials, servants, and chattels. However, basic logic, which dictated that blacks could stop Confederate bullets just as easily as whites could, overcame such bias. This thread of reasoning quickly made many a Northern segregationist into a closet abolitionist.[16]

The immediate reaction of the Southern government to the arming of blacks by federal forces was to declare that any black found in arms against the South, and any white federal officer found leading such men, would be executed upon capture. Few individual Confederate soldiers acknowledged killing blacks in their letters and diaries. Nor did they express much racist sentiment. The cases of massive race-based retaliation were reserved for the battles at Fort Pillow, Tennessee; Poison Springs, Arkansas; Plymouth, North Carolina; and the "Crater" at Petersburg, Virginia. In each of these instances it is quite certain that blacks were purposely killed after they had surrendered to Confederate troops.

Southern forces used blacks almost exclusively as laborers and servants. A Southern woman noted, "We have never made the cowardly Negro fight, and it is strange, passing strange, that the all-powerful Yankee nation with the whole world to back them . . . should at last take the poor Negro to help them out against this little Confederacy." Nonetheless, a vocal minority in the South had called for the arming of blacks from the beginning of the war, and even General Lee called for their enlistment. At the end of March 1865, the Confederate Congress, sorely pressed for manpower, approved the enrollment of armed blacks in the Southern forces, offering freedom as a reward. This promise lured many blacks, even in the face of the Emancipation Proclamation, and a number actually came to serve under arms in the Confederate army. The question of what effect black Confederate soldiers would have had on the white Southerners fighting beside them was made moot by the collapse of the war effort almost immediately thereafter.[17]

With the exception of their indefensible attitude toward blacks, and prejudicial statements by individuals, the Southern government was remarkably open to adherents to their cause from many ethnic and religious groups. It is a paradox of the war that the South was more accepting of ethnic and religious differences than the North. This paradoxical open-ness dates from the beginning of the conflict and may have been forced upon the South by its own geographic and demographic character. Mex-ican-Americans and those of mixed ethnic parentage, particularly those of French and Spanish background from the Gulf Coast, were common in the service of the South. Religious diversity found greater acceptance in the South than in many Northern cities. Two members of the Richmond cabinet and a number of soldiers and officers of the Confederate army were Jewish. Moreover, the Confederate forces boasted several brigades of Native Americans composed of Cherokees, Choctaws, and Seminoles, and several generals were of mixed or nonwhite heritage: General Pierre G. T. Beauregard (Creole-French), General William B. Taliaferro (Italian-English), General Patrick Cleburne (Irish-English), General Stand Wati (Native American). If the Confederate forces exhibited any bias, it was that of favoring Virginians for high-ranking positions. In 1863 10 of the 15 highest-ranking Confederate officers were from Virginia—a situation that was found intolerable by many outspoken officers from the other states.[18]

The North, by contrast, was replete with anti-Catholic and anti-Semitic feeling, and few whites in the North, even those who espoused the aboli-tion of slavery, believed that they shared any equality with the black race. Northerners were generally intolerant of immigrants, especially the Irish. Moreover, the federal government had a history of poor relationships with Indian groups, and Washington raised only a single Native American bri-gade, most of whom were Creeks. Other tribal groups generally remained aloof from the war. The Santee Sioux of Minnesota took advantage of the weakened federal presence on the plains to rise up and attack the local white settlers in 1862.

The most conspicuous case of overt anti-Semitism to take place in the war was the promulgation of General Order No. 11 by General U. S. Grant in December 1862. Grant ordered all Jews "as a class" expelled from the Department of Tennessee (a war zone dissected for the purpose of com-mand and supply). This order—misdirected at Jewish merchants deal-ing with the army commissary, and certainly inappropriate on the part of Grant—caused severe hardship for the local Jewish community and raised a wail of protest in the North. Nonetheless, the highest-ranking Jewish officer in the Army of the Tennessee, Colonel Marcus M. Spiegel, took no note of the order in his letters and continued to express a growing admi-ration for Grant. Under direction from the Lincoln administration, Grant rescinded the order in less than a fortnight.[19]

BOYS IN WAR

The enlistment of minors in the 19th century was based on tradition; boys had served in armies and aboard vessels for centuries. Minors under 16 were allowed to enlist in the armies and navies of both forces. More

than 40,000 minors may have served in the war, and the majority managed to survive. Many boys considerably younger than 14 served. While
figures for the Confederacy are unavailable or incomplete, in the federal
army alone there were 300 boys aged 13 or under and 2 dozen who were
10 or under. Most served as musicians, for there were places for 40,000 in
the Union armies alone. There are numerous tales of buglers too small to
climb into saddles unaided, who rode into pistol-and-saber battles with
their regiments.

Parental consent was needed in both the federal and Confederate forces
for minors to enlist. On this subject Lincoln wrote to the secretary of the
navy: "The United States don't need the services of boys who disobey
their parents." It is hard to imagine under what circumstances parents
would send such young children to war. Yet it was not until March 1864
that the federal Congress prohibited the enlistment of persons under 16
under any circumstances.[20]

Nonetheless, underage youths managed to scheme their way into the
ranks of both armies. One of Francis Scott Key's young grandsons, Billings
Steele, who lived near Annapolis, Maryland, stole across the Potomac to
join the rangers of Colonel John S. Mosby. Hard-pressed enlistment officers often turned a blind eye to the evident youth of willing recruits in
order to fill their recruitment quotas. Up to 300,000 boys, clearly under
age 17, may have served in front line organizations. Many boys entered
the Confederate state militias as railroad and bridge guards or served in
the mounted guerrilla units. They often performed necessary but routine
duties that freed older soldiers to fight. However, most boys served as
musicians, drummers, or buglers. These helped to organize the daily routine of the camp by signaling reveille, assembly, officers' call, sick call, and
taps; and their music provided a form of entertainment for the troops and
a festive flare on formal occasions such as regimental reviews. The primary purpose of music on the battlefield, however, was to communicate
orders over the din of warfare. Precisely blown bugle calls and accurately
played drumbeats carried commands over great distances more clearly
than could the human voice and more quickly than could the fleetest runner or mounted courier. Drummers were generally assigned to infantry
regiments behind which they marched into battle. Buglers were allocated
to the cavalry or horse artillery, as the bugle is more convenient to carry
and play while mounted and riding across the field than the drum.

Thousands of boys from age 12 to 16 years fought in the ranks face-
to-face against grown men. Some went to war over regional issues such
as slavery or states rights. Others went to protect their families or their
homes. Many went to escape the boredom of home and have an adventure. They quickly learned the facts of military life. Soldiers were often
bored, spending more time marching from one place to another looking
for a fight than fighting. A modest amount of discipline was just the start,
and many boys had to deal with teasing, harassment, and abuse from

older men in both armies. One officer noted that some of the boys were getting quite angry, and for good reason. Young Elisha Stockwell noted that a "big husky man" in his unit, who was "handy with his fists," had proceed "to cuff [him] around" to see what he was made of.[21]

Many older boys were tough and fit, and quickly showed that they could outmarch or outride their older comrades. However, very young or small boys faced some unique obstacles in these positions. Some cavalry buglers were too short to mount a horse and had to be hoisted into the saddle, and young drummers often had great difficulty in maintaining the regulation 28-inch pace while marching beside the troops carrying a regulation size drum. Moreover, small uniforms needed to be secured and replaced periodically. This was usually done at the expense of the officers, who sometimes provided elaborate and impractical outfits. Properly enlisted boys were paid and drew supplies like the soldier, but frequently needed items such as child-sized shoes, socks, and shirts were often difficult to re-supply.

John Lincoln Clem (1852–1937) was reportedly nine years old in June 1861 when he stowed away in a regimental baggage car and attached himself to the 22nd Michigan, whose officers appointed him the drummer for Company C. At the Battle of Shiloh a shell shattered his drum, earning him the sobriquet "Johnny Shiloh." Clem became a mounted orderly on the staff of General George H. Thomas, with the "rank" of lance sergeant. At the age of thirteen, he was discharged, only to return to the army as an officer in 1871. He retired as a major general at age sixty-five, and in 1916 was the last man then active in the service who had served in the Civil War.[22]

No one knows the identity of the South's youngest soldier, but on the Confederate side, in particular, there is a rash of claimants. George S. Lamkin of Winona, Mississippi, joined Stanford's Mississippi Battery when he was 11, and before his 12th birthday was severely wounded at Shiloh. T. D. Claiborne left Virginia Military Institute at 13 in 1861 and was killed in 1864, at the age of 17. E. G. Baxter, of Clark County, Kentucky, is recorded as enlisting in Company A, 7th Kentucky Cavalry in June, 1862, when he was not quite 13. John Bailey Tyler, of D Troop, 1st Maryland Cavalry, born in Frederick, Maryland, in 1849, was 12 when he joined. He fought with his regiment until the end, without a wound. T. G. Bean, of Pickensville, Alabama, was probably the South's most youthful recruiter. He organized two companies of cadet volunteers at the University of Alabama in 1861, when he was only 13. Though Bean did not get into service until two years later, he served as adjutant of the cadet corps taken into the Confederate armies.[23]

PARTISAN WARFARE

In the spring of 1861 enthusiasm for secession spurred Southerners to join the Confederate army. The expectation of an eyeball-to-eyeball stand-off across the Potomac or an early Southern victory convinced the South that few men would actually be needed. Enlistments of from six months to one year were common in these early days. Volunteers swelled the recruiting offices, and the Confederate War Department had to turn away more than 200,000 men because they could not adequately provide supplies for them.

The most devoted to the cause enlisted at once, and early volunteers usually joined a local company raised by some prominent citizen in the neighborhood. Following the traditions of the militia, or citizen soldiers, of the Revolutionary Era, most of the men furnished their own weapons; in a few cases, weapons were furnished by the person forming the company. The Southern press glorified these small local commands, and Northern newspapers defamed them, often associating their operations with depredations and irregularities. The scores of small companies, raised in the Revolutionary tradition and operating independently, drained the manpower pool of the main army.

CONSCRIPTION

Ultimately, the South was forced to resort to conscription to preserve its forces in the field. The Confederate Conscription Act was the first general draft of soldiers in America. Neither the Confederate Congress nor Jefferson Davis wanted it, but conscription was seen as an absolute necessity. Its purpose was twofold. The 12-month enlistments entered into in the spring of 1861 were about to run out. It was feared that these men, now veterans of war and free from many of the romantic notions they had brought to their first muster, would fail to reenlist. The Conscription Act ensured that the Confederacy would retain the men it had in the army, and, since the war had already lasted longer than anyone had predicted, it provided for the additional men that would be needed.

The Confederate Congress passed the Conscription Act of 1862 by more than a two to one vote. The act made all white males from the ages of 18 to 35 eligible for three years of service. Men who had already served one year were made responsible for two more. The U.S. Congress followed with its own Conscription Act in August of the same year, but Lincoln refused to sign it into law until March 1863. The draft, almost identical in its characteristics both North and South, was universally unpopular, but it was accepted with a certain equanimity, rather than reservation, in the South. In the North, the first drawing of names in July 1863 set off a violent four-day riot, with a mob of over 50,000 working men swarming through New York. Federal troops, just back from the grim scene at Gettysburg, were called upon to quell the riots, which left more than 1,000 rioters dead. Small disturbances also broke out in Boston, Troy, New York, and other towns in the East and in Ohio.

Failure to comply with the draft could end in arrest and imprisonment. Conscripts were generally brought to training camps, given cursory medical exams, vaccinated, and given some basic military instruction. Their time in camp and the extent of their training were dependent in large part on the immediate needs of the army. Now considered soldiers, they were shipped off to join regiments from their own states in the field. It has been estimated that over 300,000 men, from 25 to 30 percent of the army, were conscripts during the course of the war.

There were a number of ways by which a man could avoid the draft. If he was found to have a physical disability, he would be exempt. Disqualifying disabilities included genuine health problems like blindness, missing limbs, lung disease, venereal disease, or an unsound heart. Other genuine problems were less evident. Urine samples were taken; a man's balance and coordination were tested; and even if he could see, his eyesight needed to be normal or at least correctable with the use of glasses. Those who were epileptic or insane were exempt. Chronic conditions such as coughing, shortness of breath, and back pain were more difficult to prove and harder for the authorities to evaluate. Two very simple physical characteristics also freed a man from conscription. First, he could not be less than five feet six inches tall, which suggests that people were not really shorter in the 19th century than they are today. Second, as a purely practical matter, he needed at least two opposed teeth because the bullet cartridge needed to be torn open with the teeth in firing the musket.

A man could have an exemption from the draft based on a war-related occupation considered more critical to the cause than his service at the

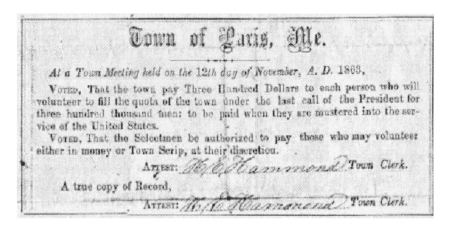

An enlistment bounty of $300 was to be paid in cash or town scrip by the town of Paris, Maine, in order to help fill the local recruitment quota. From the authors' collection

front. Among those exempt from the draft were iron founders, machinists, miners, and railroad workers; ferrymen, pilots, and steamboat workers; government officials, clerks, and telegraphers; ministers, professors, teachers of the handicapped, and private teachers with more than twenty pupils. There were protests over the exemptions, but the only outcome of a public outcry was an extension of the exemption to physicians, leather workers, blacksmiths, millers, munitions workers, shipyard workers, salt makers, charcoal burners, some stockmen, some printers, and one editor for each paper. Conscientious objectors who belonged to recognized nonviolent sects did not have to serve if they provided a substitute or paid $500 to the government.

One of the more flagrant exemptions was that one slaveowner, or a slave overseer who had more than twenty slaves under his care, would be exempt from each plantation. White overseers were exempt because of a practical consideration—the ever-present fear of slave uprisings. Many felt that this exemption led to "a rich man's war and a poor man's fight." Although this attitude was strongly held in many circles, many slaveowners and their sons voluntarily served in the war, very often as well-placed officers and leaders of local partisan groups. As an example, Wade Hampton, a leading slaveowner considered to be the richest man in the South before the war, served with great distinction throughout and was wounded several times. Both his brother and his son lost their lives in battle.

Finally, a man could buy his way out of the draft by finding a substitute. As much as $400 in gold was offered in 1863 for a draft substitute. There was a tremendous amount of fraud perpetrated in the hiring of substitutes, and this may have been the greatest weakness of the draft system. Physically unsound men were found to replace sound substitutes before they reached the training camps, underaged boys and overaged men were used in the same manner, and many paid substitutes simply deserted, often repeating the process over and over again under different names.

The Conscription Acts and the exemptions were modified as the war progressed, and more and more men became eligible for the draft. The federal act made all men 20 to 45 eligible. The manpower-starved Confederates accepted boys of 17 years of age and men between 46 and 50 as local defense forces or as railroad guards. These men who were too young or too old to fight on the front lines were able to free thousands of soldiers to do so. The draft had the positive effect of retaining veteran soldiers in the ranks. Without these, the Southern armies would soon have collapsed. The conscription system was nonetheless amazingly inefficient and filled with abuses; moreover, it provided a rallying point for antiwar sentiment.

PRISONERS OF WAR

At the beginning of the war, prisoners were released upon their parole, or promise, not to fight again until legitimately exchanged for a prisoner from the other side. Parolees were generally sent home or placed on re-stricted duty until the exchange could be affected. Some federal soldiers, wishing to avoid serving in the field for an extended period of time in subfreezing temperatures, contrived their own capture in order to obtain a parole. An investigation was called when the number of parolees sud-denly increased as the first winter of the war wore on. It was found in one case that local residents of Northern Virginia kept a supply of blank pa-roles on hand, all authentically signed by proper Confederate officers, at-testing that the bearer had been captured and released. These were traded to federal soldiers for such rare items as coffee and sugar. In this way the civilians had founded a lucrative business with a willing clientele. The practice was ended when the Washington government refused to ex-change prisoners with the manpower-hungry South. Thereafter, federal and Confederate prisoners were denied parole and held in prison camps for the duration. The unsavory reputations of Libby Prison and Anderson-ville, in which thousands died of neglect, quickly dissuaded many federal soldiers from voluntarily being made a prisoner.

DISBANDING THE ARMIES

For some concerned officials the disbandment of the armies at the end of the war was not an encouraging prospect. The federal army alone had just over one million men under arms at the war's end. Besides the sud-den influx into the peacetime economy of almost two million soldiers, the close of hostilities also meant the end of a large number of war-related industries in the North. Thousands of men would be thrown out of work. Although there were many fewer Southerners under arms at the end of the war—men had been abandoning the Confederate cause for some months—the South, with its economy all but destroyed, faced massive unemployment. Even agricultural workers had to face the destruction of their farm buildings and livestock. Wells and fields had been fouled, and almost every fence rail in the South had been torn down or burned. The cost of replacing the fences on Southern farms alone proved a substantial economic burden estimated to be in the millions.[24]

In the North, "all the anticipations of evil proved groundless." Freed of the sectional controversies of the antebellum period, massive economic growth seemed to take hold after the war. The war destroyed the hold that the anti-industrial South had on federal policy and paved the way for industrial development by placing factions sympathetic to business in undisputed control of the country. The federal soldiers who left the army in late 1865 and early 1866 "reentered civilian life with apparent content-ment and even with certain advantages." Speaker of the House James G. Blaine noted that veterans "were found to be models of industry and in-telligence." The experience of war had "proved an admirable school" and given the soldiers "habits of promptness and punctuality, order and neatness, which added largely to their efficiency in what ever field they were called to labor."[25]

The war had ended, but any cogent plan for bringing the South back into the Union died with Lincoln in April 1865. There was no plan to deal with the former rebellious states and their people, nor was there any idea of what to do with millions of suddenly freed slaves. Accustomed to being taken care of and told what to do, many freedmen did not know how to proceed. Others interpreted freedom as meaning that they would be fed and housed without having to work. As one historian has noted, the Southern veteran and the black former slave both faced "a ruined home, desolate fields, no money, no laborers—and bitterness."[26]

NOTES

1. The origins of the terms "Billy Yank" and "Johnny Reb" in reference to Civil War soldiers are not quite apparent. It is evident, however, that the soldiers referred to themselves and their enemies using these terms.

2. James H. Croushore, ed., *A Volunteer's Adventure, by Captain John W. De Forest* (New Haven: Yale University Press, 1949), 190. De Forest uses the unfortunate term "redskins" at this point.

3. McPherson, *For Cause*, preface.

4. Stephen W. Sears, *For Country, Cause, and Leader, The Civil War Journal of Charles B. Haydon* (New York: Ticknor & Fields, 1993), ix.

5. Croushore, 46.

6. David Hanson, *A War Like No Other: How the Athenians and Spartans Fought the Peloponnesian War* (New York: Random House, 2005), 141–142.

7. See John Keegan, *The Mask of Command* (New York: Vintage, 1987), 191; McPherson, *For Cause*, 94. John Keegan may have exaggerated this characteristic of Civil War armies in his study, but there is general truth in the statement.

8. McPherson, *For Cause*, 24.

9. Ibid.

10. Thomas A. Ashby, *The Life of Turner Ashby* (New York: Neal Publishing, 1914), 29–30.

11. Sears, 9.

12. Caroline C. Richards, *Village Life in America, 1852–1872* (Gansevoort, NY: Corner Book, 1997), 131.

13. Ashby, 34, 40.

14. Thomas A. Lewis, *The Guns of Cedar Creek* (New York: Bantam, 1991), 36.

15. Croushore, 50–51.

16. McPherson, *For Cause*, 126.

17. Dolly Sumner Lunt, *A Woman's Wartime Journal* (Atlanta: Cherokee, 1994), 37.

18. Gen. Wade Hampton was particularly outspoken against Gen. J.E.B. Stuart's attitude toward officers who were not from Virginia. In fairness, Lee's second in command was a non-Virginian, James Longstreet. See John S. Mosby, *Stuart's Cavalry in the Gettysburg Campaign* (New York: Moffat, Yard & Co., 1908), 90–119, 191–200.

19. Frank L. Byrne and Jean Powers Soman, eds., *A Jewish Colonel in the Civil War: Marcus M. Spiegel of the Ohio Volunteers* (Lincoln: University of Nebraska Press, 1994), 191–193.

20. David Mallinson, "Armed with Only Their Drums," *America's Civil War,* November 1992, 8.

21. Jim Murphy, *The Boys' War: Confederate and Union Soldiers Talk About the Civil War* (New York: Scholastic, 1990), 21–22.

22. Ibid., 70–73.

23. LSU Civil War Center , "Boys in the Civil War!" http://www.civilwarhome.com/boysinwar.htm (Accessed April 2008).

24. Virgil Carrington Jones, *Gray Ghosts and Rebel Raiders* (New York: Galahad, 1956), 45.

25. James G. Blaine, "The Disbanding of the Northern Army, 1865," in Francis W. Halsey, ed., *Great Epochs in American History* (New York: Funk & Wagnalls, 1884), 201–204. Blaine was Speaker in 1861–62 and again beginning in 1869.

26. James Truslow Adams, *Album of American History,* vol. 3 (New York: Charles Scribner's Sons, 1946), 191.

8

HARDTACK AND COFFEE

"It seemed at first that we would starve."
—Federal Private Rice C. Bull

SUPPLYING THE ARMY WITH GRUB

The federal soldier had the most abundant food allowance of any fighting man in the world at the time, and shortages were commonly short-lived. Most of the food ration was grown in the North and shipped to the theater of operations by using a diverse network of railways and roads and by taking advantage of an almost unchallenged ability to ship supplies by water. A volunteer from Michigan awaiting transportation to the front noted, "Our victuals are cooked and served out by a contractor at one of the Fair [grounds] buildings. The quantity is ample & the quality before cooking is good enough. There is a good deal of dirt mixed with it when we get it & some of it comes in very bad shape."[1] The soldiers commonly referred to the food that they ate as "grub."[2]

Southern soldiers, serving in the midst of a largely agricultural area, began the war with sufficient foodstuffs. However, living off the land and relying on seasonal harvests led alternately to a superabundance of food or almost none. The Confederacy was hampered in its effort to ship foodstuffs by a lack of adequate railway facilities, by an inability to maintain control of the major water arteries within its own territory, and by the increasingly successful interdiction efforts of federal forces. "Sometimes there was an abundant issue of bread, and no meat; then meat in any quantity, and no flour or meal; sugar in abundance, and no coffee to be had for love or money."[3]

"A soldier in the Army of Northern Virginia was fortunate when he had his flour, meat, sugar, and coffee all at the same time and in proper quantity."[4] Although blessed with widespread fields tended by an army of slaves, most plantations produced cash crops of tobacco or cotton, not food. Foodstuffs were provided predominantly by small farms with few or no slaves. With the increased demand for manpower on the battlefield, white Southern farmers were increasingly becoming fighters, leaving the farm work to less productive old men, boys, and women. The farms of the Shenandoah Valley in Virginia and of middle Tennessee served as bread-baskets for the Rebel army for almost four years. Most farm families in these areas managed to raise a garden crop or fatten a hog specifically for the troops, and they gladly shared their food surplus with them when they had it. Many citizens gave handouts to soldiers from their own tables, and city dwellers reduced the number of their daily meals in an effort to support the cause.

ARMY FOOD

Standard rations were issued in bulk by the company. The company cooks were generally appointed, and arrangements were made for company cooking with company cooking utensils. In his basic kit, each Civil War soldier had a tin cup and plate as well as a spoon, knife, and fork which he kept in his haversack. One federal private recalled his first company meal: "The rice was badly burned and unedible; the hardtack, the first we had ever seen, was of good quality but we had not yet learned to appreciate its value. The pork was very salty, and the coffee had not been made by an expert. . . It seemed at first that we would starve."[5]

Southern men initially formed messes, each consisting of about 10 men, many employing a Negro man as a cook. These cooks quickly disappeared from the line of march, and rarely were any soldiers other than officers so served. A Virginia foot soldier provided an insight into early Rebel eating etiquette once the Negro cook for his mess was gone: "We made a fire under the shade of a tree, made up our bread of meal, sliced our fat meat, and commenced to cook. In about two minutes both meat and bread were burned on one side . . . We were disgusted; but the next day we had better success, and in a few days we got along all right."[6]

COOKWARE

Initially the government in Richmond ignored the need for the wide-scale provision of camp equipment, and little beyond firearms, bayonets, and canteens was issued. On the other hand, the federal authorities encumbered their troops with several standard items of camp equipment, including kettles, mess pans, and coffeepots. A set of metal crutches with a sturdy crossbar served to hang the pots over the fire. The kettles were made of tinned sheet iron in sizes that allowed them to be nested within each other for ease of transportation. Large iron mess pans were used to serve the food. The company mess kettles were provided to make coffee, soups, and stews, but in typical soldierly fashion, they proved excellent for washing clothes. The mess pans were made to fry pork and bacon, yet they also served as washbasins. Such double duty was less than polite society would have tolerated, but for the soldiers any other course was considered impractical.

Each company was initially issued a mule upon which the company cookware was to be carried on the march. Camp cooking equipment was cumbersome and took up much of the limited space assigned to each company in the regimental baggage train. As the mules required careful attention, they quickly disappeared from the line of march, and the company cooking gear, whether through design or by accident, frequently deteriorated or was purposely abandoned. The concept of company cooking quickly disappeared under all but the most favorable of circumstances.

In this manner both Johnny Reb and Billy Yank found themselves in surprisingly similar situations. Each soldier was obliged to use only the limited array of cookware that he could carry. A coffee boiler of some sort was considered a necessity, and any utensil that could serve as a frying pan became indispensable. Small groups of men would pool their money to purchase a coffee boiler or a real frying pan from the sutler, and each would take turns carrying it on the march. The person so designated often was entitled to the utensil's first use when camp was made. If one of the owners was wounded, killed, or otherwise removed from the companionship of his fellow investors, his share could be sold to an outsider.

A particularly common cookware solution was to unsolder the seam between the two halves of an extra canteen acquired from the battlefield. Each half served as a tolerable lightweight frying pan or plate and could be carried strapped over the canteen. Tin cans with wire handles served as tolerable coffee boilers. As with the soldiers of most wars, Civil War soldiers quickly adopted any serviceable device that proved light to carry and easy to replace.

THE COMMISSARY

Hundreds of officers and men were engaged in the day-to-day duty of providing food for the troops. The overall responsibility fell to the Subsistence Department in Washington, headed by a commissary general who contracted for the various types of rations with private manufacturers or packers. The foodstuffs were then apportioned to the respective army commissaries, and by them, in turn, to the corps, brigade, and regimental commissaries. They were then distributed to the troops. Washington

The massive logistical support available to federal troops is made clear in this illustration of a New York City wharf in 1861.

continued, from the beginning of the war until its end, to let contracts to private suppliers for all of its rations in this manner.

The Richmond government tried to institute a Confederate Subsistence Department, but found that the independent spirit of the state governments hampered such unified efforts. Although the problem existed in different degrees from state to state, supplies were greedily guarded for consumption by only the troops of the state that provided them. Individual states exacerbated the supply problem by competing for the same scarce resources. As Confederate currency became inflated and prices soared, the Subsistence Department found it necessary to purchase foodstuffs with cotton bonds. The secretary of war made no secret of the fact that it was not possible to provision the troops as Richmond wished, yet the soldiers seem to have taken the shortages in stride.

FOODSTUFFS

The government rations distributed to the troops varied slightly with the season and the availability of local supply. Nonetheless, a complete list of all the possibilities is short. These included hardtack, coffee, sugar, soft bread, flour, rice, cornmeal, dried peas, dried beans, desiccated vegetables or dried fruits, fresh or dried potatoes (called chips), salt pork, bacon or ham, pickled beef (called salt horse), fresh meat, and occasionally onions, molasses, salt, pepper, and vinegar.

With only a rudimentary understanding of balanced nutrition, it is a wonder that any soldier survived the war on such a diet. However, the standard ration provided a daily average of over 3,000 calories, heavy in carbohydrates and fats, but providing few vitamins or complete proteins. The vitamin deficiencies and the lack of protein could have been devastating. An unrelieved diet of cornmeal and salt pork, while sufficient in calories, would ultimately produce such diseases as scurvy and pellagra. Fresh meats will provide protein but cannot afford sufficient protein to make up the deficit alone. Both beans and cornmeal are high protein sources but are individually incomplete in amino acids; yet in combination, they are complementary and provide all the essentials needed to sustain health. Rice and peas form another complementary pair with similar characteristics. In offering these pairs among a small variety of foodstuffs, the government unwittingly supplied a nearly complete diet to its soldiers, yet the unresolved question of a lack of essential vitamins had serious health consequences that cost many lives.

The lack of variety in the soldiers' diet resulted from the need to keep the rations from spoiling while they were being shipped and stored for use. In the absence of refrigeration, meats, if not freshly slaughtered, had to be salted or pickled; and breads, vegetables, and fruits, if not for immediate consumption, had to be dried. Salting and drying retarded the growth of bacteria, as did pickling, smoking, and sugar curing. With the exception of meals aboard naval vessels, there is an amazing absence from the records of cheese being issued as a regular part of the army ration.

CANNED FOODS

Some canned foods were utilized by the army. The technology of preserving foods in tinned iron cans had been developed by the French in the first decade of the century and was first patented in America by Ezra Daggett in 1825. The heat used in preparing the contents destroyed the bacteria, and the sealed container prevented new contamination. Although the process was decades old, some enlisted men saw their very first canned foods during the war, and they demanded their use at home when the war ended. Commercial canned food production soared in the 1860s and 1870s.

The officers' mess and hospitals seemed to have had a significant variety of canned items, but they were seldom available to the troops unless they were purchased from the sutlers. By 1861 the list of common canned items had expanded to include several types of meat, peas, sardines, peaches, and other fruits; but the most common canned item encountered in the field was condensed milk, much of which was purchased by contract from Gail Borden.

CAMP RATIONS

There were two standard rations in the federal army. One was the camp ration, and the other was the campaign or marching ration. The camp ration tended to be more diverse, and for one soldier in the federal army consisted of meat (1¼ lbs. of salted or fresh beef, or ¾ lb. of pork or bacon) and bread (1 lb., 6 oz. of soft bread or flour, or 1 lb. of hardtack, or 1¼ lbs. of cornmeal). He also received approximately 1½ ounces of dried vegetables, rice, dried potatoes, peas, or beans. Fresh potatoes were to be had, but fresh vegetables were rare and allotted in only very small quantities. Salt and pepper were allowed in minuscule quantities. About ½ ounce of vinegar was provided for each man daily to help prevent scurvy. About the same amount of molasses was allowed when available.

MARCHING RATIONS

The marching ration consisted of 1 lb., or 8 crackers, of hard bread; ¾ lb. of salt pork, or 1¼ lbs. of fresh meat; sugar, coffee, and salt. The beans, rice, and so on, were not issued to the soldier when on the march, as he could not carry them. The other parts of the camp ration "were forfeited, and reverted to the government." The revenue from the uncollected rations was supposed to revert to the regiment and be distributed to the rank and file as cash, but few soldiers saw a cent of the money. This was seen by some observers as "an injustice to the rank and file."[7]

The soldier added both quantity and variety to his diet in many ways. Gifts of food from home were always welcome. These included hams, smoked meats and cheeses, pickles, onions, potatoes, chocolate, condensed milk, sugar, salt butter, coffee, tea, cakes, cookies, applesauce, and preserves. Due to delays in delivery, many times the baked goods proved to be stale, the butter rancid, and the preserves, put up in glass jars, too fragile to ship to the front lines without breaking. Intoxicating liquors were frowned upon by the army hierarchy, but were often smuggled through hidden in other packages.

SUTLERS

Sutlers were businessmen and storekeepers who set up their enterprises within the army camps, and sometimes traveled with the army on campaign. With and without the sanction of the government, sutlers provided a variety of items to the federal forces in the form of pies, cakes, cookies, fudge, raisins, eggs, fresh fruits, salted or smoked fish, and soda pop. Clinton Parkhurst, 16th Iowa Volunteers, described a camp sutlery in 1862: "There was a sutler shop, with its gaudily adorned cans of fruits and jelly and the breath of rumor hinted that the peach cans . . . contained brandy. . . . Cheese, butter, crackers, nuts, candy, sardines, oysters, euchre

The sutler's shop was a favorite place for soldiers to spend their pay and find "luxury" items.

decks, boot blacking, paper collars, and a myriad other luxuries of civilization reposed within our grasp." The sutlers often took advantage of the men by charging premium prices, but in general, the sutlery provided a worthwhile, if expensive, service to the troops. The sutlers' tents and wagons quickly became a favorite haunt of off-duty soldiers with a few dollars in their pockets.[8]

Confederates were almost always on the edge of starvation once the first days of the war were past. A federal soldier noted that his opponents were "very seldom well supplied, [but] they often bravely fought when even weak with hunger."[9] They were known to have depended on cowpeas, or field peas, to round out their sparse rations. General Lee considered these field legumes one of the Confederacy's best friends. The men also grubbed for wild onions, scallions, dandelions, and groundnuts. Swamp cabbage could be made palatable by having the unpleasant flavor boiled out of it. The closest thing to a sutler's wagon seen by most Confederate troops was a cider cart or fruit wagon pushed by a slave or a roadside display of pies and cakes set up by a civilian.

OFFICERS' MESS

Officers, of course, fared better than the enlisted men. Negro cooks, some slaves and others freemen, were a common feature of the officers' mess of both armies. Southern gentlemen tended to support their own needs, including that of food, from private resources, although they received a pay based on their rank. Federal officers were given a monthly cash allowance for the purchase of food from the brigade commissary. In addition, each field officer was given an allowance for staff, servants, tents, wagons, horses, and forage in proportion to his rank. General officers required significantly more elaborate quarters than their juniors and were paid accordingly. These gentlemen could afford to have imported items, canned delicacies, cheeses, brandied fruits, wines, and liquor on their tables. The Union officers' mess at Manassas in 1862 contained lobster salad, canned peaches, pickled and smoked oysters, and a stock of Rhine wine. The federal authorities furnished no rations to company officers without payment and would not honor their credit. If the officers were too prodigal, or if the paymaster's cash was withheld by unforeseen circumstances, they "went hungry for lack of money."[10]

FORAGING

Both sides resorted to foraging for foodstuffs, and sent out groups of men, usually cavalry, to strip the countryside of provisions—a standard practice of armies since ancient times. Many farms were visited repeatedly and stripped bare by friend and foe alike. The farms in middle Tennessee and the Shenandoah Valley became the prime focus of foragers time and again. The area around Winchester, Virginia, changing hands more than a dozen times, was left sorely pressed and economically destitute by constant foraging. "It was a woeful sight for civilized eyes," wrote a federal soldier.[11]

Although both sides initially tried to moderate the activities of their foragers to keep from alienating the local residents, a good deal of unofficial foraging was practiced by individual soldiers. A federal soldier wrote in his diary, "I succeeded in getting a meal from a lusty colored woman who lived in a small cabin; gave her fifty cents and had a fine meal of fresh pork, sweet potatoes, and pones."[12]

In the final year of the war, federal troops systematically and vigorously searched even the poverty-stricken homes of Southern sympathizers to remove any provisions that could be of use to the Rebel army. In a conscious attempt to disable the Army of Northern Virginia the effort was carried out with ruthless efficiency. The incredibly large herds of army horses, requiring unending amounts of fodder, stripped the valleys of hay and grass. Provisions that could not be carried off were destroyed, livestock were slaughtered, freshwater wells were fouled, 2,000 barns were destroyed, and fields were burned. "As a warlike measure it was very effective."[13]

Gathering provisions from the countryside had both advantages and disadvantages. Fresh meat and vegetables were joyfully received by men who had nothing but salted and dried foods to eat. But foraging could slow the advance of an army. The soldiers found that it was difficult duty, and detachments were commonly gone for an entire day, leaving before dawn and returning after midnight. Seeking supplies over a wide area put a strain on the army's horses and wagons and weakened the strength of the army in the interim. Foragers needed to advance cautiously, avoiding enemy patrols, as they would inevitably be outnumbered and overwhelmed by even a small force.[14]

Foragers brought in foodstuffs common to the civilian farm diet. This usually included ham, bacon, cornmeal, roasting ears of corn, and sweet potatoes. Livestock, in the form of cattle, pigs, hogs, sheep, chickens, geese, and turkeys, was sometimes driven into camp to be slaughtered. The meat was often thin and tough, especially if taken from a Southern farm late in the war, but the soldiers usually found it possible to prepare it for consumption without extensive processing. Roasting ears were a particular favorite as they could be thrown into the fire ash with the shucks on, cooked, and retrieved with little ceremony; but recruits quickly dis-

The return of the foraging party. The entire camp rejoiced when foragers returned with fresh meat and vegetables stripped from the farms of the unfortunate local population. *Leslie's* illustration.

covered that green ears of corn, consumed without proper preparation, brought on stomach and lower bowel ailments that could have been avoided by a judicious roasting.

The troops often resorted to the unauthorized stealing and killing of livestock. "Bear hunting" seems to have been a popular pastime for foragers in both armies. Pigs, which generally were allowed to roam the scrub and woodlots of most farms, seem to have been a favorite target of the "bear" hunters. One forager, caught with a roasting pig on the spit by the enraged farmer who owned it, excused his acquisition of the meat by explaining that the pig had violated the grain allotted to the horses of his artillery battery. The horses, swore the soldier, had sensed the pig's intrusion, kicked out, and killed the pig instantly. To mollify him, the farmer was invited to partake of the meat, but he came to suspect the soldier's sincerity "after his teeth had come down hard on a pistol bullet, and continued to doubt, though assured that it was the head of a horse-shoe nail."[15]

By sending a hind-quarter to the company officers, and by similarly placating the sergeants, the soldiers "alloyed any murmurs over violated discipline."[16] Nor were the officers beyond doing a little offhand foraging. "We officers have been obliged to . . . come down to the same rations that the privates live on . . . I have a man out when on the march foraging for fresh meat, chickens, garden sauce, etc. So I think I shall make out to live."[17]

Federal foragers could wipe a Southern farmstead clean in a few minutes without the least pity. "To my smoke-house, my dairy, pantry, kitchen, and cellar, like famished wolves they came," claimed a Southern housewife in 1864, "breaking locks and whatever is in their way . . . in a twinkling my flour, my meat, my lard, butter, eggs, pickles of various kinds . . . wine, jars, and jugs are all gone. My eighteen fat turkeys, my hens, chickens, and fowls, my young pigs, are shot down in my yard and hunted as if they were rebels themselves." The woman's four horses and a mule were also taken. After pleading with the NCO in charge of the foragers to spare her something, she was told, "I cannot help you, Madam; it is orders."[18]

Soldiers were death on Southern gardens: "A five acre field of potatoes went in short order," and the fence rails "vanish[ed] as if by magic, for cooks must have firing wood, and everybody must have tent pins. Lucky is the man who has been able to steal a hatchet; he is much courted and truckled to by his comrades."[19] A federal officer noted, "It is woeful to see how this lately prosperous region is being laid waste. Negroes and runaway soldiers roam everywhere, foraging for provisions, breaking into and plundering the deserted houses, and destroying furniture, books and pictures in mere wantonness."[20]

Southern foragers understood the "terrible necessity" of depriving friendly families of most of their stock of food in order to feed the army, and some voluntarily cut cord wood, helped with the harvest, repaired farm machinery, and toiled at any other farm work in repayment for the willing donation of food. A favorite ploy of Southern foragers was to linger about the house of an unsuspecting farm family until they were at supper, "and then modestly approach and knock at the door." This procedure almost always resulted in an invitation to dinner as "honored guests."[21]

FRESH MEAT

In the summer of 1861 the Washington government decided to organize a separate and independent department within the Army of the Potomac for supplying fresh beef to the troops. The man responsible for supplying live cattle for slaughter to the army for the rest of the war was Captain John H. Woodward.

Keeping the army in fresh beef was no easy task. Woodward determined to furnish the whole army with a fresh ration of beef two days in each week, requiring that eighty to ninety animals would be killed daily. He erected a small building called the Headquarters of the Fresh Beef Department at the present site of the Washington Monument, which was incomplete at the time. "Immediately in the rear of the Headquarters there was a supply of beef cattle sufficient to subsist [an] army for a week, capable of transporting itself as fast as the army could march."[22]

As the Army of the Potomac began the failed Peninsular campaign in the spring of 1862, Woodward moved his operation to White House, Virginia. Ultimately, General McClellan ordered a withdrawal that was accompanied by an appalling destruction of supplies, but Woodward contrived to save 2,700 head of cattle in the retreat, his herders driving them across the peninsula to a new base.[23]

The cattle herds used to feed the federal armies were generally composed of essentially wild steers just off the western ranges, and a herd of 2,500 to 3,000 beef cattle could cause considerable damage to farms, fences, and growing crops. Nonetheless, Woodward was so successful in moving his cattle that by 1864 his superiors expected him to work miracles. In crossing the James River near Petersburg the beef had to cross a portion of water more than three-fourths of a mile wide. In the past, Woodward's herders had forded many small streams and rivers with large herds by having the cattle swim across, but an allowance had to be made in this case for the width and depth of the river. A pontoon bridge across the river was available, but with a width of only 12 feet and no side rails, it was considered impossible for a herd of cattle to be driven across in a body. Woodward resorted to one of the strangest solutions of the war. He put two soldiers on the bridge followed by two cattle, then two more men followed by two more cattle, and so on. The plan worked perfectly. The cattle followed the men without bunching or falling from the planking into the water. Woodward thought it "an inspiring sight, to see more than 3,000 head of wild cattle moving in close order over a bridge nearly a mile long and twelve feet wide, without a rail on either side, supported by boats. . . steadily and easily and without confusion."[24]

Of all the war escapades initiated by the Confederate cavalry, General Wade Hampton's "Beef Steak Raid" most captures the imagination. Confederate food supply had become critical by the fall of 1864. Hampton developed a well-timed and well-executed plan to capture a herd of cattle at the federal supply depot beyond General Lee's lines. Striking at 3 A.M., Hampton's men managed to rustle more than 2,400 head of cattle and re-enter Lee's lines. No more welcome raiding party ever returned to camp. The Beef Steak Raid was as brilliant an operation as any completed in the war. Hampton had brought in more than 2 million pounds of beef, or enough to feed 50,000 men for 40 days. When told of the raid, Lincoln called it the slickest piece of cattle rustling he had ever seen.[25]

PRESERVED MEATS

When fresh meat was not available the enlisted men were provided with a basic preserved meat ration of pork—boiled ham, salt pork, or bacon being most common. The South quickly realized that it would experience a meat shortage, and Richmond established an extensive government pork-packing program in close proximity to the rail and river transportation of Tennessee. These plants and their associated salt works were constantly in danger of capture or destruction by federal forces.

Federal forces also relied heavily on preserved pork. Pork's prominence as a foodstuff, when compared to preserved beef, did not lie in any intrinsic nutritional value, although the high fat content provided an excellent source of caloric intake. It was simply easier to preserve than beef and tasted better than pickled beef, which was so poor and unpalatable that the soldiers called it "salt horse." No effort was made to comply with dietary restrictions due to individual medical or religious preferences.[26]

In camp, boiled ham was often pulled from the barrel into which it had been packed for some months in a thick covering of grease that came from the boiling. The meat came out in long, "unappetizing strips," and "when brought to the surface the sound of the suction was like the noise made when one pulled his feet out of Virginia mud." The grease was scraped off and saved by many soldiers to be used as an ingredient in other recipes. The meat could be fried, roasted, or eaten sliced between two pieces of soft bread or with hardtack.[27]

Salt pork was easy to make and had been used since colonial times as a mainstay of the diet for soldiers and sailors. Salt pork was a favorite among veteran soldiers, who sometimes declined fresh beef for a good piece of salt pork, but recruits had to learn to ignore its overwhelmingly salty flavor and to appreciate its nutritional qualities. The amount of salt used in its processing was staggering, but salt pork could last, unspoiled, for a long time in a sealed barrel. However, once a barrel was opened, the meat had to be used quickly or it would spoil. One reason for the spoiling of salted meats in transit was the lack of good barrels, which sometimes opened between the staves. Southern armies suffered severely from increasing numbers of poorly made barrels as experienced coopers, white and black, were drafted to fill the ranks on the firing lines or streamed north to freedom. So great was the domestic war demand that there developed a worldwide shortage of quality American barrel staves.

Bacon was a common foodstuff reminiscent of home cooking which proved highly acceptable to the tastes of most soldiers. Bacon was made from the sides or flanks of the hog, kept in a slab, soaked in brine, and smoked. This operation cured the meat and so retarded the growth of bacteria that bacon could be kept for long periods of time. Thick slices could be cut from a single slab for several days with no noticeable deterioration of the remainder, and several rations of bacon could be carried in a haversack, wrapped in an oilcloth, without spoiling for some time.

FRESH BREAD

Fresh bread was almost unheard of on campaign in the field. However, several soldiers attest to its presence in established camps. The federal government provided a few portable regimental ovens and built bakeries where they were practical. A soldier recalled, "Our regiment built a large, double log cabin for a bakery, with brick ovens, and a professional baker from the ranks took charge. We drew flour, and every day had an abundance of as fine fresh bread as was ever laid on a millionaire's table."[28] One soldier wrote home of how he could not live by bread alone: "Of late we have drawn flour and soft bread. The flour we make biscuits and pancakes of. I think I can beat the natives making wheat pancakes. I get them as light and nice as you please and we think they make pretty good eating. But the hardest of it is we have to pay 60 cents per pound for all the butter we get. This makes it pretty high living for a soldier."[29]

HARDTACK

The staple ration of the federal army was a square cracker, 3⅛ by 2⅞ inches, with small holes in its top, known as hardtack. Referred to as both army bread and biscuit, it was a very dry, incredibly hard product without leavening, and bore little resemblance to either. The army was not being purposely cruel to its soldiers by giving them hardtack to eat. Hardtack was not a new product. It was used as ship's bread for centuries. The dryness and hardness were functional characteristics. It was dry when packaged to keep the cracker from spoiling, and hard so it could be carried in the soldier's haversack without crumbling.

Hardtack provided a good-quality ration when combined with other foods, but it took some time for the soldiers to learn to appreciate its value. Nine to ten crackers comprised a daily ration weighing only about one pound. It was therefore easy for soldiers to carry several days' rations with them in their haversacks. Hardtack was made edible by soaking it in water or coffee, or cracking it—a process that sometimes required a rock and a gun butt. Water-softened crackers were sometimes compared to gutta-percha, a sticky natural material that becomes just soft enough when boiled to be molded into shape. Crumbled hardtack was sometimes mixed with pork grease to form a hot meal called "skillygalee."[30] Soldiers with strong teeth were known to nibble at the edges of the dry cracker in camp or on the march. One soldier found this process like "biting into a wooden shingle" with the flavor of "wallpaper paste," but the taste could be improved by adding sugar or salt saved from other parts of the daily ration.[31]

A soldier wrote home to his girlfriend—with some sarcasm—about the unrelenting presence of hardtack in his diet, "Nett, I have become a model cook since entering the Army, and I think you will agree with me when I tell you how many kinds of dishes I can make out of hardtack, 1st make pancakes out of them, 2nd hoecake, 3rd flour gravy, 4th sauce, 5th coffee, 6th, fry them."[32] An officer wrote home sarcastically, "We are living very high nowadays, have pork, hardtack and coffee for breakfast and of course for dinner coffee, hardtack, and pork for a change. Then for supper we have a little coffee, pork, and fried hardtack . . . I am in danger of getting the gout on account of so high living."[33]

Federal hardtack was made by machine in a factory. Plain white flour was mixed with water and a little salt into a very stiff dough. The dough was rolled thin, about one half inch, and cut into squares by machines, sometimes with the baking company's name pressed into the top, as in "U.S. Marvin's Hardtack" and "Holmes & Coutts, Army Bread, New York."[34] The finished crackers were carefully stacked into wooden boxes in lots weighing 50 pounds.[35] Although most hardtack was made in Baltimore, contractors were located across the North, and hardtack was often months old before it was issued to the troops. When the crackers were poor, they were either too hard, or moldy and wet, or infested with maggots and weevils. It was not unusual for a man to find the surface of his pot of coffee swimming with weevils after breaking up hardtack in it. But the pests were easily skimmed off and left no distinctive flavor behind. If a soldier cared to do so, he could expel the weevils by toasting the bread at the fire. These conditions were mostly due to exposure to the weather, as thousands of boxes marked "Army Bread" piled up at some railway stations inadequately sheltered from the weather. Such wanton disregard by federal authorities rankled many Southern sympathizers conscious of their starving forces in the field.[36]

Empty hardtack boxes were common enough in the camps. Although the boxes were sometimes used whole as stools and tables, the wood panels more often became raw material for the building of shelters. They were worked into field fortifications to hold sand and dirt in place, or laid on the ground to provide better footing in the all-too-common mud. The planks were also used as temporary grave markers. Few of the original boxes survived the war, as they also provided a good source of firewood.

CORNBREAD

The supply-starved Confederates appreciated captured federal hardtack in place of the cornbread that was the staple of their daily diet. At times, the entire Southern army seemed to run on nothing but cornbread and captured hardtack. The cornbread was usually coarse, dry, and rather tasteless. Baked loaves of cornbread were sometimes available to the troops, but most often dry, ground meal was issued from which the Confederate soldier needed to make his own bread. Without an oven he needed to resort to his ingenuity. A thick corn disk, called hoecake or ashcake, could be made by mixing cornmeal with water and salt into a thick paste in an oilcloth and baking the product in a frying pan or on a hot, flat stone. Such cakes could withstand moderate abuse in a haversack and, like hardtack, were a sight common at mealtime and during breaks along the line of march.

Cornmeal could be mixed with hot water to form a mush, and was sometimes eaten with honey, molasses, or milk if they were available. Some soldiers improvised a full dinner stew called Confederate cush, or kush, of cornmeal mush, cooked meat, garlic, and bacon grease, ironically similar to a common preparation of plantation slaves. Cornmeal was also added to soups as a thickener.

COFFEE

The importance of coffee to the Civil War soldier cannot be underestimated. Their diaries and letters are full of reverent references to the hot brown liquid. Coffee was included in the official federal ration, as was sugar to sweeten it. Condensed milk of two brands, Lewis' and Borden's, and a dry powder called the "Essence of Coffee" were available through the sutlers.[37]

Federal soldiers rarely had trouble getting their regular daily ration of 1½ ounces of coffee beans. Confederate soldiers showed an equally intense liking for coffee, but due to the effectiveness of the blockade, they often had to do without coffee or find a coffee bean substitute. Several substitute materials were commonly used either to make coffee or to stretch a limited supply. Acorn coffee was made from the parched meat of the shelled nut roasted in a little bacon fat. Kernel corn, dried apples, wheat, seeds, and dried yams were tried, but wild chicory root seems to have served best. The quality of this substitute coffee was questionable, and Confederates would take great risks to trade scarce Southern tobacco for good Union coffee by trading with the enemy pickets across the lines.

The Army of the Potomac used 80 tons of coffee and sugar every week. Nonetheless, federal soldiers were very concerned lest they somehow be deprived of even the smallest part of this coffee and sugar allowance, and steps were taken to ensure that favoritism in apportioning the ration was thwarted. The appropriate amount having been issued on a company level, the orderly sergeant would place a gum blanket on the ground and make as many piles of coffee beans and sugar as there were men to receive the ration. Great care was taken to ensure that the piles were uniform. To prevent any charge of unfairness, the sergeant would turn his back, and an assistant would point to a pile randomly. The sergeant would call out the company roll by name, and the named man would retrieve his allowance. The veteran soon learned to place both the sugar and the coffee together in a cloth bag and scoop out the two together without ceremony, but some men preferred to keep them separate and use each in proportion to their taste.

Coffee was furnished to the soldier as green beans from the sack. Roasting was done in a camp kettle, which often meant the beans were burned rather than roasted. To "grind" the beans the soldier seized his musket by the barrel and used the butt as a tamper. The ground coffee more properly should have been called "cracked coffee," as many of the grains were halved, more quartered, and the rest of a very coarse texture. Yet an army surgeon believed that army coffee had "no equal as a preparation for a hard day's march, nor any rival as a restorative after one."[38]

The army recognized this value, and each soldier was issued a tin dipper in which to boil his coffee. This was a large metal cup holding between a pint and a quart of liquid. The ground coffee was placed directly into the water without a filter of any sort. With little enthusiasm, Pvt. John D. Billings recalled making coffee with the tin dipper, which proved "an unfortunate dish for that purpose, forever tipping over and spilling the coffee into the fire." Such utensils soon disappeared, to be replaced by a tin can with an improvised wire handle. Astonished recruits were amazed to see veteran soldiers holding this improvisation on the end of a stick, boiling their coffee at the campfire in happy security.[39] For those who recoiled at resorting to cast-off tin cans, sutlers offered an improved device for boiling coffee with a hinged lid and a stout wire handle by which it might be hung over the fire. The price of such an article could strain the financial resources of a single soldier, but several men might pool their money to purchase one and take turns carrying it.

The Civil War soldier would not be denied his coffee. If an early morning march was intended, and fires were permitted, the march was preceded by a pot of coffee. If a halt was ordered in mid-afternoon, coffee was made. Coffee making equipment was generally carried strapped to the outside of the kit where it was easily accessible. The movement of an army could be heard from far off by the resulting unmuffled rattling of countless coffee boilers and tin cups. So significant was this noise that special orders were frequently issued prior to stealthy movements of the army to place these items inside the haversack. At the end of each day's march, as soon as the army began to bivouac, small groups of men would invariably make the preparation of coffee their first task. A supper of hardtack and coffee followed, and then each man would roll up in his blankets for the night.

In camp, company cooks were issued large coffeepots holding several gallons. John Billings recalled, "It was coffee at meals and between meals; and men going on guard and coming off guard drank it at all hours of the night."[40] The U.S. Christian Commission made the rounds of the camps with "coffee wagons" made from old artillery limbers nicknamed by the troops "the Christian Light Artillery."[41] The coffee wagon was provided with compartments for ingredients and three large coffee boilers that could produce ninety gallons of coffee every hour. Whatever grumbling there may have been about the quality of the other rations, "there was but one opinion of the coffee which was served out, and that was of unqualified approval."[42]

SALT AND LIFE

Salt was as indispensable to an army as gunpowder. Besides its use in preserving foods, heavy doses of salt were needed to maintain the health of horses and in tanning leather for shoes, saddles, belts, and cartridge boxes. Common salt could be mined or retrieved by evaporating seawater. The Federals east of the Appalachian Mountains relied extensively on the saltworks at Onondaga Lake near Syracuse, New York, for this important substance. Here the brine, which welled up naturally from the floor of the lake, had provided an extensive source of salt for decades. More than nine million barrels of salt, worth in excess of $30 million, were produced in New York in 1862 alone. The captured saltworks of the Kanawha River Valley in Virginia were also important to federal forces. On the eve of the war a new source west of the mountains at the Saginaw River site in Michigan was found. The rapid wartime development of this resource yielded more than 500,000 barrels of salt annually. So successful were the Federals at processing domestic sources that Washington did not need to import foreign salt.[43]

Southern saltworks were a priority target for the invading Federals. Only five months into the war the Southern papers began to fret over a shortage of salt. Besides hundreds of coastal evaporating operations, there were only five principal sources of salt, in Louisiana, Alabama, Virginia, and Kentucky. The major production center in the Kanawha Valley was lost to the South with the defection of western Virginia. The Louisiana saltworks were lost to occupying federal troops about halfway through the war. Saltville, Kentucky, was the largest salt supplier in the upper Confederacy, making 3,000 bushels of salt a day, and it could have supplied the needs of the entire Confederacy alone if enough workers and rail connections had been available. Saltville was continually threatened by no less than two federal armies, yet it was the only Southern provider to remain in operation throughout the conflict.

The sure sign of a veteran was the simplicity of his cooking utensils, and many wide-eyed raw recruits—weighed down with government issued pots, pans, and knapsacks—marveled at the war-weary, blanket-wrapped soldiers sitting by a fire calmly heating their coffee in a discarded tin can with a wire bail handle. Although the troops of both armies were at times very hungry, no battle or campaign of the war was lost solely due to a lack of food, and even the Southern forces, who were often at the point of starvation, were provided with at least minimal levels of nutrition to support four years of conflict. Veteran soldiers believed that they had "reached the soldierly perfection" when two or three pieces of hardtack and some coffee could be made to satisfy their hunger for an entire day.[44]

NOTES

1. Stephen W. Sears, *For Country, Cause, and Leader, The Civil War Journal of Charles B. Haydon* (New York: Ticknor & Fields, 1993), 5–6.

2. James H. Croushore, ed., *A Volunteer's Adventure, by Captain John W. De Forest* (New Haven: Yale University Press, 1949), 162.

3. Carlton McCarthy, *Detailed Minutiae of Soldier Life in the Army of Northern Virginia, 1861–1865* (1882; reprint, Lincoln: University of Nebraska Press, 1993), 55.

4. Ibid., 57.

5. K. Jack Bauer, ed., *Soldiering: The Civil War Diary of Rice C. Bull* (Novato: Presidio, 1977), 11–12.

6. James I. Robertson, Jr., ed., *One of Jackson's Foot Cavalry* (Wilmington, NC: Broadfoot Reprints, 1987), 4–5.

7. John D. Billings, *Hardtack and Coffee* (Boston: G.M. Smith, 1887), 112.

8. Clinton Parkhurst, "Corinth: Tenting on the Old Camp Ground," *Civil War Times Illustrated*, January 1987, 30–35.

9. Ibid., 33.

10. Billings, 112–113; Croushore, 161.

11. Croushore, 197.

12. Bauer, 168. One of the objectives of the Gettysburg campaign was General Lee's wish to forage in the untouched countryside of Maryland and Pennsylvania, thereby relieving the pressure on the Shenandoah Valley, which would be free to harvest its crops. Lee carefully timed his march to coincide with the ripening of the July harvest.

13. Croushore, 197.

14. Stuart's cavalry was out of touch with Lee's army for several days during the Gettysburg campaign on such a mission. Although he brought in more than 100 wagonloads of provisions, the absence of his men may have contributed to the Confederate defeat.

15. McCarthy, 66–67.

16. Parkhurst, 35.

17. William Walton, ed., *A Civil War Courtship: The Letters of Edwin Weller from Antietam to Atlanta* (New York: Doubleday, 1980), 84.

18. Dolly Sumner Lunt, *A Woman's Wartime Journal* (Atlanta: Cherokee, 1994), 35.

19. V. C. Jones, 45; Croushore, 79.

20. Croushore, 73.

21. McCarthy, 60–61.

22. John H. Woodward, "Herding Beef for the Union Army," *Civil War Times Illustrated,* December 1970, 28–39.

23. Ibid., 31.

24. Ibid., 36.

25. The Hollywood film *Alvarez Kelly* starring William Holden and Richard Widmark was loosely based on this real-life exploit.

26. Byrne and Soman, 6.

27. Bauer, 91.

28. Parkhurst, 33.

29. Walton, 28.

30. Billings,114–116.

31. Bauer, 11.

32. Walton, 28.

33. Ibid., 90.

34. Francis A. Lord, *Civil War Collector's Encyclopedia,* 5 vols. (Edison: Blue & Gray Press, 1995), 2: 58–59.

35. J. J. Scroggs, "A Tour of a Hardtack Factory: Diary of J. J. Scroggs 5th US Colored Infantry," *Civil War Times Illustrated,* October 1972, 34.

36. Billings, 114–116.

37. Lord, *Encyclopedia,* 2: 58–59.

38. A. C. Swartwelder, "This Invaluable Beverage: The Recollections of Dr. A. C. Swartwelder," *Civil War Times Illustrated,* October, 1975, 10–11.

39. Billings, 114–116.

40. Ibid.

41. Lord, *Encyclopedia,* 58–59.

42. Billings, 116.

43. Emerson David Fite, *Social and Industrial Conditions in the North During the Civil War* (Williamstown: Corner House, 1976), 26.

44. Bauer, 11–12.

9

TENTING TONIGHT:
THE SOLIDER'S LIFE

"We soon became used to the little tents and were thankful to have them."

—A federal private

SHELTER

Civil War soldiers found shelter from the elements in many ways. Which of these was used depended largely on the season of the year and the accident of location. Permanent and semi-permanent shelters, barracks or huts, made largely of wooden planks or logs, were considered to be winter or permanent quarters. When on campaign the army was constantly on the move, and permanent structures were obviously impractical. Shelter was then provided almost exclusively by canvas tents. As the campaigning season truly began in late spring or early summer and ran on into early winter, the soldiers were under some sort of canvas shelter for most of the year, under a wide variety of weather conditions ranging from dry heat to wet, snowy cold.

The science of encamping an army is called castramentation, derived from castra, the Latin word for "camp." The armies of ancient Rome were highly regarded for the regularity of their Legionary camps, which served as a model of proper Civil War castramentation. The regimental site would be broken down according to battalions and companies. A castramentation officer was usually appointed from among the subalterns to arrange the company quarters under the direction of a regimental staff officer—

usually a major who tended to the day-to-day deskwork for the unit. A standard plan was followed as well as the vagaries of the campground allowed; yet in an establishment as big as an army, so many regiments needed to be accommodated that even on the best of sites some regiments were allotted poor ground.

This led to some unfortunate consequences for the newly raised units and inexperienced officers of the volunteer regiments when the precincts of the camp reached into uneven, wet, or swampy ground. Concerning a particularly poor site, a Michigan volunteer noted, "Our grounds will be all afloat by night. I wish the state could find dry land enough for us to camp. I would rather sleep in the open air than be quartered in the mud."[1]

An effort was made to keep the company organization together, and a single company usually occupied a whole lane called a company street. These streets often ended on a main road running through the encampment. One of the more difficult tasks was to locate the latrines, which were usually no more than simple slit trenches. These needed to be within a convenient distance of the company tents but placed far enough away from the regiment and the drill, cooking, and storage areas to mask the odors that would unfortunately be present. It was also important that the latrines not pose a health threat in terms of polluting the available drinking water.

The textbook scheme dictated exactly the relative position of each billet, whether that of an officer, an NCO, or an enlisted man, in a double row along the company street. NCOs and officers were expected to maintain a certain level of social distinction and separate themselves from the private soldiers. Regimental areas such as headquarters, the hospital, and the commissary were also carefully dictated so that those new to a particular encampment, who were nonetheless familiar with the system, could comfortably make their way around without the least perplexity. Civilian commissions, Bible societies, missions, and sutlers usually occupied an area separate from the soldiers. Nonetheless, an "astonished" federal officer found one brigade encamped "with no boundary lines between the different regiments, all being tumbled together higgledy-piddledy, officers mixed up anyhow with the men, and the brigade commander in the middle."[2] This was particularly unusual among federal troops and was considered to be due to the inexperience of the volunteer officers. A small number of volunteer officers were dismissed from their positions due to "alleged incompetency" in running the day-to-day affairs of their commands.[3]

Winter quarters for 16 men were to be made of wooden planks or logs with a one-room layout, 16 by 20 feet. A single entrance was made at the narrow end along a company street and was opposed at the rear by a fireplace with a chimney of crossed, notched sticks coated with mud. A cord or more of firewood would be stacked outside each hut. The roof was made with riven boards split from short logs or the sides of hardtack boxes used as shingles. Canvas flies, tarps, and shelter halves were sometimes stretched over the rafters to improve the weather-resistance of the roofs. Inside, the hut was designed to have wooden bunk beds paralleling the long walls, and was supposed to accommodate sixteen men. The bunks were "simply broad shelves one above the other, wide enough to accommodate two men spoon fashion." Straw-filled canvas sacks, called ticking, served as mattresses. Commonly no provision was made for any flooring other than the packed earth.[4]

The soldiers were expected to build their own winter shelters with the tools given to them. No provision was made for furnishings beyond the creativity of the occupants. "We built bunks clear of the ground, to sleep on; made rustic arbors about our streets . . . every rude improvement was encouraged by the company officers." The hut could be furnished with tables and chairs in the form of discarded barrels and hardtack crates; a shelf was usually made for the all-important fresh water bucket of tinned iron. The ingenuity of the occupants usually provided for a small section of wall or a part of a log to be removed to provide light and ventilation if a real window could not be "found" or "liberated" for the purpose. The soldiers sometimes crowned the chimney with a nail keg or flour barrel to improve the draw of the fireplace, but as these caught fire with frustrating regularity only constant attention kept the entire structure from burning.[5]

A sergeant described the NCO hut that he built in a letter to his friend: "We have been at work for about a week past building log huts to make us comfortable. We have about half of them finished. I have succeeded in getting one built for myself and a very comfortable one too. It is about as large as Molly Walker's front room, with a good fireplace in it. Two nice bunks and a stationary table built up on one side, and stools around it, these with other little conveniences make it quite comfortable."[6]

Officers' huts were constructed by details of soldiers in a similar fashion and were of the same dimensions, with the exception that the layout called for two rooms with separate doors and fireplaces. Company captains and adjutants rated separate rooms, while junior officers were normally expected to double up. A federal officer wrote in 1864, "I am not as nicely furnished as regards furniture as I was at Atlanta, but I still have enough to be quite comfortably situated. My furniture consists of a bedstead, bedding, etc. three chairs, one camp stool, one table and my office desk and table, also a wash bowl and pitcher. My room has a good fireplace in it." Not infrequently, officers absented themselves from the army during the winter to sleep in private residences. "Since I wrote you last our regiment and brigade have moved camp about a mile and a half. . . . My office is [now] located in a dwelling house and I again have a parlor of the house for my office room and a room just across the hall for storing my things in."[7]

During most of the year, and in much of the South even during the winter, the troops found shelter under canvas. Tents came in various standard

patterns, but the ingenuity of the individual soldier provided infinite variations. An officer noted the vagaries of living under canvas for long periods.
"Rain streams at will through numerous rents and holes in the moldy, rot-
ten canvas. Nearly every night half the men are wet through while asleep
unless they wake up, stack their clothing in the darkness, and sit on it with
their rubber blankets over their heads." The image of soggy soldiers squat-
ting on their kits in a leaky tent while trying to catch some sleep was not
that which recruiters commonly suggested to willing youths.[8]

"There is an alarming amount of sickness in camp if the men are to be
believed at roll call," wrote one NCO. "We can muster near 100 men at dinner but 60 is a large yield for drill . . . This dodge is getting so threadbare
that good soldiers sometimes suffer much pain & inconvenience rather
than incur the suspicion of shirking duty."[9] Under these wet and damp
conditions clean clothes quickly became a rarity. "I have ventured to sleep
with pants off but once or twice [and] it is now almost impossible to get a
chance to wash your body or even to take off your shoes . . . This is partly
due to the [clean] water being so far from camp. I have sent my only shirt
to be washed & [to hide its absence] have to wear my coat closely buttoned. [W]e are all lousy & covered with sores and blotches."[10]

The Sibley tent was invented by Henry Sibley in 1857 while he was an
active duty officer with the U.S. Army. When the war arrived, Sibley joined
the South, ultimately attaining the rank of Brigadier. Nonetheless, the Sibley, or Bell Tent, went to war on the side of the Federals and was a favorite
among volunteer units. The pattern resembled a Native American tepee
with a large canvas cone eighteen feet in diameter and twelve high with
a single entrance and a smoke hole at the top one foot in diameter. This
served the dual purposes of providing ventilation and emitting smoke in
cold weather. A canvas cap was provided to close the hole in foul weather.
Unlike the tepee with its numerous long poles, the Sibley tent sported a
unique design innovation that provided for a single nine-foot center pole
resting on an iron tripod. The tripod could be adjusted to tighten or relieve
the tension in the canvas. The area under the tripod provided a place for
a conical sheet-iron stove. With its several short lengths of stovepipe pro-
truding through the opening at the top, the Sibley stove provided a good
deal of smoke-free heat.

Sibley tents were comfortable and capacious for a dozen men under
moderate weather conditions, but they quickly disappeared from the line
of march principally because their large canvas sheathing proved cumbersome to transport. Even in moderate weather, the tents could become foul
and unwholesome if closed up for long periods. In some cases, only the
tripods were retained to be used over the company fireplace. Though the
federal government withdrew the tent from active campaigning, it continued to be popular with the state militias camped outside the war zone.

The "A" or wedge tent was quite common during the Civil War. The
one-piece canvas tent was stretched over a horizontal bar six to seven feet

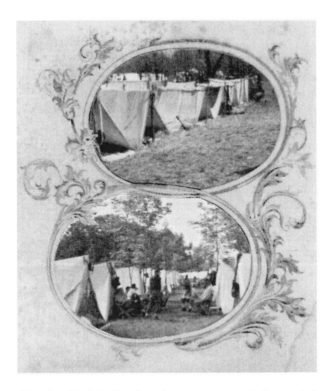

"Tenting Tonight," a favorite camp song of the period, may have envisioned neat company streets such as these, with dog tents (above) and wedge tents (below), set up by modern Civil War enthusiasts in Pennsylvania. James Volo photo.

long supported at each end by an upright pole of about the same length. One end of the wedge was split up the center into flaps, which could be opened and fixed back to provide ventilation or tied closed in foul weather. The rectangular floor was about seven feet square. The shape permitted standing only in the very center, but six men could comfortably occupy the floor space with their equipment by "spooning" together to fit. The tent was widely used during the war, but took up too much room on the march, and was most often seen in camps of instruction and used by troops permanently located near important military centers.

Wall tents were often used by officers for their quarters or as headquarters tents. An extra piece of canvas fly, of the same size as the roof of the tent, could be stretched over it to provide extra protection from the sun and rain. The air space between the fly and the actual roof of the tent also served tolerably well as insulation. The fly was sometimes placed in front of the entrance, creating a porch-like area, or set alone as an airy canopy or sunscreen. The wall tent used poles much like those of the wedge tent, but it required more than two dozen tent stakes and a dozen supporting ropes to erect properly. The all-around canvas wall served well, "as one could stand erect and move about in them with tolerable freedom." In long-term camps, wall tents were often provided with platform floors made of wooden planking.[11]

The dog tent, or shelter tent, was used almost exclusively by the Federals, and its squat shape became symbolic of the rank and file federal soldier on campaign. Open at both ends, the dog tent was composed of two shelter halves joined by an overlapping seam fastened with a series of brass buttons and buttonholes provided for the purpose. Each half was approximately 5½–4½ feet fitted with loops for tent stakes on the long side. In an open field two muskets with bayonets fixed could be stuck into the ground and a stout guy rope tied between the trigger guards to support the ridge of the tent. "As you make by leaning two cards against each other," the buttoned pair of shelter halves was quickly draped over the rope and fixed to the ground by stakes. This was not the use the military had visualized for muskets and bayonets, but it was more practical than carrying tent poles or having thousands of men trying to find new ones each night.[12] In wooded areas the guy rope might be tied between two trees, and artillerymen commonly draped the shelter halves over the wagon tongue of their limber. The dog tent provided a space about six feet square on the ground and not quite four feet high at the apex. The small size of these shelters forced the men to crawl in and out on hands and knees, but the tents could be erected in a matter of minutes by veteran troops.[13]

If time and material permitted, the soldiers used tree limbs and green boughs to build canopies over their little structures to keep off the sun, or they raised the entire enterprise off the ground several feet and built a platform on which to rest away from the ground. It was not uncommon to see the bottom of dog tents raised several feet on a stockade of logs or planks, which made them very spacious and comfortable for winter quarters. "In stockading a tent the posts were split in halves, and the cleft sides all turned inward so as to make a clean and comely inside." By far the most common way of "logging up a tent" was by notching the logs together at the corners like a cabin. This took much less time and material than splitting out planks.[14]

A favorite alternative was to place a large bed of straw, hay, or leaves a foot or more thick between two large logs. Over this snug nest the tent could be pitched. Covered with a rubber blanket in case of rain, such "straw pens" could provide a comfortable shelter for a season. In cold, dry weather some men burrowed into the ground, digging a trench under the shelter. This "lowering the floor instead of raising the ceiling" concept had several drawbacks, as digging was hard work and rain quickly filled the trenches with water in all but the best locations. Since the army might move at any moment, most men chose not to invest the physical effort needed to make these modifications until they had gone into winter quarters.

Although the dog tent was designed for two men, ice in the washbasin, numb fingers, and frosty breath often brought three men to bunk together. This allowed a third shelter half to be draped over the open end of the tent or over the seam at the top, or placed on the ground with the gum blanket as an additional barrier against dampness. Three blankets were now available. One was spread beneath and the other two on top of the men, who spooned together to conserve body heat. Shelter tents were otherwise free of all creature comforts. As one soldier noted, "These tents were to be used chiefly for sleeping, as one could barely sit erect at the highest place in the center. They were far from comfortable living quarters. Yet they were the only kind of shelter we would have in the field during our term of service . . . and we soon became used to the little tents and were thankful to have them."[15]

The success of the shelter tent lay in the ease with which it could be erected and carried. Recruits rolled it with the blanket on top of the knapsack. Besides the convenience of always having the tent in their possession, soldiers understood that the elimination of baggage allowed more wagons to be used to bring food to the front. Veterans, having dispensed with their knapsacks as useless impedimenta, commonly rolled their blanket, shelter half, and rubber blanket lengthwise and wore them as a tube over their left shoulder in bandolier fashion with the ends tied at the right hip. Some men of macabre disposition abandoned their shelter halves on the morning of battle in the knowledge that they could re-supply themselves at day's end from the unclaimed baggage of those killed in the engagement.[16]

In the early days of the war several Confederate units provided themselves with tents, but these quickly disappeared. Shelters of any kind were rarely seen in the field. Rather, two men generally slept together, each having a blanket and an oilcloth. The oilcloth served as an inferior alternative to the gum rubber blankets carried by the Federals, which were considered great prizes if they could be "captured." Generally, one oilcloth (or gum blanket) went on the ground to impede moisture. The two bunkmates then covered themselves with one or both blankets, with the second oilcloth on top to protect them from the elements. Their haversacks served as pillows. Confederate encampments came to be characterized by numerous small "mounds" of sleeping men rather than neatly arranged tent lines.[17] One Southerner noted in a letter, "Bivouacked for the night in an open field. The night was very cold and the only way we could keep warm was to build up a good fire and sit or wrap ourselves up in our blankets and lay down beside it."[18]

EQUIPMENT

While Confederates were characteristically destitute of equipment, federal recruits came to the war zone overloaded with useless articles of convenience. However, the equipment retained and valued by veteran soldiers of both armies was remarkably similar. Woolen uniforms—jackets and trousers—were almost universal, as wool retains its insulating qualities even when wet. Armies on the march in warm weather "could be smelled before they were seen." Soldiers were issued unbleached cotton or linen shirts, but wore a variety of civilian colors and patterns many of which had been brought or sent from home. The most characteristic hat of the period was the cloth kepi, which was a cap fashioned after a style made popular in European armies. Slouch hats, with a wide brim all around, were issued to some regiments and were particularly popular with troops in the western theater.[19]

Uniforms came in a variety of colors, and the lack of a standard color scheme quickly proved the cause of serious confusion. In the Battle of Bull Run, Southern troops were fired upon by their own side after being identified as Federals because of their blue jackets, and vice versa. As the war continued, the Confederates generally limited their colors to gray and butternut. The Federals commonly resorted to dark blue jackets, but in some cases, as with Zouaves and Berdan's Sharpshooters, vivid red or forest

The men of the Stone family, from the cartes de viste album of Margie Stone, exhibit a number of uniform types worn by federal officers. The man at the lower right appears to be wearing a naval uniform. From the authors' collection.

green might predominate. Federal trousers, of heavy kersey wool held up by tape suspenders, were sky blue in color. Confederate trousers were black, blue, gray, or butternut. As the war progressed, the South relied increasingly on captured federal clothing supplies or undyed cloth. By 1863, many Southerners were wearing sky blue trousers or trousers made of linen canvas, cottonade, or tent cloth.

Shoes were issued to the infantry and were made of leather—uppers, soles, and heels. Leather laces were worked through as few as two sets of unreinforced eyelets. The most common shoe was the so-called brogan, or workman's shoe of European design. The brogan covered the entire foot, coming up to the anklebone. It was often fitted with metal plates on the heels to protect against wear and metal tacks on the soles to increase traction on sometimes slick grass. Leather or cloth leggings were often buckled on over brogans to protect the lower leg. Federal shoes were dyed black, as were Confederate ones at first. Later in the war, when black dye became unavailable, Southern leather goods were done in russet brown. A severe leather shortage caused some Rebel shoes to be made with wooden soles.

Both shoes and boots were issued to the cavalry, the horse artillery, and mounted officers to protect the leg from the chafing of the stirrup leathers. Very stylish boots, hearkening back to the days of the English cavaliers, were very popular among the gallants of the Confederate and federal cavalry, but by the end of the war many riders found that shoes were more comfortable and serviceable. Federal riders were issued pants with a double layer of fabric on the inseam to be worn with shoes when astride.

The prescribed uniform allowance for a one-year enlistment in 1861 was identical in both armies and included the following items: hat (1); kepi or cap (2); havelock, or cap cover (1); coat (2); trousers (3); shirt (3); blouse (1); drawers (3); shoes, pair (2); stockings, pair (2); stock, or tie (1); greatcoat (1); wool blanket (1); ground sheet, gum rubber blanket or oilcloth (1). Theoretically, the year's allotment was divided into two batches, one for issue in the spring and one in the fall. The Confederacy quickly found that it was unable to provide many of these items, and Southern troops often equipped themselves with captured federal equipment.

With the exception of the cavalry, who were provided with a wide assortment of firearms including pistols and rapid-fire repeaters, both armies issued muzzle-loading rifled muskets with percussion cap ignition to the infantry. Most commonly, they were American-made .58 caliber Springfields or British .577 caliber Enfields. The soldiers found Enfields more accurate than Springfields. "At long range we are rather afraid of them," admitted a federal officer in 1864. Troops would "trade" their weapon for an Enfield on the battlefield if the opportunity presented itself, and whole companies were sometimes rearmed in such a manner after a major engagement.[20]

The similarity in musket calibers proved a great advantage in distributing supplies and was a godsend to the Confederacy, which could use captured federal ammunition. The ammunition for Springfields and Enfields was interchangeable for all practical purposes, but cavalry ammunition was generally made in a smaller caliber, .52 caliber being a popular size, to relieve some of the recoil experienced with lighter weapons. Weapons like the Spencer carbine or less common Henry repeater that fired pre-primed brass cartridges were almost exclusively used by the Federals. The South simply did not have the machinery to make precision cartridges in large numbers. The most common pistol calibers were .36, .44, and .45, but almost any size bullet might be fired in anger from the hundreds of private weapons carried to the battlefield by recruits. Thousands of pistols, sometimes advertised as "lifesavers," were carried on the battlefield, but many were small caliber cartridge weapons of .22 and .32 caliber of little power that proved useless in day-to-day operations. They were often mailed home to families in the North by Federals who found them useless encumbrances once they had become veterans.

With the minié ball, a conical bullet with a hollowed base, the rifled musket was capable of hitting a man-sized target at 800 yards and had plain sights that were adjustable to that range. Effectively, a target the size of a man could barely be seen at 800 yards. However, used in a volley—hundreds of muskets firing simultaneously—the musket could be deadly over open ground. The need to ram down the charge before firing slowed the sustained rate of fire of most veteran troops to about three aimed shots per minute.

Sharpshooting, the use of carefully aimed shots by individuals designated to pick off officers, artillerymen, or other conspicuous persons, was a peculiar characteristic of the Civil War battlefield that hearkened back to the activities of the fringe-shirted riflemen of the Revolution. Generally, no special weapon was used for this purpose, though many sharpshooters were equipped with Enfields with telescopic sights.

Breechloaders like the Sharps or Smith carbines could fire nine rounds a minute, and the fully self-contained brass cartridge of the Spencer repeating rifle allowed for twenty. There was a genuine concern among military experts, lasting through World War I and diminishing only after World War II, that the soldiers would quickly expend all of their available ammunition with repeating weapons. Nonetheless, breechloading designs and revolvers were widely issued to the cavalry and other specialty troops. Dismounted federal cavalry using such weapons proved significant in retarding the Southern advance on the first day of the Battle of Gettysburg and allowed the Federal army to occupy the strategic heights outside the town known as Cemetery Ridge.[21]

The majority of muskets were fitted with a socket bayonet about eighteen inches long. Some regiments were issued short swords, instead of bayonets, that could be fitted to the barrel of the musket. Although great reliance was placed by military tacticians on the ability of "cold steel" to drive the enemy from the field, in practice very few combatants came to such close quarters before the psychological effect of the bayonet caused one side or the other to flee. Captain J. W. De Forest noted that "bayonet fighting occurs mainly in newspaper and other works of fiction." Bayonets, however, proved to be excellent digging tools, skewers for roasting meat and potatoes, and good candle holders.[22]

The deadly accuracy of the rifled musket at a distance, combined with the use of entrenchments and fortified positions, caused bayonet wounds to account for a very small percentage of injuries. As the war progressed and troops settled into trenches and fortifications for prolonged sieges, head wounds "between the brim of the hat and the top of the head" predominated, and most of these occurred in the first day after entrenching as the enemy sharpshooters probed for defensive weaknesses and the occupants had not yet identified the "dangerous locations." The soldiers learned to cut "loopholes" in the works or erect "head logs" to defend against these wounds. Placed on the top of the parapet with widely separated supports, the head log provided a small space beneath which the men could fire without exposing the top of their heads.[23]

Woolen blankets were issued in warm weather, and lined woolen greatcoats, weighing several pounds, were provided for winter. The greatcoats were particularly effective in retaining body heat, but having both blanket and greatcoat simultaneously was thought to be too cumbersome.

This *Leslie's* illustration by A. Berghaus clearly shows the euphoria with which the 6th Massachusetts Regiment was greeted when mounting the "cars" in Jersey City. Note the greatcoats with their elbow-length capes.

While most men cherished their blankets, some threw them away on a hot march and regretted their actions when the weather changed. Green troops marched poorly, "straggling about the roads . . . and the fields." Their columns, flanked by discarded equipment, were described as "a spectacle of disorder."[24]

All federal troops were issued a thin canvas ground sheet coated with gum rubber, called a "rubber blanket" by most men. Some soldiers carried two, as they could be rolled very tightly. There is some disagreement among historians as to whether rubber blankets were designed to be worn as ponchos in case of rain or if the soldiers altered them to be used in this manner. About 6½ feet long and 3½ feet wide, rubber blankets were provided with eyelets in the sides and ends which allowed them to be used in the same manner as the shelter half. Confederates were issued oilcloths to ward off rain and damp, but they highly prized gum rubber blankets.

Soldiers were expected to carry their field equipment, extra clothing, and personal items in a knapsack. Blankets and dog tents were rolled and fastened to the top of the knapsack. Numerous knapsack designs were patented during the war, but most proved uncomfortable on long marches. On going into battle it was common for the troops to pile their marching gear and knapsacks in a remote spot to which they would return if they were victorious. Should the encounter go against them, the baggage would almost certainly pass into the hands of the enemy.

Private Jay Butler recalled his headlong retreat at the Battle of Stones River: "When we got back as far as my knapsack, I picked it up and attempted to carry it and did so for a quarter of a mile when I found that I was getting behind and that the bullets came nearer and thicker, so I dropped it, took out my rubber blanket and went on my way feeling very downhearted at leaving so many good and useful articles to the enemy."[25]

The string of Confederate victories in the first two years of the war helped supply the Rebel army with captured equipment and conveniences otherwise unavailable to Southern soldiers. Breechloading weapons, shoes, blankets, and gum rubber blankets were particularly valued prizes. Captured brass-cartridge weapons proved less valuable to Confederates than one would suppose, as the South was incapable of producing replacement ammunition.

UNIFORMS

Confederate soldiers acquired so much federal equipment that it was difficult to discriminate between friend and foe simply by uniform. "A Rebel Captain and some of his men were clothed in our uniform," wrote a frustrated federal officer, "a growing practice, so reprehensible that it should be met with condign [well-deserved] punishment, as the deception engendered is always apt to cost lives and disasters." In winter, large contingents of Southern troops were seen sporting sky blue federal trou-

sers and greatcoats. Federal commanders insisted that Southern troops
captured wearing federal equipment be treated as spies. The South countered that such items were legitimate objects of capture under the rules of
war, to be used at the pleasure of the captors, leaving a dispute that was
never resolved.[26]

A resident of Winchester, Virginia, Cornelia McDonald, described the
uniform of a fallen Southern gallant with the rank of major in 1862. "He
was dressed in a beautiful new uniform, gray and buff; a splendid red
silk scarf was around his waist." As the officer was dead, "his sword was
lying by his side . . . not a drop of blood stained his clothing." He was
a young man with "fine soft hair" and a "long jet black beard" through
which he had received a death wound, shot in the chin.[27] However, young
Sarah Morgan, in describing the uniform of two Southern officers serving in Louisiana, may have come closer to a picture of reality: "Yesterday
two Colonels . . . dined here. Their personal appearance was by no means
calculated to fill one with awe, or even to give one an idea of their rank;
for their dress consisted of merely cottonade pants, flannel shirts, and extremely short jackets, which, however, is rapidly becoming the uniform of
the Confederate States."[28]

Morgan recorded the following description of the enlisted men in the
fall of 1862. "What a sad site [*sic*] . . . Men that had fought at Shiloh and
Baton R., were barefooted. Rags was their only uniform, for very few possessed a complete suit, and those wore all varieties of colors and cuts.
Hats could be seen of every style and shape."[29] A Federal writer described
the clothing of a fallen foe in 1864: "His feet, wrapped in rags, had coarse
shoes upon them, so worn and full of holes that they were only held together by many pieces of thick twine. Ragged trousers, a jacket, and a shirt
of . . . 'tow cloth,' a straw hat, which had lost a large portion of both crown
and brim."[30]

By way of comparison, federal general Philip Sheridan was said to be
neatly and properly uniformed even in the hottest weather in "a double-
breasted frock coat; pantaloons outside his boots, strapped down, and
chafing against small brass spurs." He frequently eschewed his kepi for
a slouch hat.[31] Nonetheless, a federal officer wrote from the field in August 1864, "We are the seediest and most disreputable gang to look at that
you can imagine. I have but one shirt and one pair of socks, and my coat
and trousers are as ragged as a tramp's, and my shoes are innocent of
blacking."[32]

Each soldier was furnished with a canteen, cartridge box, and haversack, which were worn on his body over the shoulder along with the musket. Most veteran troops quickly discarded all other encumbrances and
reveled in campaigning with as little equipment as possible. "Everyone is
stripped for the march, carrying his own blanket, shelter tent, haversack
and canteen, whether he be captain or private." Such discrimination in
the choice of equipment quickly distinguished veteran units from new

recruits in the federal armies, while a lack of equipment became characteristic of the largely destitute Confederate forces.[33]

Most soldiers kept their most personal items in their haversacks or in their pockets, along with two or three days' rations, a so-called "housewife" or sewing kit, a tin cup, and any extra ammunition. A Confederate haversack found on the field in 1864 contained "a jack-knife, a plug twist of tobacco, a tin cup, and about two quarts of coarsely cracked corn, with perhaps an ounce of salt tied in a rag."[34]

CAMP LIFE AND RECREATION

The single complaint most often expressed by Civil War soldiers was that of being bored. Camp life was "one everlasting monotone, yesterday, today, and tomorrow." Burial and fatigue details took up much of a soldier's remaining time not devoted to drill. Pickets, or sentries, went on duty at the front for two days in every six. A federal officer noted that guard duty was the very last duty that soldiers learned to perform "accurately and thoroughly," as they were required to shoot any man, including comrades, found running the guard. An NCO remarked, "Standing guard is a very necessary duty but by no means a pleasant one . . . Two men sentinels were found asleep on their posts & nailed."[35]

If there was anything that the troops needed to excel in, it was tactical evolution. The battalion drill was often fatiguing. After a particularly grueling afternoon session an NCO noted, "Some of the men said they could scarcely drag themselves along & it was impossible to keep them up to their places in line. I acted as left guide as usual & am somewhat tired myself."[36] An officer noted with remarkable pride, "We had been drilled in battalion and drilled in brigade till we went like a machine." Yet the soldiers repudiated such regimental pride and complained, "The first thing in the morning is drill, then drill again. Between drills . . . we sometimes stop . . . and have a roll call." If things went wrong during drill, especially if an officer blundered, the general quickly moved to "the scene of confusion with a face of anguish." By the time the camp was established, firewood gathered, cooking finished, and weapons cleaned, the soldier had little free daylight time for entertainment.[37]

A federal officer observed, "I had no amusement beyond occasional old newspapers and rare walks to the position of some neighboring battery or regiment."[38] Nonetheless, individuals and groups did find some time for entertaining activities. Letter and journal writing, reading, whittling, drawing, and painting were common entertainments. Games such as checkers, chess, dice, and dominoes were popular with small groups, as were card games such as poker, cribbage, euchre, and "old sledge." Game boards were often drawn on the inside of the ever-present gum blanket, and stones, bones, and corncobs served as game pieces.

The advertising section of many Northern newspapers offered an amazing variety of goods for the soldier volunteer.

Large group activities of a more accepted tenor included snowball fights, chasing greased pigs or climbing poles, and playing football and baseball. Singing was a very popular activity. Generally speaking, the soldiers were interested in sentimental rather than patriotic tunes. Ballads such as "Just Before the Battle, Mother" and "Somebody's Darling" were very popular. The men sang about their sweethearts in "Aura Lea," "Lorena," and "The Yellow Rose of Texas." A Rebel favorite was "All Quiet Along the Potomac," and "Tenting Tonight on the Old Camp Ground" was a Northern favorite. "Dixie," "John Brown's Body," "The Bonnie Blue Flag," and "The Battle Cry of Freedom" were sung less often by the toil-weary troops than by the patriotic populace.[39]

The men were not as well behaved as could be hoped. Gambling was strictly forbidden by military law, but the prohibition was almost impossible to enforce. Soldiers were reluctant to have dice and cards found among any personal effects that might be sent home upon their death, and often disposed of them before going into battle. A popular, but probably specious, story that made the rounds of the camps was that of an inveterate card player who received a ball to his chest which passed through all the cards of a deck he was carrying save one, the ace of spades, which saved his life.[40]

An NCO from a Midwestern volunteer unit noted that about a dozen men were arrested for "pissing on forbidden ground" during a frosty night, and the air of the cantonment was loaded "with shouts and curses" during the day despite their "present state of discipline." Military life was somewhat different than the young man expected. "Card playing, profanity, & stealing of provisions are among the most noted characteristics outside of the [soldierly] duties [and] the rascals steal anything they can put their hands on." Finally, he remarked, "Some very pretty ladies visit us at camp nowadays. They are *all* looking for brothers or cousins who they heard had enlisted. They are . . . sure to find them but the boys are so hard up for money . . . [that] the meetings terminate unsatisfactorily . . . If the men pursue the enemy as vigorously as they do the whores they will make very efficient soldiers."[41]

In sharp contrast with the romantic image of groups of soldiers huddled in comradeship around the campfire, many men separated themselves from the group each night and settled at small solitary fires at the edge of the camp. After a full day of marching between twenty and thirty miles, the men's feet were often blistered nearly all over so that they could hardly take a step further. Edwin Weller, 107th New York Volunteers, found that "on taking some salt and water and bathing my feet thoroughly and then applying liquor I managed to get myself in tolerably good marching order for the next day."[42] Other men simply fell to the ground to rest, too tired to invest the further effort of pitching a tent, and happy to go to their blankets to sleep supperless and unsheltered. "The march done, the fevered feet bare to the evening breeze, the aching limbs outstretched, the head laid on the blanket roll which had been such a burden through the day, the pipe in the mouth, nature revived a little and found that life retained some of its sweetness." One Federal noted of day-to-day soldiering, "It is a healthy, monotonous, stupid life, and makes one long to go somewhere, even at the risk of being shot."[43]

NOTES

1. Stephen W. Sears, *For Country, Cause, and Leader, The Civil War Journal of Charles B. Haydon* (New York: Ticknor & Fields, 1993), 6.

2. James H. Croushore, ed., *A Volunteer's Adventure, by Captain John W. De Forest* (New Haven: Yale University Press, 1949), 165.

3. Sears, 9.

4. Carlton McCarthy, *Detailed Minutiae of Soldier Life in the Army of Northern Virginia, 1861–1865* (1882; reprint, Lincoln: University of Nebraska Press, 1993), 84.

5. Clinton Parkhurst. "Corinth: Tenting on the Old Camp Ground," *Civil War Times Illustrated,* January 1987, 30–35.

6. William Walton, ed., *A Civil War Courtship: The Letters of Edwin Weller from Antietam to Atlanta* (New York: Doubleday, 1980), 17.

7. Ibid., 141–142.

8. Croushore, 44.

9. Sears, 15.

10. Sears, 251.

11. Billings, 50.

12. These so-called shelter halves were so near to those used in the World Wars as to be identical. The 20th-century soldier was supplied with a three-part tent pole that screwed together to make a single upright. Two men teamed together to erect a single "pup" tent.

13. Croushore, 164.

14. Billings, 49.

15. Bauer, 10.

16. Gregory A. Coco, *The Civil War Infantryman: In Camp, on the March, and in Battle* (Gettysburg: Thomas, 1996), 54.

17. McCarthy, 25.

18. Walton, 18.

19. Lewis, 6.

20. Croushore, 196.

21. Many military historians consider this position to be the key to winning the battle.

22. Croushore, 117–118.

23. Ibid., 66.

24. Ibid., 56.

25. Peter Cozzens, *No Better Place to Die: The Battle of Stones River* (Urbana: University of Illinois Press, 1990), 99. Quoting a private letter made public in 1930.

26. V. C. Jones, chap. 13, note 4, 388.

27. Minrose C. Gwin, ed., *Cornelia Peake McDonald: A Woman's Civil War. A Diary with Reminiscences of the War from March 1862* (Madison: University of Wisconsin, 1992), 53.

28. Charles East, ed., *Sarah Morgan: The Civil War Diary of a Southern Woman* (New York: Simon & Schuster, 1991), 218.

29. Ibid., 274.

30. Millard K. Bushrod, *Old Jube: A Biography of General Jubal A. Early* (Shippensburg, PA: Beidel, 1955), 247. Bushrod quotes E. Merton Coulter.

31. Lewis, 33.

32. Croushore, 167.

33. Ibid., 165.

34. Bushrod, 247.

35. Croushore, 54; Sears, 10.

36. Sears, 11.

37. Bruce Catton, *The Picture History of the Civil War* (New York: American Heritage, 1960), 369, 375.

38. Croushore, 144.

39. Catton, 379.

40. Virgil Carrington Jones, *Gray Ghosts and Rebel Raiders* (New York: Galahad, 1956), 102.

41. Sears, 4–5, 12.

42. Walton, 18, 23–24.

43. Croushore, 7, 96.

10

TACTICS AND STRATEGY

"I used to think. . .that I knew what muddy roads was."
—Private Edwin Weller

STRATEGY

There was little strategic direction given to federal forces beyond a roughly drawn plan by Lt. Gen. Winfield Scott to exhaust the resources of the Confederacy by blockading its ports and controlling the flow of goods on the Mississippi River. Known as the Anaconda Plan, this general outline was supplemented by the direct guidance provided by Lincoln from the White House. The strategy was essentially geographic and offensive. The South considered it an invasion, and the plan most certainly had all of the required defining characteristics. Although Scott was quickly replaced as the army commander, the three-pronged drive into the South he envisioned was essentially the strategic plan that won the war for the North.

   The Confederacy would effectively be cut into thirds. One prong was to operate along the Mississippi—simultaneously driving north through New Orleans and south from Kentucky. The objective, unrealistically optimistic in light of future events, was to control the river with a considerable economy of force. While not conquering extensive areas on either side of the river, the joint military and inland naval operations would effectively isolate the considerable agricultural resources of the western third of the Confederacy from the rest and make importation of foreign provisions from Europe through Mexico and Texas very difficult for the supply-starved Southerners.

   The second prong visualized an attack from Kentucky into middle and eastern Tennessee. This would remove the agricultural breadbasket of Tennessee from Confederate control, cut the railways between west and east, and support the pro-Union sympathizers who inhabited much of Kentucky and eastern Tennessee. The hard core of the South's nominal industrial base was found in a corridor from central Virginia south to Alabama with its few factories, powder mills, and blast furnaces. With a foothold in Tennessee firmly established, a great advance through this region would sweep into Georgia, through Atlanta, and into the Carolinas. Upon completion of this phase, the main Rebel army in Virginia would be isolated and placed between the pincer of federal armies driving from the north and the southwest.

   Finally, there was to be an advance down the eastern seaboard with Richmond as its objective. The South would be denied its capital as well as munitions plants, iron foundries, and a major railroad hub. It was hoped that with Richmond gone, Virginia, and possibly the entire South, might be driven from the war quickly. This eastern offensive particularly caught the popular sentiment of the North, and "On to Richmond" became a common rallying cry. However, it seemed to some observers that the drive to Richmond might be the least advisable strategy. The terrain of Northern Virginia was well suited to defense, obstructed by rivers, areas of dense undergrowth, mountains to the west, and the great bay of the Chesapeake to the east. Moreover, a major defeat of federal forces might expose Washington to counterattack and capture.

   The inability of the Federals to prosecute a more vigorous offensive in Northern Virginia was symptomatic of a defensive attitude among the political and military leaders in the capital, particularly Army Chief of Staff Henry W. Halleck, Secretary of War Edwin Stanton, and Abraham Lincoln. The federal army commanders were required to protect the capital, the lines of supply wagons, and an avenue of retreat, and at the same time counteract any initiatives of the enemy. The forces entombed in the Washington defenses under these policies, over 100,000 men, more than matched the size of all of Lee's forces, and the main federal field army was almost twice this number. Moreover, federal commanders were required to maintain armies of occupation in quickly conquered areas such as western Virginia and New Orleans.[1]

   The Confederate strategy was essentially defensive. To maintain their quest for independence, the Southern states needed only to resist the invading forces of the North until their infant government was recognized by the world community. For this reason they wished to be viewed as the victims of aggression. It was obvious to the Confederate leaders, if not the general public, that the Confederate government could function equally well anywhere within the Southern states and need not occupy any territory that they did not already hold. While no point was vital to the existence of the government, any successful attack on the lifeblood of the Confederacy's economic and physical infrastructure could easily disrupt the new nation.

Southern governors were somewhat taken aback by the concurrent disposition of state forces under their own officers and those delegated by the central government, but they acquiesced to the arrangement due to the exigent
circumstance of fending off Federal attacks. Unfortunately, Confederate
strategy continued to emphasize a total defense of its territory throughout
the war. Southern leaders were particularly worried about losing control
of areas where local Unionists might free the slaves and thereby instigate
widespread slave insurrections. They also feared the vast economic cost
represented by seized cotton, destroyed manors, and burned fields. These
factors caused the Confederates to disperse their forces somewhat more
widely than current military strategy would have dictated. Consequently,
the country was organized into an array of impracticably large departments
and districts based on state lines and geographical imperatives that were
not always adapted to the prosecution of the war.[2]

GEOGRAPHY

The state of Virginia immediately took on a leading role in the war because it faced the Federal capital at Washington directly across the Potomac River. The Confederate capital—transferred from Montgomery to
Richmond and surrounded by friendly secessionists—was a mere 100
miles from Washington. The Federal capital, however, was firmly set in a
niche on the Potomac cut out from the generally pro-Southern landscape
of Maryland. The 6th Michigan Infantry passing through Baltimore in
April 1861was stoned by a pro-secessionist mob and forced to reply with
musketry. Aware of its tenuous position, the Federal government rushed
troops from the North—particularly from Massachusetts and New York—
into the district to secure it.

Virginia experienced more than its fair share of the war. Four pivotal
military campaigns were fought on Virginia soil, making the region known
as northern Virginia the main theater of the Civil War in the east. These
campaigns were the First Manassas (Bull Run) campaign of 1861; the 1862
Peninsular campaign between the York and James Rivers; the Second Manassas, Fredericksburg, and Chancellorsville engagements of 1862; and
the series of battles from the Wilderness to Petersburg in 1864–65. The
major incursions of Southern forces into Maryland (1862) and Pennsylvania (1863), which ended in the battles of Antietam and Gettysburg, respectively, were initiated from bases in Virginia. Moreover, the Confederate
capital at Richmond was guarded primarily by General Robert E. Lee and
the Army of Northern Virginia.

As a primary theater of the war, Virginia's geography posed one of
the most important variables to Civil War operations. The mountainous
northwestern part of the state defected to the Union, and a Confederate attempt to regain it in July 1861 failed when U.S. Gen. George B. McClellan
won small battles at Rich Mountain and Carrick's Ford. What remained
of the commonwealth of Virginia, after the breakaway region became the

new pro-Union state of West Virginia,[3] was divided into eastern and western regions by the Blue Ridge Mountains, which rise at Harper's Ferry
and proceed southwesterly, dividing the Shenandoah Valley from the rest
of the state. With the exception of the line of hills pretentiously called the
Bull Run Mountains, the area was relatively flat. In the southeastern portion of the state was the Great Dismal Swamp, a 700-square mile bog that
historically provided a refuge for runaway slaves and made major military operations in the region difficult.

To the east of the Blue Ridge were two discernible areas, the tidewater
and the piedmont. The tidewater was on the coastal plain that bordered
the Chesapeake Bay, and it was from here to the south along the coast
that most of the large-scale cotton and tobacco plantations were located
along with their population of free blacks and slaves. The state was cut by
numerous rivers which flowed generally from the mountains of the west
to the Atlantic coast, each posing a natural obstacle to an invading army
from the North. The major rivers that flowed through the piedmont to the
tidewater had their origins in the Blue Ridge and included the Potomac,
the Rappahannock and the Rapidan, the York, and the James. The piedmont, although fairly open, was dissected by streams, creeks, and runs,
and had a large area of dense woods and scrub known as the Wilderness.

The rivers and their tributaries had worn gaps in the mountain ranges and hills that served as connections to the great valley of the Shenandoah River in the west. This river flowed northeast into the upper reaches of the Potomac at Harper's Ferry. The Shenandoah Valley pointed like a dagger at the city of Washington, yet it angled away to the southwest of Richmond to connect with the heart of the Confederate rail system. The valley boasted a good road, a branch of the Manassas Gap Railroad, and two waterways: the North and South Branches of the Shenandoah River. Although impractical for navigation, these branches joined at Front Royal after coming around the major topographical feature of the valley, Massanutten Mountain. This large ridge split the valley from Front Royal in the lower valley to Cross Keys in the upper valley, leaving a width of barely four miles. A federal line officer noted, "Its eastern flank and a long stretch of its front are covered by the winding gorge of the North Fork of the Shenandoah River. The only feasible road of attack is from the west over successive ranges of wooded hills which are themselves easily defensible." The geography of the valley was used with great effect by General Jackson to bewilder and evade the superior Federal forces sent against him in 1862.[4]

Of secondary importance to Virginia as a field of battle was the western theater, which centered on Tennessee. While the people of Tennessee voted overwhelmingly for secession, the eastern half of the state was decidedly pro-Union. This split in sentiment and the effort to bring Kentucky into the Confederate fold brought forth much of the guerrilla warfare that came to characterize the western theater of operations. Tennessee provided more troops to the war effort than any other Southern state—a total of 145,000 men, of whom 30,000 served with the Federals. Although Kentucky remained in the Union, a large pro-Southern sentiment in the state caused a number of its citizens to join the Confederate forces. So split was the population of the state that late in the war two 4th Kentucky Infantry regiments, one from each side, faced off in battle. Missouri was also divided in its sympathies, but the state was overrun by Federal forces by 1862. Nonetheless, one-quarter of all those who fought from Missouri did so for the South.

More than 450 large engagements and thousands of skirmishes were fought in Tennessee and the surrounding border areas of Kentucky, Mississippi, Georgia, and Alabama. While many were minor affairs in the ultimate scheme of things, several pivotal battles were fought there. These included the Battles of Forts Henry and Donelson, Shiloh, Chickamauga, Stones River, Chattanooga, Franklin, and Nashville.[5]

Geographically, Tennessee is divided into three regions: east, middle, and west Tennessee. Stretching across the state from Alabama to Kentucky is the Cumberland plateau of middle Tennessee, which includes the capital at Nashville and the Stones River Valley. This valley, along with its adjacent area, was a rich agricultural region in the 1860s and served as an important source of food supply for the Confederate forces.

The state was cut by both the Tennessee River and the Cumberland, which flowed into the Ohio River in its northwest corner. The Cumberland River allowed access across the heartland of the state. Unlike the waterways of Virginia, which could be used as defensive lines and might serve to hamper federal movements toward the south, the Mississippi and the western Tennessee Rivers were a "double barrel shotgun pointed at the heart of the South" because they had the potential of allowing deep penetrations by Union forces.[6]

The ability of the U.S. Navy ironclads and gunboats to exploit these waterways characterized many of the engagements in the western theater of the war. The South attempted to confound the Federal advantage in gunboats by building forts along the riverbanks. The battles at Fort Henry on the Tennessee, Fort Donelson on the Cumberland, Island Number 10, Vicksburg, and Port Hudson on the Mississippi were fought to provide free navigation by Union forces. The battle of Shiloh (Pittsburgh Landing) was fought on the banks of the Tennessee River, and Federal gunboats were able to bring fire to bear on the Confederates from the banks of the river at a pivotal point in the battle.

RAIDERS

Several of the most successful Confederate commanders were to take on the mantle of legend by prosecuting guerrilla warfare. Among these was Turner Ashby of the 7th Virginia Cavalry, who, "leaping over stone fences" and "crying out to his men to charge the enemy," was so impetuous that his recklessness sometimes caused him to be separated from his men. Ashby's early death in June 1862 left his unit and the entire South "heartbroken." The general's remains were "wrapped in a Confederate flag and tended by a guard of honor" to be buried at the University of Virginia.[7]

Another audacious small unit commander was John Singleton Mosby, the Gray Ghost. Mosby's name was feared by Federal privates because of his lightning attacks on their outposts and pickets across Northern Virginia. Lee recognized the partisan leader's boldness and tactical genius but berated him for centering his attention on supply wagons instead of the enemy's communications. Mosby's operations so frustrated General George A. Custer that he ordered six of Mosby's men executed after they were captured. One of these was a teenage boy. Mosby proposed hanging an equal number of Custer's men in retaliation. Lee sanctioned the executions of the Federals, who were chosen by lot from a group of prisoners. Mosby survived the war and wrote one of the more controversial histories of the conflict.[8]

Widely regarded as one of the most brilliant generals on either side, Nathan Bedford Forrest recruited and equipped a cavalry battalion at his own expense that destroyed railroads, captured stores, and generally disrupted Federal plans in the western theater. Federal soldiers feared this man, who killed in single combat more men than any other general officer of the war. He was said to have had 29 horses shot out from under him. Nonetheless, Forrest's reputation was tainted by his association with the massacre of black soldiers at Fort Pillow and his founding of the Ku Klux Klan.[9]

John Hunt Morgan raised a brigade of pro-Southern Kentucky horsemen and first achieved fame in 1862 by making a 1,000-mile raid through Kentucky and middle Tennessee. In 1863, just as the Confederacy was reeling from its loss at Gettysburg, Morgan crossed the Ohio River into the North and raided through Southern Indiana and Ohio. He was finally captured, but in November of the same year he made a daring escape back into the South.[10]

These raiders illustrated the South's advantage in fighting on the defensive in its own territory. With 2,500 men, Morgan and Forrest immobilized an invading army of 40,000. By successfully destroying lines of communication and worrying the flanks of federal columns, so-called "partisan rangers" became heroes in the eyes of the Southern public but came to be frowned upon by the Richmond government. Partisans were accused, with some justification, of acting the role of highwaymen and plunderers, especially in the border states.

The border states should have been ripe with recruits for the Confederate armies, but they were not. Most of the estimated 90,000 border residents who joined the Confederacy did so in the first year of the war. When

Southern raiders, or guerrillas, were tremendously successful in acquiring supplies destined for federal troops. The continued success of these raiders proved an embarrassment to federal commanders in areas of the South that had been occupied by Northern troops.

Gen. Braxton Bragg entered Kentucky in 1862, John Hunt Morgan, severely misreading the temper of his state, assured him that thousands of previously neutral Kentuckians would join him. In anticipation of being greeted as a liberator, Bragg brought wagonloads of spare rifles and ammunition with him to arm these men, but only a few hundred recruits were drawn to the Confederate banner. When the rebels withdrew to Tennessee after the battle of Perryville in October, Bragg took with him the same wagonloads of rifles "mostly still in their packing cases." Ironically, when Union forces entered and solidified their hold on the border South in 1863, they were rewarded by almost 100,000 recruits to the Federal army from among a formerly neutral population that had turned against the Confederacy after being exposed to the "frightful disorder" imposed on them by Southern guerrilla raids during the previous year. These added to an almost equal number of Unionists that had joined the federal cause at the beginning of the war, virtually replacing all of the Union casualties from the first two years of the war.[11]

Conversely, the Confederacy had depleted its recruitment base and eaten deeply into the larders of the pro-slavery, white non-combatants in the region. Never before in American history had civilian resources been so hard pressed by their fellows. Previously "the South, with its chivalric traditions and romantic self image, had been avidly solicitous of non-combatants." This view of warfare might be considered quaint by today's standards, yet the men who fought the Civil War felt that the unwritten rules of civilized combat should be honored. The raiders in their unbridled devotion to the cause had violated this principle. At Lee's insistence, orders were issued to combine all local partisan groups into the regular organization of the Confederate army in order to stem "irregularities" in partisan operations. The Confederate forces simply could not afford to lose the support of the civilian population.[12]

RAILROADS

The abominable condition of Southern roads during the rainy season and in the winter added to the importance of its railways. Although the South controlled only one-third of the railway mileage of the North, the Southern railways were strategically located within the theater of operations and were used with great tactical skill by Confederate commanders. Virginia was crossed by several important railways that could be used with great effect to move supplies and manpower throughout the eastern theater. At First Bull Run, Confederate reinforcements were brought to the field by rail in time to turn the tide of battle and rout the Federals.

Much of the northern rail mileage was used for the distribution of manufactures in the Northeast. The most prominent railways—the Pennsylvania, the Erie, and the New York Central—were outside the war zone. Those in New England were almost entirely shut off from army transport.

However, the north-south lines—the Illinois Central and the Cleveland, Columbus, and Cincinnati—prospered on army business.

Baltimore became the hub of federal railroad activities, and the federal authorities located most of their repair facilities in and around the city. The Baltimore and Ohio Railway, with a right of way in the war zone, was strategically the most important line of communications between Washington and Ohio. In May 1861, General Jackson was able to "steal" 300 railroad cars and 56 locomotives from the B. & O. in a single operation. Much of this rolling stock was horse-drawn down the Shenandoah Valley Pike from Winchester to Strasburg to be used on the Southern railways. At a later date, when loss of the line to federal forces seemed imminent, Jackson was given the task of destroying the 400-mile railway. He burned the bridges, derailed the freight cars, and burned more than forty engines. The Federals learned to repair the damage quickly, but raids along the B. & O. were a constant source of trouble to Federal commanders.

The railways of the western theater, which had been built in the 1850s, far in advance of any immediate need, proved very important. The line between Louisville, Kentucky, and Nashville, Tennessee, provided a vital link for the invading Federals. Yet no strategic railways were built, and no thought was given to the development of the principles of military operations and maintenance of railways. "In no direction could cars run long distances without changes and delays." Freight, as well as passen-

A *Leslie's* illustration of a group of five new locomotive engines produced by the U.S. Military Rail Road (note the USMMR on the tender) in 1864. Sketch by F. B. Schell.

Confederate Railways
in the Western Theater

gers and their luggage, often had to detrain and cross town from one line to another either by wagon or on foot. The construction of five short connections between competing lines, for a total of 140 miles, would have provided the Federals with an uninterrupted railway from Washington to the entire North.[13]

An obstacle to rail transport in all parts of the country was the different gauges, or track widths, used on different lines. In New York and New England a gauge of 4 feet 8½ inches was used. In Ohio, and to the west and south of Philadelphia, the gauge was 4 feet 10 inches. Some rails were placed as much as 6 feet apart in special cases. Many ingenious expedients were used to overcome this problem. These included third rails, wide wheels that would accommodate both narrow and wide track, and adjustable train axles. The longest single gauge track of the war belonged to the

Atlantic and Great Western line, which connected New York with St. Louis more than 1,000 miles away.[14]

There was an attempt by Richmond to adopt a standard gauge of five feet throughout the nation,[15] but a national dedication to the ideal of states' rights generally got in the way of any standardization. The length of Southern railway mileage, the tonnage of rolling stock and engines, and the number of interconnecting systems were severely limited throughout the war. Nonetheless, there were more than 1,000 miles of strategically important track in Tennessee alone with connections passing to the southeast. The heart of this rail network lay in Corinth, Mississippi. The line connecting Cairo, Illinois, with Corinth drove directly south and continued on to New Orleans, creating a network that pumped vital supplies from the Gulf north to Tennessee and east to Virginia. The Confederates were therefore theoretically able to use their railways to bring troops from the Deep South into Virginia or the western theater. In 1862, more than 2,500 men and their equipment were brought to Nashville from Louisiana in just two weeks—a remarkable feat given the dilapidated state of the railways and the fact that the troops had to wait for available cars or march between unconnected lines.

A major limitation on the use of Southern railways for military purposes remained a lack of maintenance. In April 1863, Lee wrote to the War Office that "unless the railroads be repaired, so as to admit of speedier transportation of supplies," he could not maintain his position.[16] Damaged cars and worn-out engines became the victims of the South's limited industrial technology. A damaged locomotive boiler might take more than a thousand man-hours to repair if the boiler plate were found to do the job. Tracks and especially wooden ties were simply unable to withstand the wear and tear of wartime demand. "There were no means at hand for their repair. The wooden ties rotted, the machinery was almost exhausted, the rails were worn out, and thus the speed and capacity of the trains were greatly reduced." An engine could be required to lug a supply train weighing up to 120 tons.[17]

ROADS

If railroads were the arteries of the nation, then the roads were its veins.[18] A long march on dirt roads was almost inevitable for the soldiers of both armies. The very poor condition of Southern roads and turnpikes was one of the few circumstances for which the Federal army did not provide in its initial offensive planning. The Confederates understood the defensive qualities of many of the roads in northern Virginia, which were "very narrow—mere ditches," surrounded by dense forests of second growth pine or virgin oak that would snarl the movement of an invading army with its wagons and artillery.[19] "We were not able to march but three miles . . . as we are never allowed to march any faster than the artillery and baggage train can move." With high humidity and abundant vegetation, the rain-soaked road surfaces of Virginia remained wet and were churned into a sticky morass that was barely passable. "Yesterday we had another very hard rain storm which makes the roads much worse than before," wrote a soldier in March 1863. "I used to think when at the North that I knew what muddy roads was, but they do not compare at all with the roads here."[20]

Northern commanders greatly anticipated the improvement of the roads when the mud froze as it did in the North during November and December, providing a supportive surface on which to march troops, haul supplies, or move artillery. However, increased daytime temperatures prevented the freezing of the roadways until much later in the season than Northerners expected. Federal operations in the early winter of 1863, therefore, encountered an unforeseen obstacle. "We have experienced a severe snow storm," wrote a soldier in a letter home, "but the last two days have been so warm that it has all nearly disappeared making the mud much deeper than it was before. It will now be impossible for the Army of the Potomac to make a forward movement short of five or six weeks."[21]

The armies spent considerable time and effort building "corduroy" roads by laying bundles of saplings and small tree trunks across the muddiest parts of the road surface. Although uneven and bumpy, they allowed the wheeled vehicles to pass without sinking into the mud. Corduroy was very hard on the foot soldier and almost impossible for the cavalry, who often opted to ride across the open fields. Plank roads, as the name suggests, were municipal roads built with several layers of wooden planking covered with dirt. The Orange Plank Road and the Orange Turnpike, connecting Fredericksburg and Chancellorsville with the valley of western Virginia, were two of the good roads that proved critical to the strategy of the opposing forces.

The Columbia Pike south out of Nashville was a well-maintained road of macadam—a type of compressed broken stone. The Valley Pike, the main road that ran down the center of the Shenandoah Valley, was also of macadam and proved a veritable highway for the South. Flanked by the North Branch of the Shenandoah River and the western part of the Manassas Gap Railroad, the advantages of such a surface to the movement of military forces were obvious. The Valley Pike played a prominent role in Jackson's Valley campaign of 1862, and in subsequent years it figured prominently in the operations of Confederate general Jubal Early no less than it did in the operations of federal generals Franz Sigel, David Hunter, and Philip Sheridan. The battles at Cross Keys, Port Republic, New Market, Front Royal, Cedar Creek, and Kernstown were overshadowed only by the more than a dozen seesaw occupations of the city of Winchester, which straddled the pike.[22]

MILITARY ORGANIZATION

The organization of the Federal and Confederate armies was based upon the division of the available number of infantry soldiers into manageable tactical units. A clerk in the Confederate War Office wrote in April 1861: "A great many separate companies are accepted [for enlistment] . . . provided they have arms. . . What a deal of annoyance and labor it will be to organize these into battalions, regiments, brigades, and divisions. And then comes the appointment of staff and field officers."[23]

Regiments were often raised geographically with all or almost all of the men and officers coming from the same community. The commanding officer of the regiment was its colonel. While many of these men were political appointees, a great number were active leaders on the field of battle. In the absence of losses among the officers due to battle or disease, the lieutenant colonel was the second-in-command and was in charge of preparing the troops for battle in terms of drill. A major—a headquarters staff officer whose responsibilities were still being developed during the Civil War—usually tended to the regimental paperwork and dealt with the commissary. Captains commanded individual companies through a network of subalterns (lieutenants) and NCOs. The regiment might also have a chaplain, a surgeon, a quartermaster, and a number of assistants.

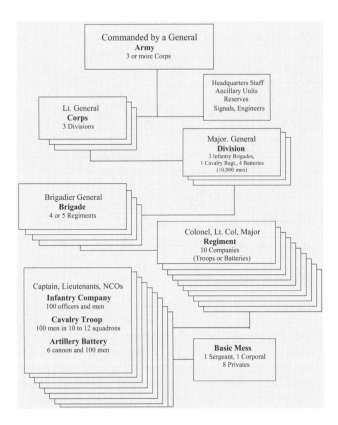

Typical Organization of a Federal Army in the Civil War

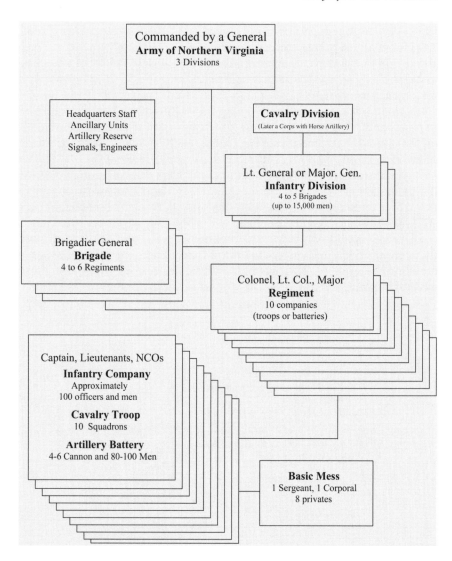

Typical Organization of a Confederate Army in the Civil War

In the first major battle of the war, First Manassas or Bull Run, 60,000 men were divided into numerous divisions and brigades composed of regiments. Both sides had about 30,000 men available to fight—the largest forces seen on the North American continent up to that time. None of the senior field officers or generals, even those with combat experience, had ever directed one-tenth of this number. The Federals were organized under General Irvin McDowell into five divisions, representing ten brigades of four to seven regiments or batteries of artillery. The South fielded two similarly configured armies, under P.G.T. Beauregard and Joseph E.

Johnston, divided into six and four brigades, respectively. There were also numerous legions, companies of volunteers, and militias that defy placement in an ordinary structural organization. In a blend of confusion, incompetence, and providence only 60 percent of these men saw action in the first major battle of the war, yet almost 10 percent of these became casualties. This result taught many lessons to both sides about organization. By 1863 army organization had become somewhat standardized, and enlistments for three years, or the duration of the war, were common.

To the individual soldier, the 8 or 10 men who were his messmates were the most important part of the army organization. Several messes formed a battalion, or half a company, under the command of a junior officer and various company NCOs. "Each sergeant except the 1st [sergeant] has the general supervision of 2 corporals & their squads" and these NCOs "have to look after the provisions, clothing, washing, equipments & in short all the wants of the men." While the company was regarded as the main unit of maneuver, the squad was the basic unit for camp duties, posting guards, and daily living.[24]

In the federal army, there were 20 battalions, or 10 companies, per regiment with an approximate strength of 1,200 men. The Confederates, forsaking the battalion as a formal unit, simply had 10 companies per regiment. Two companies were designated to act as skirmishers each day and formed the advance and rear guard for each regiment. On paper, Southern regiments were larger than their federal counterparts, with strengths up to 1,550 men—an advantage that disappeared as the war progressed and the South suffered from a lack of manpower.

It was not unusual for a regiment to lose 30 percent of its men while awaiting deployment to the front. A federal officer observed, "There is a constant drain on the troops in the field, much heavier than a civilian would suppose. Something like one-fifth of the men who enlist are not tough enough nor brave enough to be soldiers." The men "disappeared" in various ways, including death by hardship and disease, through shirking and hanging back, or through outright desertion. Others were tolled off on special duties as "bakers, hospital nurses, wagoners, [or] quartermaster's drudges," and a fair number were working out the sentences of court-martial.[25]

Generally, a regiment stayed together for the duration of the war and fought without replacements until its numbers were so exhausted by death, disease, or disability that it was no longer practical for it to continue to exist. It was thought that the relative stability of the same men eating and living together for the duration of their enlistments fostered cooperation, raised morale, and sustained each soldier's courage under fire. While this system produced units composed of battle-hardened veterans, a lengthy conflict sometimes resulted in widespread mourning among the families of a single town as its young men were continually exposed to the carnage of battle. Newly raised regiments with muster rolls filled with recruits lacked the hard-won experience of veteran units and were more likely to break and run when hard pressed. Veterans quickly learned to hold their ground on defense, but they were more likely to "go to ground" or take advantage of available cover during a charge. A federal officer bemoaned the policy. "It is a pity that our new levies cannot be clapped into the old organizations . . . They would be something like veterans in a fortnight; whereas it will take six months to bring them to the same point under their own raw officers and sergeants."[26]

Regiments from the same geographical area were often brigaded together to achieve a greater feeling of unity and to maintain the fiction of state control. The brigade, commanded by a brigadier general, was the smallest practical tactical unit. Brigades were assigned to divisions, divisions to corps, and corps to armies. The brigade's several regiments tended to serve together through many campaigns, although their number varied somewhat depending on their individual strength. As few veteran regiments were ever brought up to strength, it is difficult to determine the numbers of soldiers in a brigade by simply counting the regiments on each side.

Many hundreds of men "belong to an army but never fight," observed one officer. These included "the cooks, the officers' servants, the hospital gangs, the quartermaster's people, the `present sick,' and the habitual skulkers." The last were particularly disliked by their fellows because, while they failed to have the "courage" to desert, they also lacked the courage to take their place on the front lines. After some months of active campaigning a brigade might look like a pitiable force. Even though composed of at least a dozen regiments, some brigades numbered not more than 800 men, "all jaded and dispirited."[27]

Confederates tended to identify their place in the army establishment by referring to the names of their commanders, while federal soldiers utilized the numbers and letters assigned to their units. So common was this difference that when Lt. Gen. James Longstreet, lost after a nighttime arrival on a battlefield, and calling out to some soldiers asking their unit, received their prompt numerical designations. He was quickly convinced that he had blundered into the federal lines and made a discreet retreat in the opposite direction.[28]

A Confederate soldier therefore might have his mail sent to Pvt. Jonathan Reb, Army of Northern Virginia, 43rd North Carolina Regiment, Captain Hatcher's Company, Daniel's Brigade of Rode's Division. A Northern soldier might describe his place in the federal army as Pvt. William Yank, 2nd Battalion, Company A, 124th New York Volunteers, serving in the 1st Brigade of the 2nd Division, III Corps of the Army of the Potomac.

ARMIES

To prosecute an effective war strategy it was necessary to wage war in more than one theater at a time. Due to the enormity of the boundary between the North and the South and the need to garrison the border states, both the Federals and the Confederates divided their military strength

The cavalry arm of the federal army (above) began the war with a decided disadvantage when compared to the South's mounted force. The Confederate cavalry literally rode circles around the federal army on at least three occasions during the war. Not until the Battle of Brandy Station, Virginia, did the federal cavalry show any ability to cope with Southern horsemen. James and Dorothy Volo photo.

into large groups called armies. Armies were commanded by a full general or lieutenant general.

Federal armies were designated by the names of the rivers along which they pursued their campaigns, as in the Army of the Potomac, Cumberland, James, Ohio, or Tennessee. Briefly, there was an Army of West Virginia. Not all of these existed simultaneously. The Confederates generally named their armies for the territory they were defending, as in the Army of Northern Virginia, Mississippi, or Tennessee. Overall control of federal armies resided in the Army Chief of Staff, General Henry W. Halleck, and in the President. The Confederates had no overall commander other than Jefferson Davis—each area commander reporting directly to him. Lee, therefore, had authority over only the Army of Northern Virginia. A restrained Davis, however, was less willing to interfere in strategy and day-to-day operations than the more willing Lincoln.

Federal and Confederate armies were surprisingly similar in their structure. Confederate armies were almost always smaller than federal armies, but the advantage of numbers could not always be brought to bear. In 1862 the Army of the Potomac under General Ambrose Burnside numbered up to 250,000 men. The principal Confederate force of General Robert E. Lee's Army of Northern Virginia was 70,000 men strong during most of the war, but Lee was often able to convince the Federals that he had two to three times this number.

The army headquarters was made up of the staff officers and some troops assigned to protect the establishment and the commander from attack. A troop of cavalry was usually detached to serve as couriers. A signal unit and an engineering unit were almost always present. Headquarters personnel alone could number up to 3,000 individuals. Staff duties were primarily organizational rather than directly related to combat. The adjutant general kept track of all the operations of the different branches and did most of the paperwork for the commander. The inspector general was responsible for training, discipline, and fighting efficiency. The provost, or military police, and the judge advocate's office, or courts-martial, were operated under the inspector general. The quartermaster general assumed all those duties that related to providing for the troops and controlled service units such as supply-train troops, hospital personnel, and payroll clerks.

CORPS AND DIVISIONS

An army was really too large a unit for tactical purposes. While European armies had always been subdivided in some manner, Civil War armies generally followed the structural pattern established by Napoleon in 1804 and were subdivided into corps. The corps was a major conceptual breakthrough in military science and came to be composed of "separate, self-contained, and interchangeable parts," having its own balance of infantry, artillery, and mounted components. Napoleon mastered the armies of Europe with this organization, and his methods and strategy had been emphasized at the military schools and academies in which most Civil War general officers had learned their trade.[29]

While both sides in the Civil War established a separate cavalry corps enhanced by horse artillery designed for raiding and scouting, individual cavalry regiments were often attached to corps to provide mounted scouts, flankers, or videttes. An observer of Southern cavalry organization noted: "These are the troops for quick marches, surprises, and captures. And our people, even down to little boys, are expert riders . . . We should want all our men [to] fight in the saddle who could not or would not march in the infantry. And mounted men are content to use the double-barreled shotgun—one barrel for ball, the other for buck-shot and close quarters."[30]

While the federal armies consisted of several corps, the Confederates initially resisted their adoption, relying instead on a larger and less independent unit called the division. After 1862, however, the Confederacy incorporated their divisions into corps to provide for better articulation of forces and to allow a larger number of senior field officers to be in direct control of the troops in battle. The new corps commanders, particularly Jackson and Longstreet, whose talents may have initiated the change in organization, were made more independent of the army commander than previously. They were given additional rank to complement their new status and responsibility. Some of the best soldiers of the war rose to fame as corps commanders.

Civil War forces exhibited an amazing articulation and speed of maneuver for armies that moved on foot. Military theorists believed that corps, separated by no more than a day's march, could move more rapidly than an army marching in column together. An army column might move with its rear more than a day's march from the advanced elements. A force of equal size, advancing in parallel columns as corps, extended over a larger front and a much shorter length, as the corps individually had more roads over which to travel. Such a formation could cover a wider territory when foraging, had a greater possibility of finding the enemy, and could concentrate quickly.

In the Gettysburg campaign the Federals fielded seven infantry corps, which concentrated on the sleepy town along the many roads that intersected there. In anticipation of the invasion of Pennsylvania, Lee had reorganized his army into three large corps with a total of nine divisions. The Southern corps were almost twice the size of their federal counterparts so that the South had an initial numerical advantage as the head of the column approached on the first day. The advantages of marching in corps notwithstanding, the rear of Lee's army and much of his cavalry did not arrive until the second day of the battle, a fateful circumstance for Pickett's division, chosen to make the third day's charge because it had remained unengaged. By then the Federals (93,000 men) had a small advantage in numbers over the Confederates (78,000 men).

TACTICS

Civil War commanders relied on linear tactics and the weight of the bayonet charge to fight and win their battles. The ability of long lines of troops to face each other across open rolling fields and woodlots, banging away with a deadly hail of musket fire within sight of one another, was extraordinary. Once engaged, the roar of musketry became almost continuous. Units maneuvered under the weight of this fire in great phalanxes trying to bring flanking fire on the enemy position. Either through the weight of fire or through the terror of the bayonet charge, the ultimate goal was to cause the enemy line to break, become disordered, and flee the field.

The introduction of the long-range rifled musket, considered an improvement in infantry weapons over the old smoothbore, has been identified as the cause of the mass casualties characteristic of Civil War battles where linear tactics were used. All armies acting on the defense have always had some advantage over the attacker, and period tactical theory suggested that the offense needed a three to one ratio with regard to numbers to overcome these advantages. Nonetheless, linear tactics were generally effective during the war even if they limited individual initiative and hampered the tactical decision making accorded subordinate officers. Failed mass assaults like those of the federals at Fredericksburg and Cold Harbor, or of the Confederates on the last day of Gettysburg (Pickett's charge) were not the fault of the tactical formations used but rather of the tactical decisions of the commanders who ordered them.

Certainly, the new rifled weapon was more accurate than smoothbores at short ranges (80–100 yards), which justifies the evaluation of its impact on Civil War casualties. Yet at the longer practical range of the weapon (upwards of 600 yards) the curved parabolic trajectory (arc-like path) of the relatively slow moving bullets (up to 40 percent slower than modern ones) produced for the attackers a safe-zone of between 200 and 300 yards in depth, or half the theoretical field of fire as measured from the shooter, where the bullets passed harmlessly high over the heads of the attackers. Studies suggest that the so-called primary killing zone was about 100 yards deep immediately in front of the defensive position with a secondary killing zone beginning about 300 yards further out and shrinking in lethality until it reached the practical limit of the range of the weapon. At the extreme lethal range of the weapon (900 yards), the theoretical deadly space was only 12 yards deep, and the likelihood of hitting a human target even if the shooter knew how to correct his aim became extremely small. The same characteristic of flight affected the efficiency of artillery, which was responsible nonetheless for 40 percent of all Civil War casualties largely because gunners were trained to compensate for the curved trajectory over artillery's greater overall range. Firing up or down a significant slope—as at the Battle of Missionary Ridge where it was found that the majority of shot from both attackers and defenders went into the treetops—also produced a distortion in the path of a bullet if steps were not taken to correct for the effects of gravity especially at long ranges.

Most Civil War soldiers did not spend their time in such analyses. Yet in the safe-zone, attacking veteran troops learned by experience to "hunker down" and "go to ground" behind rocks and trees or in depressions in the earth as their comrade before and behind fell to enemy fire. On the defensive, "the vast majority of soldiers in the Union and Confederate armies received no training in estimating distances and therefore were not prepared to effectively fire their muskets at long-range targets." Officers and NCOs constantly admonished the men under their command to "aim low" in order to offset this characteristic of Civil War musket fire.

Moreover, without the aid of optical devices like telescopic sights, it was difficult to identify specific targets at extreme ranges leaving soldiers the option of withholding their fire until the enemy approached or indiscriminately lobbing bullets into a distant mass of enemy troops in the hope of hitting something. "Civil War commanders and soldiers alike preferred to wait until the enemy came quite close before opening fire," a distance (between 100 and 120 yards) found by battlefield researchers to be quite consistent with the range (if not the poor accuracy) of smoothbore muskets from the previous century.[31]

Many American officers held to the optimistic idea that the rifled musket would make each soldier under their command a consummate marksmen. Yet even with improved rifled muskets, the estimated 3 million bullets fired at the Battle of Gettysburg produced fewer than 60, 000 casualties, requiring 50 musket shots to produce one hit on the enemy (a two percent efficiency of fire) even if all those wounded or killed by artillery, bayonets, and edged weapons during the battle are totally ig-

Besides adding color to the display of battle, flag bearers and drummers served a practical purpose on the battlefield. It was a great honor to be chosen as a flag bearer, and only a very brave man was willing to accept the appointment. James Volo photo.

nored. Civil War soldiers commonly brought 60 rounds into the field with them in their kit; and although additional ammunition was available from battalion wagons, a number of period studies regarding the use of rifled musket in the Crimean War of the previous decade had shown that this was the average used by a soldier shooting all day at appropriate targets. A properly trained soldier, therefore, managed in theory only to take out his opposite number in a full day's fighting—a grinding mutual attrition also characteristic of the American Civil War that may have added to the overall indecisiveness of its combat.[32]

Military opponents commonly tried to avoid battle until each saw some advantage to the possible outcome that would shift the probabilities of success in their favor. A general seeking battle commonly tried to trap the enemy against an obstacle such as a river, swamp, or mountain range or to turn his flank with the potential of forcing a battle on the enemy in a less than advantageous position. The "strategic turning maneuver" and the advantage of operating on "interior lines" gave the field commander the ability to entangle a stronger enemy in battle by concentrating his forces at a predetermined point in space or at a specified point in time. If positioned on interior lines, his forces had the inherent advantages of shorter distances to travel than the surrounding enemy. By concentrating a higher proportion of his forces than the enemy could engage at a single point, a general could defeat the enemy in detail and turn to fight at another point. Napoleon had proved the value of such maneuvers on the battlefields of Europe, and they had been part of the course of training in most military schools. Both Confederate and Federal commanders utilized these principles, and this somewhat offset the advantages inherent in such tactics.

ANCILLARY UNITS

Communications were particularly important to the management of a battle when separate parts of the army were spread across miles of war zone. The use of flag bearers and drummers was essential for the maintenance of alignment and the transmission of orders on the company and regimental level; but across greater distances, a more effective method of managing the army was needed. During the 1850s, the U.S. Army had adopted a "wig wag" flag system for field communications. Engineers sometimes built high wooden towers to increase the range of visibility for the flag system. Flags remained the principal means of passing orders and intelligence for both the federal and Confederate armies throughout the war.

At the outbreak of hostilities, both armies lacked a military telegraph system. While the Confederacy continued to rely almost solely on flags and civilian telegraph lines, the Federals established a military telegraph to supplement the older system. The Signal Corps advocated the use of "flying" telegraphic teams organized around light telegraphic wagons that would move with the army, erect telegraph lines, and gain tactical control on the battlefield with the use of dial-type message encoding equipment. The rival U.S. Military Telegraph Service obtained its equipment and personnel from the existing civilian companies and relied on the more common Morse type telegraphic equipment. The Washington office of the U.S. Military Telegraph Service quickly became a sanctuary for President Lincoln where "he could escape other cares of his office and obtain a little quiet, except for the clatter of the telegraph keys."[33]

MEDICAL SERVICE

The medical services of the armed forces were almost nonexistent. The federal army began the war with fewer than 120 surgeons and assistant surgeons, and some of these were dismissed for suspected disloyalty and served with the Confederate forces. Medical officers and their assistants were commonly assigned to individual regiments, and musicians served as stretcher bearers.[34]

Prior to the Civil War the U.S. Army had not provided ambulances for the wounded and sick. In 1859 experimental carts were tested on the western plains and a less than satisfactory two-wheel version was adopted. Not until 1863 did the federal army organize and outfit a formal ambulance corps for the Army of the Potomac. Under General Order No. 85 only four-wheel, two-horse carts would be used as ambulances. Each ambulance had five men assigned as stretcher bearers and drivers. Three ambulances were permanently allocated to each infantry regiment, two to each cavalry regiment, and one to each artillery battery. Moreover, two army wagons were designated to carry only medical supplies for each corps, and two more were placed at the division level. "Obviously, this organization was sorely needed, but it fell far short of the real need," as three ambulances were "hardly adequate" to support a regiment of 1,000 men.[35]

Once off the battlefield the plight of the wounded was complicated by limited medical knowledge, malnutrition, and disease. While American military hospitals were better than those in Europe, they were nonetheless inadequate. Civilian corpsmen, hired by the army at $20.50 per month to staff army hospitals, often proved unreliable. A nursing service, directed by Dorothea Dix and staffed by women, had been established to care for the wounded and sick in the numerous soldiers' rests and regimental hospitals, but the recruitment of nurses was hobbled by the strict "moral" requirements Dix placed on potential candidates. Women were required to be of high moral character, no less than thirty years of age, plain looking, and unadorned. There was no requirement that they be efficient or capable.

In March 1863, Secretary of War Edwin M. Stanton established a Corps of Invalids from among the "walking wounded" and "convalescent soldiers" of the army to serve as nurses and medical aides. More than 60,000 men ultimately served in the invalid corps "scattered randomly" among the regiments of the army. Although only 42 members of the corps were killed in action, more than 1,600 died of the diseases to which they were exposed in the sick wards. The invalid corps concept received little support from the army hierarchy, and General Grant opposed all plans for retaining it as a part of the postwar army.[36]

Thousands of Catholic nuns served as nurses in the federal military hospitals of Boston, New York, Philadelphia, Baltimore, Washington, and other cities. Sisters of Charity, Sisters of Mercy, and Sisters of Saint Vincent de Paul were all conspicuous in their unique religious habits. The nuns volunteered to serve without pay even though they were often abused by anti-Catholic hospital personnel and patients. Their patience, skill, and persistence won over a good number of bigots. "My mind was filled with prejudice," wrote one soldier. "I did not believe that anything good could come from the Sisters. But now I see my mistake all too clearly."[37]

Catholic sisters were "conspicuously neutral" in their attitude toward the war. Confederate hospitals in Richmond, Charleston, Nashville, and New Orleans were also staffed with at least some Catholic nuns. The sisters consistently failed to leave their work when the vagaries of war changed the nature of the occupying force from South to North, and in Vicksburg they suffered the siege and ensuing bombardment with the beleaguered of the city. The sisters proved to be expert medical and surgical nurses, as they had experienced service in asylums and civilian hospitals during their long novitiates. A Southern woman noted that the work of the sisters made "all the difference in the world" in the Confederate hospitals of Richmond.[38]

A number of civilian organizations helped to fill the need for additional medical care. The Women's American Association for Relief was closely associated with a number of eminent doctors in New York and furnished medical supplies to the army. Beyond this, the U.S. Sanitary Commission made provisions for the relief of the sick, provided ambulances, and cared for the wounded and the dead. Commission representatives, operating in the east and in the west, oversaw the diet and personal cleanliness of the soldiers in camp, provided housing for white refugee families, and raised money to expand their work. A single Sanitary Commission fundraiser in New York City raised over $1 million. A woman wrote, "The amount realized will no doubt do much toward relieving the poor wounded and suffering soldiers than all the surgeons do. No one can know how much good is done by the Sanitary Commission who is not in the Army."[39]

The South mounted a less formal assault on the medical chaos that plagued the Confederate forces. Less than thirty surgeons and surgeon's assistants from the old army chose to serve with the Confederacy, and wounded or sick men were often left to the tender care of their mates or the local populace. The military hospitals of the South were overwhelmed by the task before them, and wounded men were often shipped home to recuperate under the care of their families. Those who were capable, but still considered invalids, were formed into local militias and railroad guards, rather than hospital orderlies, by the manpower-hungry state governments.

Ambulances were provided by subscription. A newly painted Confederate ambulance, apparently donated by a well-meaning supporter from Fairfax, was among the early acquisitions of federal pickets in Northern Virginia. "This capture was an object of much curiosity around the Federal camp near Alexandria. Soldiers stood off and stared at it in awe . . . an omen of what might lie in store for them, this wagon designed for toting the wounded or the dead."[40]

MORAL AWAKENING

Sincere religious reflection characterized both armies as the war wore on. The Christian Commission and its western affiliate were late in forming, and there is some dispute over the role they played in the war. Both sprang from an association of the YMCA, the American Bible Society, and the American Tract Society, and they were somewhat more evangelical in their agenda than the Sanitary Commission. Most historians agree that the Christian Commissions provided quality reading materials for the troops and established a moral standard for the soldiers of the federal army. However, their agenda was essentially religious in nature. Although there was some friction between the various organizing groups, no less than $500 million was raised by the Christian Commissions for religious and philanthropic purposes.[41]

Most regiments had resident chaplains. One Confederate general, Leonidas Polk, was a consecrated bishop of the Episcopal Church. Religious tracts and Bibles were circulated throughout the army camps. Nonetheless, federal captain J. W. De Forest observed that "the men are not as good as they were once; they drink harder and swear more and gamble deeper." The same officer noted, however, that "the swearing mania was irrepressible. In the excitement of the charge it seemed as if every extremity of language was excusable, providing it would help toward victory." Bible societies, moral reform organizations, and social uplift associations of all kinds sent missionaries and representatives into the field in an attempt to improve the physical and moral environment of the troops.[42]

Public demonstrations of piety and religious worship, organized by ministers, priests, lay preachers, and the men themselves, were common events in camp and were well attended by the troops. General Jackson's fanatical Presbyterian evangelical devotion came to be almost stereotypical of Confederate religious sentiment. Nonetheless, when two dozen general officers of the Confederate army were seen at the same church service in 1864, it was suggested that "less piety and more drilling of commands would suit the times better."[43]

WOMEN AT WAR

Women were active in all of the efforts to improve the morality of the troops, and, for the first time, the female presence with the army was not solely represented by the traditional camp followers. While it has been proven that a substantial number of women were able to pass themselves off as men and serve in the armed forces, their number was too small to affect any advantage or disadvantage to the troops. Most women chose to act in less startling ways to support the war effort. A number of war-related jobs were filled by women. Females served as clerks in the clothing branch of the Quartermaster's Department and filled the ammunition cartridges and artillery shells with powder at the armories, laboring at this dangerous and exacting task for low wages. Both sides utilized women in these capacities.[44]

A number of wives and female relatives traveled with the army to sew, nurse, and wash clothes. Federal captain John W. De Forest was constantly plagued by his wife's requests to join him on the field, and many of his responses to her were phrased in such a way as to discourage her gently. Confederate general John B. Gordon had his beautiful young wife with him at all times on campaign. Fanny Gordon "turned her two children, aged four and six, over to Gordon's mother, climbed into a buggy, and with one of the family slaves driving she followed her man." Generals John C. Breckinridge and Thomas Rosser brought their wives along as well when things were quiet—much to the chagrin of their superior, General Jubal Early, who was driven to "distraction" by women on campaign. But Mrs. Gordon was there all the time, and Early was overheard to say, "I wish the Yankees would capture Mrs. Gordon and hold her till this war is over."[45]

Major General Benjamin Butler, in charge of the occupied city of New Orleans, may have made the most insulting gesture of the entire war with regard to women. He declared that since federal officers had been "subjected to repeated insults from the women" of that city, any lady would, upon repetition of the offense, "be regarded and held liable to be treated as a woman of the town plying her vocation." The order was severely protested in the South and in Europe.[46] Nonetheless, prostitutes and women of loose morals were much in evidence in the Army of the Potomac under General Joseph Hooker. Historians disagree on the etymology of the term "hooker," which may or may not proceed from this circumstance as a synonym for prostitute. Nonetheless, a righteous general officer from among the federal forces noted, "The condition of morals among officers who [find] congenial companionship in the society of such women is apparent and needs no coloring from pen or pencil."[47]

NOTES

1. Thomas A. Lewis, *The Guns of Cedar Creek* (New York: Bantam, 1991), 51.

2. Archer Jones, *Confederate Strategy from Shiloh to Vicksburg* (Baton Rouge: Louisiana State University Press, 1991), 8–27.

3. West Virginia was to propose a constitution in which gradual emancipation would take place after July 4, 1863. It prohibited slavery but required freed blacks to remove themselves from the state. Jordan, 20.

4. James H. Croushore, ed., *A Volunteer's Adventure, by Captain John W. De Forest* (New Haven: Yale University Press, 1949), 192.

5. General Joe Wheeler fought 26 rearguard actions in just two weeks in 1862.

6. Shelby Foote, *The Civil War: A Narrative, Fort Sumter to Perryville* (New York: Vintage, 1986), 173.

7. Richard Armstrong, *Seventh Virginia Cavalry* (Lynchburg: H. E. Howard, 1992), 32–37; Ashby, 216–220, 269–275.

8. Mosby. Mosby was almost the only defender of Stuart's actions before and after the battle. Today, Stuart's leading apologist is Mark Nesbit, *Saber and Scapegoat: J.E.B. Stuart and the Gettysburg Controversy* (Mechanicsburg: Stackpole, 1994). Nesbit dispels many "lost cause" myths surrounding Stuart's actions and attempts to justify the cavalry leader's decisions at the time of the campaign.

9. Brian Steel Wills, *A Battle from the Start: The Life of Nathan Bedford Forrest* (New York: HarperCollins, 1992), 1–3.

10. James M. McPherson, *Battle Cry of Freedom* (New York: Oxford University Press, 1988), 514–515, 763.

11. William W. Freehling, *The South vs The South: How Anti-Confederate Southerners Shaped the Course of the Civil War* (New York: Oxford University Press, 2001), 60.

12. V.C. Jones, 107; Lewis, 59.

13. Francis A. Lord, "The United States Military Railroad Service: Vehicle to Victory," *Civil War Times Illustrated, October 1962*, 6–11, 46–50.

14. Emerson David Fite, *Social and Industrial Conditions in the North During the Civil War* (Williamstown: Corner House, 1976), 56.

15. Ibid., 57n.

16. Miers, 187.

17. Cozzens, 32; David B. Sabine, "Resources Compared: North Versus South," *Civil War Times Illustrated, February 1968*, 5–15; Guernsey and Alden, 792.

18. Sabine, 12.

19. V. C. Jones, 26. Quoting the report of Gen. Philip St. George Cooke on the defenses of northern Virginia.

20. Walton, 29.

21. Ibid., 24.

22. See George E. Woodward, *Woodward's Architecture and Rural Art,* 2 vols. (New York: Privately printed, 1867–1868), 1:32–37. John L. McAdam was a Scottish engineer who had developed a road which came to be called macadam—a covering of broken stone, in three layers consolidated by the passage of surface traffic.

23. Miers, 22, 29.

24. Sears, 15.

25. Croushore, 34–36.

26. Ibid., 77–78.

27. Ibid., 141, 173.

28. J. B. Mitchell, 165.

29. Archer Jones, *The Art of War in the Western World* (New York: Oxford University Press, 1987), 314.

30. Miers, 31.

31. Earl J. Hess, *The Rifled Musket in Civil War Combat, Reality and Myth* (Lawrence: University Press of Kansas, 2008), 4.

32. Hess, 28. The rate of volley fire established for Napoleonic soldiers was about two rounds per minute, but in practice this was sustained only for short periods. In an entire 8 hour day in the field, firing amounted to about one aimed shot every 5 minutes (See Hess, 17).

33. Wilbur S. Nye, "The U.S. Military Telegraph Services," *Civil War Times Illustrated,* November 1968, 28–34; Raymond W. Smith, "Don't Cut! Signal Telegraph," *Civil War Times Illustrated,* May 1976, 18–28.

34. Robert E. Denny, *Civil War Medicine: Care and Comfort for the Wounded* (New York: Sterling, 1995), 10.

35. Ibid., 226–227.

36. Byron Stinson, "The Invalid Corps," *Civil War Times Illustrated,* May 1971, 20–27.

37. Michael F. Fitzpatrick, "The Mercy Brigade," *Civil War Times Illustrated,* October 1997, 34–40.

38. Ibid., 36.

39. Walton, 72.

40. V. C. Jones, 34. Referring to the Official Records of the Rebellion, II, 299.

41. Guernsey and Alden, 792.

42. Croushore, 65, 80.

43. John H. Woodward, "Herding Beef for the Union Army," *Civil War Times Illustrated,* December 1970, 585.

44. McPherson, *Battle Cry,* 35. Edward D.C. Campbell, Jr., and Kym S. Rice, eds., *A Woman's War: Southern Women, Civil War and the Confederate Legacy* (Charlottesville: University Press of Virginia, 1996), 102. "Camp followers" were not necessarily prostitutes.

45. See Croushore, 148–152, "Don't come on here unless I write for you. You could sleep in a tent, you say. Not in mine; I have none," 162–163; and Lewis, 114–116.

46. Campbell and Rice, frontispiece. From a broadside of General Order No. 28, May 15, 1862.

47. V. C. Jones, 149. Quoting General Lafayette Baker.

11

SEEING THE ELEPHANT: THE REALITIES OF LIFE IN BATTLE

"The battle . . . the dreadful splendor . . . all my description must fall vastly short."

—Col. Wm. B. Hazen, Army of the Cumberland

Civil War battlefields were much more extensive than most people would suppose. Even in small engagements, hundreds if not thousands of men might be involved. In large battles a mounted officer, who could freely gallop from place to place, could scarcely travel over the entire field during the course of a day. Dense woods choked with heavy undergrowth or crossed with streams and marshes added to the difficulty of moving large bodies of troops. Commanders were forced to rely almost entirely on the reports of aides or couriers in formulating the military situation on different parts of the field.

With upwards of 100,000 men involved in battle, the individual soldiers saw only what occurred in their own regiment or company, and they were limited to a very narrow view of what was going on. Soldiers commonly heard more than they saw and relied on the reports of those coming from the front, which were sometimes incomplete or based on rumor. A strange phenomenon, known in physics as an acoustic shadow, often kept the sound of nearby fighting and artillery from reaching soldiers within a short distance while those very far off might hear it clearly. Nonetheless, even misleading information formed part of the experience of battle for most soldiers. Although we have no way of knowing the experience of those who were killed outright, the survivors and those wounded who

lived long enough to record their feelings have left us a storehouse of journals, diaries, letters, and hastily scribbled notes containing the expression
of what a Civil War battle was like.

Civil War battles had several distinct parts. The armies roused themselves in the morning and marched out with little foreknowledge that
a fateful engagement was about to take place. The opponents sent out
scouts to probe in the direction of the enemy, and, ultimately, the armies
came into contact and began to skirmish. In each regiment of ten companies, two were detailed each day to act as skirmishers. These men fanned
out before their regiments and engaged the enemy's skirmishers or outposts. Skirmishing between outposts was a constant activity in the war
zone, but skirmishers were trained to avoid precipitating an unwanted
engagement by pressing too closely. "Skirmishing is not dangerous," observed an imperturbable federal captain. "Two men mortally and two severely wounded constituted my whole loss in something like three hours
fighting out of a company of forty-one muskets." This loss of 10 percent of
his force seemed small in contrast to the large losses of a major battle.[1]

Soldiers sometimes expressed frustration with the hesitancy of their
leaders to take on the enemy. Rarely, the opposing commanders decided to
make a major fight of a small meeting, or they had a general engagement
thrust upon them. A major engagement had many requirements beyond
intelligence of the enemy's strength and position. Tactics and strategy were
chosen to fit the particular situation, orders were dictated, and units were
informed of their part in the cataclysm. It took time for forces to be marshaled. The column, sometimes miles long, had to be brought up to the
battlefield, organized, and sent to strategic positions along the battlefront.
Artillery positions and fields of fire had to be found and exploited. The cavalry might be sent to feel out the flanks of the enemy and to determine the
possible success of a turning movement. A reserve was organized, and hospitals, signal stations, and supply units were set up. Beginning slowly, the
battle began to rage furiously as more and more troops became engaged.

Soldiers often reported a lull in battle, sometimes immediately following a remarkable effort by both sides, as if both adversaries had become
exhausted in the effort. Very often a series of small climaxes taken together
made it obvious that one side was dominating the field. The opposing
sides might now call a truce to care for their wounded and dead, and the
losing commander would prepare a rearguard action to cover his retreat.
The ability to disengage effectively from the victorious enemy without
exposing one's forces to renewed attacks was the true test of a battlefield
commander. Nightfall inevitably ended most active fighting in the 19th
century, but probes and reconnaissance might continue. Commanders
often moved among their troops at night to determine their condition or
encourage them for the next day's work.

A soldier's experiences in battle were at the same time common and
unique. More than 10,000 individual engagements made up the Civil War,

and no two were exactly the same. Most diaries, letters, and journals of the men who fought describe their experiences in battle. As noted by Col. William. B. Hazen, "The battle. . .the dreadful splendor . . . all my description must fall vastly short."[2] The authors have therefore chosen simply to let the soldiers speak for themselves in this chapter. In what follows no attempt has been made to describe any particular battle. The flow of the narrative imitates the characteristic development of a major engagement. Some sentence restructuring and editing of proper names and units have been done for the sake of continuity. The name of the individual, his rank, and his affiliation are provided with each report. It is hoped that the result will remain true to the spirit of what each man contributed to the written record of the Civil War battle experience.

MARCHING TO WAR

There was a most glorious battalion drill last night, our Captain [and company] never did so well before. The Colonel was delighted. He said in his peculiar blunt old fashioned way that all we wanted now was a chance to put our drill into use. I believe he is as anxious for a battle as a school boy for his dinner. An officer came up from Washington yesterday and told him that an Ohio Regiment had been driven back from a battery [of enemy artillery] which they attempted to take. "How many men were killed?" asked the colonel. "Fifteen," replied the officer. "Oh was that all," said the Colonel, "humph–and they did not take the battery." It is well understood by all who heard the remark that if we had been there the battery would have been taken—or many more than 15 men would have fallen in the attempt.[3]
—Sgt. Charles B. Haydon, 2nd MI Infantry

We have received orders to cook all our rations, strike our tents very quietly, and be ready to move at any time, which we all think means that we are going to move against the enemy[4] across the river. They, also, have been exhibiting signs of uneasiness for some days past . . . I am writing to you now for fear I may not have the opportunity again shortly. I fear not the result, am confident that we, through God, will be victorious.[5]
—Sgt. Alexander T. Barclay, 4th VA Infantry

We have been on the march since yesterday, a week . . . I would take any amount that this trip has the most beautiful scenery I ever beheld since I have been in the army, which is some time.[6]
—Lt. William B. Taylor, 11th NC Infantry

We found several patriotic ladies with small feet and big umbrellas waiting to receive us . . . One of the ladies had an enormous wreath which she was anxious to place on the neck of the
General's charger. The horse objected to it seriously.[7]
—Lt. F. W. Dawson, Staff Officer, ANV

No one who has not had the experience knows what a soldier
undergoes on a march. We start off on a march some beautiful
morning in spring. At midday slight clouds are seen floating
about; these thicken . . . the rain commences and soon pours
down. Poor fellow! He pulls down his hat, buttons up his
jacket, pulls up his collar, and tries to protect his gun. In a short
while he feels the water running down his arms and legs . . . We
went through equal trials in very dusty marches.[8]
—Pvt. J. H. Worsham, 21st VA Infantry

Civil War enthusiasts, many of whom are experts on the
period, recreate the lifestyle of federal troops and the spectacle of battle at public reenactments. James Volo photo.

We were about proceeding on our march . . . [when] the men were allowed to light fires and dry the clothes in which they had shivered all night. At 3 PM we received orders to recross the river, and all the drying of clothes had to be done again in the evening.[9]

—Col. David W. Aiken, 7th SC Infantry

We soon came to Dumfries Creek which has swollen very much during the night taking away the bridge over the stream. . .We marched between twenty and thirty miles and when night came my feet were blistered nearly all over so that fifteen minutes after we halted I could hardly walk a step but on taking some salt and water and bathing my feet thoroughly and then apply-ing liquor I managed to get myself in tolerably good marching order for the next day.[10]

—Pvt. Edwin Weller, 107th NY Volunteers

Angry was the glare of the sun during those fearful days . . . Choking, blinding were the clouds of dust that rose from be-neath the army's steady tread; parching was that unquench-able thirst which dried the tongue to its very roots. The men fell by tens, twenties, nay by hundreds along the dusty roads. Such days as these prove the true soldier.[11]

—Capt. John E. Dooley, 1st VA Infantry

I would care very little about marching if it were not for my knapsack. The straps cause some soreness about the shoulders. When we get on our blankets, overcoats, haversacks, cartridge boxes, cap boxes, and our extra clothing we feel the weight. The men began to fall out and sit down or lie down by the roadside before we had gone two miles. More than 150 men fell out before we got through. Two are reported dead, but I am inclined to think this a mistake.[12]

—Sgt. Charles B. Haydon, 2nd MI Infantry

MAKING CONTACT

The column, hitherto moving forward with the steadiness of a mighty river, hesitates, halts, steps back, then forward, hesi-tates again, halts. The colonels talk to the brigadier, the brig-adiers talk to the major-general, some officers hurry forward and others hurry to the rear. The infantry stands to one side of the road while the cavalry trots by to the front . . . Most of the men know . . . they are on the edge of battle . . . The skirmish-ers step into the woods and carefully go forward. They load,

fire, and reload rapidly while standing six to twelve feet apart,
calling to each other, laughing, shouting and cheering . . . They
have at last driven the enemy skirmishers in upon the line of
battle, and are waiting. A score of men have fallen here, some
killed outright, some slightly, some sorely and some mortally
wounded.[13]

—Pvt. Carlton McCarthy, 2nd Richmond Howitzers

At first when the boys brought news of the engagement to the
company, we were loath to believe them and had it not been
for the serious faces of those who gave us the information we
would have been tempted to treat it as an attempt at a scare.
Quite a number of the members of the company . . . returned
with a report confirming the tidings already received. Soon afterwards a number of prisoners, about 300, were marched past
where we were resting. As soon as we saw them we crowded
up close to the road to get a good look at them. They all seemed
to be in the best of spirits, evidently glad to escape the pending
battle.[14]

—Pvt. Joseph A. Lumbard, 147th PA Infantry

The orders were to be ready at a moment's notice. The lines
were forming. Batteries were being placed into position. Dark
columns stood motionless. . .Hospitals were established in the
rear, and the musicians and other non-combatants were detailed to bear the stretchers and attend the ambulances. Medical
stores were unpacked and countless rolls of bandages placed at
hand for use.[15]

—Ebenezer Hannaford, 6th OH Volunteers

I now formed my division in the woods . . . I told the General
that the column seemed to be heavily engaged. I thought I had
better go in. He replied: "I do not wish to bring on a general engagement today; the rest of the army is not up." . . . Very soon
[however] an aide came to me with orders to attack.[16]

—Mjr. Gen. Henry Heth, Division Cmdr. CSA

A DAY OF BATTLE

In general, the terror of battle is not an abiding impression, but
comes and goes like throbs of pain; and this is especially the
case with veterans who have learned to know when there is a
pressing danger and when not; the moment a peril has passed
they are as tranquil as if it had never come near.[17]

—Capt. John W. De Forest, 12th CT

Hundreds of Civil War enthusiasts recreate a column of march (above) while others defend an artillery battery (below) during a Civil War battle reenactment. James Volo photo.

We soon came to the top of a hill in full view of the field and valley and upon the hill we had the fight. Here men jumped over a fence to the left and formed in battle line. In a short time a line of the enemy came out of the woods in front of us about a mile off; soon another; and yet another. They kept steadily advancing until we could see their officers stepping in front swinging their swords. Suddenly a cloud of smoke arose from their line and almost instantly the balls began to whistle about us and the men next to my right fell. The order rang along the line . . . to load and fire at will, as they call it. I think we fired about five rounds . . . As soon as the report of our muskets were [sic] heard we knew that a very small part of our line was there. The enemy did not return our fire but came rushing down the hill yelling.[18]

—Sgt. Edwin A. Gearhart, 142nd PA Infantry

At every step some poor fellow would fall, and as his pitiful cry would come to my ear I almost imagined it the wail of some loved one he had left at home.[19]
                                        —Capt. John T. James, 11th VA Infantry

The Colonel was all impatience. "Where the hell is my flag?" He shouted [to the flagbearer], "If I can't get you killed in ten minutes, by God, I'll post you right up among the batteries!"[20]
                                        —Capt. Abner Small, 16th ME Infantry

One of our own batteries stationed on a hill in the rear of our line fired two shots which fell short and killed two of our company. I was sent back to inform the Colonel of the fact . . . I mounted an orderly's horse, a great lumbering beast. As I reached a hill I was obliged to follow the ridge for several hundred yards. The enemy sharpshooters opened fire upon me . . . I lost my hat, and as it was a new one and cost me seven and a half dollars, I drew my saber and ran the point through the hat and recovered it. I next lost my Navy Colt revolver, but if it had been made of gold, studded with diamonds I would not have stopped for it.[21]
                                        —Col. Elisha Hunt Rhodes, 2nd RI Volunteers

There was the thunder of guns, a shrieking, whistling, moaning of shells, before they burst, sometimes like rockets in the air . . . No results of this conflict could be noted; no shifting of scenes or movement of actors in the great struggle could be observed. It was simply noise, flash, and roar. I had the sensation of a lifetime.[22]
                                        —William H. Bayly, 13-year-old resident of Gettysburg

On the morning of the 3rd, a round shell entered the gable of our house on the garret. I was lying on the floor of the room directly below. The racket caused may be imagined, the impact on the wall, the crashing of brick on the garret floor, and the sundering of timber, the rolling along of the shell till it reached the open door, and thumping down the first flight of stairs, step by step, till it reached the landing where our oldest little niece had been but a few minutes previous to that time.[23]
                                        —Robert L. McClean, a boy in Gettysburg

We betook ourselves to the cellar . . . until . . . the firing ceased. During the cessation we managed to get a cold bite [to eat]. Again, the battle began with unearthly fury . . . listening to the terrific sound of the strife; more terrible never greeted human ears. We knew that with every explosion, and the scream of

A CIVILIAN FAMILY COPES WITH
THE BATTLE OF GETTYSBURG

The Hollinger family of Gettysburg spent countless hours caring for the many wounded and dying left in the town or visiting the many field hospitals in the battle's aftermath. Liberty Augusta Hollinger (Clutz) was 16 years old at the time. Hollinger's little sister, Annie, was strangely fascinated by the many piles of amputated limbs, and this morbid attraction may have been an ulterior motive for her to accompany her mother and sisters to care for the wounded soldiers. One day while passing through the abandoned battlefield, she found a small severed hand among the shallow graves. To keep Annie from finding more ghoulish treasures, Libbie took old army coats with her when passing by the fields, and covered the exposed remains with them. Libbie recalled how her family weathered the battle while trying to maintain some semblance of normalcy:

> We stayed . . . in cellar during the three days of the battle [July 1, 2, 3, 1863], and oh how glad we were for such a safe retreat . . . There was a large wheat field south of our house . . . and it seemed to be full of Union sharpshooters. We could see them pop up and fire when any Rebel rode by, especially officers. When father left the cellar to feed the chickens or to milk the cows, the bullets seemed to fix all about him. Finally, he spoke to the rebels about feeling the bullets almost graze his hair. An officer said to him, 'Why man, take off that gray suit; they think you are a Johnny Reb.' He did so and put on a black suit, and had no further trouble.

Source: Tony DeLacy, "Civilians recall the third day of the Battle of Gettysburg," *Celebrate Gettysburg* 2, no. 11 (September/October, 2008): 29.

every shell, human being were being hurried, through excruciating pain, into another world, and that many more were torn and mangled, and lying in torment worse than death, and no one able to extend relief. The thought made me very sad, and feel that, if it was God's will, I would rather be taken than to remain to see the misery that would follow.[24]
—Sarah M. Broadhead, resident of Gettysburg

The appearance of the landscape northward from this point was singular and doleful. Hundreds of noncombatants, and many who should have been in the ranks, with many whose bloody clothing showed that their fighting for that day had ended, were drifting rearward confusedly, yet with curious deliberation. Over the space of a mile square the fields, long since stripped of their rail fences, were dotted with wagons, ambulances, pack mules, army followers and stray soldiers, none of them running. . .

Chew's battery of horse artillery fires a blank round (above) and watches as the infantry line fires a volley (below). Civil War photographs were unable to catch such action shots, as the photographic plates were too slow in reacting to available light. James Volo photo.

Defeated and retreating soldiers do not fly at full speed for any considerable distance. After a run of a hundred yards, or less, even though the bullets are still whizzing around them, they drop into a walk . . . Thence forward they tramp steadily rearward, not in the least wild with fright, but discreetly.[25]
—Capt. John W. De Forest, 12th CT

It was a moment of contending emotions of pride, hope, and sadness as our gallant boys stood face to face with those heights, ready to charge upon them. At double-quick and in splendid style they crossed the plain. Our line was perfect. The men could not have made a better appearance had they been on drill.

Just in the rear of the division three batteries of Parrott guns were playing into the works of the enemy, while from the heights above, all the opposing batteries poured a terrible and

Figure 11-1
A Regiment in Typical Order of Battle: Attacking an Enemy Position

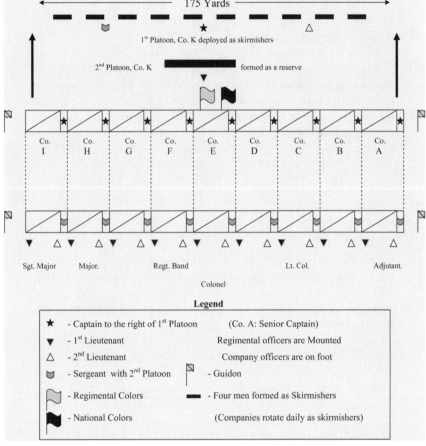

Source: Thomas. E. Griess. *The American Civil War*. The West Point Military History Series. (1987).

destructive fire upon the advancing lines. Having gained the rifle pits at the base of the hills, they pushed forward to capture the heights. . .

There were the hills, enough to fatigue any man to climb them without a load and with no one to oppose. But the boys pushed nobly, steadily on, the enemy steadily retreating . . . our men were falling in every direction . . . but with shouts and cheers . . . with bayonets fixed, mounted the heights, the enemy retreating in confusion.[26]

—George T. Stevens, Surgeon, 77th NY Volunteers

The works commenced were only piles of rails and logs not capable of resisting shells, so we got tools and commenced ditching. By 10 AM we had pretty good works . . . Soon after two lines of battle burst out of the woods in front of us, and started up, on the charge . . . They came up within 50 paces of the works, before being repulsed . . .

We have been kept close by sharpshooters, having nothing to protect us but our works. The enemy is on the edge of the woods, three or four hundred yards off while we are in an open field. We could not get out after water until dark. . . . The fire was kept up some time wounding several others, but killing no more. We have been enfiladed all day and have lost many killed and wounded—at night strengthened our works—worked all night.[27]

—Pvt. John S. Jackman, 1st KY Infantry

WOUNDED IN BATTLE

Some of the wounded from the battlefield began to arrive where I was staying. They reported hard fighting, many wounded and killed, and were afraid our troops would be defeated and perhaps routed. The first wounded soldier whom I met had his thumbs tied up. This I thought dreadful, and told him so. . . . Soon two officers carrying their arms in slings made their appearance, and I more fully began to realize that something terrible had taken place. Now the wounded began to come in greater numbers. Some limping, some with their heads and arms in bandages, some crawling, others carried on stretchers or brought in ambulances. Suffering, cast down and dejected, it was truly a pitiable gathering.[28]

—Tillie Pierce, 15-year-old resident of Gettysburg

At a distance of about one hundred and fifty yards the enemy were lying down, and rose up in masses and fired one volley. I and one other member of the Brigade fell wounded . . . the bullet cut across my bowels and made a long and ugly wound . . . I was feeling no pain, but felt somewhat dazed . . .

The grape shot and shell were pouring thick and fast in our rear, a great number falling short of their intended mark, and it made me hopeful that it would soon put an end to my existence. I turned my head to the enemy, thinking that I might be so fortunate as to get shot dead . . .[29]

As there was no sign of discharge [from the wound] . . . I thought [after a time] that possibly I was not mortally wounded.

Then fear was uppermost and I crawled about 50 feet to a well rotted stump, thinking it would protect me from shot. I was not much more than settled behind it when the idea struck me that a grape [from artillery canister] could go through, so I dragged myself to a good sized tree about 100 feet off and stayed there some time in a reclining position, with head and shoulder resting against the tree. All the while the battle was roaring across the creek.[30]

—Pvt. William A. Fletcher, 5th TX Infantry

[A] man lay near me, dying from a terrible wound through the abdomen, his fair face growing whiter with every laboring breath and his light blue eyes fixed vacantly on the glaring sky . . . I glanced at him pitifully from time to time as he patiently and silently drew towards his end. Such individual cases of suffering are far more moving than a broad spectacle of slaughter.[31]

—Captain John W. De Forest, 12th CT

A terrific explosion occurred . . . I found myself lying off from my former position and gasping for breath. Around me were brains, blood, and skull bones. The two men who lay to my left had been blown off just above the ears, and that shell had exploded almost directly over me. It had broken several ribs and bruised my left lung cutting my jacket into shreds. My Colonel asked me if I was badly hurt to which I replied I thought I was and called for that which a wounded soldier first wants, a drink of water.[32]

—Sgt. David E. Johnston, 7th VA Infantry

We were in this wheat field and the grain stood almost breast high. The enemy had their slight protection, but we were in the open, without a thing better than a wheat straw to catch a Minie bullet that weighed an ounce. Of course our men began to tumble. They lay where they fell, or, if able started for the rear. Near to me I saw a man go down, shot through the neck. I made a movement to get his gun, but at that moment I was struck in the shoulder. It did not hurt and the blow simply caused me to step back. I found that I could not work my arm, but . . . it was not serious enough to justify my leaving the fighting line. So I remained, and some time after felt a blow on my left leg, and it gave way, so that I knew the leg was broken . . . While lying here entirely helpless, and hearing those vicious bullets singing over my head, I suffered from fear.[33]

—Lt. Charles A. Fuller, 61st NY Infantry

The road where we lay was covered with our dead and wounded. A battery of the enemy came thundering along it, and when the officer commanding it saw our dead and wounded on the road, he halted his battery to avoid running over them and his men carefully lifted the dead to one side and carried the wounded to the cellar of a house, supplied them with water, and said they would return and care for them when they had caught the rest of us.[34]

—Sgt. Edward R. Bowen, 114th PA Infantry

I do not know how long it was before I became conscious but the battle was raging furiously; two dead men who were not there when I fell were lying close to me, one across my feet . . . Two stretcher-bearers came and carried me back about fifty yards to a small stream that ran parallel to our battle line. Here was a depression in the ground some three or four feet below the general level where the wounded would be protected from the musket fire . . .

When I reached the stream the banks were already lined with many dead and wounded. Some had been carried there, others had dragged themselves to the place to die. Many were needlessly bleeding to death. Many died who would have lived if only the simplest treatment had been in the hands of the men themselves.[35]

My mind was clear . . . I knew I could not get to the rear without help, so made no further attempt. Fortunately my canteen had been filled; my thirst had become great and I had some water to wash the blood from my face.

During this time the battle on our front continued with unlessening fury . . . Looking back I saw a scattered line of the enemy coming toward us on the double quick . . . They had to cross around or over the wounded and were cautioned by their officers to be careful not to disturb them more than was necessary. They passed over us carefully, without any unkind actions or words.[36]

—Pvt. Rice C. Bull, 123rd NY Volunteers

I felt a burning, stinging sensation in my thigh, and as if all the blood in my body was rushing to one spot. Finding I was falling on my face, I gave myself a sudden twist which brought me into a sitting position facing the enemy, with my broken leg doubled up over the other. Taking it up tenderly, I put it in its natural position; then tied my handkerchief above the wound, took the bayonet off my gun and made a tourniquet with it. I then took my knapsack off and put it under my head for a pil-

This period lithograph shows a much more sanitary view of a medical field station than was the case. The 19th-century public was ill prepared for the grim reality of the war.

low. Having made myself comfortable . . . every moment I expected would be my last.[37]

—Pvt. David R. Howard, 1st MD Battalion

CLIMAX

At sunrise our Division advanced against the enemy's works . . . We lay about forty yards apart . . . To expose one's person was sure death . . . Both armies were like hornets. We dug holes with our bayonets to protect ourselves and more than one poor fellow was shot before his little dugout would protect him. We lay there expecting every minute to be gobbled up. The shells passed over us both ways. Some of them fell short of going where they were started for and burst over our heads. We made ourselves in as small bulk as possible. This was a very dangerous position, but we took our chances and trusted to providence . . . Time goes slowly . . .

At 7 PM everything became as quiet as the grave, we felt it was the calm before the storm. We fixed ourselves as well as possible to be ready for what was coming, and at 8 PM it came. The enemy charged our works . . . These were long fierce charges—they came right up to the works but they could not effect a lodgment . . . We could hear their officers shouting, "Forward, forward!" On they came to be mowed down by the thousand, but we never thought of getting driven out.

At daylight all was quiet. The enemy advanced a white flag, asking permission to bury their dead, which was granted. We had an armistice of two hours. The quietness was really oppressive. It positively made us lonesome for the continual racket which we had endured for so long, both day and night. We sat on the works and let our legs dangle over the front and watched the enemy carry off their dead comrades in silence . . . When the two hours was up we got back into our holes, and they did the same.[38]

—Pvt. Daniel Chisholm, 116th PA Infantry

THE AFTERMATH

With us for a time all was quiet. There was nothing to disturb us but the occasional cries and groans of the wounded; not a word of complaint was heard . . . Nearly all knew we were not only wounded but were now prisoners . . .

The enemy's surgeons went among our wounded looking for those that required amputation . . . The arms and legs were thrown on the ground, only a few feet from the wounded who lay nearby. As each amputation was completed the wounded man was carried to an old house and laid on the floor. They said they could do nothing at that time for those others less critically wounded . . . The condition of most of these was deplorable.[39]

—Pvt. Rice C. Bull, 123rd NY Volunteers

Our men had 60 rounds of cartridges each when they went into an action and had used it nearly all when the enemy ran. Our regiment went into the fight with about 650 men and, as we lost about 100 killed and wounded, you may know that we had pretty hot work . . . I don't know the total loss in our brigade but should think about 450 killed and wounded. The enemy loss is pretty heavy but I don't believe they lost more than us as they were well protected by their breast works.[40]

—Lt. George Washington Whitman, 13th NY Militia

Some of them lay dead within twenty feet of our works—the dead look horrible all swelled up and black in the face . . . After there was nothing left but stains of blood, broken and twisted guns, old hats, canteens, every one of them reminders of the death and carnage that reigned a few short hours before.[41]

            —Pvt. Daniel Chisholm, 116th PA Infantry

The ground here is very hard, full of rocks and stones, the digging very laborious work, and the dead are many. As the time is short, they got but very shallow graves. In fact, most of them were buried in trenches dug not over 18 inches deep, and as near where they fell as was possible so as not to have to carry them far. I saw 60 buried in one trench and not one was carried more than 25 feet.[42]

            —Sgt. George A. Bowen, 12th NJ Infantry

The Pickets on both sides have agreed not to fire on each other, and are getting very friendly. They trade Tobacco for Coffee, and also exchange newspapers, etc. . . .

    This is a beautiful Sabbath day. Quiet. The regiment has marching orders and we lay around in the sun wondering where to go next. At dusk we quietly packed up and fell back

The dead were buried in shallow graves scraped out of the ground very near to where they fell. If their names were known—and many were so torn apart by artillery shells to erase their identities—markers made from cracker boxes might be inscribed with their names.

Date	Name	Union Killed	Union Wounded	Union Missing	Union Total	Confederate loss Total
July 21	Bull Run, Va.	481	1,011	1,460	2,952	1,752
Aug 10	Wilson's Creek, Mo.	223	721	291	1,235	1,095
Oct 21	Ball's Bluff, Va.	223	226	445	894	302

1862

Date	Name	Union Killed	Union Wounded	Union Missing	Union Total	Confederate loss Total
Feb 14 to 16	Fort Donelson, Tenn.	446	1,735	150	2,331	15,067
Mar 6 to 8	Pea Ridge, Ark.	203	972	174	1,349	5,200
Apr 6 and 7	Shiloh, Tenn.	1,735	7,882	3,956	13,573	10,699
May 5	Williamsburg, Va.	456	1,400	372	2,228	1,000
May 31 to June 1	Seven Pines and Fair Oaks, Va.	890	3,627	1,222	5,739	7,997
June 8	Cross Keys, Va.	125	500	---	625	287
June 26 to July 1	Seven days' retreat; includes Mechanicsville, Gaines' Mills, Chickahominy, Peach Orchard, Savage Station, Charles City Cross Roads, and Malvern Hill	1,582	7,709	5,958	15,249	17,583
Aug 8	Cedar Mountain, Va.	450	660	290	1,400	1,307
Aug 30	Bull Run, Va. (2d)	800	4,000	3,000	7,800	3,700
Sept 12 to 15	Harper's Ferry, Va.	80	120	11,583	11,783	500
Sept 14	Turner's and Crampton's Gaps, South Mountain, Md.	443	1,806	76	2,325	4,343
Sept 17	Antietam, Md.	2,010	9,416	1,043	12,469	25,899
Oct 3 and 4	Corinth, Miss.	315	1,812	232	2,359	14,221
Oct 8	Perryville, Ky.	916	2,943	489	4,348	7,000
Dec 7	Prairie Grove, Ark.	167	798	183	1,148	1,500
Dec 13	Fredericksburg, Va.	1,180	9,028	2,145	12,353	4,576
Dec 28 and 29	Chickasaw Bayou, Vicksburg, Miss.	191	982	756	1,929	207
Dec 31, 1862, to Jan 2, 1863	Stone's River, Tenn.	1,533	7,245	2,800	11,578	25,560

Date	Name	Union Killed	Union Wounded	Union Missing	Union Total	Confederate loss Total
Jan 11	Fort Hindman, Arkansas Post, Ark.	129	831	17	977	5,500
Mar 4 and 5	Thompson's Station, Tenn.	100	300	1,306	1,706	600
May 1 to 4	Chancellorsville, Va.	1,512	9,518	5,000	16,030	12,281
May 16	Champion Mills, Miss.	426	1,842	189	2,457	4,300
May 18 to July 4	Siege of Vicksburg Miss.	545	3,688	303	4,536	31,277
May 27 to July 9	Siege of Port Hudson, La.	500	2,500	---	3,000	7,208
June 6 to 8	Milliken's Bend, La.	154	223	115	492	725
June 9	Beverly Ford and Brandy Station, Va.	---	---	---	500	700
June 23 to 30	Rosecrans' campaign from Murfreesboro to Tullahoma, Tenn.	85	462	13	560	1,634
July 1 to 3	Gettysburg, Pa.	2,834	13,709	6,643	23,186	31,621
July 9 to 16	Jackson, Miss.	100	800	100	1,000	1,339
July 18	Second assault on Fort Wagner, S. C.	---	---	---	1,500	174
Sept 19 to 20	Chickamauga, Ga.	1,644	9,262	4,945	15,851	17,804
Nov 23 to 25	Chattanooga, Tenn; includes Orchard Knob, Lookout Mountain, and Missionary Ridge	757	4,529	330	5,616	8,684
Nov 26 to 28	Operations at Mine Run, Va.	100	400	---	500	500

1864

Date	Name	Union Killed	Union Wounded	Union Missing	Union Total	Confederate Loss Total
Feb 20	Olustee, Fla.	193	1,175	460	1,828	500
Apr 8	Sabine Cross Roads, La.	200	900	1,800	2,900	1,500
Apr 9	Pleasant Hills, La.	100	700	300	1,100	2,000
Apr 12	Fort Pillow, Tenn.	350	60	164	574	80

Date	Name	Union Killed	Union Wounded	Union Missing	Union Total	Confederate Loss Total
Apr 17 to 20	Plymouth, N. C.	20	80	1,500	1,600	500
Apr 30	Jenkins' Ferry, Saline River, Ark.	200	955	---	1,155	1,100
May 5 to 7	Wilderness, Va.	5,597	21,463	10,677	37,737	11,400
May 8 to 18	Spottsylvania Court House, Va; includes engagements on the Fredericksburg Road, Laurel Hill, and Nye River	4,177	19,687	2,577	26,461	9,000
May 12 to 16	Fort Darling, Drury's Bluff, Va.	422	2,380	210	3,012	2,500
May 13 to 16	Resaca, Ga.	600	2,147	---	2,747	2,800
May 15	New Market, Va.	120	560	240	920	405
May 16 to 30	Bermuda Hundred, Va.	200	1,000	---	1,200	3,000
May 23 to 27	North Anna River, Va.	223	1,460	290	1,973	2,000
June 1 to 12	Cold Harbor, Va.	1,905	10,570	2,456	14,931	1,700
June 9 to 30	Kenesaw Mountain, Ga; includes Pine Mountain, Pine Knob, Golgotha, Culp's House, general assault, June 27th; McAfee's Cross Roads, Lattemore's Mills, and Powder Springs	1,370	6,500	800	8,670	4,600
June 10	Brice's Cross Roads, near Guntown, Miss.	223	394	1,623	2,240	606
June 11and 12	Trevellian Station, Central Railroad, Va.	85	490	160	735	370
June 15 to 19	Petersburg, Va; includes Baylor's Farm, Walthal, and Weir Bottom Church	1,298	7,474	1,814	10,586	---
June 22 and 23	Weldon Railroad, Va.	604	2,494	2,217	5,315	500
June 27	Kenesaw Mountain, general assault, refer to June 9 to 30 entry	---	---	---	3,000	600
July 1 to 31	Front of Petersburg, Va; loses at the Crater and Deep Bottom not included	419	2,076	1,200	3,695	---

Date	Name	Union Killed	Union Wounded	Union Missing	Union Total	Confederate Loss Total
July 9	Monocacy, Md.	90	579	1,290	1,959	400
July 22	Atlanta, Ga; Hood's first sortie	500	2,141	1,000	3,641	8,499
July 24	Winchester, Va.	---	---	---	1,200	600
July 30	Mine explosion at Petersburg, Va.	419	1,679	1,910	4,008	1,200
Aug 1 to 31	Trenches before Petersburg, Va.	87	484	---	571	---
Aug 14 to 18	Strawberry Plains, Deep Bottom Run, Va.	400	1,755	1,400	3,555	1,100
Aug 18, 19, and 21	Six Mile House, Weldon Railroad, Va.	212	1,155	3,176	4,543	4,000
Aug 25	Ream's Station, Va.	127	546	1,769	2,442	1,500
May 5 to Sept 5	Campaign in Northern Georgia, from Chattanooga, Tenn. to Atlanta, Ga.	5,284	26,129	5,786	37,199	---
Sept 1 to Oct 30	Trenches before Petersburg, Va.	170	822	812	1,804	1,000
Sept 19	Opequan, Winchester, Va.	653	3,719	618	4,990	5,500
Sept 28 to 30	New Market Heights, Va.	400	2,029	---	2,429	2,000
Sept 30 to Oct 1	Preble's Farm, Poplar Springs Church, Va.	141	788	1,756	2,685	900
Oct 19	Cedar Creek, Va.	588	3,516	1,891	5,995	4,200
Oct 27	Hatcher's Run, South Side Railroad, Va.	156	1,047	699	1,902	1,000
Nov 30	Franklin, Tenn.	189	1,033	1,104	2,336	6,252
Dec 15 and 16	Nashville, Tenn.	400	1,740	---	2,140	15,000

1865

Date	Name	Union Killed	Union Wounded	Union Missing	Union Total	Confederate Loss Total
Jan 13 to 15	Fort Fisher, N. C.	184	749	22	955	2,483
Feb 5 to 7	Dabney's Mills, Hatcher's Run, Va.	232	1,062	186	1,480	1,200
Mar 19 to 31	Bentonville, N. C.	190	1,168	287	1,646	2,825

			1865			
Date	*Name*	*Union Killed*	*Union Wounded*	*Union Missing*	*Union Total*	*Confederate Loss Total*
Mar 25	Fort Steadman, in front of Petersburg, Va.	68	337	506	911	2,681
Mar 25	Petersburg, Va.	103	864	209	1,176	834
Mar 31	Boydton and White Oak Roads, Va.	177	1,134	556	1,867	1,235
Apr 1	Five Forks, Va.	124	706	54	884	8,500
Apr 2	Fall of Petersburg, Va.	296	2,565	500	3,361	3,000
Apr 9	Surrender of Lee	---	---	---	---	26,000
Apr 26	Johnston surrendered	---	---	---	---	29,924
May 4	Taylor surrendered	---	---	---	---	10,000
May 10	Sam Jones surrendered	---	---	---	---	8,000
May 11	Jeff Thompson surrendered	---	---	---	---	7,454

without noise or confusion and struck out through the darkness leaving the battlefield behind. This has been a hot place for us as our thinned ranks show.[43]

—Pvt. Daniel Chisholm, 116th PA Infantry

[A]n enemy officer came and took a list of all prisoners, having each one sign a parole not to enter active service again until properly exchanged . . . On returning home, after the battle, I found that my family was notified that I had been badly wounded, it was thought mortally, and was left on the battlefield. Great was their joy when two weeks later, after they had abandoned hope of my being alive, they received a letter from me sent from the hospital.[44]

—Pvt. Rice C. Bull, 123rd NY Volunteers

Tell my father I died with my face to the enemy.[45]

—Col. Isaac E. Avery, 6th NC Infantry

My Dear Papa,
When our great victory was just over the exultation was so great that one didn't think of our fearful losses, but now I can't help feeling a great weight at my heart.[46]

—Capt. Henry L. Abbott, 20th ME Infantry

Although the losses here given are generally based on official medical returns, the figures must not be taken as perfectly reliable, for in many instances the returns were based on estimates, and the totals of losses were, by later and more reliable returns, sometimes considerably reduced. Confederate losses are generally based on estimates.

NOTES

1. James H. Croushore, ed., *A Volunteer's Adventure, by Captain John W. De Forest* (New Haven: Yale University Press, 1949), 114. Casualties in excess of 50 percent were not uncommon.

2. Peter Cozzens, *No Better Place to Die: The Battle of Stones River* (Urbana: University of Illinois Press, 1990), 165.

3. Stephen W. Sears, ed. *For Country, Cause, and Leader* (New York: Ticknor & Fields, 1993), 28–29. Quoting Sgt. (later Col.) Charles B. Haydon, Kalamazoo Light Guards, Co. I, 2nd Michigan Volunteer Infantry encamped at Arlington, VA in June 1861.

4. The term "enemy" has been used to replace Yankees, Federals, Rebs, Johnnies, etc. General Robert E. Lee eschewed the use of the term "enemy." Rather, he habitually referred to the Federals as "those people."

5. Editors of Time-Life, *Voices of the Civil War* (New York: Time-Life, 1995): [1863 Maryland campaign], Sgt. Alexander T. Barclay, 4th VA Inf., 16. Hereafter cited as *Voices,* with campaign, person, unit, and page where appropriate. The excerpts from letters, diaries, and journals found in this publication were originally printed in the lifetime of their authors and can be found separately in their entirety.

6. Ibid.: [1863 Maryland campaign], Lt. William B. Taylor, 11th NC Inf., 21.

7. Ibid.: [1863 Maryland campaign], Lt. Francis W. Dawson, Staff Officer, Longstreet's Command, 33. The abbreviation "ANV" stands for Army of Northern Virginia.

8. Robertson: Pvt. John H. Worsham, 21st VA Inf., 96–97.

9. *Voices:* [Gettysburg], Col. David W. Aiken, 7th SC Inf., 22.

10. Walton: [On the March], Pvt. Edwin Weller, 107th NY Volunteers, 18, 23–24.

11. *Voices:* [Gettysburg], Capt. John E. Dooley, 1st VA Inf., 35.

12. Sears, 23. Quoting Haydon.

13. McCarthy: Pvt. Carlton McCarthy, 2nd Co., Richmond Howitzers, 94.

14. *Voices:* [Gettysburg], Pvt. Joseph A. Lumbard, 147th PA Inf., 41.

15. Ebenezer Hannaford, *The Story of a Regiment: A History of the Campaigns, and Associations in the Field of the Sixth Regiment Ohio Volunteer Infantry* (Cincinnati: Privately printed, 1868): Ebenezer Hannaford, 6th Ohio Volunteers, 811–812.

16. *Voices:* [Gettysburg], Mjr. Gen. Henry Heth, Division Commander, CSA, 40.

17. Croushore, 59.

18. *Voices:* [Gettysburg], Sgt. Edwin A. Gearhart, 142nd PA Inf., 49.

19. Ibid.: [Gettysburg], Capt. John T. James, 11th VA Inf., 121.

20. Ibid.: [Gettysburg], Capt. Abner Small, 16th ME Inf., 116.

21. Robert Hunt Rhodes, ed., *All for the Union, by Col. Elisha Hunt Rhodes* (1985; reprint, New York: Random House, 1995): Col. Elisha Hunt Rhodes, 2nd RI Volunteers, 143–144.

22. *Voices:* [Gettysburg], William H. Bayly, thirteen-year-old resident of Gettysburg, 105.

23. Tony DeLacy, "Civilians recall the third day of the Battle of Gettysburg," *Celebrate Gettysburg* Vol. 2 Issue 11 (September/October, 2008) 29.

24. Tony DeLacy, "Civilians recall the third day of the Battle of Gettysburg," *Celebrate Gettysburg* Vol. 2 Issue 11 (September/October, 2008) 29.

25. Croushore, 213–214, 220.

26. George T. Stevens, *Three Years in the Sixth Corps* (Albany: S. R. Gray, 1866), 196–197. Surgeon Stevens was a witness to the second battle of Marye's Heights (Fredericksburg) in May 1863, which was a success. The first storming of Marye's Heights in December 1862 had ended in a bloody repulse.

27. William C. Davis, ed., *Diary of a Confederate Soldier, by John S. Jackman* (Columbia: University of South Carolina Press, 1990): Pvt. John S. Jackman of the Orphan Brigade, 123–124.

28. *Voices:* [Gettysburg], Tillie Pierce, fifteen years old, 62. Tillie Pierce's memoirs of the Gettysburg battle were featured on an episode of *Civil War Journal,* a series produced by the Arts and Entertainment Network in 1997.

29. Stomach wounds were thought to end only in a long, agonizing death. Many men with such wounds attempted suicide on the field rather than endure the pain.

30. Fletcher: [Second Manassas], Pvt. William A. Fletcher, Co. F, 5th TX, 50–56.

31. Croushore, 138.

32. *Voices:* [Gettysburg], Sgt. David E. Johnston, 7th VA Inf., 117.

33. Ibid.: [Gettysburg], Lt. Charles Fuller, 61st NY Inf., 86.

34. Ibid.: Sgt. Edward R. Bowen, 114th PA Inf., 92.

35. No first aid appliances were supplied to the soldiers, although many items such as tourniquets and other "lifesavers" were available from sutlers.

36. Bauer: [Chancellorsville], Pvt. Rice C. Bull, 123rd NY, 58–63.

37. *Voices:* [Gettysburg], Pvt. David R. Howard, 1st Maryland Battalion, 110.

38. W. Springer Menge and J. August Shimrak, eds., The Civil War Notebook of Daniel Chisholm (New York: Ballantine, 1989): [Cold Harbor], Pvt. Daniel Chisholm, Co. K, 116th PA, Irish Brigade, 19–22.

39. Bauer: [Chancellorsville], Pvt. Rice C. Bull, 123rd NY, 58–63.

40. Jerome M. Loving, ed., *Civil War Letters of George Washington Whitman* (Durham: Duke University Press, 1975): [Battle of New Bern, NC], 13th Regiment of NY State Militia, 46–47.

41. Menge and Shimrak: [Cold Harbor], Pvt. Daniel Chisholm, Co. K, 116th PA, Irish Brigade, 19–22.

42. *Voices:* [Gettysburg], Sgt. George A. Bowen, 12th NJ Infantry, 147.

43. Menge and Shimrak: [Cold Harbor], Pvt. Daniel Chisholm, Co. K, 116th PA, Irish Brigade, 19–22.

44. Bauer: [Chancellorsville], Pvt. Rice C. Bull, 123rd NY, 58–63.

45. *Voices:* [Gettysburg], Col. Isaac E. Avery, 6th NC, 102. Written in a scribbled hand as he was dying.

46. Ibid.: [Gettysburg], Capt. Henry L. Abbott, 20th ME Inf., 159.

PART III
CIVILIANS' LIVES

12

BE IT EVER SO HUMBLE

What have husbands to do with housekeeping? If they furnish
the funds to supply the family, is that not sufficient?
—*The Housekeeper's Encyclopedia*

Home ownership served as an ideal during the Civil War era, but many
families, especially in cities, had to settle for apartments, boarding houses,
and tenements. Even among individual homeowners, the diversity of the
residences included mansions, villas, multistory houses, cottages, cabins,
and soddies. The Irish immigrants were noted at the time for building
shanties—structures that were virtual shacks. Architectural pattern books
abounded, containing a wide variety of house plans of different sizes and
prices. Even periodicals carried house plans. The typical middle-class
home had three types of rooms. There were public rooms such as the hall,
parlor, dining room, and library. Bedchambers were considered private
rooms and were almost exclusively located on the second floor. The mere
placement of a bedroom on the first floor of a two-story home other than
in the event of sickness was considered risqué in many circles. The final
category included workrooms such as the kitchen, pantry, laundry, scullery, and cellar.

THE FRONT HALL

In addition to the practical purposes of providing a barrier against the
cold or containing the mud and dirt from outside, the front hall of a Victo-

A floor plan from *Arthur's Home Magazine* (1855).

rian home had a very important social function. Business dealings in these times were much more likely to be done face to face, and the front hall provided a reception area where these dealings could take place without exposing the family's private quarters. In the absence of a servants' entrance, shopping purchases were often delivered here, and in urban areas, mail might be delivered several times a day.

It was important that the front hall be decorated in a fashion appropriate to the social standing of the family. The hall was likely to be furnished with a pair of chairs for visitors, a mirror for checking one's appearance, and a table to receive calling cards. Upscale homes often had massive pieces of furniture that combined several of these features. Floors could be tiled for the practical purpose of accommodating the dirt of a high-traffic area. Nonetheless, Elizabeth Blair Lee wrote in 1863, "I have enquired about carpets & oil cloth—the latter is much the cheapest for the Hall—the best quality costs $1.25 to $1.50 for square yard—a poor carpet costs that & dust makes the oil cloth best in other respects."[1]

THE PARLOR

The parlor was the most public room in the Victorian house. Parlors were common to both the North and the South and across the middle

A so-called country home from one of the many architectural magazines available in the second half of the 19th century. Bracket, pillars, and cornices made the simple rural floor plan fashionable.

class. Some more affluent homes had a front parlor solely dedicated to formal visitations and a back parlor for family use, but a single parlor was most common. The parlor was the place where visitors would be received, and therefore where the first impressions of a family were formed. Decorating decisions were made in a very calculated manner so as to project the image a family wished to convey. The parlor contained a family's "best" in every way. It would have the highest ceilings, the largest fireplace, and the most elaborate furnishings. The central feature of most parlors was a large circular table with a kerosene or oil lamp. Here the family would gather to write, read, converse, play games, or engage in needlework. The need to gather around the central light, which may have been the only one in the room, helped to foster a communal attitude. The parlor table allowed family members to be together, yet various members of the family could be engaged in a variety of pastimes. They were able to function as individuals yet remain a part of the family community as a whole.

The second focal point of the parlor was the fireplace. The mantel was often heavily decorated with pictures, collected natural objects, or mementos. What could not fit on the mantel would be placed on shelves or etageres around the room. An intense appreciation of nature prevailed during this time, leading to the collection of seashells, fossils, minerals, pinecones, and dried flowers, which were all displayed in the parlor. It

A back-to-back advertise-
ment for parlor accesso-
ries from *Arthur's Home
Magazine*, 1855.

was felt that natural objects reflected the harmony of nature and civilization. Homes decorated with objects of nature were thought to demonstrate nature's beauty in family life. Additionally, using natural objects as
decorative accents showed a wife's sense of economy, an attribute much
extolled.

Other furnishings might include an upholstered sofa, armchairs, and
a pair of easy chairs all done in matching fabric. Rocking chairs were
very much in fashion during the 1860s, and parlors were just one room in
which they might be found. Common upholstery materials included brocades, silk damask, and tapestry, which were adorned with tassels, cords,
and fringe. It was not unusual for sofa ensembles to contain a large gentleman's armchair and a smaller chair with half arms for the lady, which
accommodated her wide skirts and kept her posture properly erect. The
placement of chairs around the room allowed social groupings to change
as activities varied. A person might move from the solitary activity of reading quietly to join a game with other family members at the table. Sofas
were designed with slight curves to encourage conversation.

Ownership of a piano or parlor organ heralded solid middle-class status. In 1855 a German-born American piano maker named Henry Steinway
began to manufacture a piano with a cast-iron frame that gave its sound

Advertisements like these for piano-fortes and sewing machines continued to appear throughout the war in Northern magazines. From *Arthur's Home Magazine*, 1855.

much greater brilliance and power than earlier forms. There have been no fundamental changes in the design and construction of pianos since 1855. This improvement prompted widespread interest in pianos and musical compositions for it. More than 20,000 pianos a year were being produced in the United States by the time of the war. Retailers offered terms even for their least expensive models, which sold for as little as $300, and advertisements for pianos and organs filled period newspapers.[2]

Families enjoyed singing and listening to pieces played on the piano. The piano was generally considered to be a feminine instrument, and women actively cultivated their musical skills. The pursuit of musical excellence may not always have been motivated by a love of harmonious tones. The piano provided a reason for courting couples to be in relatively close quarters during a time when proper behavior generally forbade such intimacy. By the piano, however, the couple could exchange glances as the young woman played. The young man could bend close, as he courteously turned pages for the seated player. "Young ladies are the principal interpreters of domestic music," avowed *Macmillan's Magazine* in 1860.[3] This feminine interpretation led to the selection of many feminine accessories to adorn the piano top.

Cartes de visite are displayed on a period album. From the authors' collection

The sheet music industry was already well established and flourishing. The war created an even greater demand as people sought patriotic and war-related music. Three days after the firing upon Fort Sumter, George F. Root's "The First Gun Is Fired! May God Protect the Right!" was for sale. Two of the most popular songs, "Dixie's Land" and "The Battle Hymn of the Republic," remain favorites even today. Other popular themes for parlor music included soldier life and battlefield deaths. The sheet music itself was often beautifully lithographed, providing the additional bonus of an inexpensive piece of artwork for the parlor. With the outbreak of war, these images often contained patriotic and battlefield scenes that brought the war into the parlor. So much piano sheet music was acquired by some, that separate pieces of furniture were required to hold it. Possession of such a piece of furniture was an additional status symbol. Parlor organs tended to be an outgrowth of domestic religious worship that celebrated hymns and church music. These were particularly important to homes that actively fostered the Christian development of family.

Assorted small tables around the parlor contained additional bric-a-brac or perhaps a photograph album used to collect "cartes de visite," which were photographs a little larger than modern business cards mounted on thick cardboard stock. Filling albums with cartes de visite was quite a family hobby. Edwin Weller wrote to his fiancée, "I should be pleased to aid you in filling up your Album with nice Pictures, and will do so if I have an opportunity for I think they [other soldiers] could not place their Photographs in better hands than yours."[4] Some albums were elaborate, decorated with silver or brass clasps and covered with velvet, wood, or mother of pearl. Inside, the album contained twenty or more pages of pre-cut frames ready to receive the cartes. While the cartes became relatively inexpensive, at least one photographer advertised on the back of his work, "CARTES DE VISITE, 6 for $1.00." Filling an album was an accomplishment likely to be achieved only by a middle- or upper-class family.[5]

People generally stood for photographs at landmark times in their life such as just after marriage or betrothal, following the birth of a child, or before leaving for war. Cartes could also be purchased. Collectors acquired pictures of famous people or cartes that expressed a religious sentiment. Soldiers of both armies exchanged cartes with comrades. Weller later wrote, "I have had some new photographs sent me . . . I had these last ones taken for the officers of our Regt. who have wanted my photograph ever since I returned but I thought I would let some of my friends have the best of exchanging and giving some of the officers those I had taken first." Soldiers also purchased cartes depicting the generals of their army and prominent officers, creating a pictorial documentation of their battle experience.[6]

The walls of a home were often wallpapered. Patterns showing large bouquets tied with ribbons or of oversized fruit became popular a decade before the war and stayed in style into the 1860s. Walls were usually further ornamented with paintings and, for the less affluent, prints. Attractive prints of good quality and color became readily available during the 1860s, and many families took advantage of this new technology. Subjects included farmyard scenarios, riverscapes, European scenes, hunting vignettes, still lifes, and biblical tableaus. The popularity of farmyard pictures in homes decorated in brocade and tassels can be attributed to the passion for harmony with nature and an underlying yearning for simpler times.

European subjects might be reminders of the travels family members might have made, a fact the family would have been desirous to publicize. Another popular subject was famous people, both historical and contemporary. The prominent people came from musical, literary, political, and military venues. Representations of these people might take the form of a painting, print, engraving, or bust. Which public figures a family chose to decorate their home made a powerful statement about the owners.

Not only did the selection of these works of art show good taste and education, they served as silent but concrete reminders of revered values. George Washington, for example, was admired as a selfless leader who put the public interest above his private preferences. The presence of his picture in the parlor showed that these attributes were valued by the family. These pictures served as constant reminders to children of what was expected of them in adulthood. Many of the women depicted in this form were wives of famous men, such as Mary Todd Lincoln, or entertainers like the singer Jenny Lind. The message for young girls was one of expectation that they would be quiet movers gently working behind the scenes. Many women of the Civil War era understood this and participated in benevolent activities such as serving in hospitals, sewing for troops, and assisting orphans and needy families.

Floors were carpeted. However, carpets were sold by the linear yard and were a little more than two feet wide. They had to be pieced and sewn together much like wallpaper. Patterns tended to be floral or other naturals. Susan Evans wrote to her sister, Emma Sargent Barbour, about the installation of new carpet in July 1861. About a dozen women came to assist her in the installation. "I had to help cut the breadth, but we were not very experienced hands and consequently the carpet was cut wrong, or rather one breadth fell short. We measured it before hand, but could not seem to make the figures match any other way."[7] Carpets would additionally be covered by mats in high-traffic areas or where fireplace sparks were likely. Elizabeth Blair Lee compared prices of two merchants in Washington and Philadelphia and stated that they ranged from $150 to $262 for a carpet in October 1863.

Victorians revered intellectual pursuits. Books were therefore a must in the parlor. By 1860 more than 90 percent of white men and women could read. Diary entries refer to reading more than to any other pastime. Large, heavy Bibles were most often displayed on the central table as a symbol of family religious life. Other books were frequently displayed on tables or built-in bookshelves. Books brought learning and the world outside into the home. A parlor containing books showed that the owners valued knowledge and wished to better themselves. The information contained therein provided greater understanding of the natural world and the Lord's works. Literary allusions were not limited to pictures of famous authors or samples of their works. Statues and ceramics depicting scenes from literary works were used to decorate the parlor. Harriet Beecher Stowe's Uncle Tom and Little Eva were popular images in Northern homes.

Windows were almost buried beneath a shroud of fabrics. Closest to the window would be a thin curtain most likely of lace. This would be covered with a second layer made of heavy fabric, which could be closely drawn to block out the light entirely. The ensemble would be topped off with a valance fashionably trimmed with cords, tassels, and braid. Overall, the Victorian parlor was a place of abundant accumulation. It also gives insight into the spirit and the structure of the society of which it was a part.

THE LIBRARY

Although it was common to see period house plans showing libraries—and trade catalogs displayed library furniture—only the rich and the upper middle class could afford libraries. The library was truly a man's domain. It was a place to which he could retreat and engage in the kind of activities not traditionally associated with home life. Here a man could smoke, drink, and discuss money, politics, and war without exposing the rest of the family to such vulgarities. Libraries were usually on the ground floor but off to one side. Decorations were more subdued than in the parlor. Walls were paneled or done in dark-colored paper. Heavy bookshelves were often featured. Other furniture would include a desk or writing table, large gentlemen's chairs, and various tables. If a man had hobbies or interests, it would be here that he would pursue them. Specimen cases containing fossils or insects would be displayed among accompanying magnifying glasses and other optical aids.

THE DINING ROOM

The luxury of a room dedicated solely to the purpose of dining was another badge of middle-class status. Families of lesser means ate in the kitchen or in an area adjacent to the parlor set aside for dining. Dining room furniture tended to be massive, often of mahogany or other dark wood. Elizabeth Blair Lee wrote to her naval officer husband in October 1863, "I have look [sic] at some furniture & find that dining room furniture alone will cost four hundred dollars of oil walnut which is as cheap as oak."[8] The standard number of chairs was eight. A sideboard was common, providing an excellent place to display oversized serving pieces and candelabras. Walls tended to be dark to show up well under candlelight, the standard lighting for this room. Even during luncheons it would not be unusual to draw the draperies and eat by candlelight. The formal dining experience was one of tremendous ritual and ostentation. Books of etiquette contained pages upon pages of rules guiding proper behavior while dining. Certain foods required highly specialized serving or eating utensils, and form was extremely important. Ten of the thirty pages Martine dedicates to dining in his etiquette book pertain solely to carving. Beginning in the mid-19th century the upper class developed a passion for complicating the dining process by introducing needless table items such as spoon warmers in an attempt to ritualize the process and to distinguish those "in the know."

THE KITCHEN

The one utilitarian room in the mid-19th-century house was the kitchen. It was here that the most mundane, labor-intensive household duties took place. The kitchen was always located on the ground floor and had a door to the outside to facilitate deliveries. It was not necessary for the kitchen to be adjacent to the dining room, and in certain circles distance was considered an asset, keeping odors contained. Kitchen furnishings were

The so-called modern kitchen of the 19th century had its cast-iron cook stove, running water, and convenient pantry. The cook stove was a particular improvement over open hearths that often sent cinders into the room or caught long skirts on fire. Yet accidents persisted as housewives made adjustments in their kitchen protocols. House fires decreased as the number of cook stoves increased, but the number of reported superficial burns, especially among small children making contact with hot metal, became greater.

functional and simple. There was usually a large central work table and a cupboard for storing dishes.

Miss Beecher's *Domestic Receipt Book* advised, "The kitchen floor should be covered with an oil cloth . . . Nothing is cleansed so easily as an oil cloth, and it is much better than a painted floor, because it can be moved to be painted."[9] In many homes the kitchen was also the scullery and the laundry. If that were the case, there would also be a deep sink with a drying rack for washing vegetables and pots. Indoor sinks generally had hand pumps but no drains, so that dirty water had to be bailed out and emptied outside. Dishes were washed in a large wooden bowl as a measure to keep down breakage. Pots were stored by hanging them from racks.

In many homes the dominant feature in the kitchen would have been the wood-burning stove. Stoves had become fairly standard in Northern middle-class homes by the 1860s. In rural areas, particularly among the lower classes, cooking was still done on the hearth. There were those who felt that the hearth was the traditional heart of the home and resisted the kitchen stove.

Other furnishings included the ice chest and meat safe. The meat safe was a kind of screened cupboard that protected the meat from insects, pests, and vermin but did nothing to regulate temperature. Dry goods such as flour, sugar, and cornmeal were stored in crockery or wooden containers. Rural kitchens and those of families of lesser means were also likely to be more family oriented. They may well have been used for activities such as sewing or helping children with studies and would probably contain additional furnishings to suit their multiuse needs.

THE BEDROOMS

The bedroom of the 1860s was very different from that of the previous century. It was no longer a semi-public place in which one received close acquaintances. It was now a very private place that would not even be referred to in polite conversation. Bed curtains had disappeared.

After her husband sent her some linen samples for bed linens, Elizabeth Blair Lee wrote, "The linen is wonderfully cheap—Cotton that width costs in the city $1, 25 cts & not of the best quality—that linen here would sell for $1, 50 to 60 cts . . . you could not do better to buy than buy two pairs—they will take about 11 yards—I have 12 prs of double linen sheets & two prs single . . . & two pairs of Blankets—for we cannot get any blankets here for less than six dollars. I would like one pair."[10]

Cribs and cradles were frequently found close to the parents' bed to facilitate breastfeeding and as a precaution should the child take ill during the night. Older children in lower economic situations might also sleep in the same room. Children of wealthy families would sleep in the nursery with their nanny.

THE NURSERY

Families who could afford it had a nursery for the children. As the 1860s progressed, children came to be thought of as innocent beings in need of protection and shelter from exposure to the world outside. The nursery provided this environment. It could limit the amount and kind of stimulation a child received and might possibly protect him or her from accidents and disease. Accidents and common childhood diseases claimed nearly half of all children before the age of five. Modest households had a single nursery room, often found on the third floor. Although children of the same sex often shared a bedroom in their early years, the plan book ideal was that, if possible, each child should have their own room. Affluent households could afford both day nurseries for play and night nurseries for slumber. Furniture painted in pastels and decorated with baby animals and characters from nursery rhymes was produced in child-sized proportions.

Day nurseries were playrooms that also often doubled as schoolrooms for those children who were taught by the governess. In such cases they would also contain globes, maps and perhaps a blackboard as needed for instruction. These rooms were designed to withstand the abuse that children can sometimes inflict on furnishings. Walls were often whitewashed. Curtains were simple. There would be a table with several chairs. These might be simple pine furniture bought for the purpose or cast off furniture from other rooms. There were shelves and cupboards for books and toys and perhaps an armchair or two. The children of more affluent families enjoyed a greater degree of privacy in the home than their farming or working class counterparts. They spent most of their time in their nursery away from their parents but kept safe by their isolation. Poorer children, on the other hand, enjoyed more parental supervision and interaction inside the home, but they also had a great deal more autonomy outside where much of their play took place.

Playthings varied widely with social class, however. Manufacturing increased the number of store-bought toys and board games that were available to those who could afford them. Working class and farm children played with simple, homemade toys—usually whatever a loving father might carve from a piece of wood by a winter's fire or what a mother might fashion from her bag of material scraps. Children, too, were resourceful. Jacks might be made from corn kernels, dolls from cornhusks, and a tea set from discarded pieces of crockery. Lucy A. Weed and her sister collected acorns, the caps of which made remarkably tiny bowls and dishes. Even children from the lower rung of economic success had some exposure to simple commercially produced toys. Dolls with papier-mâché heads or those made from the same fabric as their bodies were affordable for even poorer children.

On Sundays, children were only allowed to read or to listen to the Bible or other religious literature. All toys were put away except those that were considered of a religious or moral nature, and these were called Sabbath toys. One such plaything was a Noah's Ark. Sets varied, but they all contained a boat, Noah and his wife, an assortment of pairs of animals and a dove. More extensive sets included Ham, Shem, Japheth, and their wives. Some had scores of animal pairs numbering as many as 100. Noah's Ark toys date back to the late 17th century but reached a peak during the Victorian era. Bible stories inspired other toys as well. *Jacob's Ladder*, made of six thin wooden rectangles connected by a cloth tape, was roughly reminiscent of a ladder. When held vertically and released, it created the illusion of tumbling blocks. The blocks were often covered with biblical scenes. *The Wolf in Sheep's Clothing* was a small wooden wolf hidden within a removable fleece. The Pillars of Solomon had two pillars connected with a string, which when cut, maintained the illusion that the pillars were still attached. Some doll play was permitted. Termed "church dolls" these figures could be assembled as a congregation to whom the child delivered a sermon. Some came with tiny carved coffins in which the "corpse" could be placed. Puzzle maps of Palestine (the Holy Land) were also considered appropriate.

THE NECESSARY

While wealthy families might have had inside plumbing and the accompanying bathroom facilities, most people had to make do with ceramic washbasins and pitchers on a washstand. Full baths were labor-intensive events that involved bringing up heated water from the kitchen to the bedchamber so that a compact metal tub could be filled. This relegated total-immersion baths to special occasions. Sponge baths were the more common occurrence. Outhouses were not convenient at night, so most bedrooms contained a covered chamberpot. Some chamberpots were hidden in various pieces of furniture (mostly chairs and stools), but some were merely stored beneath the bed until they were emptied into the slop jar in the morning.

Clothing was stored in chests of drawers and wardrobes. Built-in closets were just beginning to come into vogue in the 1860s. Beside the bed might be found a small table upon which to rest the chamber stick used to guide one to the bedroom upon retiring. Oil lamps were usually not found in bedrooms, as carrying an oil lamp with its liquid fuel from room to room was a dangerous endeavor. People did not sit in bed and read before sleeping, nor did they lounge about in their lingerie. Bedrooms were likely to be drafty places most of the year.

NOTES

1. Virginia Jeans Laas, ed., *Wartime Washington: Letters of Elizabeth Blair Lee* (Chicago: University of Illinois Press, 1991), 313.

2. Richard Crawford, *The Civil War Songbook* (New York: Dover, 1977), v.

3. Patricia Anderson, "Romantic Strains of the Parlor Piano," *Victorian* 3, no. 3 (1997): 22.

4. William Walton, ed., *A Civil War Courtship: The Letters of Edwin Weller from Antietam to Atlanta* (New York: Doubleday, 1980), 25.

5. Carte de visite in the authors' collection from Isaac S. Lachman, 984 North Second Street, Philadelphia.

6. Walton, 65.

7. Shirley Blotnick Moskow, *Emma's World: An Intimate Look at Lives Touched by the Civil War Era* (Far Hills, NJ: New Horizons Press, 1990), 68.

8. Laas, 212.

9. Catherine E. Beecher, *Miss Beecher's Domestic Receipt Book* (New York: Harper & Brothers, 1850), 253.

10. Laas, 313.

13

LEISURE TIME

One book, wisely selected and properly studied, can do more to improve the mind, and enrich the understanding, than skimming over the surface of an entire library.
—Reverend Doctor Joel Hawes, 1835

LITERATURE

Literacy was quite high in Civil War America. In the South at least 70 percent of the white male population could read, and in the North the ability to read may have run as high as 90 percent.[1] Prior to 1820, English texts, less expensive and more fashionable, had almost closed the literary market to American authors. The emergence of a new popularity of reading and writing among the middle class underpinned a new national interest in publishing and professional authorship. This circumstance was further fostered by the need to while away long hours of boredom created by the lack of normal social activities brought on by the war. Four types of reading material have been identified as popular with Civil War era readers: religious reading, purposeful (or instructive) reading, newspaper and magazine reading, and reading for escape. These categories, while somewhat arbitrary, can serve to describe the majority of the printed materials sought by 19th century readers.[2]

Beginning in the second decade of the 19th century, the novel, the most popular form of escapism, had a growing acceptance and appeal among the general reading public. Middle- and upper-class women have long

News, information, and entertainment. The importance
of the printed word in 19th-
century America cannot be
overestimated.

been recognized as the chief consumers of this literary form. So great was
the popularity of the novel that it drew criticism. As late as 1856 the Code
of Public Instruction for the State of New York recognized the "necessity"
of excluding from all libraries "novels, romances and other fictitious cre-
ations of the imagination, including a large proportion of the lighter literature of the day. The propriety of a peremptory and uncompromising
exclusion of those catch-penny, but revolting publications which cultivate
the taste for the marvelous, the tragic, the horrible and the supernatural
. . . [is without] the slightest argument." The code also expressed an "obvious" disgust for works dealing with "pirates, banditti and desperadoes
of every description."[3] A guide to propriety for mothers written by Lydia
Child decried "the profligate and strongly exciting works" found in the
public libraries. "The necessity of fierce excitement in reading is a sort
of intellectual intemperance" producing, in the estimation of the guide's
author, "weakness and delirium" in women and young girls. The Pelham
novels and the works of Lord Byron, Edward Maturin, Matthew G. Lewis,
and Ann Radcliffe were all identified as having "an unhealthy influence
upon the soul" that should be avoided.[4]

Of these, the only meaningful name is that of Lord Byron, who, with
Shakespeare and Charles Dickens, was among the most famous of British

authors known to those outside of Britain. Mrs. Child does not identify her reason for including him in this list, but his collected works along with his letters and journals were available to most American readers in a multivolume edition. Byron typified the Romantic movement in litera- ture, and politically he was a "genuine and burning liberal." His advanced political views may have made him suspect.[5]

The "Pelham novels" referred to by Mrs. Child may be the works of Camden Pelham, who wrote *The Chronicles of Crime,* a series of memoirs and anecdotes about British criminals "from the earliest period to 1841." They were illustrated by H. K. Browne, the famous illustrator of Dick- ens' works who went by the pseudonym "Phiz." The historical novels of Irish American author Edward Maturin were particularly steeped in the romantic. They included *Montezuma, the Last of the Aztecs,* a brilliant, if overly impassioned, history; *Benjamin, the Jew of Granada,* set in fifteenth- century Moslem Spain; and *Eva, or the Isles of Life and Death,* a romance of twelfth-century England. One of his more fiery books was Bianca, a story of a passionate love between a woman from Italy and a man from Ireland.[6]

Ann Radcliffe's novels, many written in the late 1790s, were primarily "time-fillers for literarily inclined young women who had no children and did not care for society." Although she died in 1823, Mrs. Radcliffe was the main source of "horror stories with a twist" for 19th century readers. The significance of her "horror-mongering" on later romantic literature can not be overestimated. Terror connoisseurs found her heroines melan- choly, quick to weep, and endearingly practical. In *The Italian* she created a romantic villain who brought the physical aspects of terror to perfection. This villain, repelled by the enormity of his crime, but fascinated by the looming tragedy of his fate, was the basis for similar characters used by Maturin, Byron, Lewis, and Scott. Her last novel, released in 1826, was *Gaston de Blondeville.* Actually written in 1802, this work preceded Scott's first historical novels and attempted for the first time to paint an authentic historical picture.[7]

Almost totally forgotten today, Matthew G. Lewis was a follower of Mrs. Radcliffe whose writings "ran heavily to the florid romantic." His first novel, *Ambrosio, the Monk,* was universally read and widely condemned in Britain and America. Lewis was charged with being immoral and ir- religious when it was discovered that he was recommending that certain passages from the Bible be kept from the young. His work was considered "vicious" and "terrible." Often referred to as the "immoral monk Lewis," he was, in fact, a man of genuine philanthropy and humane instincts. After inheriting a plantation in Jamaica along with 500 black slaves, Lewis instituted a series of reforms that were "regarded as mad" by his contem- poraries. He attested to their effectiveness in *The Journal of a West India Proprietor,* which was published just before his death from yellow fever. Besides several dramas, Lewis produced two romantic novels—*The Bravo of Venice* and *Feudal Tyrants*—as well as *Tales of Terror and Romantic Tales*, which were based on German and Spanish legends; and in collaboration with Scott, a collection of ballads, *Tales of Wonder*. His work is generally neglected today, but he had tremendous influence on the romantic writers of his day.[8]

Like Mrs. Child, the Reverend Doctor Joel Hawes similarly warned young men that in the choice of books there was a "great need of caution." He believed that a person's character could be "ruined by reading a single volume." Yet he confessed that one book, "wisely selected and properly studied," could "do more to improve the mind, and enrich the understanding, than skimming over the surface of an entire library."[9]

Notwithstanding such warnings, novels remained popular, and the potency of this literature to govern the mind of readers proved to have not been underestimated by the good reverend. Fictional characters possessed a remarkable ability to influence 19th-century readers. Uncle Tom, Topsy, Ivanhoe, Hawkeye, Hester Prynne, and Ebenezer Scrooge were deeply familiar characters to a society that read as much as 19th-century Americans did. These characters often seemed to become nearly as real and as influential to the reader as actual friends and relations.[10]

The works of the English novelist and social commentator Charles Dickens were widely read in America. In Dickens' very popular works both sections of the country found some character, situation, or condition that seemed to bolster the very different views of modern society Americans held. Many social reformers, like Dickens himself, championed the cause of the poor. Nonetheless, Dickens was generally unconcerned with the economic aspects of social reform, choosing rather to deal with an increased appreciation of the value of the human being. Ignorance, for him, was the great cause of human misery. In 1843 he gave a speech in the city of Manchester in which he pleaded for a heightened sense of humanitarianism and an improvement in the system of public education in Britain. In contrast to the "ragged schools" that had been set up by well-meaning but untrained volunteer teachers to give England's poor children the rudiments of an education, Dickens proposed that the surest improvement in the nation's future was tied to a public investment in education sponsored by the government.

Dickens' stories emphasized the need to change traditional ways of thinking. But many in the South misread Dickens' message and saw the misfortune, destitution, and disease that fills his works as characteristic of all urban life. Modern urban life was the great evil haunting the romantic domains of the Southern imagination. Dickens' novels mirrored the inevitable bleak future of America if Northern concepts of social progress continued to be implemented as English ones had for decades without noticeably improving society.

Although thoroughly English in its setting and personalities, *A Christmas Carol*, first published in 1843, seemed to embody the very limitations of modern society in mid-century in the interactions of Scrooge with the other characters. The story portrays a secular rather than a traditionally religious attitude toward the holidays. The spirits and ghosts of Christmas are remarkably worldly in their appearance and temporal in their outlook. The awakening of a social conscience in Scrooge is their chief endeavor. Ultimately, it is the specter of an unlamented death, a topic of great concern in the 19th century, which brings Scrooge around. Yet even a morally awakened Scrooge refuses to devote his life to social work. Instead, he acts out his reformation on a very personal level.[11]

Southerners despised such ambiguous social remedies as the poorhouses and the workhouses that filled Dickens' pages. The debtors' prison of *Little Dorrit* and the orphanage of *Oliver Twist* were obviously not sufficient to solve the social ills of an urban society. Southerners were left with a portrait of cities, like those of the North, veritably teeming with the exploited masses from which they chose to be separated.[12]

Apologists for the Southern way of life proclaimed that Scrooge's treatment of Bob Cratchit emphasized the abuses possible in an age governed by the "work for wage" system that so lacked a sense of personal involvement and family dedication. The personal responsibility many Southerners felt toward their neighbors, their workers, and even their slaves seemed noble in contrast to the socially anonymous caretaking for the unfortunates found in Dickens' works.

Southern intellectuals of the prewar period were also widely read in the literature of European Romanticism, and they used romantic allusions freely in their writing. Confederate General John B. Gordon, who rose to popular prominence when badly wounded at the Battle of Antietam, was described as being "pure as Galahad, knightly as King Arthur . . . [and] as brave as Lancelot . . . a Chevalier Bayard."[13] Southern papers spoke of heroics and crusades. The *Richmond Southern Illustrated News* reported the final minutes of General George Pickett's charge at Gettysburg as "noble and gallant."[14]

The most popular book of the war period was *Les Miserables*. This was closely followed by Tennyson's 1864 narrative poem *Enoch Arden,* in which a shipwrecked sailor returns home to find that his wife, thinking him dead, has remarried. Sir Walter Scott's Waverley novels were immensely popular. Their theme of the Scottish struggle to throw off the dominance and oppression of the English served as an analogy for the position in which the South saw itself with respect to the North. Scott's use of romantic characters, lords and ladies, knights in armor, and grand estates was particularly resonant with the Southern image of itself. So familiar was Scott's work to Southerners that in later years Mark Twain only halfjokingly blamed Scott for causing the Civil War.

Second only to Scott's in popularity were the American adventure novels of James Fenimore Cooper. Although his first novel was poorly accepted by American readers, largely because it imitated the British form,

Cooper's second work, *The Spy*, published in 1822, was an outstanding success. Cooper's subsequent novels emphasized American manners and scenes as interesting and important. Still, many Americans considered novels to be "trivial, feminine, and vaguely dishonorable" because they appealed to the emotions and aroused the imagination. Nonetheless, Cooper found that there was a great demand for adventure tales derived from the Revolution, and his writing was sufficiently manly and moral to find acceptance by a wide audience.[15]

Like Scott, Cooper promoted a social vision of a stable and genteel society governed by its natural aristocracy, "perpetuating property, order, and liberty" as represented by a reunited American gentry. That this view resonated with the Southern image of itself would have upset Cooper, with his very Northern attitudes. *The Pioneers*, Cooper's third book, was dedicated to the proposition that the American republic, poised on the verge of "demagoguery, deceit, hypocrisy, and turmoil," could be transformed into a stable, prosperous, and just society. Although the theme of "reconciliation. . .on conservative terms" was almost three decades old, Cooper's novels were very popular with the soldiers, mainly because of their masculine adventure themes, and were often found among their most prized possessions. Dog-eared copies circulated through the camps and were often read aloud around the campfire to eager audiences.

A federal officer, Captain John W. De Forest, found himself "a tolerably instructed man, having read *The Book of the Indians*, all of Cooper's novels, and some of the works of Captain Mayne Reid." Reid was a close friend of Edgar Allan Poe, and his novels were mainly adventure stories. Beginning in 1850, he published *The Rifle Rangers: Adventures of an Officer in Southern Mexico*, which was based on his own service in the 1846 war; *The Scalp Hunters; The War Trail*; and *Forest Exiles*. In 1853 he wrote a novel inspired by his 15-year-old spouse, appropriately titled *The Child Wife*, and in 1856 he wrote a play called *The Quadroon*. De Forest reported that he inexplicably found his thoughts "ranging from the expectation of a [musket] ball through the spine to a recollection of Cooper's most celebrated Indians" while under fire during the siege of Port Hudson.[16]

Nathaniel Hawthorne, convinced that most American literature ran too close to the British style, devoted himself to a uniquely symbolic and allegorical form. *The Scarlet Letter*, published in 1850, was certainly familiar to American readers, and its author was considered a literary giant. But Hawthorne's persistent dark emphasis on guilt and sorrow ran counter to the popular tastes and religious sentiment of Americans at mid-century. In 1851 and 1852, respectively, he published *The House of the Seven Gables* and *The Blithedale Romance*. This last was a study of failed utopian efforts to improve society. He served as the U.S. Consul at Liverpool, England, for four years, and was photographed by Mathew Brady before his death in 1864.

When Harriet Beecher Stowe published *Uncle Tom's Cabin* in 1852, the book sold 300,000 copies in America and Britain in one year. Mrs. Stowe's

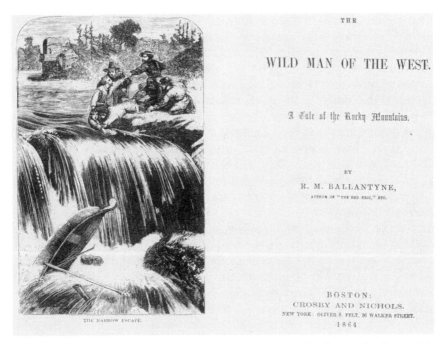

THE

WILD MAN OF THE WEST.

A Tale of the Rocky Mountains.

BY

R. M. BALLANTYNE,
AUTHOR OF "THE RED ERIC," ETC.

BOSTON:
CROSBY AND NICHOLS.
NEW YORK: OLIVER S. FELT, 36 WALKER STREET.
1864

THE NARROW ESCAPE.

The title page of a popular adventure novel from 1864. Similar works drew criticism from more conservative quarters of society.

work was one of total fiction; it stressed the evils of slavery and presented a picture of total brutality. Mrs. Stowe had no personal knowledge of slavery. The factual basis for the story was Theodore D. Weld's radical abolitionist tract entitled *Slavery as It Is: The Testimony of a Thousand Witnesses*, which was published in 1839. *Uncle Tom's Cabin* was immensely more effective in preaching the anti-slavery message in the form of a novel than the earlier tract had ever dreamed of being.

The South considered Mrs. Stowe's work a slander and regarded it as abolitionist propaganda. A Southern woman, familiar with slavery and slaves, wrote that she could not read a book so filled with distortions as it was "too sickening" to think that any man would send "his little son to beat a human being tied to a tree." The same woman goes on to suggest, using other literary references, that Mrs. Stowe's work portrays as much fiction as Squeers beating Smike in Dickens' *Nicholas Nickleby* or the gouging of Gloucester's eyes in Shakespeare's *King Lear*. "How delightfully pharisaic a feeling it must be, to rise up superior and fancy [to] we [who] are so degraded as to defend and like to live with such degraded creatures around us . . . as Legree."[17]

Nonetheless, amicably disposed Northerners found the passages describing the murderous brutality of Simon Legree indicative of the typical behavior of Southern slaveowners. The significance of the story, as of many of the attacks on the institution of slavery, lay in its ability to dramatize and emotionalize the issue. Writing and speechmaking on the subject of slavery in particular—and of the Southern culture in general—were becoming increasingly stereotypical, and the stereotypes, even when presented in novels, were taking on a reality in the minds of the people.

Although soldiers were quick to write home about finishing *Nicholas Nickelby, The Pickwick Papers, The Deerslayer, Ivanhoe,* or other works of obvious quality, they also read a great deal of low-quality material. Many of these works have been identified. They include such masculine titles as *Con Cregan, Gold Friend, The Quadroon of Louisiana, Son of the Wilderness, Scar Chief the Wild Halfbreed, Wild West Scenes,* and *Our Own Heroes,* but also more popular works such as *Lady Audley's Secret, The Mystery, Macaria,* and *Louisa Elton.*[18]

Soldiers, "burdened by huge blocks of time during which they have nothing to do but wait," were suddenly possessed of an abundant amount of time to read, which "had previously been in short supply to American men." Of the five most common leisure-time camp activities—individual foraging, gambling, sleeping, talking, and reading—only reading was seen to be "a positive force" for the improvement of the troops.[19]

American books were in large supply for the first time during the war. In 1834 fewer than 500 titles were published in the United States. By 1862 this number had grown to almost 4,000.[20] By coincidence, the first "dime novels" were published in June 1860. These were inexpensive paperbound adventure stories. The first title, *Malaeska; the Indian Wife of the White Hunter,* by Ann Stephens, makes it abundantly clear that this was escapist literature of the lowest class. Publisher Irwin P. Beadle's dime novels and their many imitators initiated a whole era of cheap publishing just eight months prior to the war.[21]

At the time there were a number of distinguished American authors of an age to serve in the field and provide a firsthand professional description of the face of war. Theodore Winthrop had written a number of successful books prior to the war, and he volunteered to serve. Unfortunately, Winthrop was killed in one of the first engagements of the war, at Great Bethel in June 1861.

Another young author distinguished before the outbreak of hostilities was John W. De Forest. From 1851 through 1859, De Forest wrote several books, including the History of the Indians of Connecticut and the novels *Witching Times, Oriental Acquaintance, European Acquaintance,* and *Seacliff.* De Forest went to war as a captain with the 12th Connecticut Volunteers. Many of his battlefield reports were printed by *Harper's Monthly,* and in 1864 he wrote *Miss Ravenel's Conversion from Secession to Loyalty.* In these, De Forest shared the simple truth of life in the army and on the battlefield.[22]

The enormous hunger for reading material in the camps was supplied to some extent by social and religious agencies that recognized the need.

There was no lack of illustrated newspapers in Civil War America, but the quality of their artwork was not consistent.

In part, the soldiers and their comrades found their own supply of reading material, but both armies were largely at the mercy of outside sources for their books and newspapers. Much of the work involved in providing books to the troops was done by the U.S. Christian Commission, which supplied both religious and secular reading material. Almost one million Bibles were distributed to the troops, and more than 30,000 other volumes were circulated through a system of almost 300 portable libraries. Each contained from 70 to 125 volumes which were transported and stored in wooden, shelved boxes about three feet square. Many of the books were printed in smaller-than-standard size and included classical titles as well as history, poetry, science, philosophy, and religion. The Confederate Bible Society and the South Carolina Tract Society provided religious works for the Southern troops, but the South had no system of portable libraries.[23]

NEWSPAPERS

There were millions of newspaper subscribers in the country on the eve of the war, and the papers were particularly adept at bringing the war to the homefront.[24] People wanted to know what was happening to their friends and relations on faraway battlefields, and they looked to newspapers such as *Leslie's* or *Harper's* to make sense of the confusion of war reports. New York publisher Frank Leslie produced amazingly moving woodcut illustrations for his *Illustrated Newspaper* from 1861 through 1865. His use of graphics and terse prose to interpret ongoing news events was a new concept in the American newspaper business that was quickly adopted by other news agencies. In a day when a partisan press was the rule, *Leslie's* stood apart. Except for tolerating anti-Irish sentiment and portraying Negroes in a stereotypical and condescending manner, *Leslie's* condoned little that was political.

Frank Leslie, whose true name was Henry Carter, had emigrated from Britain in 1848. There he had worked as an engraver for the *Illustrated London News*, which was the first newspaper to employ graphics. In London, Leslie learned the processes for turning pencil sketches into woodcut engravings that could be transferred to newsprint. In 1852 P. T. Barnum, the famed American showman, developed a process by which the sketch was divided into several pieces to be engraved on as many blocks by individual engravers, then carefully assembled into a single printing surface.[25] Leslie was hired by Barnum as a supervising engraver for the short-lived *Illustrated News*. Leaving Barnum, by 1854 he had set up his own organization and published the first issue of *Frank Leslie's Ladies' Gazette of Paris, London, and New York*, one of the first illustrated fashion magazines in America. This was quickly followed by the *Illustrated Newspaper* in 1855. Leslie employed more than 130 engraving and print artists as well as a substantial number of roving sketch artists.

Frank Leslie introduced a number of papers to Civil War readers: the *Illustrated Zeitung*, a German-language edition aimed at the German immigrant population of the North; the *Budget of Fun*, a whimsical publication featuring cheap fiction; the *Ten Cent Monthly*; the *Lady's Illustrated Almanac*; and the *Lady's Magazine and Gazette of Fashion*. All of these bore his name: Frank Leslie's.

Within four years, two independent graphic news weeklies were launched in competition with Leslie's newspaper empire: *Harper's Weekly* and the *New York Illustrated News*. Fletcher Harper, the well-financed publisher from Harper and Brothers, actively tried to recruit *Leslie's* artists and engravers, and aggressively tried to exceed *Leslie's* circulation. Leslie provided poor and erratic pay for his artists, many of whom he lost to competitors. By the opening of the war the two newspapers were within 10,000 copies of one another, with the *New York Illustrated News* a distant third.

Two of the best sketch artists of the period were the brothers William and Alfred Waud. William worked for *Leslie's* and Alfred for *Harper's*. William proved particularly adept at ingratiating himself with the social elite of South Carolina during the secession crisis. Because of the paper's uncommitted stance, wherever Waud traveled he found individuals to be cooperative and helpful. Leslie instructed him to use the utmost care in making his sketches and to avoid giving any indication of political sympathies toward one side or the other. Nonetheless, Waud left *Leslie's* in 1863 to work at *Harper's* with brother Alfred and another fine artist, Theodore Davis.

William Waud's genius and discretion were matched by an army of artists who continued to be employed by *Leslie's,* including Eugene Benson, a young artist who eagerly went to the front to record the visual images of battle; Arthur Lumley, who was hired to follow the Army of the Potomac full-time; Henry Lovie, who found his fame in sketching George B. McClellan; C. S. Hall and F. H Schell, who recorded the war in northern Virginia; F. B. Schell, who covered the Vicksburg campaign; and Edwin Forbes, who stayed with the Army of the Potomac until 1864 and became *Leslie's* most prolific artist. This 22-year-old artist followed the federal army from 1862. Forbes was not interested in the great generals and battles of the war, but rather in the day-to-day activities and lifestyle of the soldiers. So well drawn were Forbes' sketches that "readers . . . scanned the drawings in *Leslie's* for familiar faces."[26]

Reporting from the battlefield was exacting and dangerous work. Many artists fell ill with the same maladies that afflicted the troops. Two of *Leslie's* artists were captured and released by Lee, and one part-time artist, James O'Niell, was killed in combat. C.E.F. Hillen was badly wounded in the Atlanta campaign. They often found it difficult to get their sketches from the battlefield to the engravers. *Leslie's* failed to have a correspondent with Sherman on his campaign to the sea, while *Harper's* artists accompanied the general. Consequently, by 1864 *Harper's* and other Northern journals had surged ahead of *Leslie's* in circulation.[27]

The quality of the sketches by battlefield artists was not always reproduced faithfully by the engravers, and in viewing these graphic scenes great care must be taken. What the artist drew was not so much reproduced as copied. Though the artists accompanied the army and witnessed battles, they were often in a hurry to get their work back to the engravers. Unfinished sketches of prominent figures in the scene with backgrounds and lines of soldiers "roughed in" and labeled as "trees here" or "artillery battery here" were often sent off to the engravers to be filled by hands whose eyes had never seen battle. In many cases this made the scene more one created by imagination than reality. The results were sometimes unfortunate. As a consequence, the contemporary accounts of the war were far from accurately illustrated.[28]

The South had been generally dependent on Northern publishers to print its books and newspapers. In the entire South there was only one type factory, no facilities for printing maps, and an entire inability to make inexpensive wood-pulp paper. In 1860 a well-illustrated magazine such as *Harper's* or *Leslie's* could not be published in the South. *The Southern Illus-*

trated News and other papers were often limited to a single sheet of news-print. These publications made an attempt to mimic *Harper's* and *Leslie's* with crude engravings but were obviously not comparable to the Northern news outlets.[29]

Moreover, the Confederate mails were two to three times more expensive than those in the North, severely limiting circulation. Even soldiers at the front had to pay to have newspapers and mail brought to them, and by 1864 the Confederate postal system had so completely broken down that thousands of personal letters remained undelivered. The inability of the Confederacy to establish and maintain an information system based on the printed word rather than hearsay and word of mouth had no little effect on the deterioration of Southern morale. Nonetheless, patriotic Southerners bombarded their newspapers with so much unsolicited poetry on national themes that some publications began charging to print it. Newspapers like the *Montgomery Daily Advertiser* were particularly successful in creating a wide public identification with the stirring events of the winter and spring of 1861.[30]

AVAILABILITY OF READING MATERIAL

The upper classes were particularly well positioned to enjoy the pleasures of books and writing and had greater access to the printed word than the rest of the Southern population. Consequently, the aristocratic plantation owners came to share a sense of cultural commonality through their newspapers and popular literature, while the rest of the population received its information chiefly from conversation, verbal discussion, and religious exhortation.[31]

What people read during the war was dependent on what was available. In the Northern urban centers there was an almost unlimited amount and variety of reading material, so what was read in the South becomes more interesting. Southern civilians had their literary choices disrupted not only by the vagaries of the war, but also by the blockade. Newspapers printed what was available. Confederate battlefield heroes and other men of prominence were given front-page treatment. The boredom of battle reports, advertisements, and political tracts was broken, for example, when the personal letters of federal general Custer to a young woman were captured. The Richmond papers printed them and provided "some spicy reading" for the ladies.[32]

Books were read, reread, and loaned among friends and acquaintances. Many women and men turned to instructive reading, spending time with books on history, geography, painting, foreign languages, surveying, and needlework. A number of books were available on etiquette, manners, propriety, the rearing of children, husbandry, and oratory. There was a renewed interest in the Bible and religious tracts, the plays of Shakespeare, and the novels of Dickens, Scott, and Cooper.

A Virginia judge, Nathaniel B. Tucker, had turned secessionist and dedicated a novel to the cause of Virginian secession in 1830. Titled *The Partisan Leader,* the novel portrayed a unionized but unhappy Virginia in the evil grasp of Northern masters while a newly seceded and independent Southern confederacy enjoyed freedom and prosperity. While the author did not survive to see disunion, his novel became the subject of a popular Southern literary revival.

New works were scarce in the South. Nonetheless, several popular works were printed. In 1863 the *Richmond Southern Illustrated News* offered $1,000 cash to the author of the "best illustrated romance to be submitted to them between the present date and October 1 next." Many novels first appeared as serials in weekly newspapers, to be published in book form only after their popularity had been established. This had been true of the works of Dickens in England and of Stowe in America.[33]

WOMEN WRITERS

Although authorship by women was generally frowned upon before 1850, several novels were written by Southern women in the period. Women who practiced the profession of letters seem to have been viewed with less disapprobation than those who became teachers, nurses, or lawyers. Several women were acclaimed in the Southern press for their published work. The great sensation of the Southern literary world seems to have been a novel by Augusta Jane Evans, published in 1864 and entitled *Macaria, or Altars of Sacrifice.* The author dedicated this novel, about a pair of heroines sacrificing their romantic love for dedication to the cause, to the Confederate forces.[34]

PHOTOGRAPHY

The photographers who documented the Crimean War from 1854 to 1856 would be very upset to hear that the Civil War was the first to be photographed. It was not. Nor was it the first to use observation balloons, telegraphy, rifled muskets, repeating weapons, or railroads. All of these "firsts" are reserved for European wars. Yet the Civil War was the first American war to use these advances so extensively.

Hundreds of wartime photographs of the Civil War are available, and periodically new ones are found. Photographs of wartime battlefields and personalities were shown in galleries in the major cities of the North. The photographic galleries in New York and Washington in particular were very popular, and admission was expensive. The pictures, including some of the first to show war dead on the battlefield, were poignant, and may have helped to create antiwar feeling in the North. The wet plate process used in taking them was very slow and precluded any action shots. Unfortunately, some of the pictures of battlefield dead were staged by photographers who arrived days after the conflict when most of the bodies were buried. Northern photographers arriving at Gettysburg found the Confederate dead to be more available for their work, as the Federals had buried their own dead first. As a consequence, members of the burial detail were asked to pose as Federal war dead, which they did, sprawling in grotesque positions on the rocks of Little Round Top and the Devil's Den.

Mathew Brady is possibly the best-known photographer of the period. People flocked to his studios to have photographic portraits taken in their best clothes. Cartes de visite were possibly the most popular form of civilian photograph. Thousands of such wartime photos exist. Several "cabinet photos" of Abraham Lincoln (on the order of 5' X 8') were taken by Brady. However, very few "Brady" battlefield photographs were actually taken by him. Brady was practically blind and wore dark blue glasses to protect his eyes from the light. His assistants, sent out in photographic wagons with their wet glass plates, took most of the extraordinary pictures that were credited to his studio.

One of these assistants, Alexander Gardner, left Brady's employ and struck out on his own. Gardner is said to have taken almost 75 percent of the extant photographs of the Army of the Potomac. Gardner served the army by photographically reproducing maps and other documents. By the war's end, Gardner had displaced Brady as the leading American photographer, and it was he who photographed the Lincoln funeral procession and the trial of the assassination conspirators.

Another Brady assistant was George N. Bernard, whose first war photographs were taken of the Manassas battlefield in 1862. Breaking with Brady in 1863, he moved to the western theater of war to document Sherman's march from Tennessee through Georgia and to the sea. He was the official photographer of the Military Department of the Mississippi.[35]

Captain Andrew J. Russell, noted for his Union Pacific photographs after the war, was also an official army photographer during the war. As such, he was the only soldier-photographer of the period. Russell's duties included photographing the work of the Army Engineers and the reconstruction of damaged railways in order to create a visual record for the use of similar units in the future.[36]

The South also had its photographers. George S. Cook, J. D. Edwards, and A. D. Lytle were able photographers committed to the Southern cause, but their work was much more circumspect than that of their fellows from the North, being generally limited to portraiture. The South's limited technical facilities forced the public to be content with rough woodcuts and engravings. Lytle pulled off one of the great espionage feats of the war. Concealing himself, he was able to get two photos of General Benjamin Grierson's 1,700-man Northern cavalry encamping on their raid from Vicksburg to Baton Rouge.[37]

Almost no technology existed for reproducing photographs for the print media. The usual way of reproducing a photograph for a newspa-

The carte de visite was a popular form of photography. The wedding photo on the left is particularly unusual, as the bride has a white wedding dress. This reflects a relatively new fashion at that time yet to be embraced by a majority of women.

per or magazine was to have an artist redraw it and make a woodcut or engraving, as was done with battlefield sketches. This process neutralized most of the advantages of photography for the newspapers. Only original prints were available to the public, and since enlargement equipment was as yet in a formative stage of development, prints were almost always made by placing the glass plate negative in contact with the photosensitive paper and exposing them to the sun. This results in a "contact print" the same size as the glass plate negative.

OPTICAL NOVELTIES

Americans seem to have enjoyed a variety of optical phenomena in their drawing rooms and parlors. Some photographs were stereotypes, two simultaneously recorded images set side by side, giving a three-dimensional view when seen through a viewer designed for the purpose, known as a stereoscope or stereopticon. Such devices go back to 1838, and stereotypes of period places, buildings, monuments, and naval vessels predominate. Very few stereotypes of battle dead survive, and no stereotypes of the poor or of the squalid condition of the nation's slums are known. Photographers understood that to sell their pictures they would have to appeal to well-heeled customers who did not wish to be reminded of the nation's failures.[38]

Propelled by a fascination with photography, optical novelties were very much in vogue. The magic lantern had been around for over 200 years, used by showmen and hucksters to beguile audiences with mystical images. It consisted of a metal box into which an oil lamp was placed; a polished metal reflector which focused the light on a painted slide; and a hole with a lens through which the light was projected. These lanterns were notably improved as a result of photographic discoveries, and their use became widespread. Lanterns were used by lecturers to enhance their presentations, and they became very popular as a parlor toy to show comic pictures. A number of hand-colored glass slides of the war have recently been restored.

Another optical curiosity was the zoetrope. This consisted of a revolving drum with equally spaced slits around the sides. The interior of the drum contained a series of sequential pictures. The pictures were taken by a series of still cameras activated by trip wires. Walking men and running horses were prominent subjects of the zoetrope. When the drum was rotated, the pictures gave the impression that they were moving. Because it could be viewed by many people at one time, the zoetrope enjoyed popularity as a parlor amusement.

A similar device was the phantascope. This simple contrivance was comprised of a cardboard disc with a series of slits equally spaced around the center and a handle that acted as a pivot around which the phantascope was rotated. The reverse side contained a series of pictures set between the slits. When the operator held the device in front of a mirror and rotated the disc, the pictures appeared to be moving.

CULTURAL INSTITUTIONS

The decade beginning in 1860 spawned an abundance of cultural institutions in the North and West. War involvement and subsequent poverty retarded a similar movement in the South for almost twenty years. The interest in art, music, literature, and nature that permeated the parlor surged forth, creating museums, symphonies, libraries, and parks. These, in turn, engendered a plethora of ancillary institutions such as literary societies, study groups, and reading clubs.

These organizations were gender specific. Male organizations attracted businessmen and professionals. In addition to the obvious activities such organizations would conduct, they created a venue that was ripe for the founding of additional social projects. The distaff version of these clubs provided activities for middle- and upper-class women beyond domestic and church endeavors. The clubs furnished an arena for women to pursue their intellectual development. Study clubs met twice monthly for 10 months a year to discuss such topics as literature, history, and art. Meetings commonly were held in members' homes and consisted of conversation, presentation of papers, and subsequent discussions.

READING CLUBS

Many civilians, particularly the women who were doomed to sit out the war while their husbands and lovers fought, found reading one of the few sources of entertainment available to them. Like their loved ones in the army camps, many women read in groups and met regularly to do so. Books were frequently read aloud, making it possible to share the books and newspapers that were "all too scarce in the print-starved Confederacy." Even in the North, where books were widely available, oral presentation by an articulate reader often enhanced the literature and allowed the majority of the women to do other chores such as sewing and embroidery. Reading aloud became an activity with many of the characteristics of theater. Books provided women with an almost pure escape from the realities of war, suffering, and death. More important, oral presentation discouraged continual war gossip among the women, and the camaraderie of the group helped to alleviate depression and gloom among those who were without loved ones, displaced from their homes, and anxious about their own futures.[39]

Mary Wilson Gilchrist kept an extensive list of what she believed a woman should read. Her favorites were *The Taming of the Shrew, Othello,* and *MacBeth.* Gilchrist found *Richard III* interesting but declared King Richard "a wretch." Gilchrist was not alone in her enjoyment of "The Bard." She wrote, "Mary Carpenter called and we made arrangements for reading Shakespeare together." Other items on Gilchrist's reading list were *Confessions of an Opium Eater, Vanity Fair, Lucille,* and *The Wandering Jew* as well as novels by Charlotte Bronte, poetry of Wordsworth, biographies of Luther, histories of England and Egypt, and ancient works by Virgil and Sophocles.[40]

LECTURES

To some extent, literary society or study club meetings took the place of the public lectures that had enjoyed tremendous popularity from about 1840 forward. The war had interrupted many lecture series, which were curtailed, and in some cases suspended. Lectures had been particularly popular among ambitious young men, many of whom joined their cause on the battleline. Northerners demanded that the remaining lecturers make their concern matters related to the conflict. Topics sought by lecture audiences included denunciations of the South, glorification of Union causes, and narrations detailing the reforms that would follow the Northern victory. Popular speakers included Senator Charles Sumner, Major General Cassius Clay, Theodore Tilton, and Wendell Phillips.

GAMES

Games have always been popular in America. One popular game was solitaire, played on a circular board containing 33 holes. Marbles or pegs were placed in all but the center hole. A peg was moved forward, backward, or sideways, but not diagonally, over an adjacent peg, which was then removed from the board. The game ended when the remaining pegs could not make a move. The object of the game was to have only a single peg remaining, preferably in the center hole.

Board games were just coming into their own in America. Most board game publishers were located in the Northeast, particularly in Boston and New York. *The Mansion of Happiness, an Instructive Moral and Entertaining Amusement* is generally acknowledged as the first board game published in the United States. This 1843 game closely resembles the formerly imported *The Game of Goose*, but had a distinctly moral message. Players landing on squares marked "gratitude" or "honesty" advanced more rapidly toward their goal. *The Game of Goose* was a board game distinguished by an elaborate spiral containing 63 squares. Players rolled the dice and advanced along the board, incurring a variety of changes in fortune involving penalties and bonuses. The game dated from the 18th century and served as inspiration for a host of imitators, including Milton Bradley's *Checkered Game of Life.*

American board makers copied other games as well. The Game of Pope and Pagan, or the Siege of the Stronghold of Satan by the Christian Army and Mohamet and Saladin, or the Battle for Palestine were both based on the centuries-old game fox and geese. Other published games took the form of card games and included, Dr. Busby, Yankee Trader, Uncle Tom's Cabin, Heroes, Master Redbury and His Pupils, and Trades. The last of these consisted of lithographed cards; some depicted such tradesmen as shoemakers, farriers, and taxgatherers, and others showed the symbols of each trade. The object of the game was to collect tricks that matched the tradesman and the symbol. It is thought that this game served as the inspiration for the very popular English game Happy Families.

Other popular games included cribbage, checkers, tangrams, and lotto—a forerunner of bingo—which was played with cards of three horizontal and nine vertical rows. Five numbers from 1 to 90 appeared on the cards, with the remaining spaces blank. Children's versions of the game were developed to teach spelling, multiplication, botany, and history.

CROQUET

Croquet became popular among the British elite by the 1850's. The first record of a croquet court in the United States was at Nahant, Massachusetts in 1859. The game was unique in that it is probably the first game played by both men and women in America. In 1864 James Redpath of Boston published *Croquet* by Captain Mayne Reid. That same year, the popular *Peterson's Magazine* described the game of Troco, or Lawn Billiards. The Park Place Croquet Club of Brooklyn organized with 25 members in 1864. By 1865 several croquet rulebooks were published in the United States. One of them was based on the version of croquet played at the exclusive resort in Newport, Rhode Island and while admitting that croquet taxed mental capacities less than whist or chess, it touted the game as combining the delights of out-of-doors exercise and social enjoyment, fresh air and friendship—two things, it noted, most effective for promoting happiness. Lightweight backyard croquet kits were mass-produced by American industry and spread the game into the backyards of the American middle class in the 1860's and 1870's. Winslow Homer painted a series of famous canvases of croquet players in 1865 and 1869.

SOCIAL CALLS

One activity outside the home open to women of the upper classes was visiting (calling). In addition to its recreational value, calling was a required social function that was strictly governed by convention. *Martine's Hand-Book of Etiquette* postulated that such visits were necessary, in order to maintain good feeling between the members of society; they were required by the custom of the age, and must be carefully observed. Visiting not only upheld a woman's social position, it enhanced that of her husband. Ceremonial calls were to be kept brief. Half an hour amply sufficed for a visit of ceremony. If the visitor was a lady, she could remove her victorine, but on no account either the shawl or bonnet, even if politely requested to do so by the mistress of the house. It was thought that the trouble necessarily required in replacing them, ought to be avoided. Upon exiting, the caller would leave a card, which would be placed in a cardholder kept in the front hall for that purpose. Elaborate cardholders were made from silver or china. Ladies' magazines contained patterns for crafted ones. The distribution of cards allowed a woman to keep up a ceremonious acquaintance with a circle too large for friendly visiting, as that consumed far more time than could be given to the number of persons with which she had to be acquainted.

Socially conscious women kept a list of family members and business acquaintances that formed a basic calling circle. It would be expected that persons on this list would be visited at least twice a year. Failure to reciprocate would be considered a grievous slight. Naturally, close friends and family would see each other more frequently. Martine counseled women to keep a strict account of her ceremonial visits, because time passes rapidly. It was also important to take note of how soon calls were returned, as this was, in most cases, an indicator of whether or not frequent visits are desired. Brides were kept particularly busy making rounds as they introduced themselves in their new social position. Women were reminded that it was the custom for a wife to take her husband's cards with her, and to leave one or two with her own.

During the Civil War, this pastime was sometimes affected by military conditions. In Ohio, Mary Gilchrist continued her visiting apparently unabated, but women in occupied areas of West Virginia and Kentucky often found visiting curtailed. Frances Peter noted that in Lexington, in July 1862, "secesh have had to stay at home for the last two days." Henrietta Barr wrote defiantly of an edict of Ravenswood's Yankee commander. "The all abounding topic of conversation was Don Frost's latest proclamation wherein he enjoins the `secesh' to quit visiting and stay quietly at home. I wonder if he thinks we are going to mind him."[41] Such restrictions on visiting increased the hardship of war, as women were cut off from the support of friends and family.

LADIES' CRAFTS

A woman's skill at needlework had always been considered one of her most important accomplishments. With highly decorated handmade items at the height of fashion during the mid-19th century, such skills took on an even greater importance. Needlework skills, however, shifted from plain sewing, which produced essential linens and basic garments to fancywork, which, as the name implies, was done for decoration. Women used a variety of different kinds of techniques including patchwork, embroidery, tatting, crocheting, knitting, drawn work, and Berlin work. A woman was expected to furnish her home with everything from quilts to doilies.

Crocheting gained tremendous popularity during the mid-19th century. The first American booklets featuring crochet patterns appeared in 1845. Within just a few years it had become one of the most favored kinds of fancywork. Many of the ladies' magazines like *Godey's Lady's Book* and *Peterson's* devoted one or two pages each month to crochet patterns. In addition to producing items such as jackets, capes, purses, bedspreads and doilies, crocheted edging was added to pillowcases, tablecloths and undergarments.

Hooking rugs was also fashionable. The craft began in the 1840s but took off when jute began to be imported from Asia and was used to make burlap bags. Women discovered that when the bags were slit open they

Craft projects appeared regularly in many ladies' magazines. This pair is from an issue of *Peterson's Magazine*.

proved to be the perfect size for area rugs. The wide, loose weave of the burlap grain sacks also made the hooking faster and easier. Rug hooking received another boost during the 1860s with the introduction of pre-stenciled patterns on the burlap, which proved to be the inspiration for large numbers of women to take up the craft. Hooked rugs, like quilts, appealed to many women because it enabled them to use up scraps of fabric and pieces of worn clothing to create something to beautify their home. Household economy was a valued quality throughout the Victorian period. Women who could create a well appointed home without incurring great expense were admired for their thrift. These undertakings also provided women with a creative outlet in a time when many of their expressions were repressed by social prohibitions.

Patchwork quilts were another popular activity. Women worked on quilts alone for their families and at group quilting bees as community activities. Prior to the war, groups of Northern women used their quilting talents to raise money for the cause of abolition. They renamed some traditional patchwork patterns to draw attention to the cause. *Job's Tears* became known as *Slave Chain*, *Jacob's Ladder* became *Underground Railway*, and *North Star* was so named after the star that guided runaway slaves to freedom.

Once the war commenced, Northern women mobilized relief efforts and began to produce quilts to be sent to soldiers in need. Quilt making was undertaken by many women who viewed it almost as a patriotic responsibility. The records of the U.S. Sanitary Commission (the largest private agency channeling donated supplies to soldiers) show that an estimated 250,000 quilts were distributed during the war. In Hartford, Connecticut alone, 5,459 quilts were collected during 1864.[42]

Many of the quilts were more utilitarian than those their makers had created in the past, but it is likely that they were made with no less love. To one quilt was pinned this note: "My son is in the army. Whoever is made warm by this quilt, which I have worked on for six days and most of six nights, let him remember his mother's love." Quilts were made approximately seven feet by four feet so as to fit a military cot and bedding pack. The U.S. Sanitary Commission also sponsored fairs to raise money for their relief efforts. These fairs became well-attended social events held in decorated halls in larger cities. Women, many of whom had turned away from their prewar fancywork, once again took their needles to create more elaborate items for these fundraisers.

Aid societies sprung up all across the country as women stepped up to express their patriotism and to provide comfort for the soldiers. When an aid society was formed at Ohio Female College, Gilchrist noted in her diary, "After dinner the soldiers aid society . . . met for the first time in Mrs. Day's parlor. We sewed hard all afternoon on moccasins, hemming handkerchiefs, scraping lint for the 'poor soldiers.'" The handiwork of soldiers' aid societies occasionally fell into the hands of enemy soldiers. After the fall of Lexington, a frustrated Frances Peter wrote in her diary, "A good many things that had belonged to the Aid Society . . . fell into the hands of the rebels, which might have been destroyed if we had only been told sooner how matters stood . . . They went to . . . where the Aid Society used to meet & helped themselves to hats & clothes and took everything belonging to the Society."[43]

These organizations also sponsored benefit activities, including fairs, raffles, dinners and other entrainments. These events were as much social functions as they were charitable events. Mary Gilchrist described one such occasion in her diary: "Went to an oyster supper in the church for the benefit of the soldiers . . . the *prize* of the evening was an acorn basket which was raffled for, at 2S cents a chance. It brought $12.50. & Mat Whipple drew it & gave it to me, to my surprise." Frances Peter wrote of a benefit sponsored by an aid society in Lexington, Kentucky, "I must not forget to mention that the Tableaux which the Aid Society have been preparing were exhibited last night and the night before." She also noted two dinners sponsored by women for the Union soldiers in Lexington. "Today the ladies in the vicinity of the camp gave the 33rd Indiana a picnic dinner" and "yesterday the ladies gave the soldiers at the Short Street hospital a dinner."[44]

At times local citizens would raise funds for the societies themselves. Peter noted, "Tonight the ladies and gentlemen of this city gave an amateur concert, the third one they have given this winter for the benefit of the Soldiers Aid Society." Mary Gilchrist belonged to various sewing societies. She also attempted personally to raise money for the families of Yankee soldiers: "Ellen Richards. . .& I soon after breakfast started on horseback to get subscriptions for the families of volunteers."[45]

Confederate women also made quilts for soldiers. The Southern blockade, however, severely limited the availability of the requisite materials. Confederate quilts produced during the war were made from whatever makeshift materials were available, including old sheets stuffed with newspaper.[46] The war also inspired a rash of "flag bees" where women worked to make flags for the South. A contest was held in 1861 to choose a flag to be used as the Confederate Flag.

The lack of available materials also created a revival of knitting among southern women. As the century progressed, knitting shifted from economic necessary to creative craft. The blockade-created shortages forced many southern women to turn to knitting to provide their families with necessities such as capes, gloves, socks, stockings, undergarments and braces (suspenders). Even this, however, had its challenges as the necessary yarn and threads were also in short supply, leaving many women to manufacture their own. The homemade materials were often coarse and uneven. To hide these imperfections, women would add crocheted decorations to the knitted items in order to camouflage blemishes that would be obvious in plain work. Knitting and crochet can be done in limited light and were activities which women undertook after it was too dark to sew or spin. The women even carried their knitting with them when they visited one another in order to optimize the production of items for their families and for the soldiers. In her reminiscences of plantation life during the war, Cornelia Jones Pond noted, "knitting needles were never idle except on Sunday."[47] Once the war was over, knitting returned to its prewar pastime status.

NOTES

1. David Kaser, *Books and Libraries in Camp and Battle: The Civil War Experience* (Westport: Greenwood Press, 1984), 3. In 1830 Alexis de Tocqueville reported that he did not find a man in Connecticut who could not read.

2. Ibid., 14.

3. V. M. Rice, *Code of Public Instruction* (Albany: State Printing Office, 1856), 325.

4. Lydia M. Child, *The Mother's Book* (Boston: Applewood, 1831), 93–94.

5. Stanley J. Kunitz, ed., *British Authors of the Nineteenth Century* (New York: Wilson, 1936), 105–106.

6. See Antiquarian Books, http://home.navisoft.com/blackstn/crime.htm; and E. A. Duyckinck, *Cyclopedia of American Literature* (Detroit: Gale Research, 1965).

7. Kunitz, 511–512.

8. Ibid., 383–384.

9. Joel Hawes, *Lectures to Young Men on the Formation of Character* (Hartford: 1835), 144–158.

10. Drew Gilpin Faust, *Mother of Invention: Women of the Slaveholding South in the American Civil War* (Charlotte: University of North Carolina Press, 1996), 154.

11. Tim Halliman, *A Christmas Carol Christmas Book* (New York: IBM, 1984), 111.

12. Ibid.

13. Lewis, 110.

14. "Major General George E. Pickett," *Southern Illustrated News*, August 1, 1863, 26.

15. Alan Taylor, "Fenimore Cooper's America," *History Today* 46, no. 2 (February 1996): 21–27.

16. James H. Croushore, ed., *A Volunteer's Adventure, by Captain John W. De Forest* (New Haven: Yale University Press, 1949), 130–131. See Duyckinck.

17. C. V. Woodward, 245, 307, 381.

18. Kaser, 18, 36.

19. Ibid., 13.

20. Emerson David Fite, *Social and Industrial Conditions in the North During the Civil War* (Williamstown: Corner House, 1976), 256n.

21. Kaser, 4, 5; James Morgan, "Send No Trash: Books, Libraries, and Reading During the Civil War," *Camp Chase Gazette*, July 1992, 32.

22. Croushore, vii.

23. Morgan, 32–36.

24. Lawrence A. Cremin, *American Education: The National Experience, 1783–1876* (New York: Harper, 1980), 409.

25. Careful scrutiny of such prints can reveal the boundaries between the individual blocks.

26. Edwin Forbes, *Civil War Etchings* (1876; reprint, New York: Dover, 1994), preface. Forbes may have been the archetype of the young reporter featured in the TV miniseries The Blue and the Gray.

27. John E. Stanchak, ed., *Leslie's Illustrated Civil War* (1894; reprint, Jackson: University Press of Mississippi, 1992), v-xii.

28. The lack of widespread circulation of these photographs in newspapers may have been fortunate, as there was no need to add additional fuel to the growing antiwar sentiment in the North.

29. Faust, *Creation of Confederate Nationalism*, 17.

30. Ibid., 8.

31. Ibid., 16.

32. Lewis, 86.

33. *Southern Illustrated News*, August 1, 1863, 28.

34. Faust, *Mothers of Invention*, 168–178.

35. George N. Barnard, *Photographic Views of Sherman's Campaigns* (1866; reprint, New York: Dover, 1977), preface.

36. Andrew J. Russell, *Russell's Civil War Photographs* (New York: Dover, 1982), preface.

37. Francis Trevelyan Miller, ed., *The Photographic History of the Civil War: Soldier Life and the Secret Service* (1911; reprint, New York: Castle, 1957), 30.

38. Alexander Gardner, *Photographic Sketchbook of the Civil War* (1866; New York; reprint, Dover, 1959), preface.

39. Faust, *Mothers of Invention,* 153–154, 156.

40. Claudia Lynn Lady, "Five Tri-state Women During the Civil War: Day-to-Day Life," *West Virginia History* 43, no. 4 (Summer 1982), 303.

41. Ibid., 307.

42. Roderick Kiracofe, *The American Quilt* (New York: Clarkson Potter, 1993), 109.

43. Claudia Lynn Lady, "Five Tri-state Women During the Civil War," 306.

44. Ibid., 308–9.

45. Ibid., 307.

46. Ibid., 119.

47. Josephine Bacon Martin, *Life on a Liberty County Plantation: The Journal of Cornelia Jones Pond* (Hinesfille, GA: Printex, 1983), 97–98.

14

FEAST OR FAMINE: FOOD AND COOKING

"Cold milk, thick with cream, from a dairy on the side of the mountain, fresh venison steaks, the whitest bread and the tenderest broiled chicken reveling in the sweetest butter. No king fared better than that."

—Cornelia Peake McDonald

The Civil War brought developments that would alter the patterns of American eating, from home cooking to professional cooking, and from country cooking to city cooking. The seeds of these changes had already been sown as the war approached, but the dynamics of the conflict acted to speed their growth. The war may have retarded the growth of conveniences for civilians, but when it came to providing food for the armies, it drove the technology. Specifically, three major agents of change were at work: improvement in refrigeration, increased speed of transportation, and industrialization of food processing. These served to vastly increase the variety of foods available to Americans.

STORAGE

Food storage in the mid-19th century was a problem for everyone, no matter what their economic status. In addition to recipes for preparing food and suggestions on maintaining the household, receipt books like Miss Beecher's Domestic Receipt Book customarily contained suggestions on topics such as how to restore the flavor of rancid butter. (Miss Beecher advised using chloride of lime.)[1]

Heat is a great villain when it comes to spoiling food. In the absence of practical mechanical systems for making things cold—which did not arrive until the 1870s—the easiest way to keep food from spoiling during warm weather was to use ice. Freshwater ice was cut from frozen ponds in large blocks and kept in structures called icehouses, which were constructed partially below ground. The temperature a few feet below ground rarely rises above 45° F. The ice was then covered in sawdust to help insulate it. Ice would be gathered when it was thickest, generally late January. Shielded from the heat, ice could theoretically last forever, but practically it could be expected to last through October if conditions were favorable. By the Civil War, the icehouse had become an indispensable component of the farm. Meat, poultry, and perishable fruit could be kept in good condition much longer in the cool temperatures of icehouses or iceboxes.

The icebox also gave individual city homes a means of keeping food fresh. In 1850 Godey's Lady's Book called the icebox a "necessity of life." First patented by Thomas Moore in 1803, it consisted of one wooden box inside another, insulated by charcoal or ashes, with a tin container at the top of the interior box for the ice. In 1825 Frederick Tudor and Nathaniel Wyeth solved the problem of preserving ice for long periods and made ice a commercial interest. Just prior to the war, Boston families could obtain 15 pounds of ice a day from an iceman for two dollars a month. Ice was harvested from New England ponds and shipped to the South or even to the West Indies. New Orleans increased its demand for ice 70 fold between the 1820s and the beginning of the Civil War. Once the war commenced, the South could no longer depend on this improved source of food preservation.[2]

MODERN ADVANCEMENT

By mid-century the railroads had become the prime cause of the increasing diversity of food for the American table. Perishables such as milk, oysters, and lobster were transported by rail to large cities in insulated icecars or packed in barrels of ice. The speed of the railroads not only augmented the diet, it served to improve the quality of the food. Beef was more tender, more tasty, and less expensive. The cattle no longer were driven to market on the hoof, and hence they developed less muscle. The cattle were fed on grain shipped via the railroad, thus improving the flavor of the meat. Finally, meat cost less because less weight was lost between pasture and market. A similar situation arose with pork. Before the railroads were built, long legs were a desirable breeding factor in pigs, as the hog was expected to walk to market. With the advent of rail shipping, breeders began to focus on tastier meats and fatter hogs. The railroads continued to supply the North and Northern troops with fresh meat during the war.

TO HOUSEKEEPERS & FRUIT GROWERS.
ARTHUR'S PATENT AIR-TIGHT, SELF-SEALING CANS.
For Preserving Fresh Fruits and Vegetables, by Hermetical Sealing.

Can Sealed.   *Can prepared for Sealing.*

These cans are constructed with a channel around the mouth, near the top, into which the cover fits loosely. This channel is filled with a very adhesive cement, prepared for the purpose, and allowed to harden. In order to seal the vessel hermetically, it is only necessary to heat the cover and press it into place. It may be opened with as much ease as it is closed, by warming the top. The ordinary tin cans, used for the same purpose for which this is intended, cannot be closed, as is well known, without the aid of a tinner; are difficult to open, and are generally so much injured in opening as to be useless for future service. By this simple contrivance the process of hermetical sealing is placed conveniently within the reach of every individual; and fruit, vegetables, and butter (if properly prepared) may be kept, with their natural flavor unimpaired, for an indefinite length of time.

These vessels were thoroughly tested, during the past season, and their contents, after the lapse of months, found unchanged; and this reason they are coming into general use.

☞ *Full directions for putting up fruit, tomatoes, &c., in these cans accompany them.*

ALL KINDS OF FRESH STEWED FRUITS MAY ALSO BE KEPT IN THESE CANS.

Peaches, Plums, Cherries, Blackberries, Pears, and all kinds of ripe fruits, may be put up in these cans for winter use, by simply stewing them for ten minutes, either with or without sugar, and sealing up while hot. The fruit will open months afterwards, precisely in the condition in which it is sealed up. How great a luxury this secures for winter use, need not be suggested.

Although factory canning was becoming popular, many householders still preferred home canning. This advertisement appeared in *Arthur's Home Magazine*, 1855.

The processing and preservation of food had always been a domestic activity until vacuum-packed, hermetically sealed jars were invented by a Frenchman named Nicholas Appert early in the 19th century. In 1825 the first American patent for tin cans was filed. By 1849 a machine was developed that limited the amount of hand labor needed to produce tin cans, further stimulating commercial food processing. Lobster and salmon were the first foods to be commercially canned, rapidly followed by corn, tomatoes, peas, and additional varieties of fish. By 1860, five million cans a year were being produced.

In 1863 the fledgling Great Atlantic Tea Company, destined to become the A&P stores, began to sell a line of canned groceries to supplement their tea business. Two famous brand names emerged from the war: Borden and Van Camp. Gail Borden's first efforts at canned foods met with little success, but his canned condensed milk was extremely popular. Gilbert Van Camp's pork and beans quickly became a best seller, and he was given an army contract to supply the Union troops.

Federal soldiers returning from the war had become so accustomed to canned foods that many insisted that canned foods be served at home so that they could continue to eat out-of-season products with consistent quality. Americans living in isolated western territories particularly welcomed the profusion of canned foods; prices ranged from $1.00 to $2.25 per can by the mid-1860s. A line from the song, "My Darling Clementine" describes Clementine's footwear as "herring boxes without topses," referring to the oval-shaped fish tins plentiful in mining towns.

Despite these movements toward modern food packaging, the single most important controlling factor of the Civil War era diet remained availability. Those who could afford to pay had wider choices, but even these were limited. For most people, the majority of fresh food choices continued to be governed by region and season.

FOOD ATTITUDES

Issues of vitamins, salt, fiber, and fat content were virtually nonexistent for most people during the 1860s. *Peterson's Magazine* contained the following comment on corpulence: "Dr. Radcliffe recommends that the mouth should be kept shut, and the eyes should be kept open; or, in other words, that corpulent persons should eat little food, and that the quantity of sleep should be diminished. These precautions may be followed with discretion, but it may be dangerous to carry them too far."[3] Most meals at this time contained meat, which was likely to be high in fat content, and bread in one form or another. Frances Trollope, a visitor to the United States in the 1830s, remarked on the extraordinary amount of bacon eaten in American homes: "Ham and beef steaks appear morning, noon, and night." Equally astonishing to her was the way eggs and oysters, ham and applesauce, beefsteak and stewed peaches, salt fish and onion were eaten together.[4]

COMMON FOODS

Pork was the most common kind of meat, particularly in the Southern diet. Pigs are relatively easy to maintain. They required little space and tolerated a wide variety of foodstuffs, including leavings from food preparation. Pigs did not have to be put to pasture and consumed less feed than cattle to add the same amount of weight. Pork could be easily preserved in a number of ways, including pickling, salting, and smoking, without becoming offensive in taste or texture.

Chicken was important in the South, too. Chickens required little space and turned available reserves of corn and meal into meat; but chicken meat was both difficult to preserve and prone to spoil. Like other domesticated fowl, chickens were generally eaten fresh. They had the additional appeal of being egg producers while they lived.

Lamb, or mutton, was not a popular meat in America. Sheep were kept almost exclusively for their wool, and their value as wool producers far outweighed any worth they had as food. Certainly, mutton would be eaten in place of other meats in time of scarcity if it were available, but it was not easily preserved. Moreover, the meat of mature sheep had a strong taste that had to be masked by careful preparation.

Supplements to the diet were often regional. In rural areas, hunters would supplement the family larder by bringing home such victuals as geese, rabbits, squirrels, wild turkeys, partridges, pheasants, deer, and reed birds. Contrary to popular belief, Southerners had no particular predisposition for the taste of opossums, snakes, or woodchucks in their diet. Fish and other forms of marine seafood such as clams, oysters, mussels, and eels were eaten in shore communities. Freshwater fish included bass, sturgeon, pickerel, perch, pike, whitefish, and catfish. Fish could be salted or smoked, but much of it was eaten fresh. Oysters were extremely popular. They were eaten fresh but were also pickled, smoked, and canned.

Eggs were another good source of protein. Miss Beecher advised homemakers to preserve eggs in the following ways: "Pack them in fine salt, small end down . . . [or] pack them small end down, and then pour on them a mixture of four quarts of cold water, four quarts of unslacked lime, two ounces of salt, and two ounces of cream-tartar."[5] Hard-boiled eggs were sometimes pickled in vinegar.

Vegetables were eaten fresh in season. Only in the very deep South were they available during the winter. Small amounts of vegetables could be grown in hot frames, which utilized the heat of manure to keep temperatures warm enough to produce year round as far north as Virginia. Vegetables such as beets, cabbage, carrots, cauliflower, onions, parsnips, potatoes, radishes, rutabagas, sweet potatoes, turnips, and winter squash were stored in root cellars where the climate allowed. In other areas they were packed in straw and stored in barrels. The straw acted as a barrier to prevent the spread of spoilage to the entire barrel. Carrots were often buried in sawdust boxes. Other vegetables such as corn, beans and peas were dried and used in cooking. Green corn was preserved by turning back the husk, leaving only the last, very thin layer, and then hanging it in the sun or in a warm room to dry. When it was needed for cooking, it was parboiled and cut from the cob. Sweet corn was parboiled, cut from the cob, dried in the sun, and stored in a bag which was kept in a cool, dry place. Sweet corn was also dried in the husk and then buried in salt. String beans, squash, pumpkin, and, in the South, okra were strung on thread and hung up to dry. String beans were strung whole, while other produce was sliced thinly and dried in strips.

Vegetables could also be preserved by making them into catsups and relishes. Catsup was the general name given to sauces made from vegetables and fruits. Mushroom and tomato catsups were popular. Cabbage was made into sauerkraut. In 1858 John Mason patented the Mason jar with which we are familiar today. These threaded glass jars had zinc lids with threaded ring sealers. They were a welcome improvement for both city and rural homemakers, although many still relied on older methods of sealing jars such as pouring a seal made from molten wax, or tying on leather tops with string.

FOOD PRICES

Food was still accepted in certain areas of the country as payment in kind. An account book from a doctor in Butler, Illinois showed that accounts for medical service during the war were paid by a variety of items other than cash. The doctor kept specific records of the amount and price of each item, giving some insight into prices outside of the South. Accounts were settled by "4¾ lbs. of pork—.20; 16 bushels of corn—8.00; 7½ lbs. meat—10 cts. per—.75; one bushel of apples—.40; 10 lbs. of beef 4½ cts.—.45; 13 lbs. of honey 15 cts. per lb.—1.95; 50 lbs. flour 4 cts. lb.—2.00; ½ bushel potatoes—.75; 350 pickles—2.10."[6]

THE WAR'S EFFECT

At the commencement of the war, virtually all of the South's most fertile land was devoted to agriculture. The North, which relied so much on industrialization, might thereby be seen to have been at a disadvantage with regard to food, but the reverse was true. As the war progressed and was continually fought on Southern soil, Southern crops were destroyed. Cornelia Peake McDonald described a visit by federal troops. They "began to pull up the potatoes. . .they did not stop after getting enough for dinner, but continued amid roars of laughter and defiant looks at me to pull them till all were lying on the ground. . .to wither in the sun. They were no larger than peas, and the destruction seemed so wanton that I was provoked beyond enduring."[7]

The North, however, had undeveloped land that it was now able to put into production to support the war effort. The Homestead Act was quickly passed in 1862, granting free land to anyone willing to plant it. This virgin soil produced impressive yields, unlike the overfarmed Southern soil. Northern industry developed and manufactured machinery that further improved productivity. In 1861 Cyrus McCormick's reaper was offered for sale at $150 but required only a $30 down payment. The balance was to be paid in six months if the harvest was good, or longer if it was poor.[8]

The war actually provided an impetus to the development of farming in the North. Preconceived notions of a rising wartime demand for food caused farmers to overplant in 1860. Wheat and corn production soared. Pork preservation for commercial use in 1865 was twice that of 1860. An additional boon came in the form of good weather, an event not shared by Europe, which experienced crop shortages during this period. The North was able to sell surplus wheat and flour to Europe, thus earning additional funds that could be invested in the war.[9]

SHORTAGES

The war brought about many shortages in the South. A poor system of transportation prevented the Confederacy's small resources from being effectively distributed throughout the South. Furthermore, the blockade of Southern ports caused great hardship. Blockade runners took tremendous risks and expected tremendous profits. In order to make the risk worthwhile, they tended to carry luxury items for those who could afford to pay, rather than the staples of daily life for everyone. Prices soared in proportion. In November 1862 Judith McGuire wrote, "Coffee is $4 per pound, and good tea from $18 to $20; butter ranges from $1.50 to $2 per pound; lard 50 cents; corn $15 per barrel; and wheat $4.50 per bushel."[10] In an April 1863 message to Southerners, President Jefferson Davis urged people to give priority to food crops over cotton and tobacco and to plant corn, peas, and beans.[11]

Receipt books and newspapers carried suggestions for dealing with the food shortages. When successful replacements were discovered, the revelation was readily disclosed to the public in print and by word of mouth. A handwritten receipt book gives the following suggestion for dealing with the unavailability of flour: "Rice Bread, `Southern Bread'—1 gill of rice boiled very soft, when cold mix in ¾ lbs. of wheat, 1 teacup of yeast, 1 teacup of milk, salt to taste. Mix and let it stand 3 hours then it must be kneaded in flour enough to render the outside hard enough for the oven. In an hour and a quarter after, bake it."[12]

Coffee was a popular beverage, and the blockade made it very difficult to procure. There are reports of Southern soldiers trading with their Northern counterparts for coffee across the lines during times of truce. Parthenia Hague wrote:

One of our most difficult tasks was to find a good substitute for coffee . . . Coffee soon rose to thirty dollars per pound; from that it went to sixty and seventy dollars per pound. Good workmen received thirty dollars per day; so it took two days' hard labor to buy one pound of coffee, and scarcely any could be had at that fabulous price.[13]

The best substitute for coffee was said by some to be okra seeds. This was unfortunate because okra became increasingly difficult to acquire as the war progressed and agricultural output diminished. Other alternatives included yams and carrots, either of which would be peeled, sliced, dried, parched, and ground. Acorns, wheat berries, corn, peanuts, sugar cane seed, chicory, beets, dandelion root, cotton seed, and English peas were also used in various conditions of having been browned, parched, burned, and ground. By 1862 Confederate troops had even embraced peanuts as a coffee substitute. The *Confederate Receipt Book,* which was published in 1863 and is believed to be the only cookbook published in the South dur-

A KITCHEN IN SHAMBLES

Additional hardships were caused by raids of Northern troops upon individual homes. Mary S. Mallard recorded the following in her journal:

> About four in the afternoon we heard the clash of arms and noise of horsemen, and by the time Mother and I could get downstairs we saw forty or fifty men in the pantry, flying hither and thither, ripping open the safe with their swords and breaking open the crockery cupboards. Fearing we might not have a chance to cook, Mother had some chickens and ducks roasted and put in the safe for our family. These the men seized whole, tearing them to pieces with their teeth like ravenous beasts. They were clamorous for whiskey, and ordered us to get our keys. One came to Mother to know where her meal and flour were, insisted upon opening her locked pantry, and took every particle. They threw the sacks across their horses. Mother remonstrated and pointed to her helpless family; their only reply was, "We'll take it!"

Source: Walter Sullivan, The War the Women Lived: Female Voices from the Confederate South (Nashville: J.S. Sanders, 1995), 233.

ing the war, contained the following: "Substitute for Coffee: Take sound ripe acorns, wash them in the shell, dry them, and parch until they open, take the shell off, roast with a little bacon fat, and you will have a splendid cup of coffee."[14]

Tea was also a scarce item, but there have always been many satisfactory herbal substitutes for this mainstay. Tea can be made from a wide variety of leaves, roots, and berries. Some favorites included sassafras root and blackberry. Hague wrote in her memoirs of the war:

We had several substitutes for tea . . . Prominent among these substitutes were raspberry leaves. Many during the blockade planted and cultivated the raspberry-vine all around their garden palings as much for tea as the berries for jams or pies; these leaves were considered the best substitutes for tea. The leaves of the holly-tree when dried in the shade, also made a palatable tea.[15]

Butter was also difficult to obtain because it was largely imported from the North. Many Southern dairy cows had been slaughtered for their meat by invading and local armies and even by some civilians. Judith McGuire wrote in March 1863, "Butter was $3.50 per pound in market this morning, and other things in proportion. I am sorry to say that it is true, and that it is evident we must have scarcity, particularly of such things as butter, for cattle must go to feed the army."[16] Sunflower seed oil was often used as a replacement for butter.

A related casualty in this regard was the want of milk and cream. Judith McGuire wrote, "Milk is very scarce and high, so that we have only had it once for many months."[17] The *Confederate Receipt Book* gave this solution for the undersupply of cream: "Beat the white of an egg to a froth, put to it a very small lump of butter, and mix well, then turn the coffee to it gradually, so that it may not curdle. If perfectly done it will be an excellent substitute for cream. For tea omit the butter, using only the egg."[18]

Flour, too, was scarce. Prices continued to escalate throughout the war. It was reported that in Richmond a barrel of flour sold for $250 during the closing months of the war.[19] Sarah Morgan wrote in August 1862, "I sat on the floor with my plate, and a piece of corn bread (flour not to be bought at any price) and eat with my fingers—a new experience."[20] One month later she wrote again, "If anyone had told me I could have lived off corn bread, a few months ago, I would have been incredulous: now I believe it, and return an inward grace for the blessing, at every mouthful. I have not tasted a piece of wheat bread since I left home, and shall hardly taste it again until the war is over."[21] Parthenia Hague seems less distressed:

Bolted Meal, when obtainable, made a good substitute for flour, though millers said it injured their bolting cloth to sift the corn meal through it; yet nearly every household, in sending its grist to be ground, would order a portion of the meal to be bolted for use as flour. Such bolted meal when it was sifted through a thin muslin cloth mixed up with scalding water to make it more viscid and adhesive, was as easily molded into pie crust with the aid of the rolling-pin as the pure flour. Nice muffins and waffles were made of bolted meal, and we also made a very nice cake of the same and our home-made brown sugar.[22]

Perhaps the distress over the lack of flour is somehow tied to the American housewife's extreme pride in her bread making. Miss Beecher devoted an entire chapter to bread making. She counseled: "A woman should be ashamed to have poor bread, far more so, than to speak bad grammar, or to have a dress out of fashion . . . When it is very frequently the case that a housekeeper has poor bread, she may set herself down as a slack baker and negligent housekeeper."[23] Commercially produced bread was one area in which modern convenience was strongly resisted until the early years of the following century.

Households that did not produce corn, which could be ground into meal, were often at the mercy of the war economy. Judith McGuire lamented that "meal was selling to-day at $16 per bushel. It has been bought up by speculators. Oh, that those hard-hearted creatures could be made to suffer!"[24] Mary A. H. Gray's diary records the lengths to which people would go to obtain, or in this case reclaim, corn: "We spent the preceding day in picking out grains of corn from cracks and crevices in bureau drawers, and other improvised troughs for Federal horses, as well as gathering up what was on the ground . . . about a half bushel was obtained."[25]

Salt became a highly prized commodity. Dolly Sumner Lunt Burge describes disguising a barrel of salt "which had cost me two hundred dollars" as a leaching tub to conceal it from marauders.[26] In 1862 Union forces destroyed a large saltworks on Chesapeake Bay, causing difficulty for individuals and salt pork producers alike.

The obtaining of salt became extremely difficult when the war had cut off the usual source of supply. This was true especially in regions remote from the sea-coast and border states, such as the interior of Alabama and Georgia. Here again homemakers were obliged to have recourse to whatever expedient ingenuity suggested. All the brine left in troughs and barrels, where pork had been salted down, were carefully dipped up, boiled down, and converted into salt again. In some cases the salty soil under old smokehouses was dug up and placed in hoppers, which resembled backwoods ash-hoppers, made for leaching ashes in the process of soap-manufacture. Water was then poured upon the soil, the brine of which percolated through the hopper was boiled down to the proper point, poured into vessels, and set in the sun, which by evaporation completed the rude process. Though never of immaculate whiteness, the salt that resulted from these methods served well enough for all common purposes, and Southerners accepted it without complaining.[27]

Resourceful people living near the shore could obtain salt by evaporating ocean water. Sometimes coltsfoot, a wild plant that gave a salt-like flavor to foods, was used in cooking. But lack of salt posed problems other than taste preference. Salt was used extensively as a meat preservative. Parching fish and meat Indian style was only a stopgap expedient. Meat could also be cured in brine using a lesser amount of salt than other methods. Even the availability of meat to preserve was a problem. Once Vicksburg fell in 1863, Union forces had control of the Mississippi, virtually cutting off the supply of western beef to the Confederacy.

Soda, or baking soda, used as a leavening agent, was also a victim of the blockade. Parthenia Hague wrote, "It was not long 'ere some one found out that the ashes of corncobs possessed the alkaline property essential for raising dough." She noted that it was best "to select all the red cobs as they are thought to contain more carbonate of soda than the white cobs."[28]

Sugar, too, was difficult to acquire. Even though the South possessed its own sugar plantations, most were in federally occupied Louisiana for most of the war. Honey, molasses, and sorghum were used in its stead. Parthenia Hague tells the story of a woman who even used a surplus of watermelon to make sugar and syrup. The deficit of sugar also inhibited the making of jellies, jams, and preserves. Red corncobs were again found to be useful. The cobs were boiled, and the juice was thickened into syrup. The Confederate Receipt Book gave this recipe for cider jelly: "Boil cider to the consistency of syrup, and let it cool, and you have a nice jelly."[29]

When apples to make vinegar were in too short supply, Southerners turned to molasses, honey, beets, figs, persimmons, and sorghum. The Confederate Receipt Book even had a recipe for "Apple Pie Without Apples": "To one small bowl of crackers, that have been soaked until no hard parts remain, add one teaspoon of tartaric acid, sweeten to your taste, add some butter, and very little nutmeg."[30]

Apparently not all Southerners were subject to deprivations. Mary Chesnut recorded the menu of a "luncheon to ladies" given by Mrs. Jefferson Davis in January 1864 as "gumbo, ducks and olives, supreme de volaille, chickens in jelly, oysters, lettuce salad, chocolate jelly cake, claret soup champagne, &c,&c,&c."[31]

SUPPLEMENTING THE TROOPS

The Sanitary Commission was a Northern civilian organization that co-ordinated widespread war relief. "The object of the Sanitary Commission was to do what the government could not," wrote Mary Livermore in her war memoirs.[32] Funds were raised through "Sanitary Fairs," which sold homemade pies and jellies and held raffles for quilts and other homemade crafts, and from direct solicitation. Emma Sargent Barbour received a letter in which her sister remarked, "I had a couple of pamphlets from the Sanitary Commission last week soliciting funds from the Ladies of D. [W]e have about $10 on hand we have been reserving for a fitting occasion, we shall probably send to that object this week."[33]

Children were recruited to solicit funds door to door and to collect non-perishable groceries such as jellies or crackers from merchants to be sent to soldiers at the front. In some farming communities, families set aside portions of their land for the production of easily stored crops, such as potatoes, which were delivered to the Sanitary Commission. Schools held "onion" or "potato" days to collect produce.

Dietary kitchens staffed with dietary nurses were established by the Sanitary Commission in 1862 as a result of the efforts of Annie Wittenmyer. She worked very hard to see that a system was developed to feed wounded soldiers in field hospitals. Women volunteers had been scrounging milk, eggs, and vegetables for the wounded who were too ill to eat the standard pork and beans field ration. Wittenmyer's system established the means for providing appropriate meals for the men.[34]

Similar efforts in Southern communities were unable to match the organization and productivity of the North. Southerners were equally sympathetic to the plight of their soldiers, but the South lacked the efficient transportation and resources necessary for mounting such endeavors.

NOTES

1. Catherine E. Beecher, *Miss Beecher's Domestic Receipt Book* (New York: Harper & Brothers, 1850), 286.

2. Waverly Root and Richard de Rouchemont, *Eating in America* (New York: William Morrow, 1976), 148.

3. R. L. Shep, ed., *Civil War Ladies: Fashions and Needle Arts of the Early 1860's* (Mendocino: R. L. Shep, 1987), 155. "Editor's Table," *Peterson's Magazine,* September 1861.

4. Katie Stewart, *Cooking and Eating* (London: Hart-Davis, MacGibbon, 1975), 202.

5. Beecher, 286.

6. Unpublished account book of a doctor from Butler, Illinois. 1861–1866 in the authors' collection.

7. Minrose C. Gwin, ed., *Cornelia Peake McDonald: A Woman's Civil War. A Diary with Reminiscences of the War from March 1862* (Madison: University of Wisconsin, 1992), 58.

8. James Trager, *The Food Chronology* (New York: Henry Holt, 1995), 262.

9. Root and de Rouchemont, 184.

10. Judith McGuire, *Diary of a Southern Refugee During the War by a Lady of Virginia* (Lincoln: University of Nebraska Press, 1995), 173.

11. Trager, 267.

12. Campbell and Rice, 107.

13. Parthenia Antoinette Hague, *A Blockaded Family: Life in Southern Alabama During the Civil War* (Bedford: Applewood Books, 1995), 101.

14. *Confederate Receipt Book: A Compilation of Over One Hundred Receipts, Adapted to the Times* (Richmond: West & Johnson, 1863), 16.

15. Hague, 17.

16. McGuire, 197.

17. Ibid., 257.

18. *Confederate Receipt Book,* 25–26.

19. Trager, 271.

20. East, 242.

21. Ibid., 251.

22. Hague, 25.

23. Beecher, 230–231.

24. McGuire, 203.

25. Harold Elk Straubing, ed., *Civil War Eyewitness Reports* (N.p.: Archon Books, 1985), 204. Quoting Mary A.H. Gay, *Life in Dixie During the War, 1861–1865* (Foote & Davis Co., 1894).

26. Lunt, 30.

27. Hague, 38.

28. Ibid., 48.

29. *Confederate Receipt Book,* 18.

30. Ibid., 16.

31. C. V. Woodward, 551.

32. Mary A. Livermore, *My Story of the War: A Woman's Narrative of Four Years' Personal Experience* (New York: Da Capo Press, 1995), 129.

33. Moskow, 109–110.

34. Trager, 266.

15

THE LOOK: FASHION AND WOMEN'S CLOTHING

Dresses for breakfasts, and dinners and balls;
Dresses to sit in, and stand in, and walk in;
Dresses to dance in, and flirt in, and talk in;
Dresses in which to do nothing at all.

—"Nothing at All"

Students of historic fashion find 19th-century attire particularly exciting because this is the first period for which widespread photographic documentation of what people actually wore is available. No longer is the study merely subject to interpretations of the hand drawn or engraved fashion plates to which period women may have aspired.

With the ability to print albumen photographs on paper, multiple prints could be made from a single glass negative. This method was inexpensive enough that even those of middle income could afford a photographic portrait. People of the Civil War period ordered multiple copies of these prints to give to friends and family. The prints were mounted on heavy card stock and became known as cartes de visite. Fortunately, these have survived in great numbers and provide tremendous insight into the clothing of the period.

Great care must be taken not to draw overly broad conclusions from these portraits. On the one hand, the photographs are studio portraits, and as such do not provide the informal insight of 20th-century candid snapshots, which show a variety of attire in numerous settings. On the other hand, the wardrobes of middle-class Americans of the mid-19th century did not have the breadth of those of today; thus, it would be safe to assume in most cases that the clothing worn in a studio photograph was that person's "best dress."

WOMEN'S CLOTHING

One of the greatest influences on American women's fashion during the 1860s was *Godey's Lady's Book,* a magazine founded by Louis B. Godey in July 1830. In addition to serials, essays, poems, and craft projects, it featured engraved fashion plates. Each month the magazine depicted morning dresses, walking dresses, seaside costumes, riding habits, dinner dresses, and ball gowns. Such wardrobe depth was seldom needed for the vast majority of the magazine's readers, whose clothes could generally be divided into public or social and domestic or work, with a few seasonal additions for summer and winter. As time passed, *Godey's* began to show fashions better suited to the lifestyle of the American woman. By the 1860s *Godey's* had become a fashion institution, setting the standard for fashion savvy. Other magazines such as *Peterson's, Arthur's, Graham's, Leslie's,* and *Harper's* began to follow suit, or grew in popularity on their own. Parthenia Hague, a woman living in the blockaded South, observed, "Of course we used the same style the whole four years of the war, in our secluded settlement; not a fashion plate or `ladies' magazine did we see during that entire period, so we were little troubled by the 'latest styles.'"[1]

Whether a woman could afford the extravagances touted by the fashion plates of the day or not, the "look" she was hoping to attain was the same. Women of the Civil War period wanted to create the appearance of a narrow waist. Virtually all lines of garments emphasized the smallness of the waist by creating the illusion of width at the shoulders and hips. This was further accentuated by foundation garments that altered the body's physical appearance.

THE DRESS

The dress bodices during this period can be classified by three basic styles. There was the "O" bodice, distinguished by the fullness of the fabric as it cascaded over the bust and gathered in around the waist. "O" bodices were especially popular prior to the war but continued to be worn throughout the conflict. Period photographs indicate that it was the most common style during the early war. The bodice that was becoming fashionable at this time was the "V" bodice. This very fitted style was characterized by double or triple vertical darts extending from the waist. The darts, as well as the side and back seams, were usually boned. Stays could be made from whalebone, metal, or even wood. By the end of the war this style was most popular. The third bodice style was the "Y." This style has

A compilation of fashions typical of those found in *Godey's Lady's Magazine* from the Spring of 1861. From the authors' collection.

a fanlike appearance. It had been in vogue since the early 1840s and had begun to fall out of favor. Like the "O" bodice, "Y" bodices were relatively loose-fitting.

Regardless of style, bodices ended at the natural waistline. The bodice portion of the dress fastened at the center front by hooks and eyes, while the skirt portion had a side-front closure. This created an awkward opening that extended vertically from the neck, then horizontally along the waist, and then vertically again down a few inches along the left front skirt seam. The armscye, or armhole, was almost always diagonal or horizontal to give the shoulders a sloping and wider appearance.

Sleeves were very full, particularly at the elbow, again imparting the illusion of the slender waist. Sleeves, too, came in three fundamental styles. Straight sleeves were simple and loose-fitting and were gathered together into a cuff at the wrist. Also loose were bishop sleeves, which grew wide at the elbow, causing the sleeve to hang in a curve and creating the appearance of a slightly bent arm. The pagoda sleeve tended to be found on more elaborate dresses. It was a loose sleeve that was widest at its hem and usually of bracelet length. Because of this looseness, undersleeves, which would conceal the forearm from view, were worn for modesty's sake. Undersleeves were separate, straight sleeves that fit closely at the

Examples of the pagoda and fitted sleeve are clearly seen in these cartes de visite. From the authors' collection.

wrist and extended to the upper arm, where a drawstring secured them. Most commonly they were white.

Often sleeves had sleeve caps. These were ornamental pieces of fabric that covered the top few inches of the sleeve, supporting the image of the wide, sloping shoulder. Sometimes the impression of a sleeve cap would be created through the use of trim. Short cap sleeves that revealed a woman's arm could only be found on ball gowns.

The necklines of day dresses usually came to the base of the neck. Many were trimmed by small, white collars that were sewn flat and met in the front. Some had very short stand-up collars. Collars were basted inside to protect the garment from wear and soiling. They could easily be removed for frequent launderings from which the entire garment could be saved. The collars would be constructed of sturdy white or very light-colored fabric, which could stand up to the repeated washings this portion of the garment required. Sometimes these collars had matching sets of cuffs, which were similarly attached and served the same purpose. Collars were frequently decorated with a brooch at the center of the neck. If a bow was used, the tails of the bow would extend diagonally away from the center, continuing to proffer the illusion of the broad upper torso. Ball gowns often had wide bateau necklines.

Many of the fabrics and dyes used at this time did not hold up to frequent laundering. Garments were often taken apart and resewn when cleaned. The Housekeeper's Encyclopedia provided nine pages of instructions for washing various fabrics, for example, "Take rice-water, and wash them quickly, without soap."[2] Other methods included the use of bran, oxgall, salt, elixir of vitriol, and egg yolk. Most women's dresses were never totally laundered but rather spot cleaned as needed.

Skirts were long but seldom touched the ground. An exception was the elliptical skirt popular during the late war. These skirts were shorter in the front but lengthened in the back to a point where some actually dragged on the ground. Hem tapes were common on skirts. The tapes or trims were wrapped around the finished hem and could be removed for cleaning or replacement. Skirts were very full and were either fully gathered or pleated at the waistline. No effort was made to make the stomach area appear flatter because, once again, the fuller an area away from the waist seemed the narrower the waist appeared.

Fabrics used for dresses and skirts included silk, linen, wool, and cotton. These were available in an almost infinite variety of weights and weaves, some of which are no longer available today. By far cotton and linen were the most common choices for everyday wear. Silk was expensive. If the average woman owned a silk dress, it would be saved for very special occasions. Linen, because of its extreme durability and ability to be produced at home, was considered frontier or laborer clothing. This was particularly true in the South, where it was in common use among the slave population. Wool continued to have its place because of its warmth and especially because of its fire-retardant qualities. Cotton, a status symbol earlier in the century, had become readily available and affordable for even modest households by the 1830s, thanks to the tremendous development of the textile industry after the invention of the cotton gin. From time to time, there were movements in the North among abolitionist women to avoid the use of cotton due to their belief that it was produced largely as a result of slave activity, but this tended to be confined to relatively small groups.

The blockade and the resulting interruptions in trade caused great hardships for Southern women who had once been the most fashionable element of the population. Early in the war, Virginia Barr was concerned, "Goods are getting so high we are all getting very economical. If the war continues much longer I expect we shall have to go to spinning and weaving. Better that than to be dependent upon the Yankees."[3] For many, this apprehension became reality. Parthenia Hague observed, "Every household now became a miniature factory in itself, with its cotton, cards, spinning-wheels, warping-frames, looms, and so on."[4] Cornelia Pond wrote that her husband bought her a sewing machine in 1860 but during the war she "sewed very little on it, because I had very little cloth to sew."[5] Mary Chesnut recounted the following exchange after being asked for a bottle of brandy by a visitor: "I replied, `Whenever you bring me that roll of linen cambric you said you had from a blockade-runner for me.' J. C. said gravely, after Brewster left with the brandy bottle, `Surely you did not ask that man for a bolt of linen cambric?' Surely I had."[6]

Some Southern ladies continued to dress and to dance in whatever pre-war style they could manage as a means of keeping up their courage. With Yankee gunboats anchored off Baton Rouge and Union troops occupying the city, Sarah Morgan made the following entry in her diary:

Suppose we each took a fancy to consider ourselves the most miserable of mortals, and acted accordingly, going about with our eyes streaming, groaning over our troubles, and never cease to mourn. What a jolly world this would be!—And wouldn't my white dress that Tische is ironing for me to wear to church tomorrow get woefully damp!—Ah no! let us all learn to laugh and be happy, and sing "Better days are coming," even if we don't believe it, it will make those around us happy.[7]

Drawing upon their resourcefulness and creativity, Southern women managed to rework prewar finery and to use natural materials. Mary Chesnut wrote, "Went to sell some of my colored dresses. What a scene—such piles of rubbish—and mixed up with it all, such splendid Parisian silks and satins. A mulatto woman kept the shop under the roof of an out of the way old house. The ci-devant rich, the white ladies, sell to, and the Negroes buy of, this woman."[8]

Prices soared. By 1864 Judith McGuire recorded prices that would give a purchaser pause today. "I gave $110 for ladies' Morocco boots; $22 per yard for linen; $5 apiece for spools of cotton; $5 for a paper of pins."[9] Women needing funds to keep their households together often reworked old finery to create collars, undersleeves, neckties, and other items that brought handsome prices in the inflated Confederate currency. In the face of such adversity, Mary Chesnut described the ingenuity she and her friends displayed in preparation for a wedding. "Julia Rutledge was one of the bridesmaids, and we could not for a while imagine what she would do for a dress. Kate remembers some [material] she had in the house for curtains bought before the war and laid aside as not needed now. The stuff was white and sheer, if a little coarse, but we covered it with no end of beautiful lace. It made a beautiful dress."[10] Parthenia Hague remarked, "It was really ridiculous, our way of making raids upon what remained of our fine bed-linen, pillow shams, and slips, for garments of finer texture than our own homewoven cloth."[11]

The color palette available at this time was basically that which could be achieved by natural dyes. Cornelia Jones Pond noted in her memoirs that she, "made dyes from the bark of the different trees and bushes. Of the

sweet gum we made a gray dye, gallberry a black, and walnut, a brown."
She also reported, "We dyed thread gray to make our dresses sometimes,
grey and white plaids."[12] While many Southern women preferred to wear
lighter hues, popular colors included browns, soft blues, greens, laven-
ders, and grays. Yellows and deep berry-toned reds were also in use. Black
was a common color for trim and detailing. Even though chemical dyes
had been introduced by the end of the 1850s, these colors were mostly
found in decorative fabrics for the home. Although some showy young
women in the North did wear them, proper ladies did not. *Peterson's* counseled against the use of bright colors: "Though they may gratify the sav-
age, [they] will not please the educated eye." Readers were warned about
wearing yellow and yellow-greens: "It is scarcely necessary to observe
that, of all complexions, those which turn upon the yellow are the most
unpleasant in their effect—and probably for this reason, that in this climate it is always a sign of bad health."[13]

Popular patterns included geometrics such as dots, checks, and stripes.
Sometimes these were combined with small floral motifs or grouped into
small clusters. Large florals were not in style, nor were very small floral
calicoes, which were not popular until later in the century. Patterns were
also created by variations in the weave or with the use of shiny and dull
threads.

Trim for dresses was generally placed in horizontal or diagonal lines
continuing the illusion of the narrow waist. Day dresses had little trim
except on the sleeves or bodice. Skirts, if trimmed, were done so near the
hemline. The trims used included braid, piping, binding, and ribbon. Ribbons were commonly gathered, pleated, or ruched. Some skirts appeared
to be trimmed at the hem but had actually been fitted with a tape wrapped
around the hem to protect it from wear. It was much less expensive to replace a worn hem tape than to replace the garment, and the process was
less labor-intensive than turning the skirt. Some ball gowns had flounces
or even a series of ruffles along the skirt. Trims on gowns tended to be
more expensive and elaborate than those on everyday dresses.

Dresses were updated or embellished by the use of accessories. A dress
might be given a different look by the addition of a fichu. Fichus were
often made of sheer, gauze-like fabrics. They were decorated with ruffles,
ribbons, lace, and bows. Fichus were particularly popular in warmer cli-
mates at a time when propriety dictated that a lady's shoulders be fully
covered until evening. A cooler dress with a scooped neckline could be
worn and covered by the lightweight fichu. Older women often wore fichus with their ball gowns. Once again, practicality dictated that the fichu
be a separate piece that could be cleaned more easily than the entire dress.
This also allowed dresses to be easily changed to reflect new trends in
fashion. There were several styles of fichu, but, basically, they covered the
upper back much like a shawl collar and extended over the front in long
tails that either met at the waist or crossed over each other. Some extended

down the skirt a foot or so. Berthes served a similar purpose, but were like oversized collars rather than wraparounds.

Sashes and waistbands were made of rich fabrics often embroidered or trimmed. They extended well down the length of the dress. Belts of many different styles were worn. Some were quite elaborate. The Medici belt stands out as perhaps the most notable style. It was several inches wide at the sides and back, but the front flared out into two exaggerated points that extended up to the area between the breasts and down to mid-stomach. The bretelle corset was similarly shaped, with shoulder straps almost like braces.

Ball gowns, naturally, would not have been found in the majority of women's wardrobes, but their splendor and overstated nature demand some comment. Ball gowns had scooped necklines, short sleeves, and extremely full skirts. Silk was the fabric of choice. Ball gowns were elaborately decorated with long sashes, tiers of laced ruffles, flower garlands, or whatever extravagance might have struck the wearer.

Skirts worn with shirts and jackets, or with vests and jackets, were popular among young women in their teens and twenties. It was not until the very end of the war that the skirt and blouse were seen unaccompanied by the jacket. The jackets were similar to what is called the bolero today. Jackets frequently matched the skirt fabric. One of the most popular styles was the Zouave jacket, which was copied from the French military uniform of the same name. As the fashion grew more popular, the jackets became decorated with more and more black braid in increasingly ornate patterns. Vests were generally of a solid fabric.

Blouses were white and generally closed by buttons rather than hooks and eyes. The end of the blouse was sewn into a waistband as opposed to hanging loose. The Garibaldi shirt—based on the unique garment of the freedom fighters who succeeded in uniting Italy in 1860—was a very distinctive style of shirt worn during the Civil War. It was characterized by trim at the center front, the waistband, the shoulders, and the cuffs. As a rule, they were made of colored fabric.

Riding habits consisted of a skirt, jacket, blouse, and occasionally a vest. Hats were small and frequently had a veil. Jackets were decidedly plainer and more masculine during this time than they had been during the previous decade. The fabric was closely woven to withstand snags on branches, and dark colors were preferred for practicality. Of course, not all women rode for exercise. Some rode in parks to "be seen," and these ladies often preferred more elaborately decorated outfits. *Godey's Lady's Book* gives us this description of an illustration: "Riding habit of black cloth with fluted worsted braid and large gilt buttons; white cashmere vest; scarlet cravat; black felt hat with black feather and scarlet bow."[14]

By the 1860s white wedding dresses had come into fashion. However, many women still followed older traditions and were married in their "best" dress. Mary Chesnut wrote, "The bridesmaids were dressed in black and the bride in Confederate gray homespun. She had worn the dress all winter, but it had been washed and turned for the wedding. . . [S]he wore a cameo breastpin. Her bonnet was self-made."[15] Those fortunate enough to be able to afford such a specialized garment tended to choose dresses that might be considered plain by ballroom standards. Expense was more likely to be put into the fabric rather than trim. Generally, weddings were held during the day. Wedding dresses were therefore day dresses with jewel necklines and long sleeves. In keeping with the "look" of the day, head-dresses and veils tended to lie flat on the head to avoid adding height. Coronets of real or artificial flowers were arranged so that they framed the face and added width. Mary Chesnut described another bride: "Maggie dressed the bride's hair beautifully, they said, but it was all covered by her veil. Which was blonde lace—and the dress tulle and blond lace."[16] She also recorded the details of a "Negro wedding." "The bride and her bridesmaids in white Swiss muslin, the gayest of sashes—and bonnets too wonderful to be described. They had on red blanket shawls which they re-moved as they entered the aisle . . . The bride's gloves were white."[17]

UNDERGARMENTS

Quite possibly, undergarments reached the highest level of complexity in fashion history during this period. Undergarments served to protect the outer garment from body soiling, molded the body to create the ideal "look," and served to distribute the weight of the extremely full skirts. Like the previously discussed collars and cuffs, undergarments were constructed of serviceable fabrics that could be laundered. They were usually white.

The garment worn closest to the skin was the chemise—a knee-length, loose-fitting shift. The body was almost triangular in shape due to the gussets on the sides. This basic garment had changed little in the previous 600 years. During this period, the neck was so wide that it was almost off the shoulders, and the sleeves were short, "infant sleeves." Trim, if any, would be found at the neck or sleeve cuff. Sometimes the yoke would be decorated with small tucks. Its prime purpose was to help absorb perspiration and protect outer garments. It was sometimes affectionately called a "shimmy."

A number of garments were worn with the chemise. Drawers, known as pantalettes, were worn beneath the chemise. They were constructed of two independent legs attached to a waistband and extended to just below the knee. Sometimes they were decorated with tucks, fancy stitching, or eyelet.

The corset was worn on top of the chemise. The purpose of this garment was to make the waist look small compared to other parts of the body and to shape the upper portion of the body upward and outward from the waist to the bust. Corsets were lightly boned and usually had steel clasps at the front and lacing up the back to allow for adjustment. Some had laces in the front with a busk inserted for rigidity. Light corsets were introduced to girls around age 12 and certainly by the age of puberty. Over the corset was worn a corset cover or camisole. These were sleeveless and extended to the waist.

The next layer of undergarment is perhaps the single garment most associated with women's clothing during the Civil War, the crinoline or hoop. Crinolines could be covered or caged. Caged crinolines were composed of a series of hoops of varying sizes suspended from strips of tape that descended from the waist. Covered crinolines were fabric petticoats, which contained casings to hold the hoops. Crinolines were worn beneath petticoats in order to make the skirt appear more full. They also helped in the practical task of distributing the weight of the skirt, which could become quite oppressive depending on the type and amount of fabric used. Generally, crinolines for day dresses were somewhat smaller than those for evening wear. Atop the crinoline were placed one or more petticoats for added fullness and to soften the ridges that could be created by the hoops. Skirts tended to be so much greater in circumference than the crinolines that they tended to drape over this support in folds.

Even a small sampling of period photographs would indicate that few women actually wore hoops with the extreme proportions depicted in fashion plates of the day. Normally, the diameter of the hoop was approximately 50 to 70 percent of the wearer's height. Women engaged in vigor-

---

INNOVATIVE FASHION: THE HOOPED SKIRT

The October 1861 issue of *Peterson's Magazine* offers insight into hooped skirts:

> Five years ago when hooped skirts were first introduced, every one predicted for them a speedy decline, and fall; but after encountering the shafts of ridicule and opposition in every conceivable form, they still not only remain a fixed fact, but have become a permanent institution, which no caprice of fashion will be likely wholly to destroy.
>
> The reason of this constant and increased appreciation is found in the acknowledged principle of comfort and utility upon which the idea was based. . .ladies realized what they needed—something to extend their dresses to proper and becoming dimensions, and save the oppressive weight of a mass of clothing upon the hips.
>
> When a mode, no matter how excellent in itself, becomes a fashion, the tendency is always toward an extreme, and it is not surprising that this was the case with hooped skirts, and that at a certain period the size became absurdly and preposterously large. At the present time a happy medium seems to have been reached.

Source: Peterson's Magazine, 1861.

ous work would decline to wear them. Hoops did wear out, posing a great problem for women in the blockaded South. The hoop was often made of a long, thin strip of whalebone, called baleen, turned back on itself in a circle. Baleen was also used to make buggy whips, and since it was generally acquired from New England, it was largely unavailable during the war. The cloth of the hoops also wore. Parthenia Hague recounted the detailed process followed by a resourceful woman who "devised a means of weaving the hoopskirt on the common house-loom."[18]

The nightdress was ankle-length white cotton and approximately two and a half to three yards wide at the hem. The collar, cuffs, and yoke were often decorated with embroidery, lace, ruching, and tucks. Nightcaps were still worn and were often decorated with lace and bows. Prior to dressing, a woman might wear a morning robe over her nightdress. This was likely to have a shawl or cape collar and wide, loose sleeves. It was tied at the waist.

OUTERWEAR

When it came to outerwear, women had a wide variety of options, including capes, cloaks, shawls, jackets, and coats. Capes varied in length from just below the hip to just above the ankle. Consistent with the fashion ideal of sloping shoulders, they fit the top portion of the torso closely. Some capes had arm slits for ease of movement. Cloaks were extremely full in order to accommodate the full sleeves and skirts.

Jackets and coats naturally followed dress lines, making them many times wider at the hem than at the shoulder. Jackets or paletots, as they were called, may have been more popular than coats due to the weight the latter would have added. Even coats tended to be 6 to 10 inches shorter than the hem of the skirt.

Shawls were very popular. They were oversized and extended well down the back of the skirt. Commonly, two-yard squares were folded into a triangle. Double square shawls could be 64 inches by 128 inches or more. Some shawls were knitted or crocheted. Others were made from wool or lace. Many were decorated with fringe, ruffles, or lace. Paisley shawls were particularly popular.

"Mantle" was the general term for other outer garments not previously mentioned. Mantles tended to be basically triangular in shape, although the back could easily have a rounded "point." They extended over the shoulders and were slightly shaped at the arms. The long ends in front assumed a variety of shapes. For summer wear, the fabrics tended to be light and unlined. Winter mantles were made of heavier, lined fabrics.

HEADGEAR

The bonnet style specific to the 1860s was the spoon bonnet, so named because the brim curved high over the forehead, causing the wearer's face

Ladies' outerwear from cartes de visite. From the authors' collection.

to look as though it was cradled in a large spoon. This style began to be seen in fashion magazines in 1862 to 1863. Some older women still favored the coal scuttle bonnet popular during the 1840s. These bonnets fit the head closely on the sides and extended straight out on all three sides, creating almost a tunnel effect for the wearer. Bonnets were one item of apparel women could constantly update by reworking the trim or decorations to meet the current vogue. Favored decorative features included ribbon, lace, and clusters of silk flowers or berries. These were used on the outside of the bonnet as well as inside the brim to frame the face. Huge ribbons several inches wide were tied in large bows beneath the chin. The outsides of bonnets were covered in silk, or more commonly, polished cotton, which was then pleated, ruched, piped, or quilted. A gathered flounce or skirt was often found attached to the base of the bonnet at the nape of the neck. For summer wear, bonnets were often made of straw.

For country wear, there was the flat-crowned, wide-brimmed "picture" hat made from felt or straw. This often had a lace edging that hung down, almost like a veil. These hats were decorated with materials similar to those used on bonnets, but less elaborately. As the decade progressed, the brim shrank and curved slightly over the eyes, the lace was removed, and the crown became more rounded. Hats continued to shrink as the decade progressed. A popular style was the "pork pie," which resembled a turban in shape with very little space between the brim and the crown. Another type of walking hat had a round crown and a small, rolling brim often decorated by a drooping ostrich feather.

Once again, the blockade required southern women to be resourceful. Pond recalled, "From our friends on the coast, we got the long leaf palmetto, a yard and a half long and stripped it into fine strips and plaited braids for hats both for ourselves, my little girls and the gentlemen of the family. We learned several kinds of plaits. We made the braids into hats. I had Cudjo, our carpenter to make me two blocks the size of my head, and the little girls, upon which I put the hats and pressed them into shape . . . We dyed some of the straw black and made either black hats or mixed it with white straw."[19]

When serious protection from the sun was needed, the slatted bonnet came to the rescue. These work garments were made of cotton or linen and bore neither decorations nor trim. They had long back pieces that extended over the shoulders, and the front could be folded back or fully extended to shade the entire face. Women were seldom photographed in sunbonnets due to their unflattering appearance. During the first federal occupation of Winchester, Laura Lee reported that Master Provost Phileborn opposed the wearing of sunbonnets by women on the street: "Calico and gingham sunbonnets are worn by all the ladies here and styled secession bonnets. They were adopted for their cheapness and for their defense against staring soldiers, but they [the soldiers] resent it and say they are intended as an insult by intimating that we do not care how we dress while they are here."[20]

Indoors, women frequently wore morning caps. These were dainty caps made of muslin, lace tulle, and ribbon. They would never be worn outdoors. Crocheted nets were also worn, but they were generally not considered suitable for dress occasions. Some conservative older women wore more substantial caps, often with lappets, which fully covered the head and were reminiscent of the caps worn during the previous century.

ANCILLARY CLOTHING

Aprons were an important item in a 19th-century wardrobe. Household aprons were extremely large, enveloping almost the entire skirt from front to back and extending down to within a few inches of the hem. Often they had rectangular tops, known as pinners because they were held in place by pins rather than a neck strap as we see in the 20th-century. Aprons would often be made from fabrics with small plaids or checks to help hide stains. While they could be solid, they were seldom white. Aprons were made from linen, flannel, wool, or cotton. Wool was greatly preferred for safety around fires. It does not burn as quickly as linen, and its odor when burning gives fair warning. Burns were the second leading cause of death for women at this time, surpassed only by death during childbirth. Smaller aprons would be worn for mealtimes, unless the meals were served by servants. Separate aprons were kept for particularly dirty household chores.

Fancy, decorative aprons were sometimes worn only for show. These were made of fine-quality fabrics and were sometimes decorated with lace, embroidery, or ruffles. *Godey's Lady's Book* illustrates an apron "one breadth of bright plaid silk trimmed with lace and quilled ribbon; black moire d'antique on each side." These aprons would be much shorter than their functional counterparts, extending only two-thirds to three-fourths of the way down to the hem. Light-colored fabrics were often used, and many were made of polished cotton fabric. Ladies' magazines of the period gave patterns for decorative aprons as sewing projects. These aprons would be worn when doing needlework or when receiving guests at home.[21]

Gloves were essential to a 19th-century woman's wardrobe. Arthur Martine, in his *Hand-Book of Etiquette, and Guide to True Politeness,* remarks, "When dancing is expected to take place, no one should go without new kid gloves: nothing is so revolting as to see one person in an assembly un-gloved, especially where the heat of the room, and the exercise together, are sure to make the hands of the wearer redder than usual. Always wear your gloves in church or in a theater."[22]

Civil War period gloves were short. They extended to the wrist even for evening wear. Commonly, they were joined by a button at the wrist. Some were secured by short lacing. Kid was the most common material, but fabric and lace were also used. For day wear, gloves would be found in a wide variety of colors, but only white was proper for evening and formal wear. Some were embellished with decorative stitching or embroi-dery. Older women sometimes wore netted, lace, or silk mitts. These fin-gerless gloves were popular during the 1840s and 1850s and continued to be worn by less fashionable women who perhaps became enamored with this style in their youth. Pond noted that during the war she "learned to make gloves both with fingers and without."[23]

FOOTWEAR

Shoes had small heels of one inch or less and flat, square toes. For or-dinary wear they were made from leather or cloth and were black, light brown, or gray. Some southerners, affected by the blockade, "made black-ening for shoes by boiling the chinaberries and skimming off the oil and mixing it with soot."[24] Formal day dress shoes would be made of fancier fabrics such as satin. Evening shoes came in a variety of styles. Some had ribbon ties that wrapped around the ankle. Others displayed embroidered tops. Evening shoes were often in bright colors to match the ensemble.

Women's boots were ankle height and laced up the sides at the inside with elastic gussets at each side. Some buttoned at the sides. Dressy boots might be made from kid or satin. Congress gaiters were made of cloth, came in a variety of colors, and were tipped in patent leather. They were a rather low-cut boot and finished with a wide piece of elastic on the side. Balmoral boots were very popular. They laced up the front and were considered very stylish.

House slippers were low-heeled mule-like foot coverings commonly done in Berlin work featured in patterns from ladies' magazines. Slippers were also crocheted in a low, bootie style. *Peterson's Magazine* gave a pattern that directed the maker to finish it in the following manner: "Sew the slipper to a cork-sole, and run an elastic in the top of the slipper."[25]

ACCESSORIES

As in the previous century, fans were a popular accessory. The traditional semicircular fan was often covered in paper or silk. Some were beautifully painted. A popular style during the 1860s had oval-shaped fabric leaves attached to the sticks. The average fan length of this period was 6 to 10 inches. Circular fans were also fashionable. Their handles, when folded backwards, revealed an accordion-pleated fabric fan. Round or spade-shaped palmetto or straw fans were less expensive and were sometimes homemade.

Umbrellas and parasols were two different accessories, and each served a separate purpose. Umbrellas were for use in inclement weather. They were large and black and were meant to protect the carrier. Parasols were small, ladylike contrivances. Their purpose was to protect the carrier from both the sun and unwanted glances. Frames were made of metal. Handles were ivory or wood. Parasols designed for carriage rides often had a hinge at the top of the stick that allowed the top to tip in order to better fit the confined space. They varied in length from 16 to 22 inches. Parasols used for walking were generally larger, 22 to 26 inches. Silk was the most common fabric. Trimming was lace or ruching. Oriental-style paper parasols with cane ribs were used at the seaside or for informal occasions.

Purses came in a variety of styles during the 1860s. Some were carried by short handles; others, sometimes referred to as waist pouches, were suspended from the waistband. *Peterson's Magazine* presented two patterns for waist pouches:

We have just received two patterns from Paris of the little pouches, which still continue to be worn, suspended from the waistband by a chain and hook, and sometimes by a cord. They are made in all kinds of materials, and are embroidered in gold, silver, and jet; or they are made of the same material as the dress with which they are worn, and trimmed in the same manner. Last year, it will be remembered, we gave a pattern of one of those Pouches, when they first came up.[26]

Patterns for crocheted, knitted, or Berlin work purses abound in period ladies' magazines. Purses were decorated with tassels, cording, and embroidery. Shapes were round or rectangular, but the six-inch-square bag was most popular. One of the most interesting kinds of purses was a long, thin knit or netted cylinder closed at both ends with a slit in the center. These were called miser purses or long purses and were quite popular. Formal purses often had beading or were made with metallic thread.

JEWELRY

Many photographs from the period show women wearing some jewelry. Popular materials included jet, ivory, bone, onyx, jade, amber, garnet, and pearl. Still living in the shadow of its discovery in California, gold was the order of the day. Particularly fashionable was the brooch worn at the center of the neckline. Brooches varied in size from large to small and were worn both vertically and horizontally. They closed by simple "C" clasps without safety catches. Cameos were highly favored. They often bore images of mythological figures. The female head, almost synonymous with the modern cameo, was just coming into fashion toward the end of the war. Cameos were made from sardonyx, shell, lava, ivory, and coral.

The mid-19th century was a very romantic and sentimental era. It was a common practice to have a lock of hair as a keepsake from a loved one. Many period brooches contained a lock of a beloved's under glass in the center of the brooch. Other brooch materials included goldstone, agate, bog oak, enamel, horn, and mosaics. The mosaic pieces were very small and portrayed classical scenes or floral sprays. Enameled pieces were usually blue or black with a gold figure in the center.

Other neckline decorations included short necklaces of single-sized pearls or beads, especially jet. Long chains were popular in the previous decade and were still being worn by some. Both a beaded and a long chain necklace might be worn at the same time.

Other forms of jewelry were prevalent. Bracelets were also stylish and often were worn in pairs, one on each wrist. They tended to be large, almost chunky, bangle style. Serpents were one motif much in vogue. Jet beads strung on wire were also worn. Dangling earrings with long ear wires were worn. These were usually shorter than those worn later in the century. Many earrings were made of hollow wear, an inexpensive rolled gold that appears almost puffed, or formed into hollow tubes. Naturally, this made the earrings very light in weight. Use of acorns as a motif was widespread. Often earrings and brooches came in matched sets.

The wearing of rings was widespread. Unmarried females would wear a ring on the first finger of their left hand, no doubt in hope that they would soon be wearing one on the third digit of that same hand. A simple gold band was the prevalent sign of a married woman. Generally, diamond rings were not worn. The diamond mines of South Africa were not discovered until 1870, and not until then would diamonds become affordable to anyone but the most affluent. Rings were likely to bear garnets, amethysts, pearls, onyx, amber, jade, red coral, or cameos.

Watch ownership was fairly common by this time even for women. Watches were worn on watch chains and were tucked in the belt or carried in a watch pocket at the waist. Patterns for crochet, beaded, and braidwork watch pockets appeared in period ladies' magazines. Watches were hung on a long, fine chain worn around the neck that extended well below the waist. Some were suspended on a short chain from the belt.

HAIRSTYLES

As with other fashion items, hairstyles wanted to emphasize a broad upper body. To that end, the center part is almost universal in period photographs. This allows for a wide, bare forehead, making the face appear broad while adding no height on top. To continue this illusion, the fullest part of the hairstyle was at or below the ears. Some teens wore their hair cut blunt just below the earlobes. Most women, however, had long hair, which they wore rolled, braided, or otherwise confined and pulled toward the back of the head. If the hair was not confined, it was generally fixed in long finger curls and pulled to the side of the face. The variety of curls

A variety of hairstyles from cartes de visite. From the authors' collection.

and hair rolls was as rich as the ingenuity of the women who styled them. As the war drew to a close, hairstyles were beginning to change to include tendrils and greater height.

Ladies' magazines of the period offered many suggestions for elaborate hair dressing for evening wear and suggested incorporating such items as flower blossoms, pins, combs, chains, feathers, and false curls. The "Editor's Table" of *Peterson's* offered this counsel to its readers:

Perfect cleanliness is indispensable for the preservation of the health, beauty, and color of the hair, as well as its duration; this is attained by frequently washing it in tepid soft water, using those soaps which have the smallest portion of alkali in their composition, as this substance renders the hair too dry, and by depriving it of its moist coloring matter, impairs at once its strength and beauty. After washing, the hair should be immediately dried; and when the towel has ceased to imbibe moisture, brushed constantly in the sun or before the fire until its lightness and elasticity are fully restored; and in dressing it, a little marrow pomatum, bear's grease, or fragrant oil should be used. The belief that washing the hair induces catarrh, or headache, or injures the hair is erroneous.[27]

Of course, women's clothing styles changed rapidly during this period; but interest in the Civil War era has frozen many of the archetypes of women's apparel in time. While Civil War era photographs and engravings lock the view of an instant in time, nothing has had greater influence in this regard than the film *Gone With the Wind*. Care must be taken in drawing conclusions from this film, not only about the clothing worn during the period, but also about the lifestyle portrayed and the interpersonal relations among the characters.

NOTES

1. Parthenia Antoinette Hague, *A Blockaded Family: Life in Southern Alabama During the Civil War* (Bedford: Applewood Books, 1995), 81.

2. Mrs. E. F. Haskell, *The Housekeeper's Encyclopedia* (Mendocino: R. L. Shep, 1992), 15–23.

3. Claudia Lynn Lady, "Five Tri-state Women During the Civil War: Day-to-Day Life," *West Virginia History* 43, no. 4 (Summer 1982), 307.

4. Hague, 39.

5. Josephine Bacon Martin, ed., *Life on a Liberty County Plantation: the Journal of Cornelia Jones Pond* (Hinesville, Georgia: Printgraphix, 1983), 97.

6. C. Van Woodward, *Mary Chesnut's Civil War* (New Haven: Yale University Press, 1981), 565.

7. Charles East, ed., *Sarah Morgan: The Civil War Diary of a Southern Woman* (New York: Simon & Schuster, 1991), 132–133.

8. C. V. Woodward, 588.

9. Judith McGuire, *Diary of a Southern Refugee During the War by a Lady of Virginia* (Lincoln: University of Nebraska Press, 1995), 292.

10. C. V. Woodward, 456.

11. Hague, 115.

12. Josephine Bacon Martin, ed., *Life on a Liberty County Plantation: the Journal of Cornelia Jones Pond* (Hinesville, Georgia: Printgraphix, 1983), 98.

13. Shep, 127–129. Mrs. Merrifield, "The Use and Abuse of Colors in Dress," *Peterson's Magazine,* September 1861.

14. From a *Godey's Lady's Book* print in the authors' collection.

15. C.V. Woodward, 559–560.

16. Ibid., 649.

17. Ibid., 259.

18. Hague, 112.

19. Martin, ed., 98.

20. Campbell and Rice, 83.

21. From a print in the authors' collection taken from *Godey's Lady's Book,* July 1861.

22. Martine, 55.

23. Martin, ed., 98.

24. Martin, ed., 98.

25. Shep, 64–65. Jane Weaver, "Crochet Slipper," *Peterson's Magazine,* April 1861.

26. Shep, 151. Jane Weaver, " Waist-Pouches," *Peterson's Magazine,* September, 1861.

27. Shep, 326. "Editor's Table," *Peterson's Magazine,* September 1864.

16

DRESSED FOR THE PART: MEN'S, CHILDREN'S, AND SLAVES CLOTHING

"Well-bred people do not often dress in what is called the `height of fashion,' that is generally left to dandies and pretenders."
—*Martine's Hand-Book of Etiquette*

MEN'S CLOTHING

In his handbook of etiquette, Martine remarks, "There are four kinds of coats which a man must have: a business coat, a frock-coat, a dress-coat, and an over-coat. A well dressed man may do well with four of the first, and one each of the others per annum. An economical man can get along with less." Nonetheless, Martine's idea of "getting along" was nowhere near reality. Just as the average woman did not have a specialized outfit for every task of the day, most men did not enjoy the wardrobe depth detailed by Martine. Like women's clothing, men's clothing in practical application tended to fall into formal and informal, summer and winter. New clothes would be considered "best" dress until they became worn, and they would then be relegated to work status.[1] A shirt, vest, and trousers would be the very least in which a man would allow himself to be seen. A man appearing with anything less was considered to be in a state of undress. Even laborers and farmers would not allow themselves to go with less. It was the basest menial or workman who would not be so attired, such as the blacksmith, who would wear a heavy leather apron, which covered him above the waist.

Even when faced with shortages during the war, women continued to make sure that their spouses appeared well attired. Eugenia Thackston wrote her husband from Virginia, "I have delayed making your vest on account of not having material for a back, but I will soon make that as our cloth is now in the loom."[2] Eugenia Thackston's letters are full of concern for her war clerk husband. She made a shirt for him from flannel he had purchased for the baby. The following year, still worried about his clothing, she wrote, "I wish much you had some nice clothing. I dislike it exceedingly that you are so shabby, even if it is war times. I desire you to provide yourself with a new pair of shoes & a hat at any price . . . Now my Ben don't put off getting these articles any longer."[3]

Dress shirts were made of white cotton. Longer than the modern shirt, they were pullovers that buttoned from the mid-chest to the neck. Small vertical tucks commonly decorated either side of the buttons, but this became less favored as the 1860s progressed. Shirts had neckbands and detachable collars. For formal daywear, the collar was upright with a gap between the points, which just touched the jaw, allowing for freer movement of the head and neck than had been the style earlier in the century. For informal occasions, men wore either a shallow single collar with sloping points meeting at the center and forming a small inverted "V" opening, or a shallow double collar similar to the modern collar. Work shirts were made in a variety of colors and checks and could be made from cotton or linen.

Cravats, which more closely resemble the earlier neck stock than the modern tie, were worn around the neck. The term "necktie" was just coming into use. The cravat might have been tied in a flat, broad bow with the ends extending across the top of the waistcoat or secured with a pin. Basically, however, it was a band of fabric passed around the neck and tied in either a bow or a knot with hanging ends. Silk was the fabric of choice, and it was one area where a man might be able to display his good taste even if his purse prohibited further extravagances. The decade began with a preference for light-colored cravats, occasionally decorated with embroidery or other fancy work. As the war progressed, however, darker colors became more prominent. Striped, plaid, and dotted cravats were also worn, but with less regularity. Even laborers would simulate the look, although they may only have been able to knot a cotton kerchief around their neck. Ladies' magazines of the period offered patterns for woolen and cotton knitted cravats. A pattern for a striped tie done in brioche knitting in *Peterson's* ended with, "We recommend this for a present for the holidays."[4]

Vests or waistcoats could be made of the same fabric as the suit, or they could be of much finer, dressier fabrics such as silk taffetas, embossed silks, or brocades. Patterns ranged from tone-on-tone to stripes, checks, and paisleys. The neckline cut was moving lower than in the previous decade. Watch pockets became common. Suits were either loose-fitting, almost baggy, or very formal with knee-length frock coats. The fuller suit

Men's suits from cartes de visite.
From the authors' collection.

seems to have been favored by the average man, perhaps because it was more comfortable or needed less skilled tailoring. The formal suit appears to have been the "look" to which men of power aspired. Lapels sported a more modern single notch than earlier in the century. Frock coats sometimes had velvet collars and cuff-link style buttoning. Work trousers had buttoned, full fall fronts, while dress trousers had "French flys," which concealed the buttons.

Wool was the fabric of choice for these items, with linen being popular during the summer, especially in the South. Farmers seemed to favor tweeds and more sturdy woolens. Generally, solids dominated, with browns and grays most common. Black was the choice of professionals, who also preferred fine woolen broadcloth, serge, and twill. These fabrics often had a certain amount of silk woven in to give them a finer finish and lighter weight. Martine advises gentlemen:

If a gentleman is able to dress expensively it is very well for him to do so, but if he is not able to wear ten-dollar broadcloth, he may comfort himself with the reflection that cloth, which costs but five dollars a yard will look quite as well when made into a well-fitting coat. With this suit, and well-made shoes, clean gloves, a white pocket-handkerchief, and an easy and graceful deportment withal, he may pass muster as a gentleman.[5]

Hat styles varied. The stovepipe hat favored by Abraham Lincoln also came in a shorter version. Many Southern gentlemen favored what has come to be called the plantation hat. This is a low-crowned, stylish hat with a substantial, but not overstated, brim. The design of the plantation hat may have been brought back from Panama, where a similar hat was seen by travelers crossing the Isthmus to the gold fields of California in the late 1840s and early 1850s. Another hat commonly found had a round crown with a medium brim. The derby was not developed until later in the century. Flat-topped straw hats were popular in summer. Rural men often wore wide-brimmed high-crowned hats, which offered less in fashion but more in protection from the elements. In inclement weather, men carried large black umbrellas.

Male jewelry was not as ostentatious as it had been in earlier periods. Rings of all types were popular. They took the form of signet rings, seal rings, mourning rings, and commemorative rings. Smaller neckties made the tiepin unnecessary in most cases. The longer coats of the sixties made the watch chain, which hung below a short waistcoat, impractical. The watch chain was now displayed from the waistcoat pocket to a button at mid-chest.

Braces or suspenders were buttoned on to the trousers by means of leather tabs. It was quite the fashion for women to crochet braces or work them in Berlin woolwork. Ladies' magazines featured patterns for this work, but makers were cautioned, "This crochet should not be done too tightly, as a little elasticity is desirable."[6] Elastic, made from natural rubber, had been invented by this time, but its only apparel application was in wide panels in shoes. Men unfortunate enough to have no braces made by an attentive woman may have sported those made of plain or striped linen.

Underwear required two pieces. The undershirt was a long-sleeved pullover that buttoned to mid-chest. The drawers extended down to the ankle and had button fronts. They could be made of silk stockinette, cotton, or linen. One-piece union suits, with or without the "trap door" in the rear, were not developed until the 1890s.

When it came to lounging in the privacy of one's home, gentlemen had several specialized items of attire. Lounging or smoking caps were elaborate items made of rich fabrics and adorned with embroidery, beadwork, or braid. They generally came in three basic styles: the round pillbox style, the fitted six-panel cap, and the teardrop-shaped Scotch style. The first two styles ended with a tassel on top. The last was finished with a narrow ribbon at the back of the cap at the point. Ladies' magazines also carried patterns for making and decorating these caps. *Peterson's* suggests that a hand-made lounging cap "would make a very pretty Christmas, New Year's, or birthday gift for a gentleman."[7] In addition to slippers, which greatly resembled the woman's slipper for relaxed footwear at home, a man might have preferred the dressing, or lounging, boot. *Peterson's* ad-

The variety of men's hairstyles and facial hair was almost inexhaustible in this period. This sampling from cartes de visite illustrates some popular styles. From the authors' collection.

vises, "The Lounging Boot will almost supersede the slipper, as many gentlemen catch cold by changing from a boot to a slipper, even in the house." These boots were made of fabric and were decorated with elaborate embroidery.[8]

Nightshirts were made of white cotton and extended to the ankle. They had long sleeves and small turned-down collars. The nightcap was a bag-shaped item with a tassel on top. Some were knit or crocheted, but these were going out of style. Over his nightshirt a gentleman may have worn a wrapper. This was a long, sack-style robe with plain sleeves, confined by a cord at the waist.

Men wore their hair parted to the side. Facial hair was very stylish. Men sported beards of all styles, lengths, and degrees. Mustaches were equally in favor. Period photographs show a tremendous variety of styles. The names of most of these have become meaningless to modern observers. The term "sideburns," however, can be traced to General Ambrose Burnside, who sported distinctively bushy whiskers. The size and style of sideburns and beards varied greatly between individuals and over time.

CHILDREN'S CLOTHING

Children's clothing rivaled women's fashions in both complexity and ornateness. Some middle- and upper-class children were dressed in layers of clothing often constructed of impractical fabrics. *Godey's Lady's Book* carried the following description, accompanied by a picture: "Child's dress of green silk with narrow pinked ruffles, corselet of green silk, white muslin gimp, white felt hat with white wing."[9] Ornate as it sounds, this outfit is not classified as a party dress. Gauze, silk, wool, and taffeta were common fabric suggestions for children's dress in ladies' magazines. Print fabrics tended to be small geometric or abstract designs. These designs allowed for the economical use of material since it was easier to match such prints, and there was less waste. Braid or ribbon were popular trims even for children.

In rural areas, children's clothing was considerably more practical, much the same as their parents'. Muslin and cotton were the fabrics of choice for country and poorer folk. In order to allow for growth, it was common for seams at the shoulders and under the arms to be folded in an inch each, so that they could be let out as the child grew. Sometimes a waistband was added as the child grew to lengthen skirts and trousers. Several tucks, of an inch or so, were often made near the hems of skirts and trousers. These created an attractive detail and could later be let down to accommodate growth.

Little girls were dressed very much as were their mothers. *Godey's Lady's Book* even contained an illustration for a "corset for a little girl" which laced down the back only. This was not encouraged by everyone, however, as the "Editor's Table" in *Peterson's* points out: "Stays or tight bands about the ribs compress them readily, as these bones are not fully formed, hence readily cause deformities, and alter the natural and healthy position and action of the lungs, heart, liver and stomach, and produce a tendency to disease in these organs."[10]

The main difference between a woman's attire and a girl's was that girls' skirts were considerably shorter, ending about mid-calf. Pantalettes hung just below the edge of the dress. These would be plain for everyday wear and would be adorned with lace or eyelet for dressier occasions. These pantalettes differed from women's in that the crotches were sewn and they buttoned at the sides. Like her mother, a little girl wore a chemise as the basic undergarment. By age seven a girl would have begun to wear a hoop, although it would likely have only one hoop ring at this time. Once again, like an adult woman, she would wear under and over petticoats. One popular style for Sunday and party dresses was the bateau or "boat" neckline. This extremely wide neckline was another impractical fashion, and many photographs show one sleeve slipping off the child's shoulder.

In Margaret Mitchell's book *Gone with the Wind* and in the subsequent film of the same name, Scarlett O'Hara's dress in the opening scenes was

The variety of clothing for girls is exemplified by these cartes de visite. The picture at the lower left illustrates a common problem with bateau necklines for the very young. From the authors' collection.

considered inappropriate by the other characters, not because it was revealing, but rather because it was too juvenile for a young woman of her age, having an open neckline and a short skirt.

Like their mothers, little girls wore undersleeves and chemisettes. They also wore tuckers. A tucker was a panel of crimped muslin secured by a tape and sewn on the inside edge of the neckline and sleeve edge. Its purpose was to save wear on the fabric, and the tucker could be removed and laundered separately from the garment. Blouses and skirts were not popular for toddlers but were worn by older girls.

Fancy aprons were popular. They tied around the waist and covered almost the entire skirt portion of a dress. The top covered only part of the dress front and crossed over both shoulders on top. They were commonly decorated with flounces, bows, and other decorative details. Pinafores, which covered almost the entire dress, were more practical and much more common across all economic lines. They were constructed in such fabrics as muslin, calico, or linen. The pinafore fit closely to the chest and hung down loosely to the hem. Another layered style for young girls was the white dress covered by another jumper-like dress.

Children's jewelry tended to be modest and simple. Little girls wore strings of beads, lockets, and chains. Very young girls wore coral necklaces or pairs of coral bracelets. Infants were given elaborate coral rattles mounted in silver or teething rings also made of coral.

Boys wore a series of different types of outfits, each befitting a certain age group. Very young boys often had shirts that buttoned to the waist-band of their pants and provided a neater look. From ages one to four, boys wore a nankeen suit. This was a dresslike costume worn over white underdrawers not unlike a girl's pantalettes, although likely to be less fancy. The top portion of the suit was a blousy sack, often with a large sash or a cord tied around the waist.

Between the ages of four and seven, there was the French blouse. Essentially, it was a loose, dresslike tunic secured at the waist by a belt and large buckle or sash. This would have been worn over loose knee pants, although it was also worn over a skirt by very young boys. Boys may also have been attired in a loose jacket and waistcoat, once again with loose knee pants. Boys may also have been clad in a suitlike outfit with a slightly cut-away jacket, gently rounded in front, and very loose trousers which extended to about mid-calf.

From 7 to 12 a boy may have worn what would be thought of as a suit-like outfit comprised of loose, ankle-length trousers and waist-length sack coat with a ribbon tie fashioned into a bow. The pants might have "box plaits." Suspenders could be introduced at this point. Sailor suits were also popular for boys 7 to 14. Some boys in certain areas did not wear long pants until 14 or 15 years of age.

It is no wonder that the knickerbocker suit was welcomed by older boys who were as yet considered too young for trousers. Knickerbocker suits consisted of a button-faced jacket fastened merely with a hook and eye at the top; a ten-button waistcoat with small slits at the sides to allow for ease of movement and better fit; and knickerbockers, loose-fitting pants that came tight against the leg just below the knee. Emily May proclaimed in *Peterson's*:

The Knickerbocker costume is now the favorite style of dress for boys, when they are of that awkward age, too young to be breeched, and too old to wear frocks and pinafores. This costume has a great many recommendations: it can be made in almost any material; it always looks neat and tidy; and for the play-ground is particularly suitable, as it leaves boys the free use of their limbs, besides being rather more manly than petticoats, which used to be (particularly at school) a boy's abhorrence.[11]

As older teens, boys dressed much as adult men did. They wore pants, vests, and jackets. Jacket types included sack, frock, and a short, military style. Boys' undergarments included an undershirt and drawers that reached down to the knee. When boys graduated into longer pants, they wore longer, ankle-length drawers that fit the leg more closely.

For outerwear, children often wore coats, jackets, and cloaks similar to those worn by women. They also wore capes secured by buttoned tabs across the chest. Girls generally wore small hats, usually straw for summer and cloth for winter. As with women, slatted bonnets were worn in rural areas. Brims tended to be small, and they were very simply decorated. Boys wore caps and small hats with rounded crowns.

Girls wore leather or canvas short boots for day wear and slippers for dressy occasions. Some of the slippers had ankle straps. The boots either laced up the side or had elastic gussets on the side. Canvas boots often had toe and heel portions covered in leather for added protection and durability. Boys wore similar footwear or short pull-on boots decorated with a tassel on the front.

Girls wore their hair in a short, ear-length blunt cut that was pushed behind the ears. Some wore their hair in long finger curls. The latter style seems to have been more popular among girls of higher economic status. Occasionally ribbons were used to keep the long hair out of the face. Girls of about eight or nine began to wear hairnets. Sarah Morgan, aged 19, wrote in her diary, "The net I had gathered my hair in fell in my descent and my hair swept down half way between my knee and my ankle in one stream."[12] Like their mothers', girls' hair was center parted. Boys parted

All of these cartes de visite show young boys. In pictures of the young the way the hair is parted is often the only clue to the child's sex. Boys' hair was parted on the side. From the authors' collection.

their hair to the side. The sides and back were usually short. Because fashions for young children were not strongly differentiated by sex, when looking at photographs, the part is often the only clue to the sex of the child.

Finally, the "Editor's Table" of *Peterson's* offered the following advice to mothers about clothing children:

To guard against cold, the child should wear flannel, of varying thickness, according to the season of the year, next to the body, and fitting tolerably close, for, without this protection, the present style of dress, causing the clothes to project away, leaves the body exposed to sudden chills. The head should be lightly covered, so as to protect it from the sun, or sudden change of temperature; but it should never be covered with thick or heavy material. Anything causing fullness or congestion about the head will very commonly act by sympathy, as it is called, on the stomach, and cause obstinate and violent vomiting . . . A pin should never be used about a child's clothes at any age; buttons and strings should always be the modes of fastening.[13]

Infants wore long gowns that were often twice the length of the child. This was done to keep the child warm. Long gowns could not be cast off as loose blankets could. The gowns were generally white to withstand the frequent washings infant clothing required and were of "soft material, entirely free from starch."[14] For the first few weeks after birth, infants wore long, narrow strips of fabric known as belly bands. These were several yards long and were designed to protect the navel. In addition to diapers, or napkins, as they were called, infants wore a shirt, a pinner which con-

---

DETAILED GUIDELINES FOR INFANT CLOTHING

The Housekeeper's Encyclopedia detailed the order of operations in dressing a baby:

The first article put on, after a napkin, should be a flannel band, from four to four and a half inches wide; pin it snugly, but not tight enough to bind and make the babe uncomfortable; the little shirt is the next article of dress to be put on the child; this should be open at the front, and folded smoothly, so as to leave no wrinkles; the pinner comes next; lay the infant on its stomach, fold the shirt smoothly on its back, fasten the shirt and pinner together with a small pin, leaving the point covered, so as to prick neither child nor nurse; wrap its feet in the pinner, and pin it as close as possible without cramping its limbs; then take the flannel skirt. . . fold the shirt over, and fasten shirt, band pinner, and skirt, together with two pins, near the arms, being sure to have the points hid in the clothing. . . Fasten the dress, and the little one is ready for presentation.

Source: Mrs. E. F. Haskell, *The Housekeeper's Encyclopedia* (Mendocino: R. L. Shep), 1992.

CHILDREN'S FASHIONS—(*See description, Fashion department.*)

A *Godey's* print of a variety of children's fashions, 1861. From the authors' collection.

tained their lower limbs, a skirt or skirts, and a dress. Babies also wore caps, for which women's magazines frequently carried patterns.

As the child grew older, clothing adjustments were made. Mothers were advised, "Keep socks on after the child is two months old; before this, its pinners will be sufficient protection. . . . When a child shows a disposition to creep, shorten its clothes that it may have free use of its limbs, and protect its feet with stockings and shoes."[15]

SLAVES' CLOTHING

The clothing of slaves varied with the economic status of the slaveholder and with the tasks the slave was required to do. Slaves who worked in the household, often well dressed in suits, dresses, or "colonial" outfits, were seen by visitors to the home, and therefore their appearance would have been a reflection on the slaveholder. Slaves who worked in the fields needed serviceable clothing that would survive the rigors of the work being done. Any benefit that the slave gained in the way of clothing was an accidental advantage of the owner's desire to run an efficient plantation and a model household.

Sarah Stone was the daughter of a Mississippi plantation owner who held 150 slaves. In her diary she described the semiannual process of getting clothes ready for the slaves, which she admits "was no light work."

When the time would come to have everything cut out; a room would be cleared out and the great bolts of white woolen jeans, Osnabergs, with bolt after bolt of red flannel for the little ones, would be rolled in and the women with great shears would commence their work. There were several sets of patterns with individual ones for the very tall and the very fat, but there was not much attention paid to the fit, I fancy.[16]

Male slaves were furnished with only two or three suits a year. Women were supplied with a calico or linsey dress, head handkerchiefs, and ging- ham aprons for Christmas. The fabric was sturdy and became as soft as flannel as it was washed. The slaves often dyed the white suits tan or gray with willow bark or sweet gum.

Stone was particularly struck by the shoes the slaves were given: "Those heavy russet shoes that all clumped about in, the old and the young, men and women . . . so ugly and must have been excessively uncomfortable— about as pliable as wood. After many, many greasings, the poor darkies could at last bend their feet in them."[17]

The quality and quantity of clothing for slaves during the war varied greatly, and, generally, both suffered as the war continued. These gar- ments often represented white folks' hand-me-downs, remnants, and discards. Slaves, especially those in urban areas, could often be seen in slightly unfashionable, but serviceable, suits of clothing and dresses of cotton and wool. As whites felt the pinch of the blockade, hand-me-downs and discards took on a new value in their eyes and were rarely passed on to slaves. In this manner the slaves were made to bear the worst effects of the shortages.

Plantation slaves were often clothed in coarse but durable "Negro cloth," which was produced from linen in the mills of New England, or in coarse woolen broadcloth. Prior to the opening of hostilities, plantation owners commonly purchased cloth by the yard and allowed the slaves to fashion the clothing on the plantation. This cloth took the form of trousers and shirts for the men and boys, while slave women wore woolen dresses with cotton aprons. The wool helped to prevent the skirts from catching fire and was favored by women, both black and white, who worked near open hearths. Both sexes used straw hats and handkerchiefs in a variety of ways, but generally they were tied to form head coverings or neck cloths.

Shoes were a difficult item to provide for the slave at a reasonable cost, and most ex-slaves complained of rarely having owned shoes that fit well. Unless they owned a slave that was trained in shoemaking from raw leather, plantation owners resorted to buying shoes in bulk. There existed an entire trade in New England dedicated to the manufacture of cheap shoes for slaves. These shoes rarely gave long use without the services of a cobbler. Wooden clogs, a type of sandal with a large wooden sole, often served in place of shoes. Slaves generally preferred to go barefoot in the fields, as did their white farmer counterparts, because shoes do not hold up well in plowed fields. Contemporary illustrations from *Harper's* and *Leslie's* almost always show slaves to be shod. Slaves who were forced to go barefoot in winter greased their feet with tallow to protect the skin, but this circumstance seems to have been rare except in the Deep South. Slaves rarely went unshod in town or in the Northern border states as such a thing would have embarrassed their owners.

NOTES

1. Arthur Martine, *Martine's Hand-Book of Etiquette, and Guide to True Politeness* (New York: Dick & Fitzgerald, 1866), 49.
2. Claudia Lynn Lady, "Five Tri-state Women During the Civil War: Day-to-Day Life;" *West Virginia History* 43, no. 4 (Summer 1982), 307.
3. Ibid., 324.
4. R. L. Shep, ed., *Civil War Ladies: Fashions and Needle Arts of the Early 1860's* (Mendocino: R. L. Shep, 1987), 345; Jane Weaver, "Gentleman's Neck-Tye in Brioche Knitting," *Peterson's Magazine*, December 1864.
5. Martine, 49.
6. Shep, 290; Jane Weaver, "Gentlemen's Braces," *Peterson's Magazine*, May 1864.
7. Shep, 344; Jane Weaver, "Imperial Lounging-Cap," *Peterson's Magazine*, December 1864.
8. Shep, 275; Jane Weaver, "Gentleman's Dressing or Lounging Boot," *Peterson's Magazine*, April 1864.
9. Shep, 278.
10. Shep, 326; "Editor's Table," *Peterson's Magazine*, September 1864.
11. Shep, 189–190; Mrs. Emily May, "The Knickerbocker Suit," *Peterson's Magazine*, November 1861.
12. Charles East, ed., *Sarah Morgan: The Civil War Diary of a Southern Woman* (New York: Touchstone, 1991, 102.
13. Shep, 326; "Editor's Table," *Peterson's Magazine*, September 1864.
14. E. F. Haskell, *The Housekeeper's Encyclopedia* (Mendocino: R.L. Shep, 1992), 384.
15. Ibid., 385–386.
16. Walter Sullivan, *The War the Women Lived: Female Voices from the Confederate South*. Nashville: J. S. Sanders, 1995. Quoting Sarah Katherine Stone in *Brokenburn: The Journal of Kate Stone, 1861–1868*.
17. Sullivan, 7.

17

ELEVATING
AND EXPANDING
THE YOUNG MIND

"If a spirit of inquiry is once aroused, it will, sooner or later, find means to satisfy itself; and thus the inquisitive boy will become an energetic, capable man."

—*The Mother's Book*

It was essential that children be prepared for the intellectual and cultural life the 19th century valued so highly. A lesson titled "The Value of Education" in a school reader states, "The highest objects of a good education are to reverence and obey God, and to love and serve mankind. Every thing that helps in attaining these objects is of great value, and every thing that hinders us, is comparatively worthless."[1]

The home, of course, was the first place where these foundations were laid. *The Mother's Book* by Lydia Child—the Dr. Spock of her day—advocated the deliberate and early cultivation of a child's intellect. After describing some simple amusements for the small child, Mrs. Child advised, "But something ought to be mixed with these plays to give the child the habits of thought."[2] She then proceeded to describe situations in which basic daily activities could be converted into stimulating intellectual endeavors. She urged that as children grew older they should be told, "The more knowledge you gain, the more useful you can be, when you become a man." Additionally, it was essential that children be fortified with solid moral foundations. Mrs. Child cautioned against selecting readings for children that merely culminated in a moral. "The morality should be in the book, not tacked upon the end of it." With such home training, children entered school at age four or five with certain basic moral and cultural understandings upon which would be built a formal education.[3]

In the North and Midwest, schools were community or common schools. These schools would be open to all children from the community. Conditions in common schools varied tremendously not only from north to south but from community to community. School revenue was directly tied to the success or failure of local commerce. In an 1861 report, numerous county superintendents in Pennsylvania reported frosts in June and early July. The resulting loss of the wheat crop caused not only "more than ordinary pecuniary embarrassment"; in addition, teaching time was shortened, and in some communities the wages of the teachers were reduced. More than one superintendent lamented a false system of economy that reduced teachers' wages so much that some of the best teachers left the county or became engaged in "other pursuits." Some districts chose to suspend school for the entire year. Nonetheless, remaining teachers were applauded for their self-denial and the manner in which they bore up during a difficult time. In the same year, where lumbering districts were favored by high water, there was increased prosperity.[4]

School buildings were constructed in a number of ways and might be of brick, frame, log, or stone. In the 1861 state report, 58 percent of the Pennsylvania superintendents who responded used negative terms to describe their schools. It was not unusual to see claims that the schools were "less

The little red schoolhouse of Norwalk, Connecticut, was built in 1826. The one-room building with its simple wood-burning stove served as a grammar school into the 20th century. James Volo photo.

fit for the purpose of schooling, than would be many modern out houses for sheltering cattle." One schoolhouse was described as "a crumbling, dilapidated, damp, unwholesome stone building with a ceiling eight feet high, room about twenty-six by thirty feet into which one hundred and seventeen are crowded, and placed at long, old fashioned desks, with permanent seats, without backs." One superintendent reported finding "the teacher and pupils huddled together, shivering with cold, and striving to warm themselves by the little heat generated from a quantity of green wood in the stove." Additional complaints included a lack of "out-houses and other appliances necessary for comfort and convenience." Concern was expressed over the fact that schoolhouses were "placed far off the road and buried in the wildest forest."[5]

Michigan schoolmaster, Henry Hobart, was troubled by schoolhouse conditions. He wrote in his 1863 diary, "The schoolhouses throughout the country are poorly adapted for the grand object for which they are made. It is a rare thing to find a good well-ventilated, well-arranged, well-furnished schoolroom."[6] Hobart noted that his schoolhouse was "very wet. . .and should be moved to a better place" and was discouraged because "the District [was] not willing to incur the expense of placing it in a better place."[7]

Yet a number of new schools were described in more favorable terms. One report described a "tasteful brick building 30 x 45. . .furnished with first class iron frame furniture for 62 pupils." Other new buildings were of wood, and one was "24 x 36 with four tiers of seats for two pupils each accommodating 64 pupils." Another superintendent boasted, "All the rooms are warmed by coal stoves, most of them have ceilings of proper height, windows adapted to ventilation; plenty of black-board surface; and they are tolerably well seated." A new schoolhouse was proudly described as having an "anti-room, closets and platform and in every respect is superior to most of the other houses."[8]

The schools were supervised by a group of designated citizens who oversaw operations. Their duties included "the levying of tax, the location of school houses, the purchase and sale of school property, the appointment and dismissal of teachers, and the selection of studies and textbooks." The dedication and expertise of these directors was, however, often called into question.[9]

Rural districts were often unsuccessful in obtaining a normal school graduate and had to settle for whatever reasonably well educated person they could find. Although both men and women taught, male teachers were preferred. As the war progressed, many young men left the schoolroom to serve in the army or to fill better-paying jobs. This dearth of males opened the doors for women in education. A county superintendent of schools wrote, "The employment of female teachers caused some dissatisfaction, as they were believed inadequate to the task of controlling a winter school. But superior cleanliness and arrangement of their rooms, the effect of their natural gentleness and goodness on the scholars. . .amply compensated for their want of physical force." These qualities were appreciated even more when it was found that the generally younger women could be paid lower salaries than the male teachers. The average salary reported in 1861 for a male teacher was $24.20 per month. Women were paid $18.11.[10]

"The majority of teachers are between eighteen and twenty-five, and are spending a part of the year in attending academies and Normal School," wrote one superintendent.[11] But some of the teachers were little more than children themselves. A superintendent complained: "It is to be regretted, however, that parents will urge their sons and daughters to seek to become teachers at so early an age; and it is a great error in directors, as a general rule, to employ such young persons. Men engage persons of mature age and experience on the farm, in the shop or store, in the kitchen or dairy room; but they hire girls or boys of 15 or 16 to train up and educate their offspring."[12]

School districts established examinations to certify that teachers were competent to assume their duties. Most exams were a combination of written and oral questions. "They were held publicly, and attended by numbers of citizens, who had a desire to see and hear for themselves."[13] Emma Sargent Barbour's sister, Maria, wrote about the examination process in Washington. "[Hattie was] accompanying me as far as City Hall where I was to be examined, when she remarked that she had a good mind to try just for fun. She went in and passed an excellent examination and next Monday will take a position at my school."[14] Not all examinations were quite as simple as Maria implies. Many superintendents in Pennsylvania reported having to turn away applicants who had failed, while others indicated that, considering the rural nature of their district, they were lucky to find teachers at all. "Parents prefer to have there [sic] children work in the mines or learn a trade, and thus but few become qualified to teach school."[15]

Institutes were held periodically to help teachers to improve their skills. Some met only once a year, while others were held semi-monthly on alternate Saturdays. Naturally, not all teachers performed to the satisfaction of the districts. A Wayne County, Pennsylvania, superintendent wrote of his teachers, "Two last winter had the reputation of being of intemperate habits, and some few are rough and rowdyish in their manner."[16]

About 50 percent of children outside the South attended school with some regularity. Some areas of the Midwest and New England had enrollments as high as 90 percent. Attendance in rural areas still suffered from the fact that many parents "task their children heavily with farm labor, and [not] until such tasks are finished are they allowed to start school."[17] Not everyone was convinced that public education was beneficial, but public sentiment was gradually becoming more favorable to the system. "People are beginning to see that their children can get a sound practical. . .education in our common schools."[18]

Most Southerners were opposed to tax-supported education. The school reformers and educational advocates of the 1840s were mostly Northerners. This contributed to some skepticism on the part of Southerners, who felt that the school systems were at least partially responsible for Northern attitudes in the decade preceding the war. Most Southerners preferred to send their children to private institutions. By 1860 only four Southern states and a few isolated communities had common school systems.

Popular instructional materials included McGuffey's Eclectic Reader, Ray's Arithmetic, and Webster's "blue back" Speller. Spelling was just becoming standardized. Leach's Complete Spelling Book of 1859 contained a "Collection of Words of Various Orthography," which included words of "common use, which are spelled differently by the three most eminent Lexicographers . . . Webster, Worcester and Smart."[19] Emma Sargent Barbour's letter from her young cousin Mary gives additional insight into period texts: "I am getting along first rate, at school. I don't always get 10 tough by any means. I always get 9 in writing. I study Robinson's Arithmetic, it is a very hard one. Frost's United States History, Towen's speller, Weld's Grammar, the same almost exactly like the one I studied on east, but the Grammar is not at all like it. I read out of Sargent's Reader."[20] Students were graded by the reader from which they read. Many schools suffered from a lack of uniform class sets of texts, although the adoption

A *Harper's Weekly* conception of a 19th-century urban public school with its large class size and straight lines of desks screwed to the floor. This is a sewing class for girls. The seated adults are representatives of the school board.

of this practice was frequently a goal. "In time, however, as the old books, (some of which, carefully preserved, have descended from grand-fathers) are worn out, uniform class-books will be used, much to the advantage of teachers and pupils."[21]

In many schools sufficient blackboards were also wanting. Blackboards were made by taking smooth boards—painted black—and covering them with a chalk dust, which provided the erasable surface. Well-supported schools not only had blackboards but also outline maps, spelling and reading cards, charts, and globes. The average school had only one or two of these instructional materials. Paper was scarce in rural schools. Students commonly wrote on wood frame slates, although these were initially "confined to such as had made advancement in arithmetic; but now we find the smallest scholars engaged with their slates."[22]

Furniture was, at best, sparse in most classrooms. "It is useless to complain of school furniture," lamented one superintendent. "It seems that people would sooner see their children have spinal or pulmonary affliction, than furnish the school room with proper desks and seats." A York County, Pennsylvania, superintendent noted, "I witnessed a great deal of uneasiness, amounting in many instances to intense suffering, among the small children, from . . . being seated too high. In some instances, the desks are still attached to the wall, the scholars with their backs to the teacher."[23] Hobart echoed these concerns noting, "[M]ost of the schoolhouses are fitted to torture the children rather than add to the comfort and ease. Under such circumstances they dislike to go to school or when they are so uncomfortable that they cannot learn." He concluded, "People are very indifferent to the education of their children."[24]

There were few, if any, educational standards at this time. The length of the school day and year varied as the individual community saw fit. The average length of the school term in 1860 was five months and five and one-half days. A typical school day ran from nine to four with an hour for recess and dinner at noon. The day often commenced with a scripture reading followed by a patriotic song. Emma Sargent Barbour received a letter from her sister, Maria, addressing her teaching duties: "I am a regular schoolmarm. School commences every day at nine o'clock when they write a half hour and the lessons follow."[25] A subsequent letter provides more details of a teacher's day: "School! School!—is the cry, my daily life may almost be embraced in the following programme; rise at seven, breakfast at half past, practice my little singing lesson and ready to start for school at half past eight. Direct the youths how to behave and hear lessons until twelve, then from twenty minutes to a half an hour, hear missed lessons and eat lunch, chat with the boys until one o'clock, then proceed as before until three; prepare for dinner and sometimes attend receptions or receive company in the evening."[26]

Most learning was done via rote memorization and recitation. To motivate the students, less interesting material, such as geographic facts, was sung to popular tunes. Multiplication tables were often taught in verse; for example, "Twice 11 are 22. Mister can you mend my shoe?" or "9 times 12 are 108. See what I've drawn upon my slate." Mental arithmetic was still an innovative technique, and more than one district reveled in the fact that it was taught in their schools: "Mental arithmetic has been extensively introduced during the past two years and will soon be considered an indispensable item even in our primary schools."[27]

In Connecticut, towns with 80 families were required to have a single school for young children that taught English grammar, reading, writing, geography, and arithmetic. Towns with 500 families added a school for older students that offered algebra, American history, geometry, and surveying. Places with larger populations offered study of the physical sciences—sometimes referred to as natural or revealed philosophy—and Greek and Latin. The subjects taught depended on the competency of the teacher and varied greatly from school to school. In the annual report of Armstrong County, Pennsylvania, the superintendent boasted: "The number of schools in which geography and grammar are not taught is steadily diminishing. There is a considerable increase in the number in which mental arithmetic is taught. Algebra was taught in 11 schools; history in 4; natural philosophy in 2; Latin in 1; composition in 5 and in several there were exercises in declamation and vocal music."[28]

In the same report, Beaver County noted, "The Bible is read in 140 schools; not read in 17. I trust that all our teachers may become so deeply impressed with a sense of their duty, in the moral education of their pupils, that we may soon report the Bible read in every school."[29] In addition to the three R's, schools were expected to infuse a strong moral sense, foster polite behavior, and inspire good character. Another instructional objective, presented in a reading text, was "a desire to improve the literary taste of the learner, to impress correct moral principles, and augment his fund of knowledge."[30] An introductory geography book contained the following extraordinary attestation in its preface: "The introduction of moral and religious sentiments into books designed for the instruction of young persons, is calculated to improve the heart, and elevate and expand the youthful mind; accordingly, whenever the subject has admitted of it, such observations have been made as tend to illustrate the excellence of Christian religion, the advantages of correct moral principles, and the superiority of enlightened institutions."[31]

Readers contained lessons titled "The First Falsehood," "Effects of Evil Company," "Contrast Between Industry and Idleness," and "Dialogue between Mr. Punctual and Mr. Tardy." Stories, poems, and essays used in instruction drilled the message that good triumphed over evil, frugality surpassed extravagance, obedience superseded willfulness, and family always came first. This can be seen even in brief multiplication rhymes—"5 times 10 are 50. My Rose is very thrifty"[32] or "4 times 10 are 40. Those boys are very naughty." The last was inscribed beneath a picture of two boys fighting.[33]

Some texts published in the North during the war contained distinctly pro-Union sentiments. Hillard's Fifth Reader, printed in 1863, contained such readings as "Liberty and Union" and "The Religious Character of President Lincoln," as well as "Song of the Union," the poem "Barbara Frietchie," and an essay on the "Duty of American Citizens" among many similar patriotic themes. Caroline Cowles Richards wrote in her 1861 diary, "I recited `Scott and the Veteran' today at school, and Mary Field recited, `To Drum Beat and Heart Beat a Soldier Marches By.' Anna recited `The Virginia Mother.' Everyone learns war poems now-a-days."[34]

Rural schools were often ungraded and had no standard final examinations or report cards. Scholastic success was still given a showcase via exhibition bees and quizzes held for parents. Students demonstrated their expertise in spelling, arithmetic, geography, and history. In addition to praise, winners were given certificates and prizes such as books or prints. Gifted students could pass through the entire local system of schools by age 14 or 15, but only the most affluent could move on to college or university. A foreign visitor to New England found that most men had a basic education that stressed reading and writing, but that few exhibited the fine formal education available in Europe.

Southern teachers were even more challenged by the need for educational materials than their Northern counterparts. The South had depended on the North and Europe for texts prior to the war. Once the war began, Northern publications were held in contempt and the blockade curtailed European imports. A movement commenced in the South to produce its own texts, but shortages of materials and the destruction of printing equipment impeded implementation of the plan. What texts were published tended to be extremely propagandistic and of low quality. Marinda Branson Moore of North Carolina was probably the most audacious of Southern authors in this regard. She published *Dixie Primer for Little Folks* and *Dixie Speller*, which was "revised from Webster and adapted for Southern schools . . . leaving out all Yankee phrases and allusions." Her geography addressed the issues of slavery and secession and laid blame for the war on the North.[35]

Southerners regretted having allowed Northerners to teach their children prior to the war. Teaching was a respectable vocation, but women who taught in the South were often pitied for their obvious dire financial situation. With the outbreak of hostilities, the distaste for Northern teachers spread rapidly. Advertisements for teachers soon came to request that applicants be natives of Dixie or from Europe. Wartime dangers eventually suspended many Southern schools, and the task of educating youngsters fell to the mothers.

While common schools were well established by this time, and enrollments grew throughout the war in Northern cities, the development of high schools, slow before the war, faced even more obstacles. The lure of the military, or opportunities made available by army enlistments, siphoned off many would-be students. High schools were essentially an urban institution, founded with the intention of providing opportunity for boys who wished to become merchants or mechanics. Such an education was seen as terminal. Boston, a leader in educational matters, did not open a high school for girls until 1855. Although some Northern areas required larger cities to establish high schools, most people felt that this was a form of higher education and should not be part of the legal public school system. By 1860 there were 300 high schools in the United States, 100 of which were in Massachusetts.

College enrollments also suffered as idealistic young men rushed to join the forces of their cause. Caroline Cowles Richards listed in her diary a number of young men who "talk of leaving college and going to war."[36] She described a rally at the Canandaigua Academy and detailed how "Capt. Barry drills the Academy boys in military tactics on the campus every day. Men are constantly enlisting." Southern colleges had the additional complications of the loss of funding, physical destruction from battle, and conversion to hospitals, barracks, and headquarters.[37]

College studies were heavily classical. Students read Latin and Greek from Livy, Cicero, Homer, Plato, and others. As in primary school, recitation was the most common form of instruction. Work in the sciences, which covered physics and astronomy, with some chemistry and geology, consisted mostly of lectures along with occasional laboratory demonstrations. Mathematics explored geometry, trigonometry, and calculus and encompassed memorization of rules with some effort to apply them to problems. Rhetoric students studied composition as well as speaking. Other studies included philosophy and logic.

The year 1862 was an important one for education. The Morrill Act passed through the federal Congress, establishing the land grant colleges. It was also the year in which Washington, D.C., made the first provisions for Negro schooling. While the effects of both of these events may have been felt more after the war, they nonetheless show an extremely positive federal attitude toward education, even amid the turmoil of war.

As far back as the colonial era, many slaveholders felt it a duty to teach slaves about the Bible and even permitted them to read. As the abolitionist movement grew and tensions increased between slaveholders and abolitionists, many Southerners turned away from this practice and actually discouraged teaching slaves to read. Following Nat Turner's rebellion in 1831, most Southern states prohibited the teaching of blacks, fearing that the written word could be used as a mechanism for spreading more slave insurrections.

At the outbreak of the war only about five percent of slaves could read. As federal troops occupied an area and set the slaves free, many former slaves established schools to help others prepare for freedom. Often Union commanders occupying an area mandated the creation of such schools or allowed their creation by Northern missionaries. These practices led to the creation of the Freedmen's Bureau in 1865, through which the federal government took a formal stance toward the education of former slaves.

Northern teachers who traveled to the South during the war suffered tremendous physical and emotional hardships. Southerners deeply resented them and commonly refused them any accommodations. The Northern agencies that sent them generally overworked and underpaid them. Moreover, the condition of blacks in the South after years or decades of privation—at least some of which was due to the shortages brought on by the length of the war—greatly distressed most of the teachers, who were generally unrealistically idealistic rather than pragmatic in their expectations. What passed for schoolrooms were often worse than the most desolate of Northern facilities, and textbooks and instructional materials were all but nonexistent.

The abolitionists in the North had provided for the education of some free blacks. Some common school systems established schools for minority groups such as Amerindians, and free blacks. Yet in Boston, the cradle of the abolitionist movement, there were only two primary schools for black children in the 1840s. Considering the support that many regular schools were given, one can imagine the facilities that would have been provided when a separate school was established for a minority group.

While the North provided for the education of some free blacks, the idea of racially integrated schools was vehemently opposed. When Prudence Crandall attempted to integrate her fashionable Connecticut school for girls, the white students were quickly withdrawn by outraged parents. Crandall herself was insulted, threatened, and stoned. In the interest of the safety of her students, she ultimately acquiesced by closing the school and disbanding the student body.

Some common school systems established schools for minority groups such as Amerindians and free blacks. Considering the inadequate support many regular schools were given, one can imagine the facilities that would have been provided when a separate school was established for a minority group. An observer of a "Colored School" remarked that although the Black pupils "were not so far advanced. . . if the same facilities be afforded to them, which are given to the children in other schools in the borough, they will soon compare favorably with them, not only in the lower branches, but also in the more advanced departments."[38]

NOTES

1. Charles W. Sanders, *The School Reader Third Book* (New York: Sower, Barnes & Potts, 1860), 185–186.

2. Lydia M. Child, *The Mother's Book* (Boston: Applewood, 1831), 11.

3. Ibid., 90.

4. Thomas H. Burrowes, *Report of the Superintendent of Common Schools of Pennsylvania* (Harrisburg: A. Boyd Hamilton, 1861), 20, 24.

5. Ibid., 20–97.

6. Philip P. Mason, ed., *Copper Country Journal: The Diary of Schoolmaster Henry Hobart, 1863–1864* (Detroit: Wayne State University Press, 1991), 143.

7. Ibid., 117.

8. Burrowes, 24.

9. Ibid., 14.

10. Ibid., 4, 32.

11. Ibid., 43.

12. Ibid., 27.

13. Ibid., 40.

14. Shirley Blotnick Moskow, *Emma's World: An Intimate Look at Lives Touched by the Civil War Era* (Far Hills, NJ: New Horizons Press, 1990), 193.

15. Burrowes, 83.

16. Ibid., 91.

17. Ibid., 27.

18. Ibid., 51–52.

19. Daniel Leach, *Leach's Complete Spelling Book* (Philadelphia: H. Cowperthwait & Co., 1859), 140.

20. Moskow, 99.

21. Burrowes, 36.

22. Ibid., 80.

23. Ibid., 81, 97.

24. Mason, 143.

25. Moskow, 122.

26. Ibid., 139.

27. *Marmaduke Multiply's Merry Method of Making Minor Mathematicians* (1841; New York: Dover, 1971), 13, 65. Hereafter cited as Marmaduke; Burrowes, 42.

28. Burrowes, 21.

29. Ibid., 22.

30. Salem Town, *The Fourth Reader, or Exercises in Reading and Speaking* (Cooperstown: H. & E. Phinney, 1849), IV.

31. S. A. Mitchell, *An Easy Introduction to the Study of Geography* (Philadelphia: Thomas, Cowperthwait & Co., 1853), 5.

32. Marmaduke, 41.

33. Ibid., 33.

34. Caroline Richards, *Village Life in America, 1852–1872* (Gansevoort, NY: Corner House, 1997), 132.

35. Mary Elizabeth Massey, *Women in the Civil War* (Lincoln: University of Nebraska Press, 1966), 119.

36. Richards, 143.

37. Ibid., 136.

38. Burrowes, 67.

18

TILL THE MOURNFUL NIGHT IS GONE: DEATH AND DYING

The sorrow for the dead is the only sorrow from which we refuse to be divorced. Every other wound we seek to heal, every
other affliction to forget; but this wound we consider it a duty
to keep open; this affliction we cherish and brood over in
solitude.

—*Town's Fourth Reader*

Amid the romanticism and sentimentalism of the 19th century, death was
viewed from a different perspective than in earlier times, or even than it
is today. High infant mortality and the tragic loss of 600,000 soldiers in
war made death a part of daily living. Accidents were common in a society that had few safety regulations for industry and public transportation.
Charles Baldwin of Catskill, New York, kept an 1860s diary that contained
a special section headed "Accidents, Catastrophes, Etc." Some of his entries involving fatalities included the following:

Explosion of Powder Mills at High Falls; Wesley Sitser severely injured by machinery at Broom Corn Factory; explosion of the boiler on the "Isaac Newton." Honora
Barrigan horribly crushed in machinery in Woolen Mills at Leeds; explosion of locomotive at Catskill Station, fireman died; fall at a span of the old bridge; a drown-
ing in a bleach-vat at the paper mill; an explosion of the soda water generator at
Smith's Drug Store.[1]

Death simply was not the taboo topic it is in modern society. Children's stories and poems contained references to death. Battlefield deaths provided inspiration for songwriters. Numerous examples of then popular piano sheet music detail and sentimentalize the final moments of dying heroes. "Comrades, I Am Dying," contains the following lines:

Comrades, comrades, I am dying! I see my mother now:
See her coming down from heaven with a wreath upon her brow.
God has sent her to the soldier, she will teach him how to die;
And when He has called my spirit, she will bear it to the sky.[2]

It is difficult to imagine a family wanting to gather around the piano in the parlor to sing about a soldier's final moments with "The Drummer Boy of Shiloh" or "Little Major," but to the 19th-century mind this was not the morbid activity it would be labeled today. Death was the final scene of life's drama as written by God.

Following the Great Awakening of the late 18th century, religious belief allowed man to anticipate his salvation with pleasure. In the short story "The Star Vision" a dying boy describes a dream foretelling his death. He says, "Then I wished to be a star, Mother."[3] Death was, in a certain way, a joyous occasion, an opportunity to be joined once again to family who had already passed on to their reward. Following the untimely death of her brother, Hal, in a duel, nineteen-year-old Sarah Morgan recorded these thoughts:

There is no disappointment in the tomb . . . better to be laying in your grave, Hal, with all your noble longings unsatisfied, than to have your heart filled with bitterness as it would have been . . . Those glorious eyes, with God's truth sparkling in them, are now dimmed forever, Hal. Yet, not forever; I shall see them at the Last Day; bury me where I may see them again. O please God, let me die as calmly as he. And let Hal be the first to welcome me, and lead me before Thee.[4]

Attitudes toward cemeteries changed. Even nomenclature began to change. Romanticism, with its emphasis on the boundary between life and death, found the location of the grave profoundly symbolic. The term "cemetery," from the Greek for "sleeping chamber," replaced the earlier phrase, "burying ground." During the 1830s a phenomenon known as the rural cemetery movement emerged. The deplorable conditions in crowded and neglected city cemeteries created a desolate setting for loved ones making their final farewells. This coincided with a general concern that society was changing too rapidly. The once almost inseparable concepts of family, community, and church were being torn asunder. Urbanization was pulling men away from a home that was becoming an isolated and romanticized refuge from society's tumult. The church was increasingly the province of women. Domestic tranquility was closely identified with agriculture and horticulture, in reaction to the urbanization that was taking place. The rural cemetery created an idyllic place where peace and calm would reign and the family bond could remain forever unbroken. The layout created a sort of garden of graves. Cemetery paths meandered over landscaped hills and valleys. Benches were placed at grave sites, providing an inviting place for contemplation. The landscape offered air and light, safety and nature, joy and optimism. It facilitated acceptance of the physical separation of the dead from the living. In the rural cemetery death had been transformed from grotesque to beautiful.

Mary Chesnut's diary records this exchange between two women following the death of Rebecca Haskell. "[Annie said] 'This is the saddest thing for Alex.' 'No,' said his mother, 'death is never the saddest thing. If he were not a good man that would be a far worse thing.' Annie, in utter amazement, whimpered, 'But Alex is so good already.' 'Yes—seven years ago the death of one of his sisters that he dearly loved made him a Christian. That death in our family was worth a thousand lives.'"[5] Death could indeed be a cause for somber celebration.

Rural cemeteries continued to expand into the 1850s. By the time of the Civil War, virtually every sizable city in both the North and South had its own rural cemetery. The primary focus of the rural cemetery was the family plot. It provided a safe, secure resting place where the remains of loved ones would not be moved, abandoned, or vandalized. Sections in cemeteries were designed to highlight family plots. The winding roads, constructed so that many family plots would be able to have highly desired roadside locations, were built wide enough to accommodate carriages. Grave site visitations were akin to afternoons in the park. "But the grave of those we loved, what a place for meditation!"[6]

The entire institution was designed to honor, strengthen, and maintain the family. *Frank Leslie's Illustrated Newspaper* carried a lead story in the April 25, 1863 issue on the increasing volume of mourners at cemeteries. "The cemeteries of New Orleans are very interesting places for almost every day may be seen parties of mourning relatives and friends decking the grave of some loved one, who, by an early death, has been spared the pangs of regret."[7]

Family monuments were the most obvious man-made structures in the designed landscapes. They were a physical manifestation of the philosophical shift in attitudes toward death from the 18th to the 19th century. The tombstone skeletons and death's-heads of previous times, meant to instill fear in the living, were replaced with angels and cherubs who would lead the departed to heaven. Charlotte Selleck's gravestone bears a common 18th-century epitaph, found in several variations into the first third of the following century.

Behold and see as you pass by
As you are now so once was I

As I am now you soon shall be
Prepare for death and follow me.[8]

It was not uncommon for 19th-century tombstones to bear more reassuring epitaphs, such as the following:

Harriet Miles
Fell asleep in Jesus
January 16, 1857
Aged 15 years
Her last word was HAPPY.[9]

Following the death of Mary Barnwell, Mary Chesnut wrote the following in her diary: "Not in anger—not in wrath—came the angel of death that day. He came to set her free from a world grown too hard to bear." Earlier grave markers had elaborate epitaphs and flat carvings. Mid-century monuments were three-dimensional works carved in imitation of the work of European sculptors, creating a virtual museum of memorials. The new monuments depicted symbols of hope, immortality, and life. Ivy was used to symbolize memory, an important component of mid-19th-century mourning. The poppy represented sleep. The anchor symbolized hope. Oak denoted immortality, and the acorn was life. This symbolic language became so complex that writers even interpreted their meanings.

A book on rural cemeteries by Edward Fitzgerald included an "Appendix on Emblems" that detailed the significance of 26 such symbols, much like the more popular "language of flowers." Equally common were representations of the trappings of home and family. Books, hats, dogs, chairs, even home facades, were carved in loving memory of the departed. "The world outside was changing, and seemed to be turning upside down. But at least in the permanence of graveyard, traditions could be maintained—indeed maintained, exaggerated, and sentimentalized—if not for those still living, at least for posterity, and for posterity's remembrance of the dead, and preserved, and sentimentalized."[10]

Children's graves received unprecedented attention. Popular literature such as Harriet Beecher Stowe's *Uncle Tom's Cabin* celebrated the passing of young innocents. Early death provided the assurance of being "free from the sin and stain of this low earth."[11] Children's brief existence protected them from corruption. Upon the passing of her infant child, Cornelia Peake McDonald recalled her friend's words, "You may live to thank Him for taking your precious little babe from the sorrow and evil to come."[12]

Rural cemeteries provided separate sections in which young families not yet able to afford a family plot would bury their children. These young or stillborn children could be reinterred later, when the family was more established and could afford a family plot. Families that could afford it, however, often created gravestone markers steeped in sentiment and imagery. The most common image was that of the sleeping child. Sleep as a tie between life and death was a recurring theme of the period. The image makes a connection back to the home where the youth once slept. It brought to mind the comforting picture of a child safely tucked away in his bed. The child with a lamb was another recurring image that reinforced the belief in the closeness of children and nature. Empty furniture was also depicted on memorials. An unfilled chair or bed was commonly used to symbolize the child's unfilled life. The song "The Vacant Chair" reinforces this graveyard imagery, as does "Sleep today, O early fallen, In thy green and narrow bed."[13] Judith McGuire reflected, "In all the broad South there will scarcely be a fold without its missing lamb, a fireside without its vacant chair."[14]

Other items appearing on memorials included rattles, dolls, or favorite playthings. The use of toys in such a permanent form reflects the period's recognition of the naturalness of play and was a lasting reminder of the separate worlds of children and adults. Sculptural portrayals of children and their belongings ensured that they would remain forever one with the goodness of the home. They would be undisturbed and constant, forever innocent in the world.

Months after the loss of her own child, Cornelia Peake McDonald recorded an incident wherein she was told that she should be thankful that

This memorial carte de visite from the author's collection may seem morbid to the modern eye, but in its time it was considered a lasting memorial devotion to the deceased.

her babe had been taken: "I thought of that when I looked at old Mrs. Dailey's face when she stood by her son's corpse. Would my darling's forehead ever have looked so dim and weary? Her work was finished, and she went to rest 'while yet 'twas early day.' I would not bring her back if I could to resume the burden her Savior removed that day when she fled from my arms as the sun was setting."[15]

Such thoughts must have been a great consolation to the parents who lost child after child to sickness and accidents. Both Abraham Lincoln and Jefferson Davis had to cope with the devastation of the loss of a child while dealing with the complex issues of the Civil War. Lincoln lost his youngest son, Willie, to a fever on February 20, 1862. Willie was the second of the Lincoln children to succumb to sickness. Twelve years earlier the Lincolns had lost four-year-old Eddy to diphtheria. Davis lost his "Little Joe" when the boy fell from the north piazza of the Southern White House on April 30, 1864.

When a child died, the family felt the loss deeply. The death rate among the young remained relatively high throughout the war years. Family separation and a lower birth rate during the conflict led people to value surviving children all the more.

The fear death held was less for the ending of life and more that of never having been loved or lamented. When asked by a surviving soldier to see to the proper care of a dead companion whom she had never known, Cornelia Peake McDonald wrote, "Betty and I wept over him tears of sincere sorrow, the more so as we thought that perhaps ours and those of the poor soldier would be all that would fall on his lonely bier." Mourners of the 1860s went to great lengths to demonstrate their love and devotion to the deceased. The loss of family members and the personal trauma of death became the focus of mourning and ritual. To this end, mourning became an extended, almost institutionalized process.[16]

Writing elegies for departed friends was popular. Sometimes these black-bordered tributes were attached to the coffin or to the hearse. Other times, they were decorated with designs abundant with death imagery and distributed as souvenirs to the mourners. It was not uncommon for them to be printed in local newspapers.

Widows were expected to remain in mourning for two and a half years. This time was divided into three segments. During heavy mourning the widow wore only black, with collars and cuffs of folded untrimmed black crepe. No other trim was used. She might wear a simple bonnet but never a hat. Her face would be covered entirely in a long, heavy black crepe veil whenever she left home. Silk fabrics used for dresses, bonnets, or capes had to have matte finishes. Not even ribbons were allowed to have a gloss. Kid gloves were not permitted. Gloves had to be made from cotton or silk, or crocheted or knit from thread. Handkerchiefs were made of the sheerest white linen with a broad, deep border. Jewelry was restricted to black jet—usually unpolished—and even that would not be worn during the initial months. Dark furs were permitted in cold weather. Throughout the entire mourning period, a widow's hair had to be worn simply.

This period was followed by full mourning, which still required the wearing of black, but permitted black lace collars and cuffs. Veils were permitted to be shortened and could be made of net or tulle. Lighter veils were also allowed. Handkerchiefs needed only to have a narrow black band border. Polished jet jewelry was allowed as well as some gold or glass beads.

Half mourning was the final stage. During this period, print and solid-colored dresses of gray or lavender were permitted. A bonnet might be trimmed with lace and adorned with white or violet flowers. Emma Sargent Barbour received a letter with the following comment about a dress: "Mrs. Hutchens bought her a purple and black [half mourning] mohair."[17] *Godey's Lady's Book* carried a literary selection that contained a scene where a young woman was preparing to attend her first party since the death of her father. Her mother "opened a jewel case . . . and taking from the velvet cushion a necklace and bracelets of pearl, she clasped them around the throat and wrists of her daughter. 'Oh, Mother! Your bridal jewels?' 'They are not misplaced here, I think, Ellen, for your dress is simple; and these will be a happy relief.'" The young woman declined to wear the pearls, fearing she would be too conspicuous. Although fiction, the story illustrates the strong sense of fashion propriety.[18]

Some women, of course, chose to remain in mourning for longer periods, even the rest of their lives. For a woman who wanted to remarry in a period of less than two and a half years, an accommodation was made. She was permitted to be married in a conservative gray dress. However, she was expected to complete the period of mourning following the new union out of respect for the first husband. If a woman married a widower, she was expected to dress in half mourning for the remainder of her husband's mourning period.

Not so surprisingly, men were not as restricted as women. Their period of mourning lasted as little as three months to a year. Fashion required them to wear a plain white shirt with black clothes, shoes, gloves, and hat. This differed little from what the properly dressed businessman would wear in any case. Some men followed this with a period of gray. The only distinguishing additions would be a black crepe band on their hat or black-bordered cuffs. Widowers were encouraged to remarry following a respectable period, particularly if they had young children. Mourning attire was suspended for the wedding day but reestablished immediately thereafter.

Children were not sheltered from death and mourning. In *The Mother's Book*, Lydia Child advises mothers not to allow their children to be frightened by death. She encourages them to share the beautiful imagery of returning to heaven to be with the angels with even very young children. Older children wore black and crepe upon the death of a parent for six months, followed by three months each of full and half mourning with lessening degrees of black. Children in mourning under the age of 12 wore white in the summer and gray in the winter. Suits were trimmed with black buttons, belts, and ribbons. Even infant robes were trimmed in black. Often, out of practicality, children's regular clothing was dyed for mourning rather than purchased new.

A woman mourning the death of her father, mother, or child wore black for a period of one year. For grandparents, siblings, or someone having left the mourner an inheritance, the proper period was six months. The obligation for an aunt, uncle, niece, or nephew extended for only three months, and white trim was allowed throughout this time. Families in mourning often restricted their contacts with the outside world. Following the death of her mother-in-law, Mary Chesnut made the following diary entry: "Mr. Chesnut being in such deep mourning for his mother, we see no company."[19]

Martine's Hand-Book of Etiquette, and Guide to True Politeness detailed the proper protocol for condolence visitation:

Visits of condolence should be paid within a week after the event which occasions them; but if the acquaintance be slight, immediately after the family appear at public worship. A card should be sent up; and if your friends are able to receive you, let your manners and conversation be in harmony with the character of your visit. It is courteous to send up a mourning card; and for ladies to make their call in black silk or plain-colored apparel. It denotes that they sympathize with the afflictions of the family; and such attentions are always pleasing.[20]

Mourning dress was one of the first areas where mass-produced clothing gained acceptance. The need for the proper attire to conform to the rigid rules regarding dress often came unexpectedly. There were many people who felt that it was unlucky to keep black crepe in the home between deaths. Surviving items from previous losses were often discarded when no longer required. Providing mourning attire and accessories became a worthwhile commercial endeavor. Some retailers, such as J. S. Chase and Company of Boston, dealt exclusively in mourning goods. There was a great demand for black crepe for veils, collars, cuffs, skirt trim, and armbands. Other needed items included black hat pins, straight pins, and buttons. Millinery and jewelry that met the expectations of society were equally in demand. Mourning caps were such a common item, with virtually no design differences for age or demand for customization, that milliners commonly made them when they had nothing else to do. Those in mourning also required stationery and calling cards bordered in black. Many companies made fortunes on mourning clothing and related ancillary materials.

Perhaps the most favored of these goods was mourning jewelry. Sentimental melancholy for its own sake was a hallmark of gentility and refinement. The simple wearing of mourning jewelry transferred virtue to the wearer. Mourning pins and rings were given to mourners as keepsakes. Frequently, in the interest of economy, the gifts were of two price levels. The more expensive gifts were given to close friends and family, while less expensive items could be more widely distributed.

Jet, onyx, and black glass or "French jet" were extensively used, but it was jet that reached an unprecedented popularity. While French jet is black glass, true jet is fossilized driftwood formed, like coal, by decaying vegetation over hundreds of thousands of years. Jet is found in stagnant water—often seawater—and the greater the depth of the water, the harder the jet. Jet was made into carved beads for necklaces, brooches, bracelets, and earrings. Its inherent lightness allowed for the creation of pieces that would have been impractical had they been made from another material. Additionally, jet was relatively inexpensive, yet it was attractive and properly somber.

Another jewelry trend that came into full flower in this period was "hair work." This was not a new fashion. To some degree, hair jewelry had been popular since the beginning of the century, but during the war it reached new heights. Rings, lockets, brooches, bracelets, watch chains—almost any kind of jewelry was likely to include human hair in one way or an-

An advertisement from the Boston Directory particularizes a wide selection of mourning attire.

other. Sometimes the hair was that of a living person, but more often it was from a departed loved one. The period song "Bear Gently, So Gently, Roughly Made Bier," subtitled "Burial at Camp," contains the following line: "From the damp clotted hair sever one precious tress."[21] Judith McGuire concluded her tale of the burial of a Confederate soldier thus: "We cut a lock of his hair, as the only thing we could do for his mother."[22]

Godey's Lady's Book championed the use of hair jewelry, quoting an English writer, Leigh Hunt, in saying, "Hair is at once the most delicate and lasting of our materials, and survives us, like love. It is so light, so gentle, so escaping from the idea of death, that with a lock of hair belonging to a child or friend, we may almost look up to heaven and compare notes with the angelic nature—may almost say: `I have a piece of thee here, not unworthy of thy being now.'"[23]

The simplest way to prepare such a relic was to encase a lock of hair under a crystal that would be mounted in a ring, brooch, or locket. More elaborate pieces contained miniature allegories of grief. Often parts of designs, or their entirety, were made of human hair. Sometimes the miniatures were portraits of the deceased mounted on a background of their hair. Another variation of this form was "hair painting." This lost art appears to have used finely chopped hair mixed into the pigments of the paint, but no description of the exact process seems to have survived. Finally, hair was sometimes plaited in many strands and then formed into watch chains, fobs, brooches, rings, necklaces, earrings, and bracelets. These items might have been made for oneself from the hair of a loved one or made as a gift using the giver's hair.

Pattern books like *Campbell's Self-Instructor* contained numerous patterns for incredibly intricate hair jewelry designs. *Godey's Lady's Book* offered designs, instructions, and even finished pieces. If a woman lacked the talent to create a piece herself, she could give the hair to a jeweler who would then create the desired item based on hundreds of available designs.

Some photographers specialized in posthumous photographs. Period advertisements carried the names of many photographers who offered this specialty. The photographer normally came to the home, but it was not unusual for the deceased to be taken to the studio. Future president James Garfield, as a soldier in the Civil War, hurried home to have a picture taken with his dead infant in his arms. Infants were the most common subject of this type of photograph. Perhaps this was because there had been little opportunity to capture the child's likeness in life. Perhaps it provided a concrete reminder of a life that had passed too quickly. Sometimes the deceased child would be posed cradled in the mother's arms. Other poses might show the child resting on a pillow. Photographers sometimes borrowed from the imagery of portrait painters and included a cut rose in the picture, symbolizing a bloom cut early—the death of a child. The family of Maria Jane Hurd created a memorial card for the deceased twelve-year-

A hair watch fob and jet mourning pins on black-bordered mourning stationary. From the authors' collection.

old. Beneath her portrait, copied from a daguerreotype taken at age six, were enumerated her "Resolutions for the New Year," which were "found in her little portfolio after her death."[24]

A woman in mourning often occupied herself with stitchery, paperwork, or other memorial projects. Memorial work abounded with symbolism. A butterfly symbolized the passing from this world to the next. A sheaf of wheat denoted the passing of an elderly person. Pansies, in the language of flowers, meant "Think of me." The most persistent symbol by far was the weeping willow. The very shape of the willow brought to mind the image of a mourner bent over with grief. Willow branches were often carried by mourners at funerals as symbols of resurrection. Personalized items such as pets, ships, churches, and distant towns were also memorialized.

Memorial pictures worked in silk embroidery were most common. A typical scene contained black-clad mourners beside an urn-topped gravestone beneath the hanging boughs of a weeping willow tree. Some memorial pictures were painted, frequently by young girls still in school. These could be for a relative long deceased or could be kept and then completed by inscribing the name of that person on the waiting tomb at a later date. Occasionally, they were used for the painter herself. During the late 1830s memorial pictures published by Nathaniel Currier could be purchased as lithographs. A mourning card could then be pasted on to complete the

A period postmortem memorial card of a young child from Hopkinsville, Kentucky. From the authors' collection.

scene. Another form of memorial, although less popular, was cut paperwork. The cut paperwork contained similar imagery, and the contrast of white against black was stark and visually effective. These items could either be done by the mourner or purchased and personalized by inserting a memorial card identifying the deceased.

Theorem paintings, oils, and pen and ink sketches were also done as memorials, but less frequently. Watercolors were also used to create memorials. These tended to be gayer than some other kinds of works due to the colors. Watercolors were even used in conjunction with other forms of artwork. Some embroidered pictures contained watercolor skies or had watercolor faces pasted or sewn on to the needlework. As many as four different media could be used in the creation of a single work.

Immortals were fairly large, ornate floral arrangements made from wax, cloth, beads, or hair and were covered by tall glass cases. The complex designs incorporated flowers, often made by weaving or braiding the hair of the deceased over wire. Wreaths might also include yarn, seeds, berries, feathers, or dried flowers; they were later framed in shadowboxes to be displayed in parlors. Sheaves of wheat used to decorate the casket were often preserved in a similar fashion.

Death rituals among slaves and Southern free blacks still retained their African meanings. In dying, one "went home." To a slave, this was a reason to celebrate, for it meant freedom. Graves were decorated, as they were in Africa, with the last items that the deceased had used. The most common articles were pottery or glass containers, but medicine bottles, toys, dolls, and quilts were also found. It was essential that the items be broken in order to break the tie to the living. Failure to do so was believed to invite a similar fate for the surviving family. Some slaveowners gave a portion of the day off for the funeral of a departed slave and even allotted food for the following celebration. Others required that the funeral be held at night. Mourning clothing restrictions were not likely a part of slave mourning traditions; however, some slaves were known to have had mourning clothing. It is very likely that these items were initially purchased for them following the death of "the master" and could later be used for their own personal losses.

As the war progressed, the Union blockade made the acquisition of manufactured mourning goods in the South difficult, if not impossible. Women had to borrow from one another; however, as so many were in need of mourning attire themselves, availability was limited. Many women had to resort to dying fabrics in order to be properly outfitted.

Battlefield casualties brought about altered mourning practices. Families were accustomed to living and dying in close proximity, and this was the first time many experienced the loss of someone far away from home. The horrendous numbers of deceased soldiers involved affected almost every family. The inability to recover loved one's remains after a battle, a frequent occurrence, presented a kind of eternal separation that compounded the sense of loss. Soldiers went to great lengths to identify themselves so that their remains could be returned to their loved ones at home. In a time before "dog tags," some soldiers purchased brass or wooden identity discs to wear around their necks. Others attached slips of paper to their backs. However, many soldiers were interred in mass graves. Others were left in shallow pits near where they fell. Some families traveled to battle sites in the vain hope of being able to retrieve their loved one's remains. Few were successful.

Getting the remains of fallen soldiers home presented other problems. Although the process of embalming had long been known, the effort to preserve physical remains had not been practiced beyond the needs of medical research. During the Civil War, however, a new market was opened. Itinerant embalmers, mostly doctors, traveled to battlefields and used arterial embalming to preserve bodies for shipment home. In some instances, these embalmers contracted their services to soldiers prior to battle in the event of their demise. This process created a professionalism not found in "undertaking" before the war. Undertakers now required a special skill that set them apart from the carpenters and casket makers who preceded them. It was no longer enough to provide a coffin, a horse, and a special carriage.

Perhaps the most famous battlefield identification of a departed soldier was that of Amos Humiston, a sergeant in the 154th New York Volunteers.

Humiston's body was found on the battlefield, following the Battle of Gettysburg, clutching in his hand an ambrotype of his three little children. His name remained a mystery for months. Francis Bourns, a physician, obtained the picture, had it copied on an engraving plate so that it could be circulated in the hope of learning the identity of the fallen soldier, and set up a fund for the orphaned children. Many newspapers across the country supported the effort. Finally, it was learned that a woman in western New York had read the account in the religious newspaper *American Presbyterian*. She had sent her husband a picture of their three small children and had not heard from him since July. A copy of the picture was sent, and her worst fears came to fruition. James G. Clark wrote a poem set to music based on the story, called "The Children of the Battlefield." The net proceeds of the sales of the music, which contained an introductory sketch melodramatically detailing the entire incident, were "reserved for the support and education of the Orphan Children," Frank, Frederick, and Alice.[25]

The Civil War also created a new category of sacred ground, the national cemetery. Congress authorized the first nationally managed cemetery as early as 1862. Former army post cemeteries were rededicated for the use of the increasing number of Union army dead. As early as 1863, the battle sites of Gettysburg and Antietam were named national cemeteries for the Union dead. Battlefield cemeteries continued to grow as the war progressed. The earliest burials were quick and rough, but as casualties escalated, an attempt was made to provide each grave with a wooden marker. After the conflict, the War Department set out upon a campaign to reinter the dead in appropriate locations and to formalize the markers. This striking act of democracy, where men of varied backgrounds and means were memorialized side by side with uniform markers, set these areas very much apart from secular cemeteries of the day.

The death of President Lincoln in April 1865 sent the Union into the deepest mourning. As Washington prepared for a state funeral, citizens streamed to the capital. Extra trains had to be added to accommodate the mourners. Reportedly, 100,000 people came to bid the president farewell. Mourning decorations quickly sold out, and residents combed ever widening areas to find sufficient amounts of black crepe. Even the poorest families gathered what bits of black cloth they could to drape their homes. Tens of thousands of people lined the trackside as the president's body was carried by train back to Springfield, Illinois.

Mrs. Alexander Major left a rare insight to the reaction of Southerners in the hours following the news of the president's death:

The stores were ransacked for black material to hang forth as symbols of mourning. Every house was ordered to be draped in black, and where the rebel inmates refused, it was done for them by the Union boys . . . We had nothing black whatever in our possession except my husband's coat, and as he had to wear that, I asked him to go down the street to buy a few yards of some black goods, which I intended to hang out from our bedroom window as a token that we grieved at the terrible calamity that had befallen a great and good man.[26]

This compassion was not shared by all Southerners. Mrs. Major continues to relate how the woman in whose house she resided as a boarder refused to comply with the directive. When a committee of soldiers came by to ensure that the order was being observed, an ugly scene ensued. Angry soldiers ransacked the landlady's belongings, searching for something black. When they emerged with the mourning veil she had worn for her husband and son, both of whom had perished in the Confederate cause, she determined that she had endured too much. Asking that she be left alone to acquiesce, she carried the veil to her veranda and mounted a chair so that she could reach the fretwork above. Only then was it noticed that she had changed her clothes and was now dressed all in black. With deliberate action and to the horror of those watching, she pushed away the chair and hanged herself. The dictate had been satisfied.[27]

NOTES

1. Margaret M. Coffin, *Death in Early America* (New York: Thomas Nelson, 1976), 19.

2. Thomas Manahan, *"Comrades, I Am Dying"* (Boston: Henry Talman & Co., 1864). A sheet music cover.

3. Charley Hunt, "The Star Vision," *Christian Parlor Magazine* 9, no. 12 (1852), 370.

4. Charles East, ed., *Sarah Morgan: The Civil War Diary of a Southern Woman* (New York: Simon & Schuster, 1991), 11.

5. C. V. Woodward, *Mary Chesnut's Civil War* (New Haven, CT: Yale University Press, 1981), 397.

6. Salem Town, *The Fourth Reader, or Exercises in Reading and Speaking* (Cooperstown: H. & E. Phinney, 1849), 218.

7. "Mourners Strewing Flowers on the Graves of the Slain," *Frank Leslie's Illustrated Newspaper*, April 25, 1863, 1.

8. The gravestone of Charlotte Selleck, who died on January 1, 1806, stands in the cemetery at Mill Hill Historic Complex in Norwalk, Connecticut.

9. Coffin, 183.

10. David Stannard, "Calm Dwellings," *American Heritage*, September 1979, 47.

11. Mrs. L. G. Abell, "The Dying Girl," *Christian Parlor Magazine* 9, no. 12 (1852): 274.

12. Minrose C. Gwin, ed., *Cornelia Peake McDonald: A Woman's Civil War. A Diary with Reminiscences of the War from March 1862* (Madison: University of Wisconsin, 1992), 72.

13. George F. Root, *The Vacant Chair (or We Shall Meet but We Shall Miss Him)* (Chicago: Root & Cady, 1862). A sheet music cover.

14. Judith W. McGuire, *Diary of a Southern Refugee During the War by a Lady of Virginia* (Lincoln: University of Nebraska Press, 1995), 250.

15. Gwin, 91.

16. Ibid., 53.

17. Moskow, 163.

18. Martha Gandy Fales, *Jewelry in America* (London: Antique Collector's Club, 1995), 211. Quoting Godey's Lady's Book, Book 54, 1857.

19. C. V. Woodward, 589.

20. Arthur Martine, *Martine's Hand-Book of Etiquette, and Guide to True Politeness* (New York: Dick & Fitzgerald, 1866), 122.

21. E.A.B. Mitchell, *Bear Gently, So Gently, Roughly Made Bier* (Louisville: Wm. McCaroll, 1864). A sheet music cover.

22. McGuire, 143.

23. Fales, 215.

24. From a memorial card in the authors' collection of twelve-year-old Maria Jane Hurd, who died in Springfield, Massachusetts, on March 12, 1848.

25. James G. Clark, *The Children of the Battlefield* (Philadelphia: Lee & Walker, 1864). A sheet music cover.

26. Sullivan, 274.

27. Ibid., 275–276.

19

THE EFFECTS OF WARFARE ON FAMILIES

Virginia has become "a world of femininity with a line of boys and octogenarians."
—Margaret Junkin Preston, a Virginia Mother

In these days some entertain the wicked delusion that he who dies for his country will be saved by virtue of his patriotism.
—Rev. W. H. McIntosh, "The Young Soldier Ready for Death"

A DEVASTATED LANDSCAPE

Before the Civil War, the American landscape had largely been spared the damage that internecine conflicts had wrought in other parts of the world. During the Thirty Years War (1618–1648)—a European war that was inspired by religious sectarianism—the landscape in some regions was so altered by war that it was hardly recognizable. Nearly one-half of the residents of central Europe (generally present-day Germany and Austria) were killed and everywhere the countryside was devastated and stripped of its resources with no clear winner emerging from either side. By way of contrast, during the colonial wars of 17th-century in America, the French and their Native American allies had burned a few isolated cabins or small villages, and the British red coats of the revolutionary period had done some minor physical damage to New York, Philadelphia, and Charleston. Ironically, a devastating fire that burned one-third of the buildings in New York city in 1776 was probably set by over-zealous American patriots. So limited was the catalog of war damage in America prior to 1861 that the burning of the executive mansion (White House) in the nation's capital by the British during the War of 1812 stood out as a virtual calamity out of proportion to the devastation left behind by even moderate European conflicts.

During America's Civil War, however, 19th century photographers were able to record a disturbing panorama of dead bodies, mutilated animals, twisted rails, overturned locomotives, and other war damage done in the South from 1861–1865—a devastation generally spared Northern urban centers. Images of Southern cities once under siege by Federal forces, such as Atlanta, Savannah, Richmond, or Charleston, showed that they were left mere skeletons. These moving and disturbing images of a defeated South were far removed from its picturesque antebellum grandeur with columned verandas, elegant carriages, hanging Spanish moss, and laconic river steamers.

Artillery fire, especially during sieges and great battles, destroyed trees in unimaginable numbers leaving behind forests of useless stumps and splintered wood. The collective picture of a scorched and broken landscape, noted in this image taken of the Wilderness battlefield in Virginia, suggested the end of rural life as it had previously been known in the South. Courtesy of Library of Congress.

Yet while the most impressive photographic images of the Civil War were taken of devastated cities and plantation houses, most of the battles had actually taken place on farms, in plowed fields and pastures, or among orchards and woodlots where their effects had lasting but largely unreported consequences. A group of glass-plate photographs unearthed in the last decade at the Library of Congress shows the splintered stumps of what had been a Middle Tennessee forest prior to its becoming a battlefield. Not a tree is standing.

The economic cost of the devastation wrought in these battles was almost incalculable and historians have been hard pressed to attach a specific dollar amount to the sufferings that it caused in rural America.[1] Farmhouses, barns, and other outbuildings were blown up, burned, or left mere skeletons stripped of boards by the troops of both sides. Farm fences everywhere disappeared in the smoke of a thousand nightly campfires. The loss of these alone has been estimated at several millions of dollars not to mention that their replacement placed a labor-intensive strain on a region of the country already stressed by a lack of white laborers and the removal of thousands of former slaves. Digging postholes, splitting fence rails, and fashioning gates is incredibly time consuming even when the appropriate wood and labor are available.

Moreover, throughout the South and Confederate West—and especially among the modest farmsteads—soldiers had felled whole stands of forest, killed fruit-bearing trees in orchards, and used the trunks to build campsites, fortifications, and so-called corduroy roads. Winter quarters, field breastworks, and temporary bridges were almost always constructed of newly felled logs. The South had supported a significant timber, wood products, and turpentine industry in the antebellum years. It would take decades for the South to recover the produce of these economic resources.[2]

The war also affected livestock production. Farm animals—the horses and mules who were essential to 19th-century warfare and also the local meat animals like cattle, sheep, chickens, and hogs—died in appalling numbers wherever armies marched. Besides those consumed directly by the opposing armies, animals—confined together for the first time in their hundreds in depots, camps, and fortified positions—exchanged pathogens for diseases that they had not before been exposed and died by the thousands before they could be used. Disease deaths among draft animals, added to the natural loss in battle, necessitated their re-supply from farther and farther away from the battlefront, especially from the American West, so that the war's animal impact became continental in scope. As expected, many horses and mules were maimed and killed by bullets and exploding shells. Since their carcasses were so much larger than those of dead men, horses and mules presented daunting sanitary challenges on the battlefield, and onsite burials were usually hasty and incomplete. Parts of the South smelled of death.[3]

AN ABSENCE OF MEN

The Civil War involved the entire population in a way unparalleled by any conflict since the American Revolution. The military mobilization of close to four million men in as many years—the largest attempted in American history to that time—generally affected the ability of heads of households to properly support their families in ways that even the few experts in warfare had envisioned. Before a single man had been killed in battle, the absence of men from the counting-houses, factories, plantations, and farms had had an immediate negative effect on their families as well as their communities. The official population of the North and South combined, according to the 1860 U.S. Census, was somewhat over 32 million, including four million black slaves largely confined to the seceded states. The majority of service-aged young men would go to war, and over 600, 000 would never return.[4]

Mobilization was especially difficult in the manpower-hungry South where a larger proportion of white men were pulled into service than in the North. Louisa Walton reported that her region of South Carolina had been thinned out of men by 1862, and in Shelby County, Alabama, it was reported that 1600 of the 1800 male residents (89 percent) were in the army. Consequently, many women were trying to do a man's business, managing businesses and farms, or working for wages for the first time. In some cases they seemed to have usurped their husbands' places–a situation that created somewhat of a gender crisis during the war and a transformation among the roles of men and women that may have had a destabilizing effect in the postwar aftermath.[5]

With their means of making a living gone and their place in the community ripped asunder after the war, Southern men returning from war, in particular, were left with little of their former gender identities beyond their personal honor and their continued allegiance to the "lost cause" of Southern independence. Immediately after the war, the public was swamped with war stories, journals, memoirs, and battle descriptions that attempted to support the antebellum Southern cultural identity and to justify the holocaust brought on by secession. Former army commanders renewed wartime arguments about tactics and strategies in print in an attempt to dissemble the reasons for their failure to secure disunion in the name of Southern independence. Many pointed to the exhausted condition of the Southern manpower pool and its damaged infrastructure as proximate causes for the South's surrender.[6]

The fact was that the South had not merely lost the war. It had been beaten and beaten badly. Its economy, industry, agriculture, and population had been sorely pressed. Its cities had been invaded and ravaged. Southern manhood—taken as a corporate identity—was generally considered to have failed to defend hearth and home. This was a massive psychological failure in terms of an antebellum paradigm that viewed Southern men as protectors and guardians of women, children, and the elderly. Unlike most southern men, many Northerners avoided this gender identity confrontation and came home to cities untarnished by war and festooned with red, white, and blue ribbons with the sustaining knowledge of having rescued the enslaved from cruel bondage while maintaining the sacred union. As in the aftermath of other wars, an entire generation of American men shared a common set of battlefield experiences, and surely a similar collection of recurring nightmares, that bound them together.

Women too shared a physiological bond brought on by the war. Both Northern and Southern women had attempted to readjust their lives as well as possible to the extended absences of husbands and fathers during the war years, and many widows and daughters would have to do so permanently. Rev. Wm. H. McIntosh of Charleston, Tennessee noted that "especially of late [1862] . . . the illustrations of the uncertainty of life have been multiplied in our community, and in our church. But a few days ago this bell rung out in doleful tones the solemn news that another 'goeth to his long home'–not the infirm, the aged, but the young, with the flush of early manhood on his cheek, and before the hopes of youth had passed the vanity of life."[7]

So common were the battlefield deaths on both sides that whole communities of women were in simultaneous mourning. Ironically, this sharing of affliction tended to create a sense of unity among the community of matrons and their daughters. The absence of a so-called "bread winner" or other male source of income particularly stressed middle- and lower-class families who had few financial resources or reserves. Many upper-class women had servants, hired help, or slaves on which to rely in the absence of their men, but they found their situations strained nonetheless. After watching her brothers depart for the war, Kate Stone correctly speculated that those who stayed home might find it harder than those who left.[8]

The task was generally more difficult for Confederate women than for those in the North or the loyal Midwest because the real shooting war was often taking place in their front yard where they were trying to raise their children and care for their homes. Partisan warfare in the border states was virtually unending. It was equally difficult to maintain some facsimile of family stability in the main theaters of the war in northern Virginia and Tennessee and in Southern cities under siege such as Vicksburg, Atlanta, or Charleston. Annie M. Sehon of Nashville wrote, "O my precious sister . . . We are in hourly expectation of hearing the approach of the Northern Army . . . [and] all our Government officers fly tonight for their lives . . . I cannot tell you how my heart is almost breaking to part from my precious Husband who is far more than life to me. Without him I would pray, pray for death, pray that God would take me from this prison world to my husband in Heaven for I know he will be there if he falls, he is so good, so pure, so noble."[9]

MARCH 18, 1865.]   FRANK LESLIE'S ILLUSTRATED NEWSPAPER.   405

CONTRABANDS ACCOMPANYING THE LINE OF SHERMAN'S MARCH THROUGH GEORGIA.—FROM A SKETCH BY OUR SPECIAL ARTIST.

Thousands of slaves attached themselves to the Union forces during the Civil War. A nearby battle insured that hundreds of blacks would come flooding across the Federal lines as soon as the firing had stopped regardless of which side had won the battle. Federal military commanders were hard-pressed as to what to do with so many refugees, who often required food, shelter, medical care, clothing, and protection from Southern forces. Courtesy of Library of Congress.

Women in disputed areas of the rural South also had to cope with the additional threats posed by runaway slaves, uncompromising foragers, and unrestrained deserters. The Confederate military often used its scant reserve forces to hunt them, offered rewards for their capture, and relied on home guard patrols and local law enforcement officials to arrest them or at least drive them from the region. The Southern military also hoped to stop men from deserting by threatening severe punishments like whippings, brandings, and imprisonment. Death was an empty threat in an army so bereft of manpower.[10]

The loss of male farm workers and hired hands to the war effort particularly increased the burdens sustained by the farming families who made up the overwhelming majority of U.S. households. The Confederacy was the first to initiate a mandatory draft that removed many poor white farm workers from the soil, but it exempted many of those employed in the mechanical trades and slaveowners with more than 20 slaves. This left the lowest class of farm families (so-called poor whites) at a distinct man-power disadvantage, and brought forth in many quarters accusations of "Rich man's war, Poor man's fight!" The Federal government followed with its own draft that also exempted tradesmen and mechanics, but the North padded its ranks from the multitude of unemployed immigrants from the cities.

Lacking men to hire in place of absent fathers and brothers, children were often forced to fill the need for adult labor. Adolescent boys (under 16 years of age) were exempt from the draft, but their assistance had always been calculated as part of available labor force on the family farm or in the manufactory. Girls and young women often found that they now had to take the place of their fathers and husbands clearing fields, making hay, and cutting firewood. At age 12 Marion Drury had to assume the work and responsibilities of a man because most of her mother's farm-hands had gone into the army. Anna Shaw was only 14 when she took on her father and brothers' jobs in addition to teaching school, sewing, cleaning, and tending to boarders. At 15 Helen Brock was branding calves and erecting fences, and Fannie Eisele began to plow the family fields when she was only 10 years old.[11]

Between late 1862 and early 1865, Southerners struggled with an appalling rate of inflation. The price of wheat rose nearly 1,700 percent; bacon 2,500 percent; and flour almost 2,800 percent. By the final stages of the war, it was recorded that a pair of shoes cost at least $600 (CSD) and that $1,500 (CSD) was needed to purchase a simple wool overcoat.[12] Nonetheless, living in a Northern city did not make life any easier for families destitute of their men. The cost of rent, fuel, food, and clothing was higher in the city, and urban dwellers did not have the option of "living off the land." When pressed for payment by landlords or shopkeepers, they generally depended on their husband's military pay or the benevolence of relatives. While many men wrote regularly to their families expressing pitiable longing and loneliness for them and sending home money, the military mail services—especially in the South—were not entirely reliable, and soldiers were often out of touch with their families for extended periods. One federal officer testified about receiving a letter from a destitute young wife, anxious for news of her husband. She had received no word of him in months and only nine dollars since he had enlisted. She and her children had therefore been evicted from their home. "Here are four pages of pathos that make me want. . .to kick him for not deserving them," wrote the officer after investigating the case and finding the man pathetically irresponsible. "Apparently a fairly educated and quite worthy girl has married a good-looking youth of inferior nature and breeding who has not the energy to toil effectively for her, nor the affection to endure privations for her sake." Certainly similar scenes were played out many times, and many other inquiries from worried wives had tragic endings.[13]

CHILDREN OF WAR

Photographs of war dead and almost instantaneous reports from the front by telegraph made the war years difficult for both parents and children. In imitation of the news headlines, children often played at soldiers and held mock parades, drills, and skirmishes. Margaret Junkin Preston, a Virginia mother, wrote that her children's entire sets of play were referenced to a state of war. She reported that five-year-old George got sticks and hobbled about saying that he lost a leg at the second battle of Manassas. He also fabricated stories of how he cut off Yankee heads and bayoneted them—disturbing behavior in a child so young that would not be tolerated today. Lilly Martin Spencer's painting, "War Spirit at Home," shows three Northern children marching about while beating a pot and blowing a horn as their mother reads to them the newspaper account of the battle of Vicksburg. Future president, Theodore Roosevelt, who had two uncles fighting for the Confederacy, enjoyed playing "Running the Blockade" when he was seven.[14]

THE BATTLE OF GETTYSBURG INVADES CIVILIAN LIFE

In 1888, Tillie Pierce (Alleman) published one of the most comprehensive narratives of civilian experiences during the Battle of Gettysburg. An excerpt from her memoir reads:

> As I often stood . . . gazing to the distant South Mountains, or the nearer Round Tops, or Culp's Hill, little did I dream that from those summits the engines of war would, in a few years, belch forth their missiles of destruction; that through those sylvan aisles would reverberate the clash of arms, the roar of musketry, and the booming of cannon, to be followed by the groans of the wounded and dying. Little did I think that those lovely valleys teeming with verdure and the rich harvest would soon be strewn with the distorted and mangled bodies of American brothers . . .
>
> My native townsmen, during that terrible struggle, acted as patriotic and bravely as it was possible for citizens to act, who had suddenly thrust upon them the most gigantic battle of modern times . . . They had none of the weapons or munitions of war . . . and were totally unprepared for such an unthought of experience. They were civilians.
>
> To all was presented the opportunity of caring for the wounded and dying after the battle had passed, and nobly and freely did they administer the tender and loving acts of charity even in their own homes as well as upon the field and in the hospital.
>
> Let those disposed to cavil and doubt the patriotism of the citizens of Gettysburg at the time of the battle forever cease, for what I have written is correct.

Source: Tillie Pierce Allemen, "At Gettysburg: Or What a Girl Saw and Heard at the Battle," http://www.angelfire.com/pa4/gettysburg/tilliepierce.html (Accessed September, 2008).

The reality of war for most urban working-class children was work—not an increase in simple household chores, but hard, sweat producing, back-breaking labor. American industry consciously sought the cheap labor of children, and millions of children ages 10 to 15 were "gainfully" employed. Most of the child labor was agricultural, but approximately one child in six worked in coalmines, textile mills, garment industry sweatshops, or factories of all kinds. Children between the ages of 10 and 19 often provided a quarter of family income. Many youngsters—especially urban boys—were forced by circumstances to leave school, or home, or both in order to make a living for themselves on the streets as bootblacks, scrap collectors, dishwashers, construction drudges, manure collectors, and newsboys.

Newsboys, as a discrete class, were a particularly common sight in most cities. They were first employed in the 1830s to hawk the penny-paper dailies, whose low initial price made selling them financially feasible for poor boys. Due to shortages of paper, ink, and lead for type, however, Southern newspapers were quickly reduced to a single sheet of newsprint and a minimal circulation easily handled through adult conduits; but in northern cities the expanding popularity of newspapers offered a form of self-employment to many boys. The headline cries of the newsboys soon became an integral part of the sounds of the city.

Johnny Morrow's memoirs give insight into the finances of the newspaper trade from the perspective of a child. Newsboys bought papers at a small discount early in the morning and were unable to return unsold copies. Morrow generally had 56 papers for his morning's stock, for which he paid 84 cents. His sales totaled 1 dollar and 12 cents, leaving him a profit of 28 cents. Nine cents were spent for breakfast, and he had nineteen to spare. As profits accrued only after they had covered their initial investment, successful newsboys turned into clever businessmen who assessed the weather and the events of the day prior to purchasing their day's stock. The First Annual Report of the Children's Aid Society in 1860 called the newsboys the "shrewdest and sharpest" of street children.

While some of these street-wise entrepreneurs had families, many street-children were orphans, actually or in effect, having been abandoned or left orphaned by the war or other circumstances. Those who had no homes found shelter in the alleys and back streets, fighting for warm spots around grated vent-holes that let out the heat and steam from the underground press-rooms. Others went to live in one of a number of Newsboys' Lodging Houses that were set up in several cities to provide shelter and safety for the lads. The boys were free to come and go in the lodging houses as long as they behaved. The homes were like hotels and, as such, the boys were asked to pay a small amount (six to eight cents nightly) for their bed and their meals. Additionally, these homes offered the boys classes in reading and writing. The path to educational refinement through such means was likely to have been a difficult one, however. The Second Annual Report on the Children's Aid Society reported that the newsboys were apparently the most wild and vicious set of lads in the city. Their money, which was reportedly "easily earned," was more quickly spent in gambling, theaters, and low pleasures, for which, though children, they had a man's aptitude. The superintendent of the Newsboys' Lodging House in New York acknowledged that although its arrangements were popular with the boys, the temptations of a street life and its excitements were so strong that it was exceedingly difficult to get them into the homes or induce them to stay.[15]

SOLDIERS' ORPHANS

The death of 600,000 young men in the Civil War left many children fatherless, and the high incidence of death among young women of childbearing years created many so-called "full orphans" having no living parent whatsoever. Other parentless children, "half orphans," had mothers (or fathers) who simply could not afford to work while paying for someone to watch over the children and still put food on the table. Many orphaned children found homes with relatives; others relied on community aid; and still others had to fend for themselves on the streets.

It is estimated that up to 2,700 children were orphaned by the Civil War in Pennsylvania alone, and Ohio had 2,300 additional children made orphans by the war. Orphanage records are often incomplete or missing, but there may have been 20,000 to 30,000 soldiers' orphans nationwide. The total number of soldiers' orphans in the former Confederate States can only be surmised when compared to the less than complete records found in the North. It is certain that the war created thousands of full- and half-orphans in the South who were suddenly thrust upon a society ill equipped to care for them. The breadth of the problem can be estimated by the reaction to it, which seemingly peaked in July 1863 after the Battle of Gettysburg.

Many states dealt with the orphan crisis by erecting new institutions, or enlisting existing orphanages, asylums, and elder care institutions to look after the children of fallen soldiers. Nine northern states—Ohio, New Jersey, Pennsylvania, Illinois, Indiana, Iowa, Kansas, Wisconsin, and Minnesota—founded state-run soldiers' orphans homes. Other states relied on a large number of pre-existing and privately funded institutions. In all, Americans built as many orphanages—both public and private—in the 1860s as the nation had founded in the two decades prior to the war. In addition, many older institutions were pressed into service to meet the need. These were essentially the only recourse for orphans in the former Confederate states because southern communities were largely destitute of money and materials for such humanitarian endeavors. Many of these orphaned and displaced children were forced to find refuge in poorhouses, reformatories, and prisons.[16]

War widows with children often tried to cope with the situation faced by their fatherless brood, and the federal government began to award pensions to the widows of soldiers and sailors as early as July 1862. Yet the wife of a private soldier received only $8 per month without regard to the number of her children. This was the same pension given to wounded men disabled in the war, but it was simply not enough. Many single parents were forced to place some or all of their children into institutional care. In 1866, Congress increased the monthly payment by adding $2 for each child under the age of 16. This left a gap in the federal safety net for those orphans who had no parent to make or receive the claim. Two years later Congress extended the $2 monthly payment directly to children under 16. Southern widows and orphans, lacking any government intervention, relied on family or local care and generosity.[17]

Among the orphaned children of the Northeast region were a large number of Irish, indirect causalities of the brave stands made by the poor immigrant Irish who had joined the army. The 63rd and 69th New York (Fighting Irish), the 9th and 28th Massachusetts, and the 116th Pennsylvania Infantry made up the so-called Irish Brigade. A Second Irish Brigade (155th, 164th, 170th, and 180th New York Infantry) was formed by war's end. Of the 140,000 immigrant Irish in the Federal army one-third came from eastern cities (chiefly Boston, Philadelphia, and Pittsburgh), one-third came from New York City alone, and the remainder served in scattered units raised in the Midwest and Western theaters of the war. Most Irish immigrants had only a skeletal kinship network to fall back upon in America and were exceedingly poor when they entered service. This left their widows and children largely without a means of support.

The deaths of Irish soldiers were particularly high at Fredericksburg in the week before Christmas 1862. The Irish Brigade was involved in the assault on the stone wall in the sunken road in front of Marye's Heights. In this action the brigade suffered its most severe casualties of the war with its fighting force reduced from over 1600 to only 256. Ironically, one of the regiments manning the sunken road defenses was a predominantly Irish regiment commanded by Confederate Gen. Thomas Cobb. Knowing that Cobb's men manned the wall, and that both Northern and Southern units contained members of the Fenian Brotherhood—an organization dedicated to gaining military experience in the United States in order to later free Ireland from Britain—Lee ordered non-Irish Southern reserves sent to the position lest Cobb's men shrink from firing on their countrymen. He need not have worried. Before the Confederate reinforcements could settle in place, Cobb's men had more than decimated the 69th New York— the federal regiment closest to reaching the stone wall. It was in this action that the 69th regiment received its sobriquet: the Fighting Irish.

The Catholic Church in New York took one of the earliest solutions to the orphan problem created by all this mayhem. In 1863, the Catholic Protectory for Homeless and Wayward Children in New York City opened its doors to soldiers' orphans in response to the loss of their fathers in the crucial battles of the 1862 campaign in the Eastern theater: the Peninsular Campaign (June and July), Antietam (September), and Fredericksburg (December). By the end of 1863, the Catholic Protectory was caring for more than 1000 city youngsters many of whom had lost parents at the battles of Chancellorsville (May, 1863) or Gettysburg (July, 1863).

May of 1864 was the bloodiest month of the Civil War with more than 100,000 total casualties in the Eastern Theater alone. Gen. Ulysses Grant was called a butcher, but he continued to fight through the Wilderness and Spotsylvania Campaigns ending up in front of Petersburg in July 1864. In response, the Pennsylvania Soldiers' Orphan Schools Association was established. In one of the most comprehensive soldiers' orphans responses, the state provided educational instruction for the children as well as food, clothing, furnishings, and care until age 16. There were 46 individual member sites in Pennsylvania including those sponsored and staffed by Protestant and Catholic churches. As of 1887, the number of children who had received care through the Pennsylvania system numbered more than 14,000.

In his Second Inaugural Address (March 4, 1865), Abraham Lincoln had pledged "to care for him who shall have borne the battle and for his widow and his orphans." Less than six weeks later Lincoln was dead, felled by an assassin's bullet. Andrew Johnson, now President, took up the call and the promise, and in June 1866 Congress passed an act forming the National Soldiers' and Sailors' Orphans Home in Washington, D.C. In 1869, the Grand Army of the Republic (GAR)—a society of Union Civil War veterans—founded the Ohio Soldiers' and Sailors' Orphans Home on 100 acres of land donated by the people of Xenia, Ohio. The home had beds for only 75 children, but over 900 children were housed in the institution through 1900.

WHOSE CHILDREN ARE THESE?

One dead Federal soldier found on the Gettysburg battlefield presented a sad puzzle with regard to his children. The man's body was unidentified except for a photograph in his pocket of three children that were presumed to be his. In October 1863, the *Philadelphia Enquirer* ran a story that described the children in detail in an effort to discover their identity. Newspapers at that time did not have the technical ability to reproduce photographs in print. Other newspapers reprinted the story. Philinda Humiston of Portville, New York read the article in the *American Presbyterian* a month later, and strongly suspected that the description fit a photograph sent to her husband, Amos some months before the battle. She was able to confirm that the children Frank, Alice, and Fred were in fact the children in the picture. Amos Humiston had been a sergeant in the 154th New York Volunteer Infantry. The incident led to the founding of the National Homestead at Gettysburg in October 1866 with funds coming in from businessman Jay Gould. The three Humiston children became residents there when their mother was given a position helping to run the home.

In the 1870s and 1880s, a number of Soldiers' Orphans homes closed due to the fact that the children had grown to adulthood. The Wisconsin Soldiers' Orphans Home closed in 1874, after the trustees found foster care for the children remaining there. The National Homestead at Gettysburg was closed in 1879 after several scandals involving physical abuse and mismanagement of funds. Other institutions continued to serve the orphans of U. S. servicemen killed in action in other conflicts.

THE ORPHAN TRAINS

In 1853, a group of ministers looking for a better way to help orphaned or destitute urban youth formed the Children's Aid Society. Chief among these was Charles Loring Brace, a minister from Connecticut working in the tenement neighborhoods of New York City. In 1851, Brace had worked at the Ladies' Methodist Home Missionary Society founded in 1848 in the city's Five Points neighborhood. This was one of the poorest and most crime-ridden areas of the city, and it was filled with an immense number of boys and girls floating and drifting about in the streets with no occupation other than petty crime, prostitution, and gang membership. Few had any assignable home or guiding parents.

Brace and his comrades in the Children's Aid Society understood that children needed a secure loving home free from the filth of the city and its corrupting influences. The board of the Society decided that part of the solution to the problem was to remove orphans from the urban environment and find homes for them in the country where they would have enough to eat, warm beds and clothing, and fresh air and a cleaner environment. The Society began in 1853 to place children with willing families in central New York and in New England. In 1854 they expanded their program by rounding up 46 children between the ages of 7 and 15 from the slums and sending them by train to the Midwest. Here the children were put on display at a church meeting so that farm families could choose among them.

The so-called Orphan Train was very successful, and two more were established in 1855. In return for a home in the rural countryside the children were expected to do the same work that was expected of the natural progeny of farm parents. However, the "foster" parents were not screened in any way. Their willingness to take children was their only qualification, and no follow-up was done by the Society to find out if the children were thriving in their adoptive homes or being abused. Yet the society had great difficulty in placing children under ten years old, who were seen as less able to do a full day's work. Black children were particularly difficult to place with white families, and the Society made no concerted effort to find willing black families to provide foster homes.

By 1860, the Children's Aid Society had placed approximately 5,000 children. The exact number is unknown because the Society kept only fragmentary or contradictory records. During the war, Children's Aid Societies in other Eastern cities—particularly Boston and Philadelphia—again sent out orphans by train including many of the so-called Soldiers' Orphans of the Civil War. By 1884, Brace was able to claim 60,000 successful placements by means of the Orphan Trains. Brace served as president of the Children's Aid Society of New York for 40 years.

NOTES

1. Estimates range from $6.6 to 10.3 billion with the South bearing 60 percent of the total cost. On a per capita basis, the costs to the Northern population were about $150—or roughly equal to one year's income. The Southern burden (with $2 billion figured as the loss of slave property due to emancipation) was two and a half times that amount—$376 per man, woman and child. See Roger Ransom, "Economics of the Civil War," *EH.Net Encyclopedia,* ed. Robert Whaples, http://eh.net/encyclopedia/article/ransom.civil.war.us (Accessed April 2009).

2. Jack Temple Kirby, "An Environmental View on the American Civil War," http://www.eoearth.org/article/Environmental_view_on_the_American_Civil_War (Accessed April 2008).

3. See Kirby.

4. David Woodward, *Armies on the World, 1854–1914* (New York: G. P. Putnam's Sons, 1978.

5. James M. Volo and Dorothy Denneen Volo, eds., *The Greenwood Encyclopedia of Daily Life in America,* Vol. 2, ed. Randal M. Miller (Westport, CT: Greenwood Press, 2008), 38–39.

6. James M. Volo and Dorothy Denneen Volo, *Family Life in 19th-Century America* (Westport, CT: Greenwood Press, 2007), 47.

7. W. H. McIntosh, "James C. Sumner, the Young Soldier Ready for Death," Rare Book Collection, University of North Carolina at Chapel Hill, http://docsouth.unc.edu/imls/mcintosh/mcintosh.html (Accessed April 2008).

8. Ray B. Browne, and Lawrence A. Kreiser, Jr. *The Civil War and Reconstruction* (Westport, CT: Greenwood Press, 2003), 11.

9. Annie M. Sehon, Nashville, Feb 16, 1862. Kimberly Family Personal Correspondence, Manuscripts Dept., Southern Historical Collection, University of North Carolina at Chapel Hill, http://docsouth.unc.edu/imls/kimberly/kimberly.html (Accessed April 2008).

10. Paul Randolph Dotson Jr., "The Effects of Confederate Deserters on the Floyd County Homefront," http://scholar.lib.vt.edu/theses/public/etd-4019122049721391/materials/CHAPTER2.PDF (Accessed April 2008).

11. Volo and Volo, (2007), 319.

12. R. Neil Fulghum, "Moneys for the Southern Cause," *The Southern Homefront, 1861–1865.* Accessed April 2008. URL: http://docsouth.unc.edu/imls/currency/index.html.

13. James H. Croushore, ed., *A Volunteer's Adventure, by Captain John W. De Forest* (New Haven: Yale University Press, 1949), 46.

14. Margaret M. Lothrop, *The Wayside: Home of Authors* (New York: American Book Company, 1968), 51.

15. Volo and Volo, (2007), 327.

16. Catherine Reef, *Alone in the World: Orphans and Orphanages in America* (New York: Clarion Books, 2005), 76.

17. Reef, 65–66.

20

COPPERHEADS

In these days some entertain the wicked delusion that he who
dies for his country will be saved by virtue of his patriotism.
—Rev. W. H. McIntosh, "The Young Soldier Ready for Death"

During the secession crisis many Democrats in the North were more con-
ciliatory toward the South than were their Republican rivals preferring
political compromise rather than military action to resolve the problem
of secession. The majority of Northern Democrats supported the effort to
save the Union, but a strong and active minority asserted that the Republicans had provoked the South into secession and were waging war in
order to establish their own domination, suppress civil and states rights,
and impose racial equality.

These Peace Democrats, as they called themselves, believed that military
means would never restore the Union. Their Republican opponents nicknamed them Copperheads, describing the antiwar Democrats as poison-
ous snakes waiting in the weeds to strike a blow in favor of the South. The
first reference to these peace proponents as "Copperheads" occurred in an
Ohio newspaper in 1861. Accepting the Copperhead name as a badge of
honor, many opponents of the war began to use the portrait side (Goddess
of Liberty) of copper pennies as badges and tokens for identification and
promotion of their cause. This gave a second meaning to the term Copperhead, one which Peace Democrats cherished. Copperheads should not
be confused with Quakers, Mennonites, or other conscientious objectors
who followed absolute pacifism based on their religious beliefs, nor were

This image ran in the February 28, 1863 issue of *Harper's Weekly* above the caption: "The Copperhead Party–In Favor of a Vigorous Prosecution of Peace!" Courtesy of Library of Congress.

they traitors and spies. On the contrary they seem to have been sincere in their belief that the Lincoln administration and the majority Republic Congress were overstepping their constitutional bounds in waging war on the South.

There were three distinct types of Copperhead: those who believed the war could not be won, those who were alarmed by Lincoln's actions with reference to emancipation, and those who supported the Confederate right to secede from the very first. The first group was least dedicated to antiwar pacifism and quickly abandoned their positions and returned to supporting the war with every dramatic Confederate reversal on the battlefield. The deeply racist Democrats had often supported the war when its purpose was maintaining the Union, but many of them jumped to the Copperhead side when confronted with the reality of black emancipation. Those who supported the concept of secession from the onset grew increasingly distressed as Lincoln took unprecedented steps to force the seceded states back into the union. These last made up the stable inner core of the Copperhead movement throughout the war.

Several of these Democrats participated in a peace convention held in Washington, D.C. during early 1861. The delegates hoped to convince

President Lincoln to either agree to the Confederacy's demands in order to get it to rejoin the Union or simply to let the Southern states go. Politically, most people who participated in the peace convention affiliated themselves with the so-called Peace Democrats. They were unhappy with Lincoln's preparations to invade the South that included calling up 75,000 volunteers, but mostly they reflected a long-standing dislike for a number of Republican policies especially their dedication to the universal abolition of slavery.

Peace Democrats were most numerous in the Midwest (especially in the southern tier of Ohio, Indiana, and Illinois), a region that had traditionally distrusted the Northeast and that had economic, cultural, and sometimes kinship ties with the South. Many of the residents here were so-called *butternuts*–Southern-born migrants to the Midwest much like Lincoln's own father. As much as 12 percent of the population originally may have been from the South. The Lincoln administration's arbitrary treatment of dissenters caused great bitterness in the region. Above all, anti-abolitionist Midwesterners feared that emancipation would result in a great migration of blacks into their states. Some objected to slavery's end fearing that freedmen would flood the North looking for jobs forcing whites to compete with them for employment.

CLEMENT VALLANDIGHAM

Representative Clement Vallandigham of Ohio was the best-known Peace Democrat. He helped organize a rally for the Democratic Party at Mount Vernon, Ohio, on May 1, 1863 that caused a great stir among Lincoln supporters. Vallandigham, Samuel S. Cox, and George H. Pendleton all delivered speeches denouncing General Order No. 38 that had been issued by General Ambrose Burnside, commander of the Department of Ohio in April 1863. Burnside hoped to intimidate Confederate sympathizers with General Order No. 38, which stated:

The habit of declaring sympathy for the enemy will not be allowed in this department. Persons committing such offenses will be at once arrested with a view of being tried . . . or sent beyond our lines into the lines of their friends. It must be understood that treason, expressed or implied, will not be tolerated in this department.

Burnside also declared that, in certain cases, violations of General Order No. 38 could result in a sentence of death.[1]

Vallandigham was so opposed to the order that he allegedly said that he "despised it, spit upon it, trampled it under his feet." He also supposedly encouraged his fellow Peace Democrats to openly resist Burnside. Vallandigham went on to chastise Lincoln for allowing Burnside to thwart citizen rights under a free government. Federal agents wearing civilian

THE CHICAGO PLATFORM AND CANDIDATE.

As a Presidential candidate in 1864, McClellan was branded a hypocrite by many critics who saw his public stance on the war issue as ambiguous and deceptive. Nominated because of his military record, he nevertheless ran on a peace platform, written by Copperhead leader Clement Laird Vallandigham, but then asserted his support for the war in his letter accepting the nomination. Here the platform rests on the shoulders of (clockwise from left): a devil, Confederate president Jefferson Davis, New York Copperhead Fernando Wood, and Vallandigham. Courtesy of Library of Congress.

clothes attended the meeting and took careful notes. Made aware of Vallandigham's protests, Burnside ordered his immediate arrest. On May 5, 1863, a company of soldiers arrested Vallandigham at his home in Dayton and brought him to Cincinnati to stand trial before a military tribunal.[2]

Vallandigham offered no serious defense against the charges contending instead that military courts had no jurisdiction over his case. Judge Humphrey Leavitt of the federal circuit court rejected Vallandigham's argument. He agreed with Burnside that military authority was necessary during a time of war to ensure that opponents to the United States Constitution would not succeed in overthrowing it and the rights that it guaranteed its citizens. The military tribunal found Vallandigham guilty of treason and sentenced him to remain in a federal prison for the remainder of the war. Cox, a newspaper editor from Ohio and former U.S. ambassador to Peru, wrote a moving letter to the president asking for Vallandigham's release "If not accounted magnanimous, by reason of the bitterness of the times, [such a course] may nevertheless prevent that ill will and distrust between the people and its agents, which the wisest of Statesmen ever seek to avert."[3] Cox, considered moderate among Copperheads, was one of the most vehement and outspoken in terms of his verbal attacks against the president and the war. Lincoln knew that confining Vallandigham might make the Ohioan a rallying point for opposition and cause Peace Democrats across the North to rise up to prevent his detention. The president, therefore, commuted Vallandigham's sentence to exile in the Confederacy, and on May 25, Burnside sent Vallandigham into Confederate lines. Vallandigham made his way to Canada and proceeded to run for Governor of Ohio from that distance, but lost the race.

The influence of the Peace Democrats varied with the fortunes of war on the battlefield. When things were going badly for the Union on the battlefield, larger numbers of people were willing to entertain the notion of making peace with the Confederacy. When things were going well, Peace Democrats could more easily be dismissed as defeatists. But no matter how the war progressed, Peace Democrats constantly had to defend themselves against charges of disloyalty. Revelations that a few had ties with secret organizations such as the Knights of the Golden Circle, or the Sons of Liberty helped smear the rest. The administration exaggerated the Copperhead menace for political advantage, but their stories of secret plots and treasonous association were most false. Government officials estimated that more than 100,000 persons belonged to these organizations, but most historians discount the figure as being dramatically higher than the group's actual numbers.

The Copperheads mobilized behind the 1864 election to throw Lincoln from office and gain their objectives at the ballot box, but they generally opposed the Democratic party's nomination of General George McClellan, a War Democrat for president in 1864 on the grounds that he refused to accept their demands for an immediate peace. They were influential enough in the party, however, to set a peace plank in the party platform and place a Copperhead, George H. Pendleton, of Ohio as the vice-presidential candidate. Pendleton had begun his political career during the 1850s. He first served in the Ohio Senate, and in 1856 voters elected him to the U.S. House of Representatives. He held his seat until March 1865. He was a committed Peace Democrat and strongly opposed the Union war effort. He was a close associate of Vallandigham.

The Peace Democrats made a good deal of headway among Democratic voters in the North with an argument that the war could not be won and was not worth winning, but this line of attack generally infuriated the soldiers serving in the federal armies who wanted to win the war. These men voted in increased numbers for Lincoln and helped to persuade their family and friends at home to do so. Historian James M. MacPherson has noted that the demands made by the Peace Democrats for "peace at any price, even the price of defeat and disunion," exemplified "the naïveté of the Copperheads insistence that an armistice and negotiations would bring the Confederate states back into the Union." Southern leaders had consistently set Confederate independence as a first condition for any formal talks.[4] Due largely to major Northern victories at Savanah and Atlanta, the McClellan-Pendleton ticket lost the election. With the successful conclusion of the war in 1865, the Peace Democrats were thoroughly discredited. Most Northerners believed, not without reason, that the Copperheads had prolonged the war by encouraging the South to continue fighting in the hope that the North would abandon the struggle.

ANTI-CONFEDERATE SOUTHERNERS

The Lincoln administration could not wage a war effectively in the South without neutralizing the pro-confederate sentiment in the border states. If the border states insisted on proclaiming their states' rights, they could refuse to allow federal forces to pass through and across their boundaries to bring the Confederates to battle. Lincoln, hoping to recruit border residents in the fight to suppress the Confederacy, first attempted to attract white support in the region to the cause of *perpetual union.*

Although Tennessee had seceded more than 30,000 men from the eastern part of the state ultimately served in the federal forces. Five times this number–mostly from the western and central regions–served the Confederacy, yet no border state donated more men to the Union cause. By downplaying abolition, emancipation, and citizenship for blacks, and by treating escaped slaves as so-called *contrabands,* Lincoln was generally successful in attracting manpower, resources, and positive public opinion in the white belt border regions. This was especially true in 1861 and 1862 when Lincoln most needed the border states as staging areas for the incursion of federal forces into the Confederacy. He also needed to secure, with a minimum of force, better access to the Ohio, Tennessee, Mississippi, and other rivers for the operations of the federal gunboat navy.

Only in September 1862, after the marginal success at Antietam in Sharpsburg, Maryland had ended the Confederate Army of Northern Virginia's first invasion into the borderland, did Lincoln tactfully broach the idea of using the war as an opportunity to free slaves. In introducing the Emancipation Proclamation (taking effect January, 1863) he carefully "freed" only those slaves residing in areas *not* held by federal forces. He thereby exempted the federally controlled border regions from the proclamation and salved the sometimes racists propensities of borderland residents. White Marylanders in convention chose the Union by a two to one margin.

In March 1861, Captain Nathaniel Lyon arrived in St. Louis, Missouri in command of a company-sized detachment of the 2nd U.S. Infantry. Prior to the secession of South Carolina, Lyon had been extensively involved in establishing the St. Louis Wide Awakes, a pro-union paramilitary organization composed of anti-secessionist Missouri residents. He realized that pro-secession forces under command of the state governor, Clairborne "Fox" Jackson intended to arm his forces from the federal arsenal in the city and muster them into the ranks of the Confederate army. Upon obtaining command of the arsenal, Lyon armed the Wide Awake units and had most of the excess weapons in the arsenal secretly moved to Illinois. Lyon was also aware that secessionists had shipped captured artillery from the U.S. arsenal in Baton Rouge to the Missouri State Militia camp near the city. On May 10, he led the Missouri volunteers and the 2nd U.S. Infantry to the camp, forcing its surrender. Riots broke out in St. Louis as Lyon marched his prisoners through the city, and he ordered his men to fire on the demonstrators, killing 28 and wounding approximately 50. Lyon was promoted to brigadier general and oversaw the instillation of a pro-Union state government. He was killed on August 10 at the Battle of Wilson's Creek while dramatically rallying his badly outnumbered men, the first Union general to be killed in the Civil War.

In July 1861, John C. Fremont had taken command of the Western Department of the Federal Army headquartered in St. Louis, Missouri. Lyon had secured the federal arsenal in the city, but Fremont found disorder everywhere. The terms of enlistment of the three-months' militia who were holding the state for the Union, were expiring, and they were unwilling to reenlist because they had not been paid. Fremont had very little money or arms at his disposal to battle the active Confederate minority in the southwestern portion of the State. He applied to the U.S. Treasurer at St. Louis for $100,000 of the cash on hand and, with the money, Fremont secured the reenlistment of many of the home guards. He strongly fortified St. Louis and proceeded to garrison the nearby river city of Cairo, Illinois by moving nearly 4,000 troops to the city on river steamers. The bodies of Confederate troops in Kentucky and Missouri that were gathered for the purpose of seizing Cairo were dissuaded from the attempt.

Fremont immediately proclaimed martial law in Missouri, and appointed a provost-marshal in St. Louis. Some of the most active secessionists were arrested, and the publication of newspapers charged with disloyalty was suspended. Because of Fremont's avowed determination to confiscate the property and free the slaves of those disloyal to the Union, a storm of indignation suddenly arose among the residents of the border states. This alarmed the national government, and the President, wishing to placate the rebellious spirit of those states, requested Fremont to modify his position on these points. Fremont declined to do so, and his military career was suddenly placed in check. False accusers, public and private, ultimately cost Fremont his command. Meanwhile, the Missouri state convention defrocked the pro-secessionist governor (Jackson), rejected any lingering idea of disunion, and declared itself the permanent wartime government of the state. The quick actions of Lyon and Fremont had secured Missouri to the Union.

In sharp contrast to the situation in Missouri, the state of Kentucky was so divided politically that only neutrality seemed possible. The state legislature voted two to one "to take no part in the civil war now being waged except as mediators and friends to the belligerent parties." State Governor Beriah Magoffin issued a strong Neutrality Proclamation warning that only death awaited any who defied Kentucky's decision. Hundreds of Kentuckians immediately enrolled in the state guard ready to enforce its neutrality. Lincoln carefully stayed away, but Confederate General Leonidas Polk violated Kentucky's neutrality by seizing first Columbus and then Bowling Green. Two days later, General Ulysses Grant entered Kentucky with federal forces claiming that he came to save the state. The state legislature, in a lopsided vote, insisted that Polk retire across the border, but invited Grant to stay. The state was safe for the Union, and in the next election Unionists carried three of every four seats in the Kentucky house. More than 70 percent of the state's young men remained out of the fighting. Nonetheless, Kentuckians served in both armies. Federal recruiters did better in bringing men into the army, but Confederate raiders found the southwest section of the state a prime recruiting ground for guerillas.[5]

Bitter guerilla raids were conducted in many of the border states. With its history of Missouri-Kansas border conflicts from the 1850s, Missouri was possibly the most terrorized region in the Yankee-occupied South. No other border state had "such entrenched antislavery and proslavery regions or such experience with the nighttime raid and the daytime ambush. . . Its embittered black belt offered guerillas their launching pad against the Federal dominion."[6] Western Virginia and eastern Tennessee had no convenient marshalling areas for guerilla activity, but their mountainous topography was ideal for cross-border irregular operations. Delaware with less than 1800 slaves and fewer than 600 slaveowners in a population of 90,000 hardly needed any force to quell secessionist sentiment, and almost all the anti-government activity in Maryland centered in Baltimore raising its head on a single day (April 19, 1861) when Massachusetts troops were attacked by a mob. Thereafter, secessionists in Maryland caused little unrest besides street grumbling. They called Ben Butler a beast and Lincoln a despot; a few hundred crossed to Virginia to enlist in the Southern cause, but they raised no local forces to oppose the federal occupation of the state.

The white belt areas of the border states overwhelmingly supported the Union in the Civil War thereby allowing the federal forces to secure important avenues into the Confederate breadbasket in the Shenandoah Valley and the strategic heartland of the Mississippi Valley. A wall of border states loyal to the Union now faced the South. Only a combination of minimal federal forces with an anti-Confederate local sentiment could have so swiftly secured these regions. Lincoln's army had imposed little or no coercive force on the majority population of the white belt regions, and a minimum of federal repression had been applied to borderites, who on their own had chosen to remain in the Union. Only with the support of loyal border residents could Lincoln expect to guard these borderland winnings against Confederate insult.[7]

WATCHING A FREE GOVERNMENT DIE

Antiwar sentiments were not peripheral issues during the Civil War. They were argued over on the national stage and in the newspapers as well as on the tenement steps and across farmyard fences. The rhetoric used against Lincoln, and the hostility that it engendered in some quarters, was quite similar to that used against the presidents who oversaw America's 20th-century wars. Copperheads claimed that Lincoln had brought the war on and had made the situation worse by fighting, or that the war would not have happened except for some presidential dedication by the government to a hidden agenda: to strip Americans of their rights. On the day after the firing on Ft. Sumter the editor of the *Dubuque Herald* wrote:

Nothing will satisfy the fanatics of the North but a provocation to civil war, in which they may accomplish their darling object that which they have toiled for many years: the incitement of slaves to insurrection against their masters, and. . . the consequent emancipation of those slaves, the abolition of slavery, and the ruin and subjugation of the South to the political thralldom of Northern fanaticism.[8]

Matthew Bulkley of Connecticut, an antiwar Democrat, was astounded that his fellow citizens in New England could not perceive the dangers inherent in Lincoln's disregard for the Constitution. "If we have any desire to maintain and preserve our government, and free institutions. . . Sacrifice everything, but honor and principle and unite as brothers, and give this corrupt, imbecile and . . . God abhorred administration to understand that they can no longer usurp power and trample upon the sacred rights guaranteed to us by our constitution and laws."[9]

The fact that Copperheads existed also caused a flurry of accusations regarding disloyalty and treason even in the states that remained in the Union. The county sheriff of Hartford City, Indiana and 21 other men were accused of inciting and participating in a riot to prevent the draft when they argued with the enrolling officers over just who should supervise the proceeding. The sheriff refused to have anything to do with conscription and the mob tore up the enrollment records, destroyed the lottery wheel, and chased the enrolling officers out of the local courthouse. Two pro-union men in Union County, Illinois, disturbed by the level of southern sympathy they detected, claimed that their region was the most pro-slavery in the state. Secessionists were making speeches against the government, claiming that Jefferson Davis was a better president than Lincoln and holding secret meetings in the woods. Many Democrats—ostensibly unionists—readily admitted forming units for the personal safety of the residents in their area from runaway slaves, deserters, and foragers. Former president Franklin Pierce was accused of being a member of a group whose secret objective was to overthrow the federal government. Secretary of State William H. Seward wrote to Pierce for an acceptable explanation of the rumor. Reports of widespread disaffection among the military-age male population were made to state governors already scrambling to fill the rolls of their volunteer units and find dependable leaders to serve as officers. Governors, especially in the border regions and the states of the Midwest, were earnestly urged to send troops to disband newly formed Copperhead militias that may or may not have existed, and for which task they had no available troops in any case.[10]

Under Lincoln's Executive Order of April 25, 1961, the administration had 19 pro-secession or antiwar members of the Maryland legislature arrested so that they could not vote for secession. On May 25, 1861, Lieutenant John Merryman, an officer in the Maryland state cavalry and a dedicated Copperhead, took a leading role in demolishing a bridge so as to block any federal troop movements through his state. Merryman was arrested at his home by Union troops, indicted for treason, and confined in Fort McHenry. A proferred writ of habeus corpus was obtained from a state judge, but it was ignored by Merryman's jailers. As a petitioner to the courts for relief from imprisonment, Merryman became one of the earliest and best-known habeas corpus cases of the American Civil War.

Chief Justice Roger Taney ruled against Lincoln in the federal district court with regard to the suspension of habeus corpus and the arrest of civilians by the military, but the full Supreme Court never heard the case (*Ex parte Merryman*, 17 F. Cas. 144 1861). Lincoln ignored the ruling, maintaining that he had no choice but to bend the law in response to the gravity of the secession crisis. "Must a government . . . be too strong for the liberties of its own people, or too weak to maintain its own existence?" he asked.[11] Besides, the Constitution clearly stated that habeus corpus could be "suspended" (Article 1, Section 9) in the case of a rebellion or an attack on the nation, but it was equally unclear over which branch, or branches of government were empowered to enact the suspension. Until the president issued the suspension, no one had ever considered that the executive might act on his own. Lincoln, immediately faced with the greatest threat ever to face to the United States, had no time to finesse a highly articulated response to secession. The crisis had come on too quickly to allow for extensive debate on these questions, and Lincoln had rolled out the war powers of the executive branch to insure the Union's preservation and resist its destruction by force. Asserting his prerogative, Lincoln asked rhetorically, "Are all the laws, but one [habeus corpus], to go unexecuted, and the government itself to go to pieces, lest the one be violated?"[12]

The details surrounding the administration of Jefferson Davis in the South have attracted a good deal of second-thinking concerning his abilities as a political leader and the government's ideological roots. The Confederate government lasted somewhat less than the six years its constitution had envisioned, making scholarly arguments concerning the lack of a two-party system, a single-term presidency, and the effects of state's rights on a centralized system of governance somewhat superfluous. In the Confederacy, Jefferson Davis had also suspended habeas corpus and imposed martial law, in part to maintain order during the secession crisis and the marshalling of Southern defense forces. This fact left Lincoln with some modicum of political cover.

After the war, the Supreme Court held (*Ex Parte Milligan*, 71 U.S.C. 2, 1866) that Lincoln had exceeded his powers as commander-in-chief by declaring martial law in *those parts of the country not in rebellion where the ordinary civil courts were open and well-functioning.* Lamdin P. Mulligan was arrested, tried, and sentenced to death in a military court for joining and aiding, between October, 1863, and August, 1864, a secret society known as the Order of American Knights, or Sons of Liberty (a Copperhead group), for the purpose of overthrowing the government of the United States. The Court found it significant that the petitioner was a private citizen not connected with military service who lived in Indiana, was arrested there in 1864, and had not been a resident of any of the states in the rebellion or a prisoner of war. The court found that the guarantee of trial by jury contained in the Constitution was intended for a state of war as well as a state of peace; and is equally binding upon rulers and people, at all times and under all circumstances. The court also found that Congress had power, under the Constitution, to provide for the organization of military commissions and for trial by those commissions of persons engaged in conspiracy against the US, if they chose to use it. The authority of federal courts to review claims of habeus corpus was not clearly established until Congress adopted a statute (28 U.S.C.§ 2254) granting federal courts that authority in 1867, as part of the post-Civil War Reconstruction.

Absent decisions like these, there was, in fact, little that opponents of the administration in Congress could do in 1861–1865 to thwart Lincoln's prosecution of the war *in any manner he found acceptable.* The Peace Democrats in the 37th Congress (1861 and 1862) were at a severe disadvantage politically. With the secession of 11 states, the number of Democrats in the House (44) and Senate (15) had been significantly diminished. The House alone lost 55 members due to secession. Some of the remaining members were Unionists or War Democrats, generally unfriendly to the antiwar position of others in their party, but equally interested in weakening the Republicans in the next two-year election cycle.

Despite the exit of 21 Southern senators during the Civil War, the U.S. Senate continued to push forward with its legislative duties. Some senators left the body in order to aid the military efforts of the war, while others attempted to balance careers in the Senate and on the battlefield. When the Senate convened, the seats from all 11 Confederate states were vacant with the single exception of Andrew Johnson, of Tennessee. Johnson denied the right of a state to secede and maintained his allegiance to the Union. He left the Senate in March 1862 to become the military governor of his state and later (1865) Vice-president and President of the United States.

The Republican Party that had elected Lincoln in 1860, was for the first time in US history the majority party in both houses (In the House: Republican 108, Democrat 44, Unionist 28, Constitutional unionist 2, Ind. 1. In the Senate: Republican 31, Democrat 15, Unionist 3, vacant 1). In an admittedly unlikely scenario where the Southern states had maintained their representation in the Congress, in the manner that Tennessee had a sitting representative in Andrew Johnson, Lincoln's power in Congress, and in the executive roll, might have been curtailed somewhat. Yet such a course would have weakened the cause of secession and undermined the clean break that the Confederate states were trying to make with the Union. As it was, the few Copperheads remaining in Congress would have to speak their piece against the war and hope for the best.

Through an innocuous bill to increase the soldiers' pay passed by both Houses without significant further debate, the 37th Congress quickly added a conspiracy provision with a penalty of death to Lincoln's Executive Order of April 25. It was argued that the provision was ostensibly meant to thwart "rebellious activities," but it was actually aimed at suppressing antiwar protests particularly those found in opposition newspapers. No one was put to death under this provision. California Democrat James McDougall put forward the frightening contention that all civil laws were superseded in time of war, and that habeus corpus was a "peace right."[13] To ratify the President's acts, protested John Breckinridge of Kentucky, was to effectively amend the Constitution–an action clearly "beyond Congress's authority." It was of course nothing of the sort. Ratification of unauthorized acts after the fact had a long and honorable history in the law. In the end the 37th Congress found that the President had not transcended his power.[14]

In addition, the Congress made conspiracy a crime if its object was to overthrow the government, to levy war against the United States, to obstruct the execution of the laws, or to seize government property; outlawed the recruiting of soldiers to fight against the United States; authorized the President to prohibit commercial intercourse with rebel states; required federal officers to take an oath of allegiance to the nation; and removed a source of ambiguity in the President's authority to enforce the laws by empowering him to call out the armed forces and militia for that purpose whenever it was "impracticable" to enforce them by ordinary judicial means. These measures were all innocent enough in constitutional terms, and none of them met with significant constitutional objection. In contrast, a revolutionary but innocuous bill to establish a Department of Agriculture encountered heavy weather in the Senate, though it too was ultimately enacted.[15]

However, the main measures taken under consideration by the 37th Congress were financial in nature: the legal tender bill, the internal revenue bill, the confiscation bill, and various loan bills. These bills were all debated at length and their passage was generally not along party lines. Owing to the initial expectation of a short war, the Federal government raised its war chest chiefly by taking loans and issuing paper money and bonds. The government generally failed to raise enough funds through these methods, running in deficit throughout the conflict. Expenses ran eight times the revenue from taxes. A novel source of war funding was found in the adoption of a personal income tax, the first tax of its kind ever levied by the United States government. As first envisioned, it fixed a three percent tax on family incomes over $800, but by June 1864 the exemption fell to $600 and the minimum rate rose to five percent on incomes up to $5,000.

The 37th congress was also memorable for the measures by which the state of Virginia was divided and the new Commonwealth of West Virginia was formed, as well as for the Militia Act, the Homestead Act, the Morrill Tariff, the Pacific Railroad Act, and the Enrollment Act (military conscription). The nonmilitary legislation of the Civil War years also reflected a veritable revolution in the understanding of the nature of federal authority. By the end of the war the concept of central government represented "a far ampler sovereignty than it earlier had been, more powerful, more ambitious, and more besought." Indeed another observer went so far as to call the legislation of the first Civil War Congress a "blueprint for a new America."[16]

The bi-elections for 1863 were disappointing for the Lincoln administration. Many Americans had given Lincoln the benefit of the doubt for two years, but after two years of war with no seeming success, a number of them jumped to the antiwar camp. Horatio Seymour, the Democratic candidate for governor in Connecticut, ran on the slogan "Restore the Union as it was, and Maintain the Constitution as it is."[17] Republicans lost the governorships of New York, New Jersey, and Illinois; but Michigan, California, and Iowa all went Republican. Democrats gained 28 House seats, many in places that the republicans had thought safe like Indiana, Ohio, Pennsylvania and Lincoln's own home state of Illinois. Yet a closer look at the results shows that the Democrats gained seats only where they had been strong in the past and in smaller numbers than the minority party in an off-year election might expect. The Republicans maintained a majority (85 to 72) over the Democrats in the House and actually gained two seats in the Senate.

The first session of the 38th Congress was characterized by a serious confrontation between the President and Congress over control of the process for reconstructing the governments of the self-styled Confederate States. Otherwise, it was largely a repetition of the previous congress: providing troops, voting supplies, adjusting finances, and establishing the Freemen's Bureau. In June 1864 Congress enacted a brief statute with the astonishing title "*An Act to repeal the Fugitive Slave Act of eighteen hundred and fifty, and all Acts and Parts of Acts for the Rendition of Fugitive Slaves.*" A close look at the statute confirms that it did just what the title said it was intended to do. When the 38th Congress adjourned, the end of the war was not far off. In less than six weeks after the adjournment of the 38th Congress, the Confederacy collapsed.[18]

NOTES

1. Jennifer L. Weber, *Copperheads: The Rise and Fall of Lincoln's Opponents in the North* (New York: Oxford University Press, 2006), 94–95.
2. Weber, 96.
3. Samuel Cox to Abraham Lincoln, June 14, 1863, accessed on May 27, 2008. Available at http://memory.loc.gov/mss/mal/maltext/rtf_orig/mal054f.rtf.
4. See in Ibid., x.
5. William E. Freehling, *The South vs. the South: How Anti-Confederate Southerners Shaped the Course of the Civil War* (New York: Oxford University Press, 2001), 52–53.
6. Freehling, 55.
7. Freehling, 57.
8. Weber, 22.
9. Weber, 66.
10. Weber, 23–24.
11. Weber, 32.
12. Weber, 33.
13. Weber, 36.
14. David P. Currie, "The Civil War Congress," *The University of Chicago Law Review* 73. 1131–1226: 1136, http://lawreview.uchicago.edu/issues/archive/v73/fall/Currie.pdf (Accessed June 14, 2008).
15. Currie, 1141.
16. Currie, 1132.
17. Weber, 66.
18. Currie, 1174.

GLOSSARY OF CIVIL WAR PERIOD TERMS

Abolitionist—A person who wanted to do away with slavery (abolitionism). American abolitionists began to speak out in public in the 1830s.

Army—A tactical and administrative military unit consisting of a headquarters, two or more corps, and auxiliary forces.

Artillery—The branch of an army that specializes in the use of large-caliber weapons, such as cannon and howitzers that are operated by crews rather than individuals.

Berlin woolwork—Needlepoint wool yarn stitched on to canvas.

Border states—The slave states of Delaware, Maryland, Virginia, Kentucky, and Missouri that were adjacent to the free states of the North during the Civil War. Virginia joined the Confederacy in 1861, causing its western counties to form the new state of West Virginia. It and other Border States remained tied to the Union despite strong Southern sympathies.

Busk—A piece of flat bone or wood inserted into the front of a corset to make it straight and rigid. Sailors often carved busks from whalebone and decorated them with scrimshaw to present to their sweethearts when they returned from a long voyage.

Casualties (of war)—Persons injured, killed, captured, or missing in action through engagement with an enemy.

Cavalry—A highly mobile army unit composed of troops trained to fight on horseback.

Confederacy (The)—Generally, the 11 seceded states making up the Confederate States of America (CSA).

Constitutional Construction—Constitutional *interpretation,* or constitutional *construction,* a term often used by the Founders, is the process by which meanings are assigned to the words and phrases of the Constitution as to the original intent of the Founders, to enable legal decisions to be made that are justified by it.

Draftee (military)—One who is drafted (conscripted) into military service and placed under military discipline. Induction is the process of activating a draftee or a volunteer into military service.

Dragoon—A soldier intended primarily to fight on foot but trained also on horseback and in cavalry combat. Dragoons were a favorite format for mounted militia units.

Earthworks—In military engineering earthworks are specifically types of fortifications constructed from mounds of soil (sometimes supported by timber frames). Although soil is not very strong, it absorbs the force of shot and shell well. It is easily moved with simple tools and cheap enough that huge quantities can be shifted by a few troops to generate formidable structures.

Entrenchments—A trench, or series of trenches, dug into the ground especially for the purpose of fortifying or defending a position.

Federalism—A system of government in which power is divided between a central authority and the constituent political units known as states.

Fire-eater—One of the numerous radicals in the forefront of the clamor for secession who consistently and actively pursued the disunion of all the Southern states from the Federal union.

Foundry—A manufactory dedicated to the casting of metal objects particularly cannon, wheels and rails for trains, and parts for steam engines.

Franchise—Generally considered the right to vote.

Free Labor movement—In the Civil War period it became common for abolitionists to speak about "free labor." Nonetheless, the free labor movement was more than a drive for the abolition of slavery. It was an idealistic vision of a democratic society based on independent artisans owning their own means of production.

General (rank)—The rank of General of the Army is the most senior in that branch of the armed services. First in the chain of command behind the president (both of the U.S. and CS), it is followed in descending order of rank by Lt. General, Major General, and Brigadier General, who are all considered "general officers." Regimental officers included Colonel, Lt. Colonel, Major, Captain, Lieutenant, and (sometimes) Ensign, as well as a whole series of NCOs.

Gentry—People of gentle birth, good breeding, or high social position. An upper or ruling class generally outside of an hereditary aristocracy.

Greenbacks—A paper note of U.S. currency as opposed to metal (specie) money such as gold or silver.

Infantry—A soldier who fights on foot, as opposed to a cavalry trooper or artillery gunner.

Manumission—The act of manumitting, or of legally liberating a slave from bondage.

Nationalism—Aspirations for a separate national independence in a country under Northern domination.

Nativist—Although persons opposed to foreign immigration are included, the term nativist has an inherently specific meaning. Strictly speaking, nativists and *nativism* distinguishes between Americans who were born in the United States, and individuals who have immigrated or are the children of immigrants—so-called "first generation" immigrants.

Nullification—The doctrine by which certain states claimed power to declare a law of the federal government unconstitutional. It was the most important theoretical alternative to the idea that the U.S. Supreme Court is the final arbiter of constitutional controversies. Nullification was an important conceptual development on the way to secession. The most important and systematic development of nullification doctrine occurred in South Carolina in 1828 and 1832 championed by John C. Calhoun and others.

Operation (military)—A military operation is the employment of military resources to achieve a specific objective. It often involves planning, calculating, or interpreting information. It can involve the prosecution of a strategic or tactical plan such as a battle, a raid, or any form of combat; or an administrative military mission including the movement of troops and supplies; attack, defense, ruse, or maneuvers needed to achieve the objectives of a military campaign.

Papists—Generally considered adherents of the Pope, the religious leader of the Roman Catholic Church.

Partisans—A partisan was a member of an irregular military force formed to oppose control of an area by an enemy or by an army of occupation. Called "irregulars" during the warfare in the 19th century, the tactical concept of partisan warfare was the use of trained adjuncts to regular forces who could operate behind enemy lines to disrupt communications, raid logistical stockpiles, and draw enemy reserves from the front lines.

Plantation—A large estate or farm on which crops are raised, often by resident workers.

Plantation aristocracy—A class of wealthy, often hereditary land owners who dominated the lives of their subordinate classes and controlled the politics of vast areas.

Plantation economy—A plantation economy is based on agricultural mass production, usually of a few staple crops grown on large farms called plantations. Plantation economies are usually dependent on outside forces, due to the fact that their produce is being harvested as a cash crop to be exported.

Pluralism—The political theory of pluralism holds that political power in society does not lie with the electorate but is distributed between a wide number of groups formed into both formal and informal coalitions.

Propaganda—The systematic dissemination of a doctrine, cause, or other information reflecting the views and interests of those advocating such a doctrine or cause.

Reconstruction—The period (1865–1877) during which the states of the Confederacy were controlled by the federal government before being readmitted to the Union.

Red Legs—One of the free-soil guerrillas in Kansas and Missouri during the border disputes of 1854 to 1859. The term red leg originated during the Bleeding Kansas period from the red woolen or painted canvass leggings worn by these partisan militiamen. Unionist guerrillas in the Civil War were sometimes referred to as "jayhawkers."

Refugees—The entire class of persons made homeless by the Civil War, or simply fleeing the forces of the enemy.

Regulars (military)—A soldier belonging to a regular army or a unit constituting the permanent military force of a nation.

Ruching—A strip of fabric or ribbon is gathered and drawn up to form scallops or petals. It is used as an embellishment or trim on women's clothing often seen on a neckline, sleeve, hem, or bonnet.

'Secesh'—A shortening of *secession*, used to describe supporters of the Southern cause.

Secession—The withdrawal of 11 Southern states from the Union in 1860–1861, precipitating the U.S. Civil War.

Secessionists—Those who believed that the South had a right to formally leave the Union. Secession, and the founding of the Confederate States of America, was in many respects a reaction against the party politics of the 1850s with Jefferson Davis and other secession leaders reverting to an earlier political ideology and cultural vision of southern unity.

Slave power—Slave Power (sometimes referred to as the "Slaveocracy") was a term used in the North (beginning circa 1840) to characterize the political power of the slaveholding class in the South.

Sniper—A picked marksman who shot, usually from a concealed position, with the aim of killing key enemy personnel. Initially there was no clear distinction between snipers and other light troops armed with rifles whose fire was effective at greater range than that of their comrades armed with smooth-bore muskets. Both sides raised regiments of so-called "sharpshooters" who could hit targets at distances over 200 yards.

Soddie—A dwelling having thick walls of blocks cut from an upper layer of grassland. These homes were constructed by early settlers in the Great Plains in areas where timber and stone were scarce. They were often constructed partially underground, or built into the side of a hill to provide additional insulation. Interior walls were generally plastered with clay, making them dryer and more attractive.

Sovereignty—Supremacy of authority or rule as exercised by a government or state. Complete independence and self-government.

Specie—Lawful money generally considered gold or silver coins or bullion. Specie is also known as "hard" money. Lawful money stands in contrast to fiat money, to which the government assigns value although it has no intrinsic value of its own and is not backed by reserves. Fiat money includes paper money, checks, drafts, and bank notes.

States' Rights—The political position advocating strict interpretation of the Constitution (and especially the Tenth Amendment to the Bill of Rights) with regard to the limitation of federal powers and the extension of the autonomy of the individual state to the greatest possible degree. States' Rights advocates in the antebellum period believed that considerable governmental authority should be located in the separate and collective states rather than the federal government of the United States. Although various individual states and groups of states (New England, for instance) from time to time appealed to the principle of states' rights for their political and economic protection, the South is most often associated with the doctrine.

Suffrage—The right or privilege of voting; the franchise. The exercise of the right to vote.

Tariff—A list or system of duties imposed by a government on imported or exported goods. Henry Clay and the Whig Party envisioned a rapid modernization of the American economy based on highly productive factories. They sought high protective tariffs for those infant industries. The Nullification Crisis (1828 and 1832) forced an abandonment of the Whig position of higher tariffs in favor of the States' Rights position of South Carolina and other Southern states until 1842 when the Whigs took control of congress.

Temperance—A social reform movement dedicated to the control of alcohol consumption through the promotion of moderation and abstinence.

It began as a church-sponsored movement in the United States in the early 19th century. It attracted the efforts of many women, and by 1833 there were 6,000 local temperance societies in the United States.

Trenches—*See* entrenchments.

Unionists—Those Americans (especially residents of seceded states) who believed that the Union should be maintained.

Urbanization—The increase in the proportion of the population residing in towns and cities, brought about by migration of rural populations into urban areas. Increasing urbanization often indicates a change of employment structure from agriculture and cottage industries to mass production and service industries.

Victorian (Era)—the period named for Queen Victoria of Britain who reigned from 1837 until 1901. The term Victorian is often used as an adjective.

Victorine—A covering for the shoulders of women, generally made of fur, with long ends that hang in front.

Volunteers (military)—Persons who freely enrolled for military service rather than being conscripted, especially as members of a force formed by voluntary enrollment and distinct from the regular army (as in militia and partisan units).

Zouaves—Military American units dressed in fancy uniforms with baggy pants, short jackets, and turbans—a uniform largely abandoned for field service after the first year of the war. This distinctive form of light infantry was created in 1830 by the French army serving in Algeria. The name may have originated from that of a warlike tribe from the area, or derived from the Arabic for "to creep or crawl," a comment on the considerable skill of Zouaves as skirmishers.

SELECTED BIBLIOGRAPHY

Back issues of Civil War periodicals can be found online at http://www.sonofthesouth.net/.

Abell, Mrs. L. G. "The Dying Girl." *Christian Parlor Magazine* 9, no. 12 (1852).
Adams, Alice Dana. *The Neglected Period of Anti-slavery in America.* Boston: Corner House, 1973.
Albree, John, ed. *Whittier's Correspondence.* Privately published, 1911.
Anderson, Patricia. "Romantic Strains of the Parlor Piano." *Victorian* 3, no. 3 (1997).
Armstrong, Richard. *Seventh Virginia Cavalry.* Lynchburg: H. E. Howard, 1992.
Ashby, Thomas A. *The Life of Turner Ashby.* New York: Neal Publishing, 1914.
Barnard, George N. *Photographic Views of Sherman's Campaigns.* 1866. Reprint, New York: Dover, 1977.
Bauer, K. Jack, ed. *Soldiering: The Civil War Diary of Rice C. Bull.* Novato: Presidio, 1977.
Beecher, Catherine E. *Miss Beecher's Domestic Receipt Book.* New York: Harper & Brothers, 1850.
Berry, Harrison. *Slavery and Abolitionism, as Viewed by a Georgia Slave.* Atlanta: M. Lynch, 1861.
Billings, John D. *Hardtack and Coffee.* Boston: G. M. Smith, 1887.
Blassingame, John W. *Black New Orleans.* Chicago: Chicago University Press, 1973.
Blassingame, John W. *The Clarion Voice.* Washington: National Parks Service, 1976.
Bowman, John S., ed. *The Civil War Almanac.* New York: Bison Books, 1983.
Burrowes, Thomas H. *Report of the Superintendent of Common Schools of Pennsylvania.* Harrisburg: A. Boyd Hamilton, 1861.
Bushrod, Millard K. *Old Jube: A Biography of General Jubal A. Early.* Shippensburg, PA: Beidel, 1955.

Byrne, Frank L., and Jean Powers Soman, eds. *A Jewish Colonel in the Civil War: Marcus M Spiegel of the Ohio Volunteers.* Lincoln: University of Nebraska Press, 1994.

Campbell, Edward D.C. Jr., and Kym S. Rice, eds. *A Woman's War: Southern Women, Civil War and the Confederate Legacy.* Charlottesville: University Press of Virginia, 1996.

Catton, Bruce. *The Picture History of the Civil War.* New York: American Heritage, 1960.

Child, Lydia M. *The Mother's Book.* Boston: Applewood, 1831.

Clinton, Catherine. *The Plantation Mistress: Woman's World in the Old South.* New York: Pantheon Books, 1982.

Coco, Gregory A. *The Civil War Infantryman: In Camp, on the March, and in Battle.* Gettysburg: Thomas, 1996.

Coffin, Margaret M. *Death in Early America.* New York: Thomas Nelson, 1976.

Colton, Calvin, ed. *The Private Correspondence of Henry Clay.* Cincinnati: N.p., 1856.

Confederate Receipt Book: A Compilation of Over One Hundred Receipts, Adapted to the Times. Richmond: West & Johnson, 1863.

Cook, Fred J. "The Slave Ship Rebellion." *American Heritage,* February 1957.

Cornish, Dudley T. *The Sable Arm: Black Troops in the Union Army, 1861–1865.* New York: Longmans, 1956.

Cozzens, Peter. *No Better Place to Die: The Battle of Stones River.* Urbana: University of Illinois Press, 1990.

Crawford, Richard. *The Civil War Storybook.* New York: Dover, 1977.

Cremin, Lawrence A. *American Education: The National Experience, 1783–1876.* New York: Harper, 1980.

Croushore, James H., ed. *A Volunteer's Adventure, by Captain John W. De Forest.* New Haven: Yale University Press, 1949.

Davis, David Brion. *Slavery in the Colonial Chesapeake.* Williamsburg: Colonial Williamsburg Foundation, 1994.

Davis, William C., ed. *Diary of a Confederate Soldier, by John S. Jackman.* Columbia: University of South Carolina Press, 1990.

Denny, Robert E. *Civil War Medicine: Care and Comfort for the Wounded.* New York: Sterling, 1995.

DeRosa, Marshall L. *The Confederate Constitution of 1861.* Columbia: University of Missouri Press, 1991.

Donald, David. *The Civil War and Reconstruction.* Boston: Heath, 1961.

Douglass, Frederick. *Narrative of the Life of an American Slave, Written by Himself.* 1845. Reprint, New York: Penguin, 1968.

Dowdey, Clifford. *The Great Plantation.* Charles City, VA: Berkeley Plantation Press, 1957.

Duyckinck, E. A. *Cyclopedia of American Literature.* Detroit: Gale Research, 1965.

East, Charles, ed. *Sarah Morgan: The Civil War Diary of a Southern Woman.* New York: Touchstone, 1991.

Editors of Time-Life. *Voices of the Civil War.* New York: Time-Life, 1995.

Eggleston, George C. *A Rebel's Recollections.* 1874. Reprint, Bloomington: Indiana University Press, 1959.

Fales, Martha Gandy. *Jewelry in America.* London: Antique Collector's Club, 1995.

Faust, Drew Gilpin. *The Creation of Confederate Nationalism: Ideology and Identity in the Civil War South.* Baton Rouge: Louisiana State University Press, 1988.

Faust, Drew Gilpin. *Mothers of Invention: Women of the Slaveholding South in the American Civil War.* Charlotte: University of North Carolina Press, 1996.

Fehrenbacher, Don E. *The Era of Expansion, 1800–1848.* New York: John Wiley & Sons, 1969.

Fite, Emerson David. *Social and Industrial Conditions in the North During the Civil War.* Williamstown: Corner House, 1976.

Fitzpatrick, Michael F. "The Mercy Brigade." *Civil War Times Illustrated.* October 1997.

Fletcher, William A. *Rebel Private: Front and Rear.* 1908. New York: Meridian, 1997.

Foote, Shelby. *The Civil War: A Narrative. Fort Sumter to Perryville.* New York: Vintage, 1986.

Foote, Shelby. *The Civil War: A Narrative. Fredericksburg to Meridian.* New York: Vintage, 1986.

Foote, Shelby. *The Civil War: A Narrative. Red River to Appomattox.* New York: Vintage, 1986.

Frederickson, George M., ed. *Great Lives Observed: William Lloyd Garrison.* Englewood Cliffs: Prentice-Hall, 1968.

Freehling, William E. *The South vs. The South: How Anti-Confederate Southerners Shaped the Course of the Civil War.* New York: Oxford University Press, 2001.

Gardner, Alexander. *Photographic Sketchbook of the Civil War.* 1866. Reprint, New York: Dover, 1959.

Garrison, William Lloyd. *Thoughts on African Colonization.* Boston: N.p., 1832.

Genovese, Eugene D. *Roll, Jordan, Roll: The World the Slaves Made.* New York: Pantheon Books, 1976.

Grimsley, Mark. *The Hard Hand of War: Union Military Policy Toward Southern Civilians, 1861–1865.* Cambridge: Cambridge University Press, 1995.

Guernsey, Alfred H., and Henry M. Alden, eds. *Harper's History of the Great Rebellion.* New York: Gramercy Books, 1866.

Gwin, Minrose C., ed. Cornelia *Peake McDonald: A Woman's Civil War. A Diary with Reminiscences of the War from March 1862.* Madison: University of Wisconsin, 1992.

Hague, Parthenia Antoinette. *A Blockaded Family: Life in Southern Alabama During the Civil War.* Reprint. Bedford, TX: Applewood Books, 1995.

Halliman, Tim. *A Christmas Carol Christmas Book.* New York: IBM, 1984.

Halsey, Francis W., ed. "The Disbanding of the Northern Army, 1865, by James G. Blaine." *Great Epochs in American History.* New York: Funk & Wagnalls, 1884.

Handlin, Oscar, and Lilian Handlin. *Liberty and Expansion, 1760–1850.* New York: Harper & Row, 1989.

Hannaford, Ebenezer. *The Story of a Regiment: A History of the Campaigns, and Associations in the Field of the Sixth Regiment Ohio Volunteer Infantry.* Cincinnati: Privately printed, 1868.

Haskell, E. F. *The Housekeeper's Encyclopedia.* Mendocino: R. L. Shep, 1992.

Hawes, Joel. *Lectures to Young Men on the Formation of Character.* Hartford: N.p., 1835.

Hess, Earl J. *The Rifle Musket in Civil War Combat, Reality and Myth*. Lawrence: University Press of Kansas, 2008.

Hunt, Charley. "The Star Vision." *Christian Parlor Magazine* 9, no. 12 (1852).

Johnson, Robert U., and Clarence Clough Buel, eds. *Battles and Leaders of the Civil War*, 4 vols. Edison: Castle, 1887.

Jones, Archer. *The Art of War in the Western World*. New York: Oxford University Press, 1987.

Jones, Archer. *Confederate Strategy from Shiloh to Vicksburg*. Baton Rouge: Louisiana State University Press, 1991.

Jones, Howard. *Mutiny on the Amistad*. New York: Oxford University Press, 1987.

Jones, Terry L., ed. *The Civil War Memoirs of Captain William J. Seymour*. Baton Rouge: Louisiana State University Press, 1991.

Jones, Virgil Carrington. *Gray Ghosts and Rebel Raiders*. New York: Galahad, 1956.

Jordan, Ervin L., Jr. *Black Confederates and Afro-Yankees in Civil War Virginia*. Charlottesville: University Press of Virginia, 1995.

Kaser, David. *Books and Libraries in Camp and Battle: The Civil War Experience*. Westport, CT: Greenwood Press, 1984.

Keegan, John. *The Mask of Command*. New York: Vintage, 1987.

Kellar, Herbert A., ed. "The Diary of James D. Davidson." *Journal of Southern History*, 1 (1935).

Kennedy, James R., and Walter D. Kennedy. *The South Was Right*. Gretna, LA: Pelican, 1995.

Kiracofe, Roderick. *The American Quilt*. New York: Clarkson Potter, 1993.

Kunitz, Stanley J., ed. *British Authors of the Nineteenth Century*. New York: Wilson, 1936.

Laas, Virginia Jeans, ed. *Wartime Washington: Letters of Elizabeth Blair Lee*. Chicago: University of Illinois Press, 1991.

Larcom, Lucy. *A New England Girlhood*. Boston: Northeastern University Press, 1986.

Leach, Daniel. *Leach's Complete Spelling Book*. Philadelphia: H. Cowperthwait & Co., 1859.

Leech, Margaret. *Reveille in Washington*. New York: Harper & Brothers, 1941.

Lewis, Thomas A. *The Guns of Cedar Creek*. New York: Bantam, 1991.

Livermore, Mary A. *My Story of the War: A Woman's Narrative of Four Years' Personal Experience*. New York: Da Capo Press, 1995.

Lord, Francis A. *Civil War Collector's Encyclopedia*. 5 vols. Edison: Blue & Gray Press, 1995.

Lothrop, Margaret M. *The Wayside: Home Of Authors*. New York: American Book Company, 1968.

Lothrop, Margaret M. "The United States Military Railroad Service: Vehicle to Victory," *Civil War Times Illustrated*, October 1962.

Loving, Jerome M., ed. *Civil War Letters of George Washington Whitman*. Durham: Duke University Press, 1975.

Lunt, Dolly Sumner. *A Woman's Wartime Journal*. Atlanta: Cherokee, 1994.

Mallinson, David. "Armed with Only Their Drums," *America's Civil War*, November 1992.

Malone, Dumas, ed. *Dictionary of American Biography*. New York: Scribner's Sons, 1943.

Marmaduke Multiply's Merry Method of Making Minor Mathematicians. 1841. Reprint, New York: Dover, 1971.

Marten, James. *The Children's Civil War.* Chapel Hill: University of North Carolina Press, 1998.

Martine, Arthur. *Martine's Hand-Book of Etiquette, and Guide to True Politeness.* New York: Dick & Fitzgerald, 1866.

Massey, Mary Elizabeth. *Women in the Civil War.* Lincoln: University of Nebraska Press, 1966.

Mayer, J. P., ed. *Journey to America, by Alexis de Tocqueville.* Translated by George Lawrence. New Haven: Yale University Press, 1960.

McCarthy, Carlton. *Detailed Minutiae of Soldier Life in the Army of Northern Virginia, 1861–1865.* 1882. Reprint, Lincoln: University of Nebraska Press, 1993.

McGuire, Judith W. *Diary of a Southern Refugee During the War by a Lady of Virginia.* Lincoln: University of Nebraska Press, 1995.

McPherson, James M. *Battle Cry of Freedom.* New York: Oxford University Press, 1988.

McPherson, James M. *For Cause and Comrades: Why Men Fought in the Civil War.* New York: Oxford University Press, 1997.

Menge, W. Springer, and J. August Shimrak, eds. *The Civil War Notebook of Daniel Chisholm.* New York: Ballantine, 1989.

Miers, Earl Schenck, ed. *A Rebel War Clerk's Diary, by John B. Jones, 1861–1865.* New York: Sagamore Press, 1958.

Miller, Francis Trevelyan, ed. *The Photographic History of the Civil War: Soldier Life and the Secret Service.* 1911. Reprint, New York: Castle, 1957.

Mitchell, Joseph B. *Decisive Battles of the Civil War.* New York: Fawcett, 1955.

Mitchell, S. Augustus. *An Easy Introduction to the Study of Geography.* Philadelphia: Thomas, Cowperthwait & Co., 1853.

Morgan, James. "Send No Trash: Books, Libraries, and Reading During the Civil War." *Camp Chase Gazette,* July 1992, 32.

Mosby, John S. *Stuart's Cavalry in the Gettysburg Campaign.* New York: Moffat, Yard & Co., 1908.

Moskow, Shirley Blotnick. *Emma's World: An Intimate Look at Lives Touched by the Civil War Era.* Far Hills, NJ: New Horizon Press, 1990.

Nesbit, Mark. *Saber and Scapegoat: J.E.B. Stuart and the Gettysburg Controversy.* Mechanicsburg: Stackpole, 1994.

New Orleans as It Is. New Orleans: N.p., 1850.

Nye, Wilbur S. "The U.S. Military Telegraph Services." *Civil War Times Illustrated,* November 1968: 28–34.

Parkhurst, Clinton. "Corinth: Tenting on the Old Camp Ground." *Civil War Times Illustrated,* January 1987, 30–35.

Paul, James Laughery. *Pennsylvania's Soldiers' Orphan Schools.* Harrisburg, PA: Lane S. Hart Publisher, 1876.

Reef, Catherine. *Alone in the World: Orphans and Orphanages in America.* New York: Clarion Books, 2005.

Rhodes, Robert Hunt, ed. *All for the Union, by Col. Elisha Hunt Rhodes.* 1985. Reprint, New York: Random House, 1995.

Rice, V. M. *Code of Public Instruction.* Albany: State Printing Office, 1856.

Richards, Caroline C. *Village Life in America, 1852–1872.* Gansevoort, NY: Corner House, 1997.

Robertson, James I. Jr., ed. *One of Jackson's Foot Cavalry.* Wilmington, NC: Broadfoot Reprints, 1987.

Root, Waverly, and Richard de Rouchemont. *Eating in America.* New York: William Morrow, 1976.

Rose, Anne C. *Victorian America and the Civil War.* Cambridge: Cambridge University Press, 1994.

Rothman, David J. "Our Brother's Keepers." *American Heritage,* December 1972.

Russell, Andrew J. *Russell's Civil War Photographs.* New York: Dover, 1982.

Sabine, David B. "Resources Compared: North Versus South." *Civil War Times Illustrated,* February 1968.

Sanchez-Eppler, Karen. *Dependent States: The Child's Part in Nineteenth Century American Culture.* Chicago: The University of Chicago Press, 2005.

Sanders, Charles W. *The School Reader Third Book.* New York: Sower, Barnes & Potts, 1860.

Scott, Sir Walter. *The Fair Maid of Perth.* New York: Harper, 1831.

Scroggs, J. J. "A Tour of a Hardtack Factory: Diary of J. J. Scroggs 5th US Colored Infantry." *Civil War Times Illustrated,* October 1972.

Sewell, Richard H. *A House Divided: Sectionalism and the Civil War, 1848–1865.* Baltimore: Johns Hopkins University Press, 1988.

Shep, R. L., ed. *Civil War Ladies: Fashions and Needle Arts of the Early 1860's.* Mendocino: R. L. Shep, 1987.

Smith, James West. "A Confederate Soldier's Diary: Vicksburg in 1863." *Southwest Review,* 28 (1943): 304, 312.

Smith, Raymond W. "Don't Cut! Signal Telegraph." *Civil War Times Illustrated,* May 1976.

Stampp, Kenneth M. *The Imperiled Union.* New York: Oxford University Press, 1980.

Stampp, Kenneth M. *The Peculiar Institution.* New York: Vintage, 1956.

Stanchak, John E., ed. *Leslie's Illustrated Civil War.* 1894. Reprint, Jackson: University Press of Mississippi, 1992.

Stannard, David. "Calm Dwellings." *American Heritage,* September 1979.

Stevens, George T. *Three Years in the Sixth Corps.* Albany: S. R. Gray, 1866.

Stewart, Katie. *Cooking and Eating.* London: Hart-Davis, MacGibbon, 1975.

Stinson, Byron. "The Invalid Corps." *Civil War Times Illustrated,* May 1971.

Straubing, Harold Elk, ed. *Civil War Eyewitness Reports.* N.p.: Archon Books, 1985.

Strother, Horatio T. *The Underground Railroad in Connecticut.* Middletown: Wesleyan University Press, 1962.

Sullivan, Walter. *The War the Women Lived: Female Voices from the Confederate South.* Nashville: J. S. Sanders, 1995.

Swartwelder, A. C. "This Invaluable Beverage: The Recollections of Dr. A. C. Swartwelder." *Civil War Times Illustrated,* October 1975.

Taylor, Alan. "Fenimore Cooper's America." *History Today,* 46, no. 2 February 1996.

Thayer, John A. *The Practical Expedite or Time-Book Companion.* Stoughton, MA: Privately printed, 1847.

Thomas, Emory M. *The Confederacy as a Revolutionary Experience.* Columbia: University of South Carolina Press, 1991.

Tice, Douglas O. "Bread or Blood: The Richmond Bread Riot," *Civil War Times Illustrated,* February 1974.

Tosh, John. "New Men? The Bourgeois Cult of Home." *History Today,* 46 (December 1996).

Town, Salem. *The Fourth Reader, or Exercises in Reading and Speaking.* Cooperstown: H. & E. Phinney, 1849.

Trager, James. *The Food Chronology.* New York: Henry Holt, 1995.

Walton, William, ed. *A Civil War Courtship: The Letters of Edwin Weller from Antietam to Atlanta.* New York: Doubleday, 1980.

Weber, Jennifer L. *Copperheads: The Rise and Fall of Lincoln's Opponents in the North.* New York: Oxford University Press, 2006.

Weigley, Russell F. *The Age of Battles: The Quest for Decisive Warfare from Breitenfeld to Waterloo.* Bloomington: Indiana University Press, 1991.

Weld, Theodore. *American Slavery as It Is.* New York: N.p., 1839.

White, David O. *Connecticut's Black Soldiers.* Chester: Pequot Press, 1973.

Wills, Brian Steel. *A Battle from the Start: The Life of Nathan Bedford Forrest.* New York: HarperCollins, 1992.

Wise, Stephen R. *Lifeline of the Confederacy: Blockade Running During the Civil War.* Columbia: University of South Carolina Press, 1988.

Woodward, C. Vann. *Mary Chesnut's Civil War.* New Haven: Yale University Press, 1981.

Woodward, George E. *Woodward's Architecture and Rural Art.* 2 vols. New York: Privately printed, 1867–1868.

Woodward, John H. "Herding Beef for the Union Army." *Civil War Times Illustrated,* December 1970.

WARTIME PERIODICALS

Frank Leslie's Illustrated Newspaper, January 31, 1863; April 17, 1863; June 6, 1863; April 9, 1864; May 28, 1864; August 6, 1864.

Harper's Weekly, October 4, 1862; October 11, 1862; December 27, 1862; May 23, 1863; July 2, 1864.

New York Times, April 15, 1861; September 23, 1862; December 17, 1862; July 6, 1863; April 10,1865; April 15, 1865.

New York Tribune, May 1-May 9, 1863; May 16, 1864.

Southern Illustrated News, February 21, 1863; March 28, 1863; August 1, 1863; October 17, 1863.

SHEET MUSIC

Clark, James G. "The Children of the Battlefield." Philadelphia: Lee & Walker, 1864.

Manahan, Thomas. "Comrades, I Am Dying." Boston: Henry Talman & Co., 1864.

Mitchell, E.A.B. "Bear Gently, So Gently, Roughly Made Bier." Louisville: Wm. McCaroll, 1864.

Root, George F. "The Vacant Chair (or We Shall Meet but We Shall Miss Him)." Chicago: Root & Cady, 1862.

WEB SOURCES

Welcome to Civil War.com
http://www.civilwar.com/battle-summaries/gettysburg.html

African-Americans and Slavery
> http://www.civilwar.com/abolition-and-slavery/african-americans-slavery.html

Abraham Lincoln
> http://www.civilwar.com/union-government/abraham-lincoln.html

Weapons-Small Arms
> http://www.civilwar.com/weapons/weapons-small-arms.html

Gettysburg
> http://www.civilwar.com/battle-summaries/gettysburg.html

Civil-War-History
> http://www.civil-war-history.com/

American Civil War.com
> http://www.americancivilwar.com/

Music of the Civil War
> http://www.americancivilwar.com/

Historic American Sheet Music
> http://library.duke.edu/digitalcollections/hasm/browse

Primary Source Set: Civil War Music
> http://memory.loc.gov/learn/community/cc_music_kit.php

American Civil War Homepage
> http://sunsite.utk.edu/civil-war/warweb.html

INDEX

About the Authors

DOROTHY DENNEEN VOLO is a teacher, historian, and living history enthusiast. As program coordinator and president of her local historical society, she has been an active participant in numerous community historical education projects. Dr. Volo is the author, coauthor, or editor of more than a dozen historical reference works dealing with American history including a number of works from the Greenwood Daily Life and Family Life series.

JAMES M. VOLO is a teacher, lecturer, and historian. He has served as a consultant for documentary television and movie projects dealing with the American Revolution and the Civil War. He is the author, coauthor, or editor of more than a dozen historical reference works dealing with American history, including a number of works from the Greenwood Daily Life and Family Life series. Dr. Volo is presently teaching physics at Sacred Heart University in Fairfield, Connecticut.